Ruby, Between the Cracks

Ruby, Between the Cracks

BETWEEN THE CRACKS
BOOK ONE

P.D. WORKMAN

# PD WORKMAN

Copyright © 2014 by P.D. Workman

All rights reserved.

No part of this book may be reproduced in any form or by any electronic or mechanical means, including information storage and retrieval systems, without written permission from the author, except for the use of brief quotations in a book review.

ISBN: 9781926500355 (IS Hardcover)

ISBN: 9781926500249 (IS Paperback)

ISBN: 9781774688205 (KDP Paperback 2 ed)

ISBN: 9781774688212 (KDP Hardcover)

ISBN: 9780992153960 (Kindle)

ISBN: 9780993768743 (ePub)

ISBN: 9781774688229 (Lulu Paperback 2 ed)

ISBN: 9781774685280 (accessible audiobook)

Also by P.D. Workman

FIND MORE BOOKS AT PDWORKMAN.COM

YOUNG ADULT FICTION:

Medical Kidnap Files:
YA Suspense
Mito
EDS
Proxy
Toxo
Pain
Fail
Pulse

Between the Cracks:
Gritty Contemporary YA Family Saga
Ruby
June and Justin
Michelle
Chloe
Ronnie
June, Into the Light

Tamara's Teardrops:
Gritty Contemporary YA
Tattooed Teardrops
Two Teardrops
Tortured Teardrops
Vanishing Teardrops

Breaking the Pattern:
Gritty Contemporary YA

Henry

Sandy

Bobby

Stand Alone Young Adult:

Stand Alone

Don't Forget Steven

Those Who Believe

Cynthia has a Secret

Questing for a Dream

Darkness before the Dream (prequel story)

Once Brothers

Intersexion

Making Her Mark

Endless Change

Gem, Himself, Alone

AND MORE AT PDWORKMAN.COM

To those we have allowed to fall between the cracks.

CHAPTER One

Ruby lay in Chuck's arms, listening to his deep, regular breathing. She wondered fleetingly what he did the nights she didn't see him. Sometimes it was almost a week between visits. Sometimes she saw him almost every day, but sometimes it was a long time in between.

Ruby shifted to move her arm, which was falling asleep. Chuck stirred, and the hair on his arm tickled her cheek. Ruby stroked his arm with one finger, sighing. She felt safe. The nights that she ended up alone, when she couldn't find any company, were the hardest. Cold, alone, scared... Ruby's heart pounded faster just thinking about it. Ruby turned over restlessly to face Chuck. He stirred drowsily, and his eyes opened a slit.

"Are you still awake?" he murmured.

"Mmm-hmm."

"Go to sleep. It's gotta be two in the morning."

"Three-thirty," Ruby told him.

"Mmm. Come here."

He pulled her close to his chest. Ruby tucked her head under his chin and closed her eyes. He rubbed her back for a couple of minutes before he fell asleep again. After a while, Ruby finally fell asleep as well.

Ruby awoke in the morning to an empty bed. Chuck's side was cold and empty. Ruby stretched out her sleep-cramped muscles, slid out of bed, and pulled on her t-shirt and shorts. She wandered out to the kitchen, yawning.

"Hey," Chuck greeted. "You're actually up."

He was all ready for the office. Showered, dressed, curly hair perfectly coiffed. His blue eyes were bright and alert. He smiled at her and took a sip from his coffee mug.

"Yeah," Ruby smothered another yawn. "What time is it?"

"Almost nine. I'm on my way out," he glanced toward the door.

"Mmm. To work?"

"Yeah, precious. Some of us have jobs," he teased.

"I would if anyone would hire me."

"Well then, go to school," Chuck suggested.

Ruby laughed, wrinkling her nose.

"Uh-uh. What am I going to do at school?"

"Whatever the other kids are doing."

Ruby just shook her head.

"You look after yourself," Chuck said, smiling as he looked her over, "and don't forget your jacket."

"Yeah, yeah." Ruby rolled her eyes. She glanced around and picked the jacket up off of the back of the couch.

"Seriously." Chuck's voice took on a more severe tone. "Last time you left a pair of earrings on the sink. Be more careful."

"You already told me," Ruby huffed. "Sorry, okay?"

Chuck tugged at his shirt cuffs to get them a perfect half-inch below his suit jacket.

"All right, Ruby, let's go."

Ruby put her arms around his neck and pulled him in close for a good-bye kiss.

"I'll see you around," he said softly.

"Yeah. You gonna be there tonight?" Ruby questioned, picking up her backpack.

"Maybe."

Chuck rarely committed. Sometimes he'd pick her up, and sometimes he wouldn't. He never knew ahead of time. Ruby wondered if he met someone else the other nights, policing her as carefully as he policed Ruby, to make sure that she didn't leave any sign of her presence. He had his reasons, but Ruby always wondered if he was doing more than just trying to guard his reputation. Why was it so important that there were no signs in his apartment that he had a girlfriend?

They separated in the hall, Chuck going one way and Ruby the other. Ruby wandered to the coffee shop down the street and sipped a fresh cup of coffee slowly. The boy behind the counter always paid her plenty of attention, and Ruby often wondered what kind of guy he was. He was high school or college-aged, she wasn't sure which. She'd never seen him at the high school, but she didn't hang around there very much, he might go there and she just hadn't seen him.

"Running a little late today," he commented.

"Yeah," Ruby agreed. She wasn't sure what it was about her that interested him. She never did her makeup before she got there. Sometimes, like today, she didn't even have her hair combed yet. It was just a halfway point for her, between Chuck's apartment and wherever she decided to go next.

"Doing anything special today?" the boy questioned, with an interested smile.

Ruby shrugged.

"No."

He probably was intrigued because most girls Ruby's age would really be flattered by the attention of a guy his age and fawn all over him, but Ruby really didn't care. He was actually younger than the guys she usually went with. There were only a couple of guys under twenty that she really liked. He might be a better catch than the guys Ruby's own age, but he wasn't very interesting.

"What are you taking in school?" he asked.

"I don't usually go."

"Oh. Where do you go?"

Ruby shrugged.

"Around."

She put down her mug, and he moved to refill it. Ruby shook her head and waved her hand.

"No, thanks."

Ruby got up and went to the lady's room. Unzipping her knapsack, she dug for her lipstick and other makeup. She brushed her teeth before putting on the lipstick, and brushed her hair into order. Her blond hair was straight and fine and she rarely bothered to curl or style it. She pulled it back in a pony and put an elastic around it to keep it in place. She packed her bag again and moved on.

Ruby wandered through a couple of the arcades and hangouts that she usually found company at, but things were strangely quiet. She eventually gave up, and with a sigh, decided to try the school. She arrived halfway through the morning, and joined up with a couple of the girls she knew.

Kate was plain, with no figure, a girl who desperately wanted to be popular, but no amount of makeup or trendy clothes would make her so. She didn't have the personality to join the 'in' crowd. She didn't have the money, the manner, the superficiality.

Marty was a different story. Her name was really Martha, but she preferred the less feminine form. Ruby liked her better than Kate, because Marty was more boyish, more like the guys that Ruby usually spent her time with. Of course, Marty would never be mistaken for a boy. Unlike Kate, she was an early bloomer; her figure already well-developed and she had a head of wild, dark curly hair. Marty had an easy manner, the type that attracted people to her, but didn't really care for a lot of friends or attention.

Ruby felt at ease with the two of them. They were undemanding friends, and she could spend a day with them every now and then and not have them grill her on where she'd been and what she had been doing.

"Hey, Marty," Ruby greeted, and she nodded to Kate.

"Hi, Ruby. You're just in time for math."

Ruby wrinkled her nose.

"Oh, joy. What are we doing?"

"Algebra."

Ruby shook her head. They arrived in class a couple of minutes before the second bell, and Ruby and Marty talked and watched Kate trying to flirt with Robin, the boy who sat in front of her, who she'd had a crush on for a couple months.

"He's never even going to notice her," Ruby commented, watching Robin answer Kate casually, oblivious to her body language.

"I don't even know what she sees in him," Marty commented. "Or in any guy."

"Any junior high boy," Ruby agreed.

Glancing over at them, Robin noticed Marty looking at him, and his manner changed instantly.

"Hey, Marty! How about you, what'd you think of the homework?"

Marty shrugged, and rolled her eyes at Ruby. Robin didn't seem to know how to take Ruby, and didn't say anything to her.

"Did you get A-8?" Kate asked Marty.

"Yeah."

"Can I see it?"

Marty got out her book and passed it across. Kate stared at it for a moment, and scribbled the answer down in her book. The teacher walked in and looked around. He appeared surprised to see Ruby sitting there.

"Are you still in this class?" he questioned.

"Yeah."

"Where have you been the last couple of weeks?"

"Sick." Ruby shrugged.

"You have a note from your doctor?" he demanded.

"No."

"Your mom?"

"I don't live with my mom," Ruby pointed out.

"Where do you live?"

"Foster care."

"Do you have a note from your foster parents?"

"No. You can call my social worker if you want," she suggested.

He hesitated for a moment, then shrugged it off. Too much bother.

"You're going to have a lot to catch up on. Can you get the notes from one of your friends?"

"Uh-huh."

"Okay," he moved towards the middle of the front. "Kate, do your own homework. If you don't have it by now, it won't do you any good. Anyone have any questions from the homework last night?"

Ruby stretched her legs out and looked around the room, tuning the teacher out.

At lunchtime, Ruby and the other girls went over to the senior high half of the school to look for some guys to join up with. Kate would never have been able to interest any of the guys by herself, and Marty didn't really care to, but Ruby had something that attracted the older boys.

"It's because you look so much older," Kate said. "They don't think they're dating a kid, then." She sighed. "I don't look a day older than I am. If I at least had a body like Marty…"

"You're welcome to it," Marty grumbled. "I sure don't want it. But that's not what makes the guys like Ruby. She's almost as flat as you are."

"You just look… more mature," Kate told Ruby.

Ruby shrugged.

"There's Brian. Let's see what he's doing."

Brian looked happy to see them. Tall, slim, with longish hair, he had a handsome face and was almost always smiling and relaxed.

"Hey, girls," he greeted cheerfully. "Looking for some action?"

He put his arm around Ruby's shoulders and gave her a quick hug.

"Got any plans?" Ruby questioned.

"Nope. You wanna go to my place and order a pizza?"

"Sure."

A couple of Brian's friends and Kate and Marty all agreed, so they headed for his house. Brian broke out a couple of six-packs when they got there, and they lounged around drinking and watching kid's shows on TV while they waited for the pizza.

It was almost one when the pizza delivery man got there, but nobody really cared. Missing the first class after lunch was no big deal. In another hour, though, most of them were done eating and getting set to go back to school. Ruby didn't move from her spot on the couch beside Brian.

"You going back?" she asked Brian.

"Not if you'll stick around," he said, giving her a squeeze and kissing her on top of the head.

"Good. I'll see you guys around," Ruby told Kate and Marty.

"Okay. See you later," Marty agreed.

The others went back to school. Tanner, one of Brian's friends, stuck around for another hour watching TV with them. Then he got bored, and suggested they all go somewhere.

"The arcade?" Brian suggested.

"For a while," Ruby agreed. She knew how it would go. They'd play for a while, but Brian would be off his game from drinking for three hours, and he'd get frustrated.

Ruby played a few games herself, but the games or the booze were giving her a headache. She watched Brian play for a while, but he wasn't getting anywhere near his high scores and she could see his frustration mounting.

"Why don't we go shoot some pool," she suggested.

Brian slammed his hand down on the control panel and let the game end. He turned to face her.

"Yeah. Let's blow. I'm totally useless at this today."

Tanner had disappeared at some point. The pool hall was more relaxing. Ruby and Brian shot a leisurely game together, without caring who got the better shots or who won. Brian cajoled a jug of beer out of the management, and they smoked and drank and shot into the evening.

"You know, your friends are sort of strange," Brian commented.

Ruby smiled.

"Yeah, I know it. They're misfits, like me."

"That Marty—she gives me the creeps. I get the feeling she's got a voodoo doll somewhere with my name on it."

Ruby pictured it, and laughed.

"Don't mention it to her, she might think it's a good idea," she giggled.

"She hates me, doesn't she?"

"It's not you. She doesn't like any guys. I think she's got a short-circuit somewhere."

Brian looked thoughtful.

"No, it's more than that. She doesn't look at the other guys like she looks at me. I think it's because you like me. I think she's actually jealous."

"Jealous?" Ruby repeated, surprised. "Nah. If she was jealous, why go back to school? She could have said: 'let's go somewhere' and we could have gone somewhere without you. She could'a' skipped one afternoon of school to do something with all of us. We would've done something with her."

"She doesn't ever get you to herself, does she? Just the two of you?"

"Well, not much..." Ruby admitted. "You're nuts, you know? Marty isn't like that, she just doesn't like guys."

"Maybe... but I don't know."

They dropped the subject.

"I gotta be getting home," Brian commented, looking at his watch.

"It's not that late," Ruby protested.

He gave her a couple of gentle kisses, softening the parting.

"I know. But I got things going on tonight," he apologized.

"You gotta go home? Right now?"

"Sorry."

Ruby shrugged.

"All right."

"You want me to drop you off somewhere?" Brian suggested.

"No. I'll hang around here a while."

Brian took a glance around.

"I get nervous, you hanging around places like this by yourself," he said.

Ruby looked over the crowds.

"They're just kids, Bri'. And it's not like it's a gang hangout or something."

"I guess," he agreed reluctantly. "You look after yourself, though."

"Sure. See you 'round."

"Okay, babe."

He kissed her again briefly, and left. Ruby hung out there for a while before going to the bar where Chuck would meet her if he was picking her up. The bouncers knew her, but they never let her in because she was too young. If she was a few years older, they might have bent and let her in, but as it was, she had to stand outside. If it was cold out, they'd let her stand inside the door periodically to warm herself up, but otherwise she stood outside with the hookers, watching for Chuck.

"Hi, Ruby," Betty greeted cheerfully.

"Hi, Betty."

"How're you doing, girl?" Grace questioned.

"Good. Chuck ain't been by, has he?"

"Nope. You expecting him tonight?"

"Maybe. Saw him last night, so maybe not."

"Does he ever pay you anything?" Grace demanded.

"No. It's not like that," Ruby protested with a laugh. "I like to be with him."

"He's taking advantage of you."

"No, he's not. Any time I felt like that, I'd just stop coming here," Ruby pointed out.

"She's just too young to know the difference," Betty interposed. "She thinks she loves him."

"No…" Ruby said, frowning, "I just… like being with him. I don't like being alone."

"Well, you could get company that paid a lot better than that," Grace grumbled.

"Aw, leave her alone. She's better off not getting into this business."

Grace lit a cigarette, and they were quiet for a while. A car pulled up in front of the bar. Betty went up to talk to the driver.

"Hi, honey."

The man indicated Ruby. Betty glanced over at her.

"Oh, she's not interested, honey. But Grace or me…"

"No. Her."

"She's not working."

"I'll make it worth your while," the man said to Ruby, holding up a wad of cash.

Ruby shook her head.

"She's just waiting for her friend," Betty explained.

He screeched his tires when he pulled out, and shot down the street. Betty went back to stand with Ruby and Grace.

Grace shook her head.

"You stand there in shorts and a tee and sneakers and get more pick-ups than we do. I just don't know what you do."

"She's young. Men like'em young," Betty said.

"I started at her age, and I never got the attention she does."

Betty looked at Ruby and shrugged.

"Some people just got what it takes."

Ruby watched for Chuck's car. If he didn't show up, she'd have to try and find somewhere else she could spend the night. But she wasn't going to take up a new profession to do it. An hour passed, and Ruby knew he wasn't going to show up. She said goodbye to the girls, and started to walk away. She got about half a block down, and a red convertible pulled up beside her.

"Hey, sweetheart."

"Not interested."

"Slow down. How'd you like to make a little cash?"

Ruby stopped and looked at him. A small, ferret-faced man in a red convertible. She'd seen him before, but she couldn't remember where. He was well dressed, but she got a bad vibe from him.

"What're you going to pay me for?" she demanded.

"To work for me," he said vaguely.

"Doin' what?"

"Leave her alone," Betty said, catching up to Ruby. "Ruby doesn't need any help from you."

The man looked at Betty.

"Stay out of it, Betty. This doesn't concern you."

"Ruby's my friend, you'd better believe it concerns me. Ruby, you ever met my boss?"

"No. Guess I haven't."

"Well, he's a snake, so stay away from him. You see this rat, you go the other way."

"Thanks."

Ruby turned and walked away. She could hear the pimp getting after Betty as she walked away, but Ruby didn't look back. The last thing she needed was to get involved in that scene. She went back to the pool hall, but no-one that she knew was around. Ruby stayed there until the small hours of the morning before admitting to herself that her choices were either sleeping on the street or going home. She left the pool hall and started for home. Halfway there, a squad car pulled up beside her.

"Hi," the police officer said, through the open window.

"Hi there," Ruby acknowledged.

"A little late to be out wandering, isn't it?"

"I'm on my way home."

"How about if I drive you?" he offered.

"Yeah, okay."

"Hop in."

Ruby got into the squad car and shut the door. He pulled away from the curb.

"What's your name?"

"Ruby."

"Where do you live, Ruby?"

She gave him her address.

"Good. The name's Brown. What were you doing out so late?"

"Just hanging out." Ruby shrugged.

"There's lots of crazies out there. You shouldn't be out alone."

"I know."

"Your folks know where you are?"

"No."

"You do this often?"

Ruby shrugged.

"No. Not a lot."

Brown didn't say anything else. They pulled up to the house a few minutes later. Ruby glanced at the cop to see if he was going to insist on escorting her in and talking to her parents, but he was relaxed and didn't move to get out.

"Thanks for the lift," Ruby said.

"No problem," Brown took a business card out of his pocket. "If you're ever out late alone or need something, you call me. I'd rather be a taxi for a couple minutes then find you dead by the road somewhere."

Ruby took the card from him.

"Hey—thanks. That's cool."

She got out and went up to the house. The key was on a ring on her knapsack, and she waved at Brown and let herself in.

CHAPTER Two

Ruby awoke disoriented, in a fog. She rolled over and almost fell on the floor. Steadying herself, Ruby opened her eyes and looked around. She was at home, sleeping on the couch. She sat up slowly and looked around. It still smelled the same. Stale cooking, cigarette smoke, sweat, dirty shoes tumbled around the back of the door.

"Ruby's home," Chloe called out. Ruby turned and looked at her.

"Hi, Chlo'."

"Hi, Ruby. What'cha doin' here?"

Ruby shrugged. Chloe walked into the kitchen, out of sight. Their mom came down the stairs.

"What did you say, Chloe?" She saw Ruby. "Oh. You're here. What time did you get here?"

"I dunno. Two, three…"

"Why? Your foster family kick you out?"

"No. I was just out too late. They lock me out after midnight."

"Well, you shouldn't be coming back here. You should be going back to your foster family before midnight. Does your social worker know you're staying out late?"

"Sometimes."

"I'm going to call him," her mother warned.

"Okay," Ruby said, shrugging.

"Go have breakfast with Chloe. I want to talk to you before you leave. Okay?"

"Yeah."

Ruby got up and went into the kitchen. Chloe was eating a bowl of cereal. Ruby poured a cup of coffee for herself.

"Coffee's bad for you," Chloe pointed out.

"I don't want to get fat," Ruby countered.

"You're not fat."

"I plan on keeping it that way," Ruby agreed.

"You still shouldn't do it."

June and Justin came into the kitchen, and Chloe got bowls out for them. Chloe was dirty blond, with shoulder length hair. The twins both had dark hair and round faces.

"How old are they now?" Ruby questioned.

"We're six," June answered, for herself.

"I remember when they were born," Ruby told Chloe.

"Were you here?" Chloe questioned.

"Mmm... yeah. When they were born, I was."

"You must have left right after."

"Yeah. Pretty much. Where's Ronnie?" Ruby looked around for their other sister.

"Foster family," Chloe advised.

"Ronnie too? When did that happen?"

"Couple weeks ago."

"Why?"

"She wanted to. She's been getting into trouble from Mom and at school and all, and she thought it would be fun."

"Really? I never would have thought she'd have the guts. So why are you still here?"

"I get along with Mom and Dad," Chloe said loftily. "I'm responsible."

"Well, I guess every family gets one. It's your funeral."

"It's my life," Chloe corrected primly.

Ruby's mom walked in.

"You have an appointment with your social worker today."

"When?"

"Ten. If you leave now, you can still get the bus."

"Okay. See you around."

"Bye."

"Bye, Chlo'."

Ruby did make the bus, and wondered on her way to the Social Services office if she should actually bother to go or not. But her mom might follow up to see if she was there or not.

Ruby didn't have to wait long at the Social Services reception area before the woman showed her in for her appointment. Ruby had enough time to grab another cup of coffee, but not long enough to browse through the newest magazine on the side table, which happened to be a good six months old.

"Hello, Ruby," her social worker greeted without looking away from his computer.

Ruby sat down in the chair in front of his desk.

"Hi, Chuck," she crooned.

"Mr. Samuel here, Ruby. You know that," Chuck insisted his eyes darting around to make sure that no-one had heard.

Ruby just grinned. Other foster kids called their social workers by the first name, but it made Chuck really nervous. Ruby kind of liked to see him get flustered over her.

"So why did your mom call me today?" he asked, frowning down at the pink message slip on the desk.

"You weren't around last night, and I couldn't find any of the friends I stay over with, so I went home." Ruby shrugged, and leaned her chair back, looking up at the ceiling. "I told her my foster family locks me out after midnight."

"You could go to one of the shelters," he pointed out.

"They do lock their doors at midnight."

"If you can't find one of your friends before eleven," Chuck said, wording his statement carefully. "You aren't going to see them."

"I know. But I don't like the shelters. They're just... gross."

"Well, I don't think your mom minds you staying there every now and then. I just don't want her to start asking questions about your foster family. So don't do it too often," he warned.

"It's been at least a month since I was there last."

"Okay," Chuck approved, nodding.

Ruby let the front legs of her chair drop back to the floor with a thump.

"You know what?" Ruby offered. "My little sister Ronnie's in foster care now."

"I know."

"You know?" Ruby was surprised. "Why didn't you tell me?"

"Client privilege. That information is confidential."

"Client? Does that mean that you're her social worker too?"

"I've been trying to get her file. I think I would be more effective, already knowing the background she's coming from."

"Huh. That would be cool, hey? Having both of us? And you could arrange for us to meet, couldn't you? If she's not at home anymore, I can see her, right?" Ruby pressed.

"Yes, you could probably meet. I'll see if I can arrange a 'reunion' for the two of you. Saturday?"

"Yeah. That would be great. I can't believe Ronnie's in foster care! She wasn't ever a black sheep like me." Ruby laughed. She released her hair from the pony tail elastic, and ran her fingers through the length of her hair, toying with it.

"Well, everyone has their own set of problems," Chuck observed.

"Why did she leave?"

"That's confidential. You know I'm not allowed to tell you things like that."

"It's not like I don't know the 'family situation'."

"It's still not allowed. And I imagine there are things going on that you don't have any idea about. It's been quite a while since you lived there."

"Yeah. Well, Ronnie can tell me on Saturday."

"Right. Well, is there anything else we need to discuss?"

Ruby massaged her scalp, and then pulled her hair back through the elastic again.

"Just whether I'll see you tonight," she said lowly.

"Hush. I'll try, but you keep your mouth shut, all right?"

"I know," Ruby said with a smile. "You just keep me happy, and I won't say a word."

Chuck frowned, looking at her. He took out his appointment book and looked at it.

"Nine o'clock," he said shortly, and put his book back away.

Ruby smiled.

"Nine it is. You'd better be there."

He nodded. Ruby stood up.

"Bye then, Mr. Samuel," Ruby said demurely.

"Good-bye, Ruby."

Ruby waited excitedly for her meeting with Ronnie. She had arrived early so that there was no way they'd miss each other. Ruby and Ronnie had never been close at home. They were five years apart in age, so

Ronnie had hardly been more than a baby when Ruby first went into foster care. Now Ronnie was eight, and they'd really never had a conversation of more than a couple minutes in length. But with Ronnie leaving the family and going into foster care, Ruby suddenly had a longing to become close to her sister. For the first time, she felt like she had something in common with someone in her family.

It seemed like hours before Chuck's car pulled into the parking lot. Ruby stood up and waved at them. Ronnie looked different than she expected. When Ruby had left the family, she'd been wild and rebellious, and made herself appear a lot older than she really was. But Ronnie was the same little girl Ruby remembered. She didn't look any older or more mature. You could tell she was with a foster family instead of at home, because she had on designer pants and a blouse instead of cut-offs and a tank top. If anything, the clothes made her seem even younger, like a little girl going to her first day of school. Her thick brown hair was carefully braided into two pigtails, with ribbons around them. She looked like a doll, not Ruby's sister.

Ronnie submitted to being hugged, but didn't hug Ruby back. She looked uncomfortable. Ronnie sat down on the bench of the picnic table where Ruby had been waiting for them. Chuck looked hesitant, like he didn't know whether to join them or go back to his car. Ruby motioned him away, and he went back and sat in the car.

"So how come you didn't tell me you were in foster care now?" Ruby demanded.

"I don't exactly have your phone number," Ronnie pointed out.

"You could have told you social worker, they would have got in touch with me."

Ronnie shrugged.

"So is Chuck your social worker now?" Ruby questioned.

"Who?"

"Mr. Samuel," Ruby corrected quickly, realizing her mistake.

"I guess so. He's the one who picked me up."

"You'll like him. He's cool."

"Yeah, okay."

"So why did you leave? Just get tired of Mom and Dad getting on your case?"

"I guess," Ronnie avoided her eyes.

Ruby sat down, moving in close.

"Well, then, why?" she persisted. "You can tell me. It's not exactly like I'm gonna tattle to Mom. Or Social Services."

Ronnie shrugged, looking down at the grass. She dug a hole with her toe.

"Ronnie?"

"Ruby..."

"Yeah?"

"Do you like your foster family?"

"Yeah, I love my foster family," Ruby said briskly. "Why?"

"No, I mean—do you really like them? Better than Mom and Dad?"

Ruby studied her little sister, trying to see where she was going.

"I don't know. They're different," she was floundering, "I guess I like them a different way."

Ronnie looked relieved.

"Yeah, just different," she agreed.

"Are they okay? If you don't have a good family, Mr. Samuel can move you."

"No, I like them." Ronnie was silent for a few minutes. "Ruby... have you ever thought about what it would be like to be adopted?"

Ruby sat on the bench beside Ronnie.

"Adopted? By someone else? No."

"The family you're with—have you been with them since you left?"

"No."

"How long?"

"Um—a year," Ruby invented.

"Would you like them to adopt you?"

"No," Ruby said firmly. Ronnie nodded. "Why, are they talking about adopting you?"

Ronnie nodded again. Ruby understood. Ronnie's carefully braided hair and cute schoolgirl outfit, they were all part of a foster family trying to mold her into a daughter that they could adopt.

"You've only been there two weeks, and they're talking adoption?" she questioned in disbelief.

"Uh-huh."

"They're not supposed to do that. They're supposed to be working for reunification!"

"I'm not going back home."

"I know that, and you know that, but the system—they don't know that. They try to bring families back together. It doesn't mean anything, just that foster parents aren't usually allowed to adopt."

"So they can't?"

"They might be able to, but not for quite a while."

"Oh."

16

"It's all right—it's not like they're going to send you back home. But no-one's going to adopt you. Not for a few years."

Ronnie was silent for a while.

"Why did you decide not to stay with Mom and Dad?" she questioned.

Ruby thought back. It was a long time ago now. She hardly remembered the reasons, the restrictions put on her. She could remember being deeply unhappy, trapped, and angry. She remembered feeling desperately alone in a houseful of people. When Mom and Dad had started talking about having her taken out of the family, it had been such a relief. Getting out of there had been such a relief. The foster families she had gone to had been better, most of them less constricting, but she still didn't have what she needed. Now she was really on her own, making her own choices. When she could, she stayed with Chuck. If she couldn't be with Chuck, she would try to stay with one of her other friends. Foster care was really not for her. She wanted more freedom than that.

"I don't know, Ronnie. I just couldn't stay there anymore. I felt like I was being strangled," she explained.

"By Dad?" Ronnie questioned.

"No, more by Mom."

"Mom's okay…"

"We never really got along. She wished I was never born."

"Why?" Ronnie questioned, shocked.

"Well, she and Dad broke up, you know. Then she found out she was pregnant with me, so they got back together again and got married. So whenever she's unhappy about the way things turned out—it's my fault."

"I didn't know that," Ronnie said, wide-eyed.

"Yeah. Well, you weren't exactly around to know what was going on while I was there," Ruby pointed out with a shrug.

"I don't think Mom hates you."

"No, she just doesn't like having me around." Ruby thought about it and shook her head. "But you don't get along with Dad? How come? He never really was around much when I was there."

"I dunno. We just don't… get along so good."

"Well, he can't shout at you or anything now. You like your foster folks okay?"

"Yeah, they're nice," Ronnie agreed.

"What's your phone number? Can I call you?"

Ronnie gave her the phone number.

"What about yours?"

"Oh, I'm not there very often. You just call Mr. Samuels, and he can usually get a hold of me."

Chuck had gotten out of the car and was coming towards them.

"Why aren't you usually with your foster family?" Ronnie asked, puzzled.

Ruby hesitated.

"We'll talk again later. Maybe next week. But if you need anything, you find me, okay?"

"Okay."

Chuck reached them.

"You guys have a good talk?"

Both girls nodded.

"Ronnie, why don't you go back to the car. I just want to talk to Ruby for a minute."

Ronnie walked away from them. Ruby watched her make her way back to the car and get in.

"Why did she leave?" Ruby questioned.

"If she didn't tell you, I don't think it's my place."

"Well, I have some information that might interest you, as her social worker."

"What?"

"You tell me why she left, and I'll tell you what I know," Ruby bargained.

Chuck sighed.

"Don't play these games with me, Ruby. If there's something I should know about Ronnie, you'd better tell me."

Ruby considered.

"She doesn't want to be removed from the family, though, so that's not why I'm telling you."

"What, then?" he said, tilting his head to the side, waiting.

"They're talking about adopting her."

"What?" Chuck's voice came out in a yelp.

Ruby nodded.

"She wants to stay with them—but tell them to lay off a bit. She's confused, she doesn't know what to think."

Chuck nodded.

"I'll tell them, all right," he agreed. "Would you be interested in being placed in the same foster family as Ronnie? I haven't asked them if they would take you, but they've looked after sibling groups before."

Ruby shook her head resolutely.

"I don't want another foster family."

"Well, think about it. It would give you a chance to spend some time with a family member without being with your parents."

Ruby shrugged uncomfortably.

"We'll just stick to visits for now."

Chuck nodded.

"Okay. I'll see you later."

They couldn't exactly kiss good bye, with Ronnie watching out the window. Chuck touched Ruby on the arm and gave her a little smile, then returned to the car.

Ruby ran into Mike at the arcade late in the afternoon. Although she considered herself too mature to have "a crush" on any boy, she had to admit that even just the sound of Mike's voice gave her goose bumps. She had never met another man who made her feel like that.

"Hey, it's Ruby," he said from behind her, putting his arms around her. Ruby forgot her game and turned around in his embrace.

"Mike!"

"Hi, baby."

He was handsome, smooth and cool as ice. He was tall and slim, and wore the jacket of the Jaguars, a local gang. His hair was dark and lank, his eyes brilliant blue. Sharp, prominent cheekbones. If he was with one of the boys from his gang, he paid no attention to her, but on the rare days that he was alone, he treated her like she was the only person in the world.

"You looking for some company?" Ruby questioned, snuggling close.

"Are you free?"

"Yeah, always."

"Let's go back to my place."

Ruby nodded eagerly and went with him. Mike took out a couple of joints as they left the arcade.

"Smoke?"

"Sure, thanks."

She took the joint, and he lit it for her. Ruby's heart was beating quickly, and she wondered if Mike could tell she was breathing faster. He turned on the TV as soon as they walked in the door of the apartment. Ruby got a couple of beers out of the fridge for them, and they cuddled up on the couch.

Chuck pulled up in front of the bar. One of the ladies walked up to the car.

"Oh, hi, there. Looking for Ruby?" she questioned.

"Where is she?" he demanded.

"I haven't seen her tonight. Anyone seen Ruby?" she looked around at the other hookers. They all shrugged or shook their heads. Chuck looked at his watch and took an impatient glance up and down the street.

"Where is she? I can't sit around here waiting for her."

"Maybe she has other plans tonight," the girl suggested.

"Like what?" Chuck snapped irritably. He looked at his watch again, and pulled away.

Monique grinned, enjoying seeing Chuck frustrated and disappointed instead of Ruby for once.

"Good for you, Ruby," she said under her breath. "You show him who's the boss of this relationship."

Ruby turned over again and cuddled closer to Mike. She was cold, almost shivering. They must have been having trouble with the building's boiler. Mike didn't seem to notice the temperature. Ruby tried to tuck her feet under his legs to warm them up, but he shifted and moved away in his sleep. Ruby curled up in a ball. There was a noise in the hall outside the apartment, and she strained her ears trying to hear what it was. There were voices, but it was late for anyone to be out. Ruby sat up. It sounded like the voices were right outside the apartment door.

There was a crash. Ruby jumped, and so did Mike, beside her.

"What was that?" he hissed, sitting up and fumbling on the bedside table, knocking things off. There was a blinding light in Ruby's eyes, she couldn't open them. She covered her eyes with her hand.

"Get your hands up, Mikey!" a harsh voice screamed. Ruby tried to squint through her fingers to see what was going on. All that she could see was the light pointing at her eyes. She tried to shade her eyes from the light and turned aside to look at Mike. He was frozen, one hand on the nightstand, grasping for a gun that he must have knocked to the floor. He was as white as the sheet on the bed, his eyes wild.

"Mikey, Mikey… didn't you hear me? I said get your hands up!" the voice screamed.

Mike slowly raised his hands. The light divided in two and one of the lights moved towards them. Mike started to lower his hands.

"Keep'em still," the voice warned. He approached on Ruby's side of the bed. Ruby cowered back, trying to avoid him. She could just barely see his outline, his shadow, behind the light. He reached towards her. Ruby tried to avoid his grasp. He wrapped his fingers around her long, blond hair and jerked her towards him. Ruby winced in pain and couldn't resist.

"This your girlfriend? She's very cute."

"Leave her alone," Mike said shakily.

The hand in her hair jerked again, hard. Ruby choked back a cry. The light that the man was holding went out. Then there was a gun pressing against her temple. Ruby held her breath and tried not to blink her eyes, hoping that she wouldn't cry.

"How'd you like us to kill her, Mikey?" the voice taunted. "What do you think of that?"

Mike swore quietly.

"Please…"

The hand let go of her hair. He sat on the edge of the bed, running his hand provocatively down the smooth skin of Ruby's neck and shoulder.

"Mmm, I could spend some time here."

Mike swore angrily, and lunged for him. There was an explosion. Ruby yelped and closed her eyes. Her ears rang and her face burned. When she opened her eyes again, the light was no longer shining directly on her eyes, but was playing over the bed. Mike was laying across her, still. Blood was splattered everywhere.

"He dead?" a different voice questioned.

The man who was closest to Ruby leaned across her to check Mike for a pulse.

"Yep," he sat back up and touched Ruby briefly. "What do you think of that, baby?"

"What a waste," the other voice said. "Well, we'd better blow before the cops show up. What are you going to do about her?"

"Hmm. No time for what I'd like to do. Are you going to keep your mouth shut, sweetie? 'cause if you're not, we'll settle this now."

Ruby tried to answer. There was a lump in her throat and she couldn't speak. She nodded a bit, and covered her eyes.

"Good. 'cause I will find you if you talk."

He bent over and picked up her knapsack.

"This is yours?"

Ruby could see him through the cracks in her fingers. She nodded again. He unzipped the front pocket and found her wallet. He looked through it, and nodded, throwing the contents on the floor.

"I'll look you up," he promised, and he and his friend walked out of the room. Ruby cuddled up and held Mike close.

Holt was one of the first ones to the scene. They had a few brief words with the neighbors who had called in. Then they entered the apartment with their guns drawn and a shouted warning of "police!" Holt groped for a switch and flipped on the lights as they went in. The bedroom was a mess. There was blood everywhere. After clearing the apartment, Holt holstered his gun and leaned over to check that the couple in the bed were both dead. The boy was lifeless. The girl, however, flinched away when he touched her throat to check for a pulse.

"Get an ambulance," Holt told Jarislow.

Jarislow nodded, and stepped out of the room to make the call. Holt tried to separate the couple and examine the girl. She jumped every time his fingers brushed her skin. He finally got the two of them untwined.

"It's all right," he said softly to the girl. "It's okay, everything is all right. You're safe. Are you hurt?"

The girl shook her head, her hands covering her face. She was splattered and smeared with blood. She was very young.

"Can you tell me what happened?" Holt asked. She shook her head. Holt gently tugged her hands away from her face. There was an ugly bullet-path across her forehead. He took her radial pulse. It was strong. Her eyes were wide and staring.

"Are you okay?" he questioned. She couldn't answer. Holt turned his head to speak to Jarislow.

"Get me a wet cloth."

Jarislow nodded and ducked into the bathroom. He came out with a towel, and handed it to Holt. He carefully dabbed at the black and red mark across her head. She didn't seem to feel it.

"It's just a powder burn," Jarislow observed, watching.

"Yes," Holt agreed with relief. He glanced around the room, analyzing the scene. "There was only one shot reported... the shooter must have been standing here. One bullet got them both."

"She's lucky."

"Yeah. Homicide on the way?"

"Someone will be here any minute."

"See if you can find a blanket or coat or something."

Holt picked up the girl's clothes from the floor.

"Let's get you dressed, all right? So you can warm up a bit."

She had goose bumps, and she was shivering. Even fully dressed and with a jacket, Holt found the room chilly. The girl's movements were slow and clumsy, but Holt guided her hands into the shirt and helped pull on her blue-jean cut-offs. Jarislow came in with a dark jacket.

"This is all I could find. The closets are pretty bare."

Holt took the jacket and turned it around to look at the logo on the back.

"Our vic's a Jaguar. Things have been pretty hot with the Jags and other gangs lately." Holt pulled the girl gently to her feet. Her knees buckled. Holt put his arm around her and tried to get her steadied on her feet. Jarislow went over to the bed.

"Who is he?" he questioned. "I know a lot of the Jag's by sight." He turned the boy over, and gagged, covering his mouth and turning quickly away. Holt glanced over, his emotions shut off. He hadn't looked at the boy before, except to make sure that he was dead. His face had been taken off by a soft-nosed bullet. There was no way they could recognize him now. The girl moaned, wilting, and Holt took her into the bathroom. He held her up against the sink, splashing water on her face to keep her conscious.

"Come on, stay with me, here. None of that."

She shuddered, and started to come back to herself. Holt heard the homicide officers come into the bedroom. He slowly let go of the girl.

"Are you okay? Can you stand here a minute?"

She stayed steady, and he stepped out into the bedroom.

"You moved him?" one of the homicide cops questioned.

"The girl moved him. We had to shift him to get the two of them apart."

"The girl? Where was she?"

"Beside him."

"Has she told you anything?"

"No. She's scared. And hurt. Hasn't said a peep."

The homicide officer studied the scene carefully. He looked closely at the wall and the bed sheets.

"They weren't asleep."

"I don't expect so. I'd probably wake up when someone kicked the door in. His gun's on the floor. Must not have had it under the pillow."

"Dangerous if you're sleeping with someone else. I want to talk to this girl. Put her in the kitchen with a hot coffee and see if it gets rid of the shakes."

"I'll give it a try."

Holt went back into the bathroom, and found the girl hunched over on the floor, in the corner by the grungy shower.

"Oh, no. Come on. Let's go have a nice hot drink. Come on."

He pulled her to her feet again, and half-carried her into the kitchen. He settled her in a chair.

"There, you just sit there, and I'll get you a coffee. Lots of sugar."

He talked gently to her as he started the water boiling. There was only instant coffee, but it would work. A couple of paramedics came in.

"Hi, do you guys want to check her over? I'm getting her a coffee. You've got blankets with you, don't you?"

"Sure."

"She's cold."

One of the medics stayed to check her over, and the other one went back out to the hallway to take a blanket off the stretcher. The water started boiling, and Holt sloshed some into a cup with some crystals, and stirred in a couple of spoons full of sugar. The paramedic gave it to the girl, helping to steady her shaking hands. They wrapped the blanket around her. The medic continued to examine the girl while she drank.

"Is she going to be okay?" Holt questioned.

"We should take her to the hospital. She's shockie. She should be kept under observation."

"Can we keep her for just a few more minutes?"

"Sure. Not too long."

"I'll be right back, then."

Holt went back into the bedroom. He motioned to the homicide cop.

"Detective Merrill? If you want to try the girl now?"

"Thanks."

Merrill followed him into the kitchen. He sat down across the table from the girl.

"Hi there, honey. You feeling a little bit better?"

She shrugged, not looking up at him.

"What's your name?"

She mumbled something.

"What?"

"Ruby."

"Hi, Ruby. I'm Merrill, okay? How long have you been here tonight?"

She sank further into the blanket, pulling it close.

"I don't know," she said in a hoarse whisper.

"Did you just meet the boy tonight?"

"No."

"You guys know each other?"

"Uh-huh."

"Spend the day together?"

Ruby nodded.

"Part of it," she acknowledged.

"You want another coffee?"

She nodded at gave him her cup. Holt took it and put the kettle back on the burner.

"Can you tell me who came in here tonight?"

Ruby shook her head.

"How many were there?"

Ruby put her head down and didn't answer, pulling the blanket tightly around her.

"Did they threaten you?" Merrill questioned.

Ruby didn't respond.

"Of course they threatened you. And probably scared the heck out of you. Did they know who you are?"

She didn't answer.

"Her I.D. is on the floor in the bedroom," Holt contributed.

"So he found out your name and address, and he told you that if you said anything, he'd kill you."

Ruby stayed quiet. She shook her head and closed her eyes.

"I think we should get her to the hospital," one of the medics advised.

Merrill nodded.

"We can catch up again later. We need to call your parents, Ruby. What's your phone number?"

She stirred herself slightly, clearing her throat.

"Not my parents—my social worker."

"Okay. What's the number?"

Ruby gave it to him. Then she left with the medics to go the hospital. Holt went back into the bedroom.

"Jarislow. Come on, let's follow the girl to the hospital. We'll call her social worker on the way."

"Do you want me to bring her bag?"

"Yeah. Let's take a look first, though."

Jarislow brought the bag into the kitchen and emptied the contents onto the table. The two of them sorted through her stuff, and Holt nodded and they repacked. They headed to the hospital.

The phone trilled loudly, waking Chuck Samuels from a sound sleep. He fumbled for the receiver, swearing. He knocked the phone down, then picked it up, pulling the cord until he reached the receiver, and put it to his ear.

"Hello?" he growled. His heart was racing from the rude awakening.

"Is this Charles Samuels?" an official sounding voice questioned on the other end.

"Yeah," he snuffled and rubbed his eyes. "Who's this?"

"My name is Holt. You're Ruby Simpson's social worker?"

Chuck sat up straight.

"Ruby?" he repeated. "Yes—what's wrong?"

"Ruby's been in a small accident. She gave us your number."

"Yes. Where are you?"

"At the General."

"She's okay?"

"She's just under observation. I would appreciate it, though, if you could get in contact with someone who could sit with her," Holt suggested.

"I'll come down myself."

"I'll see you when you get here, then."

Holt saw the nurse motion a man in their direction, and he stood up. They walked towards each other.

"Holt?"

"You must be Mr. Samuels."

"Yeah. How's Ruby? What happened?"

"She was spending the night with a friend. Intruders came into the apartment, and her friend was shot in the scuffle."

"Shot," he said in disbelief, "and Ruby was hurt?"

"She only has some minor scrapes. It's more the scare than anything. She's pretty confused."

"Can I talk with her?"

"I think that would be a good idea."

Holt took Samuels in to see Ruby. Jarislow was sitting by the bed, and he stood up and moved back when Holt and Samuels entered. Samuels nodded to Jarislow and sat down in the visitor chair. He leaned close to Ruby, touching her arm.

"Ruby…" he said softly.

She opened her eyes.

"Chuck."

"What happened, Ruby?"

"Chuck?"

"The officer said you stayed at a friend's. Where did you stay, Ruby?"

"Mike's…" she said in a distant voice, "I was at Mike's."

"Who's Mike?"

"I been seeing him for a while…"

"What happened?"

"They came in…" her eyes searched his face. "They held the gun at my head." He squeezed her hand as they stared at each other and she tried to get the words out properly. "They shot Mike…"

Samuels swore.

"You must have been scared out of your wits, you poor kid." He stroked the bandage on her head, his fingers light. "Are you okay?"

"They shot Mike," she repeated.

"I know, Ruby. Did you see who it was?"

"They put a gun against my head," she repeated touching the bandage.

Samuels held both of Ruby's hands, trying to comfort her, to give her strength.

"It's okay, Ruby. It'll be okay. It's over."

She held his hand to her face, closing her eyes. Samuels sat with her until he figured she was falling asleep. He pulled his hand away slowly and carefully so as not to disturb her. He got up quietly to talk to Holt.

"Who is this guy she was staying with?" he questioned.

"He's in a gang. We suspect that the killing was gang-related."

Samuels shook his head.

"She should know better. She should have been home with her foster family."

"Are you sure she's still with her foster family?" Holt countered.

Samuels looked startled.

"What? Why do you ask?"

"Her knapsack. Why would a kid in a foster family need anything more than she could put in a purse? She has full changes of clothing and other overnight items. I suspect she's living on the street."

"Well... that's serious. I'll have to look into it."

"A girl her age should not be out on her own. If she is, this won't be the last time she gets mixed up in something like this."

Samuels nodded.

"I completely agree. I'll contact her foster family and find out what's going on. I know that she was staying out late some nights, but living on the street—that's another story. Has she said anything to you? About what happened?"

"No. She wasn't able to tell us anything. She didn't even say anything about them holding the gun to her head. About all she managed to get out was her name."

"How could someone do that to her?" Samuels said, shaking his head. "She's such a sweet kid."

"She's lucky they didn't kill her too. Most of the bangers I know wouldn't have hesitated to shoot all witnesses."

"That's horrible..." Nothing was said for a few awkward moments. "Do you deal much with the gangs?"

"Somewhat."

"Ruby doesn't hang around with them much, does she? You haven't seen her with them before?"

"Not that I remember. There aren't a lot of girls in with the gangs around here."

"I hope that's not what she spends her time doing."

"She's not in school?"

"She's absent a lot. She's not very academic."

"From the sounds of things, I think she needs a lot more supervision than she's getting," Holt suggested, eyes narrowed.

"I may have to recommend a different foster family for her," Samuels said.

"I suspect so."

"I appreciate you being here tonight. Ruby's a good kid, and I'm glad you were there to look out for her, and not someone who would have been rough with her, being involved in a gang shooting."

"I can see she's basically a good kid. I'd like to see her settled in with a family for a few more years yet."

"She really shouldn't be on her own like this," Samuels agreed.

Holt nodded.

"Well, we'll leave her with you tonight. We will need to talk to her about this whole thing again. The homicide officers will probably want to see her tomorrow, after they've been over the scene a little more carefully. Ruby should be up to it, I would think. Should they contact you?"

"Yes," Samuels took out a business card. "There's my daytime number. Give me a call."

"Thanks. Someone will."

Holt stepped back into the hospital stall and motioned to Jarislow. They headed back to their car.

"Now there's a social worker who really cares about his kids," Jarislow commented.

"Yes..." Holt agreed, "he seemed very attached to Ruby."

CHAPTER Three

Ruby left the hospital with Chuck in the morning. She still seemed very subdued, and the doctors recommended that she take it easy for a few days, and spend lots of time in bed. Chuck took her out to the car.

"What are we going to do with you?" he sighed.

"Can I sleep at your place?" Ruby suggested.

"No. The police are going to want to talk to you today, and I may have to assign you to a new foster family."

"I don't want a family."

"Maybe not, but the cop who took you to the hospital figured you're living on the street, and I'm going to have to do something in response to his report. I really think we need to put you in a foster home, at least for a few weeks, until things cool off."

Ruby stared out the window.

"You're trying to get rid of me, aren't you?" she complained.

"It's only for a couple of weeks. Then I'll do some more paperwork to get you out of it again."

"I'm not going."

"Do you want someone investigating your records and finding out that you haven't been with a foster family for a year and a half? Do you have any idea what would happen to me?" he demanded.

"Well, if you want to get rid of me, maybe I don't care what happens to you anymore either," she said sullenly.

"Ruby, I do care about you," Chuck assured her, touching her cheek and speaking earnestly, his clear blue eyes showing deep concern. "I want us to be together. This is only temporary."

Ruby rolled her eyes and didn't say anything else.

"I'll drop you off at the Watsons. They provide emergency shelter to kids who are between homes for a day or two. It's better than the Children's Center."

Ruby shrugged and refused to look at him. She knew that what he said made sense, but she felt hurt just the same. At the time when she needed him most, Chuck wasn't going to be there for her. She didn't really want him to get in trouble. But the added stress of having to live with a family on top of everything else was just too much.

"You'll only be there for a day," Chuck assured her, "just until I get your records straightened out. It's just a place to crash and take a break for a day. Then I'll have you in a new family. One that is used to having older girls, not little kids," he promised.

Ruby nodded to show that she had heard what he said, but not necessarily that she agreed with him. Her mouth was set in a frown. Chuck was satisfied that she would put up with it, and didn't try to convince her any further.

They got to the Watsons' place and Chuck took her in.

"Hi, Nancy," he said to the woman who answered the door. "I have someone I need you to look after today, until I get her placed again."

"Sure, Mr. Samuels. Come on in."

Chuck entered. Ruby walked in behind him. Nancy Watson was a slim, dark-haired, middle-aged woman. She looked pleasant and friendly enough, but Ruby knew better than to trust to appearances.

"Ruby, this is Nancy Watson. Nancy—Ruby was in an accident last night, and she needs somewhere to stretch out and take a long nap. The doctors told her to take it easy for a bit."

"Sure, I've got a bed she can use."

"I expect the police will be by later on today to talk to her again. Aside from that, I'm sure you'll hardly even know Ruby's here."

"We'll be just fine, Mr. Samuels. And I'll see you tonight or tomorrow. She'll be okay overnight, she's our only one today."

"I appreciate it. Ruby, don't cause any trouble."

Ruby just glared at him. Chuck left.

"Were you in a car accident?" Nancy questioned.

"What?"

Ruby studied Nancy. She knew that even the friendly ones had rules. Too many rules. And tomorrow, who knew who Ruby would be with.

"Mr. Samuels said you were in an accident," Nancy said. "Was it a car accident?"

Ruby turned away from her, not wanting to discuss it.

"I'm going to lie down, okay?"

"Oh, sure. I'll show you the bedroom. This way."

Ruby followed Nancy into a bare bedroom, and dropped her bag on the floor.

"Thanks."

"Let me know if you need anything."

"I don't need anything from you."

Nancy didn't say anything to this. She left, pulling the door almost shut behind her. She left it open a couple of inches. Ruby lay down on the bed and stared up at the ceiling.

Late in the afternoon, Nancy opened the door to a couple of large policeman. She was used to having police come by the house, but she didn't recognize these ones in particular.

"Hi," she greeted.

"We're here to talk to Ruby."

"Sure. Come in. I'll get her."

She let them in to the front room.

"Can I get you gentlemen coffee?"

They both assented. Nancy went up to the bedroom. Ruby was lying in bed flat on her back with her eyes wide open.

"Ruby?" Nancy said tentatively.

"Yeah."

"The police are here to talk to you."

Ruby got up and went down to the front room to talk to them. She sat down on the couch with her knees up to her chest. She looked at two cops and didn't say anything.

"Well, you've got a little more color than you did last night."

"I don't know your names," Ruby said.

"I'm Merrill. We talked last night. My partner is Banks."

Ruby nodded.

"So what can you tell us about what happened last night?" Merrill questioned.

"I don't remember anything."

"Why don't you start with when you and your friend met up yesterday?"

Ruby stared out the big front window. The afternoon sun shone on the window and made the room almost uncomfortably warm. But inside, Ruby felt dark. She felt closed in. Trapped.

"We just met up at the arcade," she told Merrill.

He nodded.

"Then what did you do?" he prompted.

"Went to Mike's apartment."

"What time would that have been?"

Ruby considered. She shrugged.

"Just the afternoon sometime."

"Four o'clock?" he suggested.

"Something like that."

"Earlier? Later?"

"Four."

"Were you with anyone else?"

"No, just Mike."

"Did you notice anyone hanging around? At the arcade, on the street near his apartment, anything?"

"No."

Why would she? When she was with Mike, he was all she saw. He was all she cared about. She watched his curvy lips when he talked, his beautiful blue eyes when he listened, the curve of his chin, with just a hint of a cleft, when he looked away from her.

"What did you talk about?" Merrill questioned.

"I dunno."

"Did he talk about what's been going on with the gang?"

"No. He never talks shop."

"So you don't know anything about any of the other Jaguars?"

"Not even their names," Ruby agreed, shaking her head.

"Did he talk about anyone he's not getting along with? Do you know what his family situation's like?"

"He never sees his family. I don't know where they are."

"Never talks to them? Anything?"

"No." Ruby shook her head.

"Why is that, do you know?"

"I don't talk to my family either. It doesn't mean anything. I never asked him about it."

Merrill took some notes in his notepad. He looked at Ruby. He smiled encouragingly.

"What was Mike like yesterday? What kind of mood was he in?"

"I dunno. Same as usual. Good mood."

And when he smiled at her... Ruby's heart sped up just thinking about his warm smile.

"He didn't seem uptight, tense or distracted?" Merrill suggested.

"No," Ruby shook her head. "We had a good time."

"Did you stay in the apartment all night?"

"Yeah. Just watched TV and stuff."

"Go out to eat? Order in?"

"Ordered in."

"What did you have?"

"Pizza."

"Uh-huh. What restaurant did you get it from?"

"Toni's. It's just a little place down the street."

"Who answered the door when the delivery boy came by?"

"Mike."

"Did you see the delivery boy?"

"Yeah."

"Did he see you?"

Ruby thought about it, shaking her head.

"I guess. I dunno."

"Did you recognize him?" Merrill questioned.

Ruby frowned.

"No."

"You've never had him deliver for Toni's before?"

"I don't know... I didn't notice. Who notices the delivery boy?"

"Was he wearing a jacket for Toni's?"

"They don't wear jackets."

"Did Mike talk to him?"

Ruby shook her head.

"Just hello, and give him the money, and all," she said with a shrug.

"Mike didn't seem to know him?"

"No."

Merrill took a break from the questioning for a moment, writing down whatever conclusions her answers had led him to. He looked back at Ruby.

"Did you guys see anyone else that night?"

"No."

Nancy brought the coffee in to the officers. She gave them each a mug, and handed Ruby a glass of milk. Ruby just looked at it, dumbfounded. What was she, a baby?

"I drink coffee," she told Nancy.

"You need milk. Coffee you don't need."

"I'm not drinking it."

Nancy shrugged, and left it on the coffee table for her. Ruby didn't touch it. The cops were silent until Nancy left. Merrill took a sip of the coffee, and continued with the stream of questions.

"Did you hear or see anything out of the ordinary during the evening?"

"No."

"And Mike didn't seem worried about anything?"

"No."

"What time did you guys turn out the lights?"

Ruby thought about it.

"We just finished watching a movie. Midnight or something."

"What movie was it?"

Ruby shrugged.

"They're all the same to me."

"What was it about?"

"Some guy and the girls he liked."

"What channel?"

Ruby told him the channel, and Merrill managed a dry smile.

"That's what they're all about on that station."

"Like I said."

"So you went to bed after you watched the movie."

"Yeah," Ruby agreed.

"Then what?"

"I don't remember anything after that," Ruby said flatly.

"What time did you get to sleep?"

"I don't know."

"What time did Mike get to sleep?"

"I dunno. One or something."

"Okay. How long after that did the intruders come in?"

"I don't know."

"Were you asleep?"

"I don't remember."

"Ruby... we can't help you if you won't talk to us," Merrill said, putting his coffee mug down and leaning toward her.

"You can't help me," Ruby said flatly.

"If you can help us put these guys away, you won't have to be afraid of them," he assured her.

"You think they're from one of the other gangs, don't you?" Ruby questioned.

"I suspect so, yes," he agreed.

"And how're you going to protect me from the whole gang? You going to put them all away?"

"We'll put the ones who did it in jail, and no-one will know that you helped us out."

"Right."

Merrill looked at her for a moment. He looked back down at his notebook.

"How well did you see the guys who did it?"

"I don't remember," Ruby said stubbornly.

"Hypothetically, if you could remember, how well would you have seen them?"

Ruby considered the question.

"If they were smart, they would have made sure I didn't see them good," she suggested.

"By wearing masks?"

"Yeah, or shining a light in my eyes or something."

"I see." For a few minutes, he didn't say anything. Then: "So exactly how well did you see them?"

"I don't remember," Ruby maintained.

"Ruby... these guys are animals. You know that they're just going to go on killing if we don't put them away."

"But they won't be killing me."

"Do you really want to take that chance? How do you know they won't just wait until the situation is right, and come after you?"

"They could have killed me last night. They didn't."

"They may decide that wasn't very smart once they've had a chance to think about it, and come back after you. We need to protect you."

Ruby had already thought of that. And she didn't like it. But as long as she didn't talk, they would have no reason to come after her.

"You're talking to us," Merrill said slowly, watching her carefully. "How does anyone know whether you're telling us what happened or not?"

"Because they won't get caught."

"What if they do? What if we manage to find another witness or specific suspects on our own? How do they know that we didn't get any help from you? The only way to make sure they can't come after you is to put them away."

"No."

"What are you going to do if we subpoena you or arrest you for obstruction?"

"Say that I don't remember."

"I don't think you realize just how serious that is," Merrill said sternly.

Did he think that she was just playing a game? Fooling around? This was a matter of life and death for Ruby, and she didn't want them doing to her what they had done to Mike.

"Sure I do," she said flatly.

"Let's try it from another angle," Merrill said, starting over, "What if the Jaguars get upset with you because they want to see Mike's killers punished?"

Ruby shrugged.

"They wouldn't expect me to squeal to the police."

"I don't think you know very much about them."

"I know that much," Ruby snorted.

They didn't say anything. Ruby looked for a cigarette, and found one in her pocket.

"I'm going outside," she told them, and went out on the front steps and lit up.

She went through a couple of cigarettes before they figured out that she wasn't going back in to talk to them. They joined her outside.

"Nice day," Merrill commented, squinting in the afternoon sunlight.

"Yeah."

"So... tell me a little about yourself, Ruby."

"What's to tell?"

"I just would like to know a little about you. It occurs to me that I don't even know anything about you."

"I'm nothing special," Ruby said with a shrug. "Just another foster kid."

"How long have you been in state care?"

"Five years."

"Did you and Mike spend a lot of time together?" he probed.

"Just now and then."

"How long had you known him?"

"A year, I think. Maybe a bit more. I dunno."

"He was a bit older than you, though, wasn't he?"

"Yeah—'bout seven years," Ruby agreed.

"And that makes you... how old?"

"Thirteen."

She could see that Merrill was surprised. He had thought she was older. But he didn't make a big deal of it. He went on just as if he was used to talking to thirteen year olds about homicides.

"What did you like to do together? What are you interested in?"

"We just hung out. I just... like to be with people."

"What do you do with your other friends? Same thing? Just hang out?"

Ruby nodded.

"Yeah. We go to the arcade or pool hall... or just out to eat..."

"You didn't play pool with Mike?"

"No. Sometimes we met at the arcade, but we didn't stay there."

"Why not?"

Ruby didn't answer. She frowned. Why didn't they? She never thought about what they did together, where they went... she hadn't realized that they had avoided being out where others would see them. Had they? Or was it just a coincidence?

"I don't know why."

"Did the two of you ever go out anywhere?"

"No... just to his apartment."

"Who didn't he want to be seen by?"

"We just—liked to be alone with each other," Ruby said uncomfortably, her face getting hot.

"I thought you said you didn't know why."

"Well... I don't... I just..."

Ruby took a deep breath to calm herself, and lit up another cigarette.

"I think I'm going to request that you come down to the station for us to talk to you some more," Merrill said.

"I've told you all I'm going to."

"That's not enough."

"Then I want a lawyer."

Merrill looked exasperated.

"What do you want a lawyer for?" he demanded. "You're not a suspect."

"You're talking about subpoenas, and putting me in jail. I want a lawyer."

"All right, Ruby. Do you have a lawyer?"

"No."

"Do you know how to get in touch with one?"

"I'll call my social worker. He'll get me one."

"I really don't think this is necessary."

"If you want to talk to me anymore, you're going to have to wait until I get a lawyer."

"All right. We'll finish up for now. I'll let you know if we want to ask you any more questions. We are going to have to get you to look through mug shots, though."

"I told you, I don't remember anything."

"Well, maybe a picture will jog your memory."

Ruby shrugged.

"Fine. I'll call my social worker."

"Okay. We'll be in touch," Merrill said.

Ruby nodded. They left her sitting on the steps and got back in their car. Ruby watched them drive off, and sat for a few minutes in the sun, smoking her last cigarette. She went back into the house and called Chuck.

"Hello?"

"It's Ruby."

"You shouldn't be calling me," he protested lowly.

"I want you to get me a lawyer."

"A lawyer? What for?"

"The cops were just here, asking me questions."

"Yeah, so?"

"So now they want me to go to the police station to talk to me. They're threatening to put me in jail for not remembering what happened last night. And they don't want me to get a lawyer."

"Why don't you just tell them what happened, and they'll get off your case?"

"I don't remember what happened," Ruby insisted.

Chuck breathed out heavily in exasperation.

"All right. I'll make a couple phone calls for you. But try not to get yourself in trouble, okay?"

"I'm trying to stay out of trouble," she said reasonably. "That's why I want a lawyer."

"You'd be better off just telling the truth."

"I am. Are you picking me up tonight?" Ruby suggested.

"Yes, I'll be taking you to your new foster family."

Ruby hung up the phone in his ear.

Ruby always felt like a little kid when she was dropped off with a new foster family. She was good at meeting new people, and got along all right with most, but she felt like she was no longer controlling her own life. She couldn't choose them herself, she couldn't make her own rules. All she could do was sit in the car and be driven to another house full of strangers.

This time it was Mr. and Mrs. Winters. No first names. Ruby hated the ones who didn't go by their first names. Chuck did manage to put her with a family who weren't taking care of any other kids, at least. The bedroom was cute, probably decorated by one of their own children, since grown up and moved out. It felt warmer than the families that put you in the guest room, neat and bare and you'd better keep it perfectly tidy. Ruby was dumped at the door by Chuck, and given a quick tour of the house by Mrs. Winters. There were no posted house rules, and the woman didn't say much in the tour by way of restrictions.

Ruby kept telling herself it was just for a couple of weeks until things settled down, but she felt anxious and trapped, closed in. She'd had supper at Nancy's, so after the tour, Ruby just went back to her room and lay down on the bed. She couldn't seem to shut her eyes. She was wide awake and couldn't relax. Ruby found herself jumping at the slightest noise, listening and trying to identify every creak of the old house around her. When it started to grow light outside, Ruby was still lying on top of the bed, fully clothed, stiff with tension and staring up at the ceiling. She had made it through the night, alone and maybe a little scared. Getting through the day wasn't going to be a lot easier.

"Good morning," Mrs. Winters greeted, when Ruby stepped into the kitchen.

"Hi."

Mrs. Winters turned to see her.

"Oh, you don't look like you slept too well," she observed.

"No."

"Come on in and sit down. Cereal or toast?"

Ruby sat down at the table, rubbing her temples.

"Toast. No butter."

"Coming up. There's orange juice in the fridge."

Ruby obediently got up and got out the jug of juice and put it on the table.

"Coffee?" she questioned tentatively.

"I'll put some on for you," Mrs. Winters agreed.

"The folks I stayed with yesterday wouldn't let me have coffee," Ruby offered.

"Well, it certainly isn't good for you," Mrs. Winters admitted, "but I need my coffee in the morning, good or not."

"Yeah, me too."

"What school do you go to, Ruby?"

Ruby told her.

"I'll drop you off today, and we'll find out what bus goes by there for tomorrow."

"Do I have to go?" Ruby protested.

"Of course you do. You have to keep up."

"I'm never going to use anything they're teaching."

"You go to school to learn how to learn. Otherwise, you'll go through life without being able to keep a job."

"That's the first time I've heard that one."

"Yes, well it's the one reason you never hear, but the only one that's important."

"Huh."

Mrs. Winters gave Ruby her toast, and put a jar of jam on the table.

"I'll have you your coffee in a second."

"Thanks."

Ruby rarely got to school on time. Kate and Marty were surprised to see her there so early.

"What happened to you?" Kate questioned.

Ruby really became conscious of the bandage on her head for the first time. She touched it.

"Oh—nothing. Got shot."

Their eyes widened in surprise. Kate couldn't seem to think of what to say about this. Marty raised her eyebrows.

"What jerk shot you?" she questioned.

Ruby shrugged and grinned, enjoying being the center of attention over it.

"Not someone I knew," she said.

"You're kidding, right?" Kate questioned.

"Nope."

"Why would somebody shoot you?"

"Well, it was an accident, I think."

"What happened?" Marty demanded.

Ruby tried to make light of it, but didn't manage.

"Have you ever met Mike?" she questioned. "The Jag I go with sometimes?"

"Oh, the cute one?" Kate questioned. "I've never met him, but I'd like to."

"They were aiming for him."

"Pretty bad aim," Marty said dryly.

"No, they got him, all right."

Kate's eyes got wider yet.

"Is he okay?"

"No."

Kate swore—a rare occurrence.

"I told you to stay away from the guys in gangs," Marty said, shaking her head.

"You tell me to stay away from all guys," Ruby pointed out.

"Good advice. You could have been killed."

Ruby didn't answer. It was true, but she'd been trying not to think about that part.

"I don't want to talk about it."

"So why're you here so early?" Marty questioned, changing the subject for her.

"Foster Mom dropped me off."

"I haven't heard you talking about your foster parents for a long time," Marty said.

"Yeah, I just got moved."

"What are they like?"

"I don't know yet."

"We got English. Are you coming?"

"Yeah, I guess."

They wandered into the classroom after the bell rang. The woman teacher glared at them as they took their seats. Then she started the lesson. Ruby stared out the window, and doodled in her notebook. The teacher gave them an assignment and came over to talk to Ruby.

"Where are your textbooks?" she questioned, narrowing her eyes at Ruby.

"In my locker, I guess," Ruby said with a shrug.

"Where have you been lately? You've missed a lot of classes lately."

"I had some troubles with foster families."

"Have you got them sorted out?"

"No."

"Have you talked to someone about them?" she questioned, putting on a concerned air.

"Yeah. I've been talking to my social worker and the police."
"Good. You know we have resources here if you need them."
"You can't do anything."
"If you need something…"
Ruby shook her head. The teacher moved on.

"Hey, sweetheart."

There was a heavy hand on Ruby's shoulder, and she jumped, and whirled around, tense.

"Whoa, whoa," Brian soothed. "What's the matter?"

Ruby breathed out, relieved. She hugged him and gave him a quick peck.

"Sorry—I'm sort of jumpy," she said.

"What's this?" He touched the bandage on her forehead.

"I got hurt. It's nothing."

Brian brushed his thumb gently over the bandage, looking down at her face.

"You wanna go somewhere?" he suggested.

"Sure." Ruby looked at Marty and Kate, who had come to the mall with her and were approaching after checking through some purchases. "Do you guys wanna do anything?"

Kate wasn't sure. Marty turned them down.

"We'll do something next time, right?"

"Yeah. I'll see you later this week."

"Okay."

They separated. There was a matinee movie, but it didn't start for a while, so they stopped by the arcade for a while. Ruby enjoyed playing for a while. A boy came up and started playing the game next to her. Ruby's heart started thumping fast. She glanced over at him a couple of times, and ended her game. She went over to Brian.

"Let's go," she said.

"It's not that late," he said, without looking up.

"Come on. I have to get out of here," Ruby persisted.

He glanced back at her.

"What's the matter?"

"Please, Brian?"

"Yeah, okay… just a sec'."

Ruby looked around nervously shifting her weight back and forth. Brian kept playing. Ruby didn't want to keep pressing him, but she couldn't stay there. She walked out of the arcade and went to the theater. Brian joined her ten minutes later, looking annoyed.

"Why'd you leave? I was just playing out my game."

"I just... had to get out of there."

Brian was speechless. He just stared at her. She'd never behaved that way before.

"Are you okay?" he questioned after a few moments. "You don't look so good."

Ruby was sweating, and felt light headed and faint. Brian hugged her when she didn't answer, and she could feel her heart racing as they pressed together. She pulled away and darted into the restroom, overcome with nausea. Brian waited for her, and the movie had already started by the time she got out. He could probably tell that she'd just put on fresh makeup, and the fine hair around her face was damp.

"Are you all right?" Brian questioned.

Ruby nodded, and put her arm around behind his back and squeezed up close to him. She was still shaking violently, and felt like she might faint at any moment.

"Do you want to go in?" Brian questioned uncertainly.

Ruby nodded, not trusting herself to talk. They went into the darkened theater.

"Are you sure? You don't want to go home or something?"

Ruby just held onto him, and they sat down. Ruby rested her head on his shoulder and tried to calm herself down. Brian rubbed her back soothingly, and kissed her forehead every now and then. Ruby closed her eyes and concentrated on breathing deeply, and didn't follow any of what went on in the movie.

When the movie ended, Brian waited for the lights to go back on, and studied her.

"Are you okay?" he asked again.

"Yeah."

"Are you sick?"

"A little, I guess," Ruby admitted.

Brian stroked her hair gently.

"Do you want to go home?"

"We could go back to your place," Ruby suggested.

"If you want."

Ruby nodded.

"Okay. We'll go hang out at my place. Let's go."

It was after dark when Brian dropped Ruby off at the Winters again. Ruby really dreaded going back and having to be by herself, but she knew that Chuck would get on her case if she didn't. She had to keep showing up for a couple weeks, appear to be a normal foster child, and then no-one would notice if he screwed up the paperwork. Chuck was really careful that way.

The porch light was on and the door was unlocked, which was a good sign. Some foster families locked you out completely or made you ring the bell. Ruby opened the door quietly, and swung it open. A lamp in the front room was on, and Mrs. Winters was sitting up reading a book.

"Hi," Ruby said.

"You're pretty late getting home. Have you had something to eat?" she inquired.

"Yes, ma'am."

"Well then, you'd better scoot to bed, or you're going to have a hard time getting up for school."

Ruby ducked up the stairs without another word. She sat up in bed, in the dark, and listened for them to go to bed. Once everything was quiet, she went back downstairs, and turned the TV on.

Mrs. Winters got up in the night, and went by Ruby's bedroom to check in on her. The door was open, unlike the night before, and Mrs. Winters stepped in to see if Ruby was asleep. The bed was empty, not slept in. Mrs. Winters found Ruby downstairs watching TV. Ruby's eyes were heavy, and the volume was very low. She started up when she saw Mrs. Winters, and muted the TV.

"Did I wake you up?" she said quickly.

"No, no. I was just checking on you. Why are you still up?"

"I can't sleep."

"You look beat," Mrs. Winters observed. "Why don't you give it a try?"

"I can't..."

"Come up with me. We'll talk for a bit and see if we can't get you settled in for the night."

Ruby reluctantly shut off the TV and followed Mrs. Winters up to the bedroom. Mrs. Winters folded back the blankets for her, and Ruby slipped in between the sheets. Ruby felt strange, a tightness in her stomach. She couldn't remember anyone, foster families or her own family, ever folding back the sheets and tucking her in. It made her unaccountably tense. Mrs. Winters sat on the side of the bed.

"Did you have a good day at school?" she asked.

"Okay." Ruby shrugged.

"You look so tired. You didn't sleep very well last night, did you?"

"No. I didn't sleep at all."

"Do you have something on your mind? Something bothering you?"

"Yeah."

"What's the matter?"

Ruby touched the sore on her forehead. She'd removed the dressing when she got home. It was scabbed over. Ugly, but healing.

"Did Mr. Samuels tell you how I got this?" she asked.

"No. I thought maybe you were in a fight or a car accident."

Ruby shook her head.

"I was with a friend, and he got shot."

"How horrible!" Mrs. Winters exclaimed. "No wonder you're having trouble sleeping! Why don't you just close your eyes, Ruby? I'll stay with you until you can get to sleep."

Ruby looked at her for a long moment, then she turned her cheek into the pillow and closed her eyes. Mrs. Winters watched Ruby until her muscles relaxed and her breathing got regular and deep. Mrs. Winters quietly turned off the nightstand lamp and went back to bed.

Ruby woke up in the dark, the sweat pouring off of her face. She got up and went to the bathroom and turned on the light. She looked at herself in the mirror for a long time, splashed cold water on her face, and tried to decide what to do. She was so tired she could cry. But she wasn't going to. She hadn't cried at all since Mike was shot. Ruby went to the door of the Winters' bedroom, hoping that Mrs. Winters would be up still. She stood there for a few minutes, but it was obvious that they were both fast asleep. Ruby crept up to the bed and touched Mrs. Winters on the shoulder.

"Ma'am? Mrs. Winters…?"

She stirred, and turned over.

"Oh—um, Ruby? What is it?"

Ruby bent down to talk to her.

"Can I sleep with you? Please?"

Mrs. Winters propped herself up a little and rubbed her eyes.

"You're a little old for that, Ruby."

"I can't sleep. I keep having dreams. I promise I won't kick, you won't even know I'm there. I'm a quiet sleeper."

"Ruby, why don't you bring in a blanket and pillow and sleep beside the bed."

Ruby hesitated, then agreed. She knew it wasn't very likely she'd be allowed in their bed. Most people didn't think it was okay after about ten. She was lucky to have a foster mom who would let her sleep beside the bed. There'd been those who would have locked her in her room if she gave them trouble. She got a blanket and pillow from her bed and lay down on the floor next to the bed. Mrs. Winters murmured something to her and fell asleep again. Ruby drifted off to sleep for a few minutes, and then woke again with a nightmare. This time she didn't wake Mrs. Winters up, but slipped in under the covers beside her. Mrs. Winters shifted away a little, and said something to her, but didn't really completely waken. Ruby cuddled against her, and finally fell peacefully asleep.

"Is she in bed with us?" Mr. Winters questioned. Mrs. Winters opened her eyes and shifted closer to her husband. She realized that it was true, Ruby was cuddled up against her on the other side, fast asleep. The alarm was going to go off in a few minutes.

"I guess she is. I told her she could sleep on the floor last night." She spoke quietly, not wanting to waken Rub yet.

"We could really get in trouble for something like this," he warned.

"She's just a child. And she's beside me, not you."

"Still, you know they wouldn't like it."

"I didn't tell her she could come into bed." Mrs. Winters gazed at Ruby's face, for once relaxed and un-made-up. She looked very young and defenseless. "You should have seen her last night. She was so tired, and so scared. She probably went forty-eight hours without a wink of sleep."

Mr. Winters propped himself up so that he could see her.

"What would she be so scared of?"

"Whoever shot her friend. That's how she got the mark on her head. She was that close to being shot in the head."

"Yikes. Poor kid. It's time she had a chance to just be a child. Just to be safe. She's probably been in foster care half her life and doesn't know who to trust."

"I got the feeling from Mr. Samuels that he was only placing her here temporarily. I think he has another situation in mind for her."

The radio went on and Ruby jumped and opened her eyes. She looked at Mr. and Mrs. Winters, both watching her.

"Uh—hi."

"Hi," Mrs. Winters greeted.

"I couldn't sleep," Ruby said.

"How're you feeling now? A bit better?"

"Yeah." Ruby sighed and stretched. "I wish I could sleep all day."

"Don't we all? Well, you can sleep for a few minutes while we get ready, but when I go down to get breakfast going, you'd better get dressed and ready for school. Okay?"

"Okay." Ruby closed her eyes and relaxed again. Mr. and Mrs. Winters got out of bed and got ready for their day.

Ruby tried to focus on the Language Arts assignment that they had just been given, but found it hard to concentrate. She looked up from her paper when the teacher approached.

"You're wanted in the office," the teacher said.

"Why?" Ruby questioned, frowning.

"I don't know. They just called for you."

Ruby closed her books, and got up and left. She got down to the office and found Merrill and Banks there waiting for her.

"What do you guys want?" she demanded.

"We need you looking through those mug shots at the station," Merrill advised her.

Ruby unzipped one of the pockets of her knapsack and found the card that Chuck had given to her when he picked her up from Nancy's house.

"I'm calling my lawyer," she told them. They waited while she got permission to use the phone and called him. Ruby explained the situation, looking over her shoulder at the cops and talking in a low tone. The lawyer promised to meet her at the police station when she got there. Ruby went with the officers.

"Are you going to handcuff me?" she questioned playfully. She was nervous and she needed some kind out outlet.

"Don't get mouthy," Merrill growled. Ruby shook her head.

"Somebody got up on the wrong side of the bed this morning."

"The idea of a couple murdering gang members out there free and clear gets on my nerves," he retorted.

"Well, putting them away is your job, not mine."

"It's going to be pretty hard, when our only witness refuses to talk."

"If I tell you anything, I'm gonna get killed. Not much of a choice," Ruby pointed out.

"If no-one has the courage to talk, guys like this are never going to face the consequences of what they do."

Ruby didn't have anything to say to that one. She just shrugged. She wasn't going to risk her life to put anyone away. Besides, she hadn't really seen enough to identify anyone even if she wanted to.

Ruby met her lawyer at the police station. Medium height, slender, dark hair. Blue eyes. Much younger than she had imagined. He introduced himself as John Willhelm. Ruby said hi to him nervously, and gestured to their surroundings.

"Do I have to do this?" she questioned.

"Yes. But I'll stay with you, and we'll make sure things don't get out of hand."

"I'm not going to tell them anything."

"Maybe you and I should talk alone for a few minutes." John looked at the officers, "Can we have a couple of minutes to get acquainted?"

Merrill pointed them towards an empty room that they could use. John shut the door, and the two of them sat down across the table from each other.

"So, what's the scoop here?" John questioned.

"If I tell them anything, I'm gonna get killed," Ruby said, scratching at a mark on the table top.

"Whoever did it won't be able to get at you. They'll be in jail," he echoed the party line.

"And if they're in a gang? Their boys aren't going to come after me?"

"I could see how that could be a problem. I'm sure we could get you police protection until this all blows over."

"No. I live my own life, I don't want cops around, or to have to stay in a safe house or something."

"Well, let's look through the pictures. If you see the killers in the pictures, you remember the names and tell me afterward."

Ruby shook her head.

"I'm not telling anyone."

John frowned and opened the door for her.

"Let's get this done."

"Okay."

The pictures only convinced Ruby of what she already knew—that she hadn't seen enough to identify the boys. The things that she knew about them didn't show up in the pictures—their voices, the murderer's touch on her skin. The things that she had seen—shadows in the dark, a hand here, a profile there—nothing looked anything like the pictures she was looking at. They had not shone the lights on their own faces, posing impassively for her. She would know them again only if she met them.

John drove her back to the school, without much to say. Ruby wondered what kind of a guy he was. She was surprised that he was so young. Other foster kids who talked about their lawyers always made them sound old and uninteresting. Ruby managed to get him to give her his home phone number, thinking it might come in handy at some point.

It was after lunch when she got back to school, so Ruby stayed for afternoon classes with her friends. After school, she agreed to go home with Marty. Kate went with them too. Kate didn't like to hang round at the arcade or pool halls—malls were more her speed. So when they were together, they did slower things, just hanging around at home watching movies and so on.

After ordering Chinese, they settled down in front of the TV. Ruby was aware of Kate leaving at some point, but everything seemed hazy and far away. She got bits and pieces of what was going on on the TV, but it was all muddled up. After a long time, the TV went off. Ruby roused herself drowsily. She found herself lying across Marty's lap, her head cradled in Marty's arms. She sat up slowly, rubbing her eyes.

"Sorry—I guess I fell asleep," she apologized.

"Yeah. You've been pretty out of it all night. You been popping pills?" Marty questioned, studying her closely.

"No... just not sleeping very well."

"Why not?"

Marty brushed a tendril of Ruby's hair back from her face. Ruby sighed.

"I can't sleep alone—after Mike getting shot."

"Why don't you sleep here with me?"

"This foster family…"

"Call and ask them if you can sleep over. If they think you're staying with a boy, they can talk to me. Even to my mom. They'll let you stay."

Ruby considered.

"Yeah—I'll give it a try."

She called Mrs. Winters.

"Can I sleep over at a friend's tonight?" she questioned.

"It's a school night, Ruby. You probably shouldn't."

"We won't stay up late. Marty's mom's here."

"Marty?"

"Martha. Do you want to talk to her?"

"Well, I would like to make sure it's okay with her mom."

"Okay." Ruby put down the receiver. "She wants to talk to your mom."

Marty nodded and went to find her. Mrs. Rodger picked up the receiver.

"Hi, there… oh, sure. It's fine with me. Ruby's slept over here before. She's no trouble." She listened for a few minutes, nodding. "I'll make sure they get to bed right away, and off to school in the morning. Okay. Good-bye." She hung up the phone. "No problem. But you guys had better be heading to bed."

"Yeah, Mom. Come on, Ruby."

They headed for Marty's bedroom and shut the door.

CHAPTER *Four*

Ruby's call rang for several minutes before Chuck finally picked up the phone.
"Yes?"
"It's Ruby." Which he probably already knew from the caller I.D.
"How did it go with the police?" he said coolly.
"What? Okay, I guess. I couldn't help them."
"So why are you calling me?" he asked.
"I miss you. I want to meet you tonight."
"No. You've got at least another week with the Winters. Then if things stay quiet, we'll see what arrangements we can make. Now hang up, and don't call me here. You know better."
"I'll keep calling you until you agree to meet me," Ruby threatened.
"If you start harassing me with phone calls, I'll have you assigned to another social worker."
Ruby slammed the receiver down. She exited the phone booth and walked towards the arcade. There was a boy leaning against the wall outside the arcade smoking. Nothing unusual. But she saw his black jacket and turned and went the other direction. She slipped into the fast-food joint and looked around. There were a couple of boys in the far corner of the restaurant. Ruby hurried up to them and slid into the seat next to them. They stopped talking abruptly and looked at her in consternation, surprised at her behavior.
"You're Jaguars," Ruby said breathlessly.
"Yeah," one of them said, "So what do you want, baby?"
Ruby tried to catch her breath, and she looked out the window to

see if the boy had followed her. The Jags watched her curiously, waiting for her to answer.

"I was—I was with Mike. I saw—one of the other gangs…"

"Ah, you're the chick Mike was always picking up. So you saw who did it? Who wasted him?"

"No. Not very well. I just know it was one of the other gangs."

"Yeah, we know that. You want a soda?"

Ruby shook her head. Her stomach was churning. She didn't want them to see how scared she was—how she panicked every time she saw a black jacket that wasn't the Jaguars'.

"What's your name, kid?" he prodded.

"Ruby."

"You're a lot younger than I expected. So you're looking for some protection?"

"Yeah."

"I'm Jack. This here's Joe Milner. If you want to hang around here a while, go ahead. You're a friend of Mike's, you're a friend of the Jags."

"Thanks," Ruby breathed.

"No problem." Jack took a sip of his drink "So the cops been on your case to tell you what happened?"

"Yeah. But I don't remember anything if I'm talking with them."

Jack snickered.

"Good for you. You realize you got a cop on your tail?"

Ruby followed his gaze through the window.

"I do?"

"Sure. Right there." He pointed. "Plain clothes. With the newspaper."

Ruby watched the man Jack indicated. He didn't seem to be looking their way.

"Are you sure?"

"Sure I'm sure. You watch what you do the next little while. You're going to have a shadow wherever you go."

"Why would they do that?"

"In case Mike's killers decide to take care of you. Then they got their men. You, sweetheart, are valuable. You're their live bait."

Ruby frowned, watching the man through the window.

∽

Ruby got through the week, sleeping over at Marty's some of the time, once at Brian's, when his mother wasn't around, and a couple of times at the Winters' house. She hated not being with Chuck, but she managed to get through another week without him. Chuck hesitantly agreed to let her move out from the Winters again. He picked her up from the house to make it look official, then dropped her off at the coffee shop near his apartment.

"Now you be careful, all right?" he instructed, "I don't want you to make people suspicious."

"I know. I've done it before, haven't I?"

"Sure, but not with as much attention as you've had lately. The officer who took you to the hospital after the accident figured out that you were on the streets."

"Well, no-one else is going to get shot, so that's not very likely."

"All the same…"

"I know. I'll look out," Ruby told him. "But you have to treat me right, got it? I want to see you."

"You'll see me, just not every night."

"Why not?"

He just looked at her and didn't answer. Ruby shrugged and got out of the car.

The first day after being removed was fine. Ruby started to be a little more relaxed and was recovering from the scare she got when Mike was shot. She managed to push it further and further away from herself, so that it seemed like a dream, or like something that happened to someone else. She still panicked whenever she saw a black jacket, and she spent a lot of time hanging around the Jaguars where she felt safe.

It was two days after leaving the Winters that everything fell apart.

It was late, and Ruby was walking down the street, looking for Chuck's car. She was sure that he would pick her up—after all of her coaxing, he would be nervous that she would say something she shouldn't. Besides, it had been over two weeks since they'd been together. They were never away from each other for that long. It was never more than a week. He was bound to be looking for her.

Someone grabbed Ruby by the arm, and she whirled around, expecting a drunk or something. The boy grabbed her tightly and pulled her close to himself, into the shadow of the doorway.

"Keep your mouth zipped!" he warned sharply. Ruby felt the gun shoved into her ribs. She gasped and tried to sort out the confusion fogging her mind. He clamped his other hand over her mouth, and jerked her back further into the doorway.

He backed into the building, shoving the door open and pulling her in. He threw her down on the floor, training the gun on her.

"You know who I am?" he demanded.

Ruby recognized his voice instantly. She nodded, wondering when the cop who'd been trailing her would show up. What was he doing? Calling for backup? Taking a pee? Where was he?

"Sure you know who I am," he agreed. "Now you've been a good girl and not told the cops anything, right?"

Ruby nodded again. He fired the gun, and Ruby curled up in a ball and shut her eyes, her whole body tense and waiting for the pain. He laughed and fired again. Ruby didn't move. She heard her coming closer to her, and knew he couldn't possibly miss. He touched her and she flinched, trying to escape his touch.

"You don't have to be scared of me," he said soothingly. "As long as you don't talk, I'm not gonna hurt you. There..." he touched her face, and Ruby tried weakly to push him back. Where was that cop? Couldn't he hear the shots? Didn't he know what was going on? How could they just let him do this to her? He stroked Ruby's face gently, his touch making her shudder.

"I'm not going to hurt you," he repeated.

How could he threaten her and shoot at her and then expect her to not be afraid?

"Just do what I tell you," he whispered, "and you won't get hurt."

Chuck drove slowly past the bar, looking for Ruby. She wasn't there. He had been sure that she would be. She'd been so insistent that he pick her up. She had to be there.

Flashing lights down the street caught his eye, and a strange, tight feeling crept into his stomach. He told himself that it was stupid. He was just paranoid because the last time she hadn't been there was the night that boy had been killed. Chuck was just associating bad things with her not being there. He pulled up beside one of the police cars.

"What happened?" he questioned someone who was watching from nearby.

"Some girl got messed up by one of the gangs."

"A girl? Did you see her?"

"She's still in there."

Chuck tried to convince himself to move on. It couldn't be Ruby. She wouldn't have been coming from that direction. She wouldn't be on that block.

Bryant tried to get the girl to stand up. She didn't appear to be hurt, but she wouldn't move. He coaxed her and talked to her quietly, but she flinched whenever he touched her, and she just sat there, frozen, hunched over, hugging her knees, shutting the world out. Her shirt was torn at the shoulder, but otherwise she seemed to be unharmed. It was a while before the paramedics got there. They managed to maneuver her around to lift her up onto the gurney to take her to the hospital.

Chuck watched them bring the girl out on the stretcher, and strained for a good look at her. Everyone else was trying to see, crowding as close as they could. He caught a flashing glimpse of blond hair over the side of the stretcher, and knew without a doubt that it was Ruby. He sat there, trying to decide what to do. What was he going to do? Walk up and tell them he was her social worker? That he just happened to be in the area? Chuck watched them load the stretcher into the ambulance, and went back home.

Merrill rolled over and grabbed his phone, silencing it in hopes that it wouldn't disturb his wife. He slid out of bed and stepped out into the hallway before pressing the talk button, and answering lowly.

"Yeah?"

"Detective Merrill? It's Doctor Brown at the General. We just admitted a girl, she had your card in her wallet."

Merrill rubbed his eyes, trying to focus.

"Uh-huh. A girl? Who?" he questioned.

"Ruby Simpson."

"Ruby. What's she been admitted for?"

"Apparently she ran into a gang downtown."

Merrill didn't say anything for a moment. He rubbed his forehead, already feeling a headache coming on. He closed his eyes and leaned against the hallway wall, thinking.

"Is there an officer with her?" he questioned.

"Yes, there was one at the scene," Brown said helpfully.

"Plain clothes?"

"No, beat cop who I guess found her."

"She was supposed to have a plainclothesman following her," Merrill said.

"Well… he's not here. No-one like that around."

Merrill mouthed a curse, but didn't say it out loud.

"Is she badly hurt?" he questioned, fearing the worst. Obviously Ruby hadn't been able to talk to the doctor. He hoped that didn't mean that she was intubated or in a coma.

"No. Mostly shock, it looks like," Brown assured him.

"I'll be down shortly. She should also have a number for her social worker. She's in foster care."

"Yes, we found it. I'll call him next…"

"Don't worry about it," Merrill interrupted, "I'd rather talk to him myself."

"Oh, all right then."

Merrill pressed end and stood there for a moment. He thought the matter through as he went to his study and pulled a set of clothing out of the closet to get dressed. Once ready, he called his superior.

"Frank? Merrill. I just got a call that Ruby Simpson had some trouble with one of the gangs tonight."

"Did she? What happened?" Frank sounded concerned.

"I'm just going down to the hospital to find out. Who's supposed to be on her tail tonight?"

"Uh—no-one. We took off surveillance yesterday."

"No," Merrill protested.

"Sorry. It seemed like things had gone smoothly and she was out of danger."

"They must have been waiting until she was unprotected," Merrill observed, "How obvious was the surveillance?"

"Well… not our top guys. But not bad, either."

"I'd better get up there. Can we get surveillance on her again, but a little more discreet this time?"

"I'll see to it. We'll go over the case at stand-ups in the morning."

Merrill looked up the number for the social worker and gave him a call. The phone was picked up before Merrill even heard it ring.

"Hello?"

"Mr. Samuel? I'm calling about Ruby Simpson."

"Is something wrong? Is she okay?"

Merrill frowned and didn't answer immediately.

"Ruby's up at the General. I'm just on my way up to see her now. I thought you'd like to be there."

"I'll be there."

Merrill hung up his phone thoughtfully, and headed out to the hospital.

Ruby didn't look as bad as she did after the shooting—she didn't appear to be injured at all. But the doctor seemed concerned.

"Miss Simpson is in pretty bad shape," he confided, "she's completely unresponsive—although there is no physical cause. Whatever happened, it was pretty traumatic. I'm afraid you won't be able to question her tonight."

Merrill looked down at Ruby, laying on the bed staring off into space. When he bent over her, she didn't focus. Her eyes didn't follow his movements, and she didn't even blink. He nodded.

"I'll just wait for her social worker to arrive, then," he said lowly.

Samuels was only a couple of minutes behind him, even though Merrill had come in his squad car with the lights and siren on. He hurried up to the bed and leaned over Ruby, grasping her hand.

"Ruby? Are you okay? What happened?"

He looked up at Merrill in confusion when she didn't respond.

"What's wrong? Is she hurt?"

"We're not sure what happened. But she's not going to be able to talk to us tonight. She's not hurt, just… out of it. Traumatized. She'll probably be fine in the morning."

"What happened?" Samuels questioned, shaking his head.

"Have you talked to her foster family?"

"She didn't go home tonight. Where was she?"

"I don't have the details. Something about a run-in with one of the gangs. I'm on my way over to the scene next."

Samuels nodded, and sat down in the chair beside Ruby, watching her worriedly.

There were still police cars with their lights flashing all along the street, yellow crime scene tape strung around the building, plenty of officers and investigators swarming over the site. Bryant, one of the officers who had first arrived on the scene, caught Merrill up on the details.

"We have a few witnesses who heard gunshots. No-one wanted to get too close, and no-one bothered to call it in. We responded to a routine alarm in the warehouse. One of the gangs likes to use it for their business, so we often get alarms here. Usually it's nothing. Pretty hard to get these kids for more than trespassing. No-one saw anyone come in or out, but no-one was getting too close, after the gunshots."

"But the girl wasn't shot," Merrill pointed out.

"No." Bryant motioned Merrill to follow him into the warehouse. "This is where we found her," he pointed out the 'x' that someone had drawn in chalk on the concrete to reference the spot. He then pointed to each of the smashed bullets within a few feet of the x. "He didn't shoot her. Just did a bit of target practice. Personally, I'd rather take a bullet and get it over with than have them whizzing around my head while some psycho amused himself."

"Not only that," Merrill said slowly, "but a psycho that Ruby knew wouldn't hesitate to kill her. This girl was witness to her Jag boyfriend being executed two weeks ago."

"Oh, heard about that. She was there?" Bryant whistled through his teeth and shook his head slowly, "No wonder the poor kid was so freaked out."

"Yeah," Merrill agreed, "anything else you turned up here?"

"No. It was about forty-five minutes between the alarm going off and us getting here. The shots were fired pretty close to the time the alarm went off. Probably he threatened her, then left her here alone. She's too scared to leave in case he's still out there, just stays put until we get here."

"You didn't see anyone leaving the scene?" Merrill questioned.

"Caught a glimpse of someone in the alleyway, but probably not the guy who did this. Why stick around for almost an hour? Get in, get done and get out before the heat shows up."

"Does it usually takes you forty-five minutes to respond to an alarm here?"

"Sure. Usually longer. Like I say, we can't usually bust anyone for anything more than trespassing. If there's anything else going down, it takes priority over an abandoned building alarm. Tonight was quiet, so we got here pretty quickly."

"So they would have known they had lots of time. Can you describe the suspect in the alley?"

"Hard to give you any description... slim. About my own height. I figured more likely a junkie at the time. The Terminators are rarely alone."

"Terminators?" Merrill repeated.

Bryant nodded. Being a homicide detective, Merrill was familiar with the Terminators and their work. They were one of the local juvie gangs. And it was true, they usually at least worked in pairs. One person alone was much more vulnerable. Well, at least now they knew which gang had done Mike in. That was more than they had known before.

"Who are your witnesses? That heard the shots?"

"Couple of working girls. They're in the cars out front," Bryant jerked his thumb in the right direction.

"Thanks."

Merrill went out to talk to the girls. They sat in the back of one of the squad cars talking to each other causally, like this happened every day. A black girl and a red-head. Both young, but not underage. Experienced professionals, not they type to be scared off by an interview with the cops.

"So you ladies heard gunshots?" he questioned without preamble.

"That's right," the red-head told him, "And no, we didn't bother to call the cops. You hear gunshots around here pretty regular. Usually some guy in a bar showing off to his girlfriend. Or the gangs. By the time the police can get here, everything is long over."

Merrill didn't think there was any point in disputing her judgment.

"What time did you hear the shots?"

"About eight-thirty."

"Eight-thirty?" Merrill looked at the slender black girl for confirmation. She nodded. "See or hear anything else after that?"

"No."

"Any Terminators around tonight?"

"Mmm, a couple," the redhead confirmed, frown lines appearing on her face momentarily as she thought about it. "But that's not unusual."

"Who did you see?" Merrill's pencil hovered over his notebook.

"I figure that might not be too bright. We don't want to get involved with this. With them."

It figured. They knew, but they weren't about to give any information that might get them in trouble with the locals. Considering the way that Ruby had been treated when she hadn't fingered the boys who killed Mike, he couldn't very well blame them.

"What about the girl?" he questioned. "Did you guys know her?"

"Nobody's bothered to tell us who it was."

Merrill shut his notepad, not expecting a positive response. The girls were prostitutes, and he had no indications that Ruby was in the business.

"Her name is Ruby," he said.

Both girls looked surprised.

"Ruby?" the redhead repeated, "A real young kid with blond hair?"

Merrill opened up his notebook slowly.

"Yes. Is she around here often?"

Both nodded vigorously.

"Sure. Every night, usually. Waiting for her boyfriend. But she hasn't been around for a couple of weeks."

"Not since she got shot when the Jag she was sleeping with was murdered," Merrill deduced.

"Oh, the poor girl," the black girl said, speaking for the first time. "Poor Ruby."

"You say she's here every night?"

"Yeah," the redhead agreed.

"Working?"

"No sir! Ruby's a one-man woman. Her boyfriend picks her up here."

"Why here? Why doesn't she go to his house?"

"He doesn't show up every night. He only picks her up when he feels like it. Probably has a wife the rest of the time, or another girl."

"Who is this guy?"

"Don't know much about the guy. His name is Chuck. Good looking white boy. Little white sportster."

"When did you see him last?"

"I thought I saw his car tonight," the black girl said, "About the time all the cops showed up. Might not have been him, though."

"I want you to call me if you see him again." Merrill handed them each one of his cards. "I want to know if he picks Ruby up again."

They shrugged. Merrill knew they probably wouldn't bother.

"Is Ruby okay?" the black girl questioned.

"She will be," Merrill sighed. "She's a mighty scared little girl. But she'll get through it."

Ruby still wasn't talking in the morning. She was a little more responsive, her eyes starting to follow movements, but there was no point in trying to question her. Samuels had stayed with her all night, then left for work in the morning, leaving her alone with her police guard. At that point, there were no solid leads, and all of the evidence was being reviewed by forensics, so Merrill went home to get a little shut-eye himself.

Ruby's condition improved slightly day by day. Each time Merrill and Banks went by to see her, she was a little more responsive to their presence. On the fourth day, Merrill knew immediately that she was aware of what was going on. Her lawyer, Willhelm, was there. Ruby and Willhelm looked up at the approach of the homicide officers.

"Feeling pretty good today?" Merrill questioned.

Ruby didn't say anything. Willhelm looked up at them, his face serious and composed.

"Ruby's feeling a little more like herself today," he acknowledged.

"Well then, maybe she can tell us about what happened," Merrill suggested.

"I've been trying to convince Ruby that it would be in her best interests to do so. However... with the gang involvement in this matter, I'm not having much success."

"Ruby," Merrill sat down and looked earnestly into her eyes, "this guy is going to keep terrorizing you unless you do something about it. Next time, maybe he really will shoot you."

"No, he won't," Ruby asserted in a quiet, hoarse voice, "not if I don't say anything."

"You think you can trust him to keep his promises? We know which gang he's in. It's only a matter of time until we find out which one of the Terminators it is. Then what?"

"Then I'll testify it's not him."

Willhelm looked at Ruby sharply.

"Ruby. That would be really stupid. You could end up in jail for perjury."

"I'm not putting him in jail."

"You don't want him to be convicted? This guy killed your boyfriend, and you don't want to see him behind bars?" Merrill demanded.

"No."

Merrill studied Ruby, trying to figure out what was going on in her mind. In the past, she'd been obstructive, but she had only been concerned about what would happen if she talked. Now, she was protecting the guy, vowing to lie to keep him out of prison. He could see the shock and worry on Willhelm's face. The last thing that Willhelm wanted was a client who was going to lie on the stand. Whatever had happened to change Ruby's outlook, she hadn't told him the details either.

"Are you still going to tell me that you don't remember what happened when Mike was killed?"

Ruby nodded, looking down at her knees.

"What happened Tuesday night?" Merrill asked.

The girl's eyes got distant, and Merrill watched her carefully, trying to identify her emotion. Fear? Pain? She sank back in the bed, and turned her face away.

Willhelm touched her shoulder after a moment.

"Ruby."

She turned and looked at them in confusion, as if they had awakened her from a dream.

"Are you okay?" Willhelm questioned.

Ruby shook her head, brows drawn down.

"I'm tired," she objected.

"Can we set up an appointment to talk later?" Willhelm questioned the officers.

Merrill consulted his schedule and set up a time when they could interview her.

CHAPTER *Five*

Mrs. Winters watched Ruby go past her and up the stairs without any word or acknowledgment. Ruby's face was as white as a sheet, and she looked worse than when she was staying there before. She was obviously sick and frightened. Ruby shut her bedroom door. Mrs. Winters turned and looked at Mr. Samuels.

"She asked to be brought back here," Chuck told her. "It's the first time she's ever asked for a family that she's been with before. It's the first indication we've had that there might be a chance of a more permanent placement for her."

"She's a good kid. We haven't had any trouble with her," Mrs. Winters told him. "We're happy to have her back."

"Well, I hope this means progress."

"What's happened in the last week? She looks awful."

"Yeah, she's had a pretty rough time. She hasn't really said what happened, but she had a run-in with one of the gangs."

The doctors had said not to push her to tell them what had happened. Something about post-traumatic stress. Any time they pushed her for information, she sort of phased out.

Chuck was confused about what had happened to Ruby. The doctors said that she hadn't been beaten up, but she was in the hospital for four days. She still could hardly speak to him coherently. The teasing and needling that he had grown used to from her was gone. She had been silent on the trip over. When he had told her that she would have to go back to a foster family again, she'd had little to say. She'd asked distantly if she could stay with him. Chuck told her no. She'd then surprised him by asking for the Winters. Chuck agreed to arrange it, and took her to the house. In the car, he stared at her bare legs, stretching long below her short-shorts. It just served to remind him that it had been three weeks since the two of them had been together. Now it would be at least a couple more.

"We'll look after her," Mrs. Winters promised.

Chuck nodded.

"Thanks. I'll check up later to see how she's doing."

Ruby got ready for bed, and took out the pills the doctors at the hospital had given her to help her sleep. They had told her not to take them if she didn't have to, but there was no question of need in Ruby's mind. They made her groggy in the morning, but they kept her from waking up in a cold sweat from nightmares. She had enough pills for another week. After that, Ruby didn't know how she was going to make it through the night. She took one pill and climbed into bed. She closed her eyes. Fifteen minutes later, there were quiet footsteps in the hallway and Ruby tensed. The footsteps got closer and stopped just outside the door. There was a soft knock on the door and Mrs. Winters opened the door.

"I just wanted to see how you were doing."

Ruby turned her face towards the door and didn't say anything. Mrs. Winters entered the room and went up to the bed.

"Are you okay, Ruby?" she whispered.

"Yeah."

"Are you going to be able to sleep okay?"

"Uh-huh."

Mrs. Winters straightened Ruby's blanket and smoothed out the wrinkles.

"Do you want me to stay with you for a few minutes?"

Ruby shrugged, but she did feel safer when Mrs. Winters was there. She didn't like being alone. She closed her eyes, knowing that Mrs. Winters would stay by her side until she fell asleep.

Mrs. Winters got up a couple of times in the night to check on Ruby. She was sleeping soundly. When Mrs. Winters went in to wake her up for school, she was still fast asleep.

"Ruby, time to get up."

She didn't move. Mrs. Winters touched her shoulder.

"Ruby. Wake up."

She shook Ruby's arm harder, and eventually Ruby stirred.

"Ruby..."

Ruby opened her eyes, and snuggled down under the covers.

"It's time to get up," Mrs. Winters prompted. "School today."

"I'm not going today."

"Well, let's get you up and around, and see how you feel after you've been up a while."

"Mmm-mmn," Ruby disagreed.

"Come on. Get out of bed, so I can get started on breakfast."

Ruby climbed slowly out of bed, scowling.

"Go have a shower and get dressed," Mrs. Winters encouraged, ignoring her expression. She watched to make sure that Ruby was going to stay up, and went downstairs to get breakfast ready.

Ruby slipped into one of the kitchen chairs. Mrs. Winters glanced up at her.

"Hi, there. Feeling better?"

Ruby shook her head.

"I can't go to school," she said.

"You don't look great."

Ruby knew. She'd seen herself in the mirror in the bathroom. She looked like she had two black eyes. Ruby didn't feel sick, but she didn't feel well. She just couldn't face going to school. All she wanted to do was lie in bed.

"Well, have a bite to eat. Toast?"

"I'm not hungry."

"Try some toast and juice."

Ruby sipped at the orange juice on the table. She had the corner of a piece of toast, but couldn't get anything else down. Mrs. Winters sat down with a bowl of cereal.

"Should I call the school and find out what you should be studying?" she suggested. "I take it you've missed a lot of time lately."

"I'll catch up. Don't worry about it."

"Well, I'll at least call and let them know you'll be absent today," Mrs. Winters decided.

Ruby shrugged. It would be a shock for the school, someone calling in an excuse for her.

Chuck didn't hear from Ruby for a week, which was unusual. He did, however, hear from Mrs. Winters. She kept him up to date on how Ruby was doing—the fact that she wouldn't go to school, she just stayed in her room all day. She didn't call her friends. She didn't go out. She slept in late in the mornings and watched TV in the afternoon. Mrs. Winters was concerned that Ruby needed counseling. Chuck just breathed a sigh of relief that Ruby wasn't calling him and risking giving them away. After a week, Chuck got a phone call.

"It's Ruby," she said quietly.

"Ruby? How are you? Mrs. Winters says you haven't been feeling well."

"Yeah. Can I come over tonight?"

"You know you have to stay with the Winters until things are normal again." This was familiar territory.

"They let me sleep over at Marty's whenever I want. I'll just tell them I'm there."

"I don't think that would be a good idea," he countered.

"I'm coming by your place tonight. See you then."

She hung up. Chuck stared at the receiver in disbelief. He wasn't displeased—he did want to see Ruby. But they had agreed before that she would not come directly to his place. He would pick her up if it was a good day for him. She had always complied, and had listened to his reasoning. She often complained, or pushed to get her way, but this was something new. She was coming by. She wasn't listening to any argument. She wasn't going to wait for him to pick her up. She was coming to his place and that was that. Chuck was bewildered. Ruby had never behaved that way before.

Ruby buzzed Chuck's apartment, and he released the door without talking to her on the intercom. She went upstairs, and he must have been watching for her, because he opened the door the instant she walked up to it. Ruby went in.

"Hi."

"Hi, there." Chuck smiled tentatively. He was studying her, like she was someone he'd never seen before. "Are you hungry?"

"No."

"I ordered in. Come have something to eat with me."

Ruby shrugged, and followed him into the kitchen. She had one slice of pizza, and that was it. It was the first day since that night that she had walked outside by herself, and her stomach was all queasy. She had that horrible tight feeling in her stomach like you get when you're caught at something you knew you weren't supposed to do. A feeling of impending doom.

"Have some more," Chuck urged. "I thought pizza was your favorite food."

Ruby shook her head.

"I'm not hungry."

"You're not dieting, are you?"

"No."

"You've lost weight," he pointed out.

"So?"

"You need to eat. You're too thin as it is."

"I'm not hungry," Ruby said flatly.

"Mrs. Winters thinks that maybe we should get you into counseling."

"I'm not here to talk about foster family stuff," Ruby said, looking him in the eye.

Chuck smiled and stopped trying to be her social worker.

Ruby awoke to Chuck sitting on the side of the bed and shaking her.

"Ruby. It's time to get up," he told her.

Ruby stretched and pulled the covers up further.

"Ruby."

Chuck's voice was tough, the tone he used when there was not going to be any discussion. Ruby had a tone too. A new one.

"I'm not going anywhere," she said flatly.

There was silence for a moment as Chuck took this in.

"Come on, Ruby," he said with a bit of a laugh. "You know you can't stay here."

"Exactly how are you going to get me out?" Ruby questioned, opening her eyes and turning over to look at him.

Chuck stared at her.

"You can't stay here by yourself," he repeated, not answering her question.

"Then stay with me," she invited, holding up the covers for him to climb back into bed.

"I have work, Ruby."

"You can call in sick one day," Ruby argued.

"I'm not calling in sick. Get out of bed."

"I don't feel good." Ruby snuggled under the covers, closing her eyes again.

Chuck pulled the covers back from her.

"Get up," he ordered.

Ruby didn't move. Chuck grasped her wrist firmly and pulled her up to a sitting position.

"Now get dressed and ready to go. You're already making me late."

"I'm not going," Ruby repeated.

Chuck picked up her clothes and threw them at her. Ruby flinched and curled up on the bed, shutting her eyes tightly. She hid her face in her arms, trying not to let Chuck see how the violent movement scared her. She knew it was silly, that he'd never do anything to hurt her, but the action made something inside her stomach snap, and she couldn't get up again or stop the tears that sprang to her eyes and started to stream down her cheeks. She hadn't cried since Mike got shot, but suddenly she couldn't stop the tears. Her heart beat hard and fast, and panic welled up in her. Chuck moved towards her.

"Ruby? Are you okay? I'm sorry…"

"Don't!" she pulled away from his touch. "Please don't."

She started to sob. She couldn't stand him moving towards her. She was flashing back to that night, and she couldn't bear for him to touch her.

"Ruby, what's the matter? I'm sorry. Don't cry."

"Don't touch me—please don't hurt me."

Chuck stood there looking down at her, trying to figure out what to do. He looked at his watch and left the room. Ruby tried to calm her tears and block the images out of her mind. Chuck came back after a few minutes and sat down on the bed next to her.

"I'm not going to hurt you, Ruby. I'm just going to sit here by you until you get settled down. It's all right, you're safe here."

Ruby could feel him sitting on the bed next to her. He didn't move, didn't say anything else, and after a long silence, Ruby managed to slow her tears a little.

"It's all right," he soothed, his voice low and steady. "You've been through a rough time. But it'll be okay."

Ruby nodded. She was still covering her face, but managing to relax her muscles a little bit, trying to control her breathing.

"Why don't I get you a drink?" Chuck suggested.

Ruby nodded her assent. Chuck didn't usually approve of Ruby drinking. He said she was too young. He left the room and came back in with a glass. Ruby took it from him and held it to her lips. It was strong. She didn't usually have anything more than beer. It burned at first, but it warmed her and helped her relax her muscles. Chuck picked up her clothes and handed them to her gently.

"Get dressed, Ruby. You'll catch cold."

"You sound like a mom," Ruby said with a weak smile. She still found it hard to move her hands away from her face and sit up straight. She pulled the shirt on slowly. Chuck nodded.

"Have another drink. You're okay."

Ruby nodded and had another sip of the drink. She pulled on her shorts quickly, and sat with her knees pulled up to her chest and her arms wrapped tightly around her knees.

"Feeling better?"

"Yeah."

"Come into the kitchen and have something to eat."

Ruby climbed slowly off the bed. She sat at the table and held onto her glass with both hands. Chuck made coffee and took out the pizza from the night before. No toast and juice at Chuck's place. Ruby glanced at the clock and was shocked to see that it was creeping towards noon.

"You're skipping work," she said in surprise.

"I told them I had an emergency. I'm still hoping to get in, though."

"Go ahead," she told him.

"Once you're ready to go," he agreed.

"Where am I going to go?"

"Wherever you feel like, Ruby. Come on, I'm tired of this fooling around. If you can't live with the arrangement we've always had, I guess we won't be seeing each other."

Ruby stared at him.

"What?"

Chuck didn't answer.

"You're dumping me?"

"I'm saying you're getting too demanding. You used to be independent, Ruby. Now you're clingy and want my attention all the time."

"I haven't even called you for a week!"

Chuck couldn't find anything to say to that. He shrugged.

"You have to be with the Winters for another couple weeks. Maybe then we can try to get things on track again."

"You're not going to see me at all? Even though I can tell her I'm just at Marty's?"

"It's too dangerous. I want things to go back to the way they were."

Ruby couldn't believe it. She cried once, and suddenly he couldn't stand to be around her. There was only one thing that made sense.

"You're already seeing someone else."

He didn't deny it.

"I need to get to work, if you're all right now."

Ruby sat on a stool in the kitchen and watched Mrs. Winters while she made supper.

"I have a sister in another foster family," Ruby offered suddenly. "Did you know that?"

Mrs. Winters stopped ripping lettuce and looked at Ruby for a moment.

"No, I didn't. What's her name?" she questioned.

"Ronnie. Could she come over, maybe?" Ruby questioned tentatively.

"I don't see why not, as long as it's okay with her foster family," Mrs. Winters agreed, starting in on the lettuce again.

"Could she sleep over?" Ruby suggested.

"It's okay with me. You've been spending a lot of time at Marty's lately. It would be nice to have you here."

"I'm going to call her."

Ruby went upstairs to her room, and found the phone number in her wallet. She was getting quite a collection of phone numbers and business cards. She looked through them for a moment, trying to place them all. Some of them she couldn't even remember who had given to her. She went into the master bedroom and dialed the number. It rang a few times and then a man answered it.

"Hello?"

"Is Ronnie there?" Ruby questioned.

"Just a moment."

He left the phone off the hook, and Ruby could hear people talking back and forth, though she couldn't make out the words. It sounded like a busy place. After a while her sister's voice was on the other end.

"Hello?"

"Hi, Ron'. It's Ruby."

"Ruby? Hi!" she sounded pleased.

"How're you doing?"

"Good. I told Mr. Samuels I wanted to talk to you again, but he said you were sick," Ronnie said.

"Oh, I was. But I'm better now. Do you think your foster parents would let you come here to my place? To stay overnight?"

"Just a second, I'll find out. Mom?" Ruby could hear her calling out over the other voices for permission. Strange that she should call some stranger mom. Ruby had never called any of her foster parent mom and dad. None of them had encouraged it, either. Ronnie's voice faded out as she put down the phone and went to discuss it. She came back after a while and picked it up again.

"She says as long as your foster mom says it's okay and is going to be there."

"Yeah, she already said it was all right."

"Okay. What's the address?"

Ruby read it carefully off of the paper Chuck had written it down on when he brought her there. When you were only going to be place for a couple of weeks, there was no point in memorizing another address. It was just too confusing. Ronnie repeated it back to her.

"Yeah. When will you be here?" she questioned.

"I have to eat and pack first. Then Dad'll drive me over."

Ruby got a queer feeling in her stomach hearing Ronnie talk about 'dad,' even though she knew Ronnie just meant her foster dad. Ruby didn't know why she reacted like that. Although she and her father had never particularly gotten along, they hadn't fought either. Ruby felt indifferent towards him.

"So you'll be here in a couple of hours?" she questioned.

"Yup. See you!"

"Bye."

Ruby hung up and went down to talk to Mrs. Winters.

"Ronnie's coming in a couple hours," she confirmed.

"Great. I'm looking forwards to meeting her. Is she close to you in age?"

"No, she's only eight."

"What are you guys going to do?"

"I don't know." Ruby hadn't thought about that. "Watch TV, I guess."

"You guys had better not stay up all night, or Ronnie's foster parents won't want her over again. Eight is still pretty young for a sleepover."

"Yeah, whatever. We'll go to sleep," Ruby agreed.

"Good. Do you have any other siblings, or are you two the only ones?"

"The only ones in foster care."

"Still others at home?"

"Yeah."

"Older or younger?"

"Younger than me. Chloe's between me and Ronnie. And there's some younger ones."

"How long since you've been with your family?" Mrs. Winters asked.

"Five years."

Ruby felt uneasy talking about foster care, and went back upstairs to her room to escape the questions.

The hour was getting late and the girls had been quiet for a while, so Mrs. Winters went in to see if they were getting to sleep. Ronnie, sleeping on a mattress near the door, was asleep. Mrs. Winters saw Ruby tossing and turning in bed, and slipped into the room.

"Having trouble settling in?" she questioned.

"Yeah."

It looked, in the dim light from the hall, as if Ruby might have been crying. Mrs. Winters couldn't tell for sure.

"Are you okay?" she questioned.

"Yeah."

"Do you want me to stay with you?"

Ruby shook her head. Mrs. Winters guessed that she wanted to look mature in front of Ronnie—even though the other girl was already asleep. She nodded and patted Ruby's hand.

"Try to relax, then. At least it's not a school night."

She left the two of them and went back to bed.

Chuck looked away from his computer work and answered the phone without looking at the caller I.D.

"Yeah?"

"It's Cynthia Dare, Mr. Samuels."

"Hi, Mrs. Dare. What can I do for you?"

"I'm a little bit concerned about Ronnie."

"What's she doing?" Chuck questioned, sorting through the files on the desk to find Ronnie's.

"She's been very moody since she and Ruby got together—" Mrs. Dare started out.

"That was quite a while ago. How's she acting?"

"No, I mean just this weekend."

"What? They didn't meet this weekend," Chuck said blankly.

"Ronnie spend the whole weekend at Ruby's house. They were together for two full days."

"Who set this up? Ruby is only supposed to have supervised visits with Ronnie."

There was silence on the other end for a few moments.

"Ruby called Ronnie. I assumed you had okayed it."

"No, I didn't. Was someone else around while they were together?"

"Ruby's foster mom was there."

"Okay. Good." Chuck found Ronnie's file, and opened it up. "And Ronnie's been upset since the weekend?"

"I don't know if upset is the right word," Mrs. Dare said. "Up and down; unusually quiet. Like she has something on her mind. But she won't talk about it."

"Why don't you make an appointment for her to come and talk to a counselor? I'll give Ruby's family a call and see if they know what might be bothering Ronnie."

"Okay."

Chuck hung up the phone, scowling and shaking his head. He looked up the number for the Winters and called them. Mrs. Winters answered the phone, and Chuck identified himself.

"Oh, Mr. Samuels. Ruby's not home from school yet."

"I'll talk to you first. I hear you had Ruby's sister over the weekend."

"Yes, we did," Mrs. Winters agreed. "The girls had a good time."

"Were you aware Ruby is only allowed supervised visits with her family?" Chuck questioned with a sigh.

"Nobody told me that. But one of us was here the whole time. They weren't in the house alone," she assured him.

Chuck tapped his pen on the phone, thinking.

"Whose idea was it to get them together?"

"Ruby's."

"How did you get Ronnie's phone number?"

"Ruby called Ronnie. She had it."

"What did the two of them do?"

"Talked, watched TV. They got to bed in good time. Everything was okay."

"Bed?" Chuck repeated, his voice rising. He struggled to keep it under control. "Ronnie slept over?"

"Sure. We put a mattress on the floor in Ruby's room."

"They slept separately?" Chuck verified.

There was silence on the other end of the line, and Chuck knew the answer before Mrs. Winters gave it, her voice hesitant.

"Ruby's been having trouble sleeping. She ended up on the mattress with Ronnie."

Chuck didn't say anything. Mrs. Winters was uncomfortable with the silence.

"I didn't know Ruby wasn't supposed to see Ronnie. Everything went smoothly. They got along really well."

"Have Ruby call me. I want to hear from her as soon as she gets in."

"I will."

Ruby broke away from the kiss and embrace with Brian.

"I'll call Mrs. Winters and tell'er I'm staying with Marty," she told Brian.

"She never checks up?" he questioned.

"Nope."

Ruby went to the phone and called Mrs. Winters.

"Hi—it's me. I'm going to stay over with Marty tonight."

"I think you should come home, Ruby. Mr. Samuels wants you to call him."

"I can call him from here. See you tomorrow."

Ruby hung up the phone before Mrs. Winters could protest. She tried to decide whether to call Chuck. She was angry with him after their last meeting, but maybe he had come to his senses since. She dialed his home number.

"Hello?"

"Hello Mr. Samuels," Ruby said in a sugary voice.

"Ruby," his voice was flat, not welcoming. "I hear you had Ronnie over for a sleepover on the weekend."

"Yeah, so?"

"You're supposed to go through me to set anything up."

"I can call up my own sister without your help," Ruby said.

"Wrong. You are not to contact Ronnie directly, and any visits with her have to be supervised."

"Why?" Ruby was nonplussed.

"Because I don't want Ronnie to have to deal with any more problems than she already has," Chuck said sensibly.

Ruby rolled her eyes. She kicked at the baseboard of the wall.

"I didn't do anything to her. We didn't even talk about home."

"You slept with her," he pointed out.

"Yeah, so? She's my sister. There's nothing wrong with that."

"It's confusing for Ronnie. She has enough to sort out without you interfering."

"What're you talking about?" Ruby demanded, lost.

"Do I have to spell it out for you, Ruby?" Chuck's voice was a growl. "Ronnie is not in foster care because she has problems with authority. The issues were a lot more serious than that."

Ruby was silent, trying to sort out Chuck's words, but not wanting to believe what she was hearing.

"Chloe said Ronnie was getting in trouble at school, and with Mom," she recounted.

"Chloe is one of the reasons the rest of the kids are still with your parents. If she would cooperate with our inquiries, we would likely be able to remove her and the others to foster care too."

"I don't believe anything is going on. Ronnie's just making up stories to get attention. She wanted to get out, so she made something up," Ruby explained.

"Ronnie went into foster care after the hospital made a report. She's told us very little."

"I didn't know," Ruby said in a small voice. "Why didn't you tell me before?"

"It never occurred to me that you'd be so stupid," Chuck snapped.

Ruby slammed the receiver down. She turned around to find Brian in the doorway watching her.

"Who was that?" he questioned mildly.

"My social worker."

"What's up?"

"Everything's screwed up." Ruby scowled, shaking her head.

"You still staying here tonight?" he questioned, running two fingers through her hair.

"Yeah. Of course," Ruby said, giving him a hug. "Yeah."

Chuck hadn't expected Ruby to hang up on him. But in retrospect, it had been a pretty dumb thing to say. He wouldn't have said something like that to any of the other kids he was in charge of, but he was too emotionally involved with Ruby. That was going to have to end—or he would have to transfer her file to someone else. He called Ruby back. Mrs. Winters answered the phone and Chuck asked for Ruby.

"She's not here."

"I just talked to her," Chuck said.

"She was calling from a friend's house. Just a minute, I'll get you the number."

While she looked it up, Chuck scrolled through the caller I.D. on his phone. The number that Ruby had called from had been blocked. She knew how to play the game. Mrs. Winters came back on the line.

"Okay. She's staying at Marty's. Here's the number."

Chuck thanked her and hung up. He dialed the number, and a girl answered the phone.

"Yeah?"

"Could I talk to Ruby again?"

There was silence on the other end. Then eventually,

"Who's calling?"

"Mr. Samuels. We got disconnected."

"Yeah. This line is bad sometimes. Just a minute."

The dial tone buzzed in Chuck's ear. He tried to redial, but the line was busy.

So Ruby wasn't at home, and wasn't at Marty's house. Who knew where she was staying tonight.

Ruby looked through her phone numbers, and picked a few out. One was for the cute lawyer she'd been assigned when Mike was killed. She dialed him up and arranged to meet with him for lunch. They met at a restaurant and talked casually for a little while before Willhelm asked her why she had asked to meet. Ruby had been enjoying the personal visit, and looked for a good excuse for having called Willhelm.

"I want to sue the police," she said.

"Sue the police? For what?"

"For not doing their job and helping me when the guy who killed Mike came after me."

"They did everything they could once they found you, didn't they?"

"There was a cop following me everywhere. Why didn't he come when he saw what was going on?"

Willhelm studied her, tapping his fork lightly on the plate.

"Who was following you?" he questioned with a frown.

Ruby leaned forward.

"Ever since Mike got killed, the police have had a guy following me. But he didn't do anything. I got grabbed in the middle of the street, and shot at, and stuff... and they didn't do anything."

"That's pretty serious, if it's true," Willhelm admitted. "I'll have to look into it."

"I kept waiting for him to come," Ruby said, biting her bottom lip and allowing her eyes to tear up a little. A lump came to her throat when she flashed back to the attack, but she pushed it away, trying not to really feel it, trying not to remember too clearly.

"I bet," Willhelm agreed, nodding in sympathy.

They talked on about the situation a few minutes more, and then the conversation strayed to other things and Ruby tried discreetly to find out all she could about Willhelm. He didn't seem to notice her new focus.

A few times, Willhelm tried discreetly to end the conversation to get back to his office, using his "winding up" voice, putting his cutlery and then his napkin in the center of his plate, smiling and looking away from Ruby, toward the door. Ruby managed to extend the conversation and keep him talking. Finally, Willhelm looked obviously at his watch and pushed away from the table.

"I have a very important meeting to get to. I'm glad you called me..."

"When can I meet you again?" Ruby interrupted.

He stopped short.

"What?"

"All this stuff with the gangs... I'm scared. I don't know where to go. I thought maybe..."

"I'll look into this stuff with the police, but... I can't give you a place to stay."

Ruby considered him thoughtfully. He said no, but she thought he could be convinced.

"I gotta have somewhere to go," she pleaded.

"You have a foster family."

"They know about the Winters. It's not safe there."

"You should talk to the police," Willhelm told her firmly.

"I told you, they won't protect me. They let me be attacked."

Willhelm stood looking at her. He pulled out one of his business cards and wrote on the back of it.

"I don't know. We'll try to figure out what we can work out for you," he sighed.

Ruby took his card. His address was scribbled on the back. She nodded.

"Thanks."

She tucked the card away, and headed back to the house.

Mrs. Winters didn't smile when Ruby came in the door. She raised her eyebrows.

"Where were you last night?" she questioned.

Ruby's heart raced. She swallowed, and tried to keep her breathing and voice even.

"I told you—I was at Marty's."

"You weren't at Marty's."

Ruby looked at Mrs. Winters and waited for more information. She needed to know what exactly Mrs. Winters knew before she argued the point any further.

"Mr. Samuels tried to call you there last night," Mrs. Winters said.

"I didn't want to talk to him," Ruby shrugged.

"He says you weren't there."

"I was there," Ruby said stubbornly.

Mrs. Winters studied her, saying nothing. Ruby scowled and went out onto the front steps to smoke.

Mrs. Winters watched Ruby through the door. When simply accepted for herself, Ruby acted like any normal thirteen year old. A little bit of a child and a little bit of a young woman. But push her, and she became a little girl hiding behind a sophisticated woman facade. Ruby smoked on the steps, looking like a thirty year old world-weary woman. She was easy to deal with as a child, but challenge or confront her, and she shut you out completely. Mrs. Winters let Ruby smoke and think and cool down. At least Ruby hadn't grabbed her bags and run off.

Merrill looked over the surveillance records. There were obvious patterns to Ruby's activities, as there were with anyone. Ruby's most obvious pattern was that she was never at home, where she should be. She'd only spent three nights over the last week at her foster family's. A couple were spent with her school friend, one apparently with a boyfriend, and one at an apartment building. Ruby wasn't spending time at school, either.

The surveillance team hadn't yet seen the little white sports car that the ladies had advised him Ruby's regular boyfriend drove. The boy she'd stayed with last night drove an old station wagon. Of course, there was a garage at his house that they hadn't gotten a glimpse inside of yet, but he wasn't likely to be the "man" that the women had referred to, and it wasn't likely that his parents let him drive the family's white convertible on occasion. Merrill made a note to himself to try to find out who lived in the apartment building. It was outside the neighborhood that Ruby typically stayed within. Whoever picked her up downtown obviously didn't live close by, or she would just walk or bus there.

Merrill was suspicious of all of Ruby's acquaintances. Her assertion that she would lie to protect her attacker suggested to him that she had been attacked not by a Terminator, but by someone she knew. The boyfriend's convertible had been seen that night. Maybe he was the one who had hurt her.

Ruby went back into the house, a little more relaxed after a long smoke. She went quietly upstairs and picked up the phone. She waited for a moment to make sure that Mrs. Winters wasn't paying any attention what she was up to. Then she dialed Ronnie's number.

"Hello?" a male voice answered.

"Ronnie there?" Ruby questioned.

"Who is this?"

"Her sister."

"Sorry. You can't talk to her."

"She's my sister. You can't stop me from talking to her," Ruby protested.

"Sorry. Talk to your social worker."

He hung up. Scowling, Ruby clicked the hang-up switch and dialed

Chuck. She got his voice mail, hung up, and then tried his home number.

"What's going on?" she demanded, when he picked it up.

"Ruby?"

"Yeah, it's Ruby. Why can't I talk to Ronnie?"

"You can visit Ronnie under supervision," Chuck said calmly.

"They won't even let me talk to her on the phone!"

"No. I'll set something up on the weekend. You can talk then."

"You get me in to talk to her now!" Ruby insisted, her voice screeching slightly.

"Relax, Ruby," he tried to calm her. "By the way... where were you last night?"

"What do you care?"

"It's my job to keep track of you."

"Well, keep off my case and keep Mrs. Winters off my case, or I'll tell everyone just how much you really do care," Ruby didn't even try to keep the snarl out of her voice.

"Do you know what would happen to you if you start spouting off?"

"Not as much as would happen to you," she countered, her voice extra-sweet.

"It's my word against yours. Who do you think they'll believe?"

"Why wouldn't they believe me?"

"Foster kids like to make waves. You don't have a great record in that department."

"I know what will happen if they look at my records," Ruby asserted.

That one stumped him and he was silent.

"I want to talk to Ronnie," Ruby repeated.

"Well, you won't be able to tonight, but I'll see what I can do. Okay?"

"I'll talk to you tomorrow."

CHAPTER Six

Angry at Chuck, Ruby grabbed her knapsack and went downstairs. Mrs. Winters was vacuuming in the living room. She looked up as Ruby came down the stairs.

"We're having supper soon. Where are you off to?"

"I'm going to Marty's," Ruby snapped.

"Ruby?"

Ruby didn't answer. She opened the door and walked out without another word. She couldn't believe that Chuck was keeping her from Ronnie. And Chuck had dumped her and threatened her. And he and Mrs. Winters were both harassing her about where she had been the night before. She was so furious she could hardly think. She didn't know where she was going to go or what she was going to do. She grabbed a bus and sat and watched out the window.

When the bus got up to the arcade, Ruby got out. She started towards the arcade, but changed her mind and went into the cafe instead. Jack and a few of the other Jags were there. Ruby sat down beside Jack uncertainly. He was deep in conversation, leaning forward with his elbows on the table. He didn't acknowledge her immediately. After a few minutes, he looked up.

"Hey, Ruby," he greeted, straightening up and sitting back in his seat. "Been a while since I've seen you around here."

"Yeah, I guess."

"Are you going to go out with us tonight?" he teased, knowing full well that gang stuff wasn't her speed. He was the only guy that she spent time with that treated her condescendingly, like she was a little girl. Some of the younger members of the gang were not that much older than her.

"Maybe I will," Ruby shot back.

Jack laughed.

"You wouldn't last an hour, baby."

"Yeah? I'll go with you."

"You'd just slow us down," Jack said, shaking his head.

"I learn quick."

"Sure, let'er come," Tim encouraged.

"Are you going to be responsible for her?" Jack demanded.

"Sure."

"You'll look out for her if we get in a jam?"

"Would I go back on my word?" he countered.

"Fine. You look after her," Jack said with a shrug.

Tim looked past the other boys to Ruby.

"You got a rod?" he questioned blithely.

"No." Ruby unzipped one of the pockets of her knapsack. "But I have this." She took out a switchblade and flipped it open. The boys looked surprised.

"Where'd you get that?" Tim questioned.

"It's Mike's," Jack answered for her, studying it. "How did you get your hands on that?"

"I don't know. It was in my bag after he got shot. Fell in there, or something."

"I wonder how the cops let that one by. Well, do you know how to use it?"

Ruby shrugged.

"How hard could it be? It's a knife."

He laughed.

"You are so naive, kid. Well, Tim, she's all yours."

Ruby's heart raced, even though all they were doing was hanging around looking for trouble. They had stopped in at a couple of bars and arcades picking up other Jags. Jack was looking around, his eyes narrow and suspicious, watching shadows and movements in the dark. He turned and looked at her.

"You still got a cop on your tail?"

Ruby shook her head.

"I don't think so."

"Well, I do. This is the third time I've seen that car tonight. They usually quit after a couple weeks. How come they're still watching you?"

Ruby shrugged, not wanting to talk about the second attack. Jack watched her suspiciously.

"It's been more than a month since Mike got wasted. How come they're still tailing you?"

"I don't know," Ruby insisted.

"Well, let's lose'em." He looked her over, squinting in concentration. "Give her your hat, Tim. Put your hair under the cap or inside your jacket," he told Ruby. "At least you're wearing a dark jacket."

Ruby didn't know what a dark jacket had to do with anything. Jack nodded.

"Let's go, then. The Lamplighter."

Ruby went along with them. She stayed toward the back of the group, but Tim grabbed her by the arm and pulled her into the center of the group.

"Less visible. You're too obvious. You don't want the cop to be able to see you all the time."

"Why?"

"Just trust me."

Ruby tried to stay in the center of the group. They led the way to the Lamplighter, a dance club. The bouncer let the gang in, though he glared at Ruby as she went by him. It wasn't the type of place that Ruby would have gone into without the gang. There were lots of punks, lots of black leather, studs, chains and tattooed bare skin. There had been a number of motorcycles parked out in front of the club, and Ruby picked out the burly bikers. She wouldn't have wanted to be there without the gang, but with them there, she felt safe and free to look around and see what was going on.

The gang dispersed in different directions. Ruby grabbed Tim's arm before he could leave her. He looked back at her, startled, then grimaced.

"Yeah. Sorry, forgot I was babysitting. Come on, let's get something to drink."

Ruby stuck close to him. They sat down at the bar and ordered a couple of beers. The woman bartender looked Ruby over.

"Sorry, honey. You're under age. You're not getting any drinks from me."

"Give her a drink," Tim said.

"I don't serve underage kids."

"Then give me two beers."

She topped off two mugs and put them on the bar in front of Tim. Tim slid one over to Ruby, grinning. The bartender acted like she didn't see it. Tim and Ruby had a few drinks, and watched the other members of the gang. Harlan was dancing with a girl with black makeup and an orange stripe. Other guys were hitting on girls, picking fights, or just drinking.

"What're we doing here?" Ruby questioned, shaking her head.

"Getting thrown out," Tim said with a grin.

"What?"

"Enjoy your drink and the show."

Things were sort of quiet for a while. Then Jack started to mix it up with a skinny punk on the other side of the room. Ruby tensed up, but Tim put his hand on her thigh.

"Relax. Just sit and watch the fun."

The rest of the Jags gathered from the room and joined in the fight. The bouncers moved in to clear the room. Ruby stood up. Tim stood up and put his arm around her shoulders. They watched the Jags and other fighters get thrown out of the club. There was shouting and fighting for a couple more minutes, but the fighters dispersed before police were called.

"That's our cue," Tim told her.

"For what?"

"Come on."

She went with him out the back of the club into the dark alley. They worked their way through back streets to another bar. Ruby sat down at the new bar with Tim. Tim ordered nacho chips. Ruby looked around. It was much quieter than the club. A bar that Ruby might have gone to by herself, if they would let her in.

"Where are the others?" Ruby questioned.

"They'll be here. Have a drink."

Ruby accepted another drink, although she was starting to feel light-headed. She'd probably had enough. But Tim was still chugging them back without any effect. It was about an hour when the rest of the Jags showed up. Jack was grinning, in high spirits.

"No more cop," he said, pleased.

"We lost him?" Ruby questioned.

"Yeah, you lost him. With any luck, he'll stay lost. Now we can have a good time without bein' watched. Have a drink, baby."

"I've already—"

"I said have a drink," he said sharply.

His eyes were angry, hard and cold. Ruby turned on the bar stool.

"I'll have another draft," she said quietly.

"She'll have a tequila," Jack interposed, "and I will too."

Ruby shook her head, but the bartender gave her one, and Ruby picked it up and sipped it. Jack picked up his and gulped it down. He put the glass down firmly on the bar.

"I thought you could keep up with us," he challenged.

Ruby tipped the glass up sucked down the tequila quickly. It made her choke, and it hit the beer afloat in her stomach and made her nauseated. She coughed and gagged and tried desperately to keep it down. Jack stood grinning at her. Tim thumped her on the back.

"We just gonna sit around drinking all night or are we gonna do something?" Harlan questioned impatiently.

"Yeah, we'll go. Come on. Let's find some action."

Ruby got up, a little unsteady on her feet.

"Saw you dancing at the Lamplighter," Ruby said to Harlan.

He grinned.

"Some chick, huh? I'm gonna meet her again later."

They went out on the town looking for trouble, but the night was reasonably quiet. Ruby felt really good for the first time in weeks. The tension drained away. She felt relaxed and unafraid, ready to handle anything. Tim looked at her once during the night and commented,

"I think this is the first time I've seen you smile."

Ruby put her arm around him in answer. She couldn't remember much of what happened the rest of the night, other than going back to the apartment that Tim and some of the other boys shared. Tim helped her off with her coat when she couldn't seem to get it off on her own.

"You did good tonight," he told her. "You handled yourself real well."

"Thanks."

Ruby enjoyed sleeping in without having to wake up for school. The apartment was warm, and she knew the sun must be high in the sky outside, but the windows were covered so little light leaked in, and they all just sprawled in bed. Ruby knew it was getting late, but she didn't care. She felt warm and comfortable and safe, and didn't ever want to get up. She felt Tim stir beside her a few times, but they both just readjusted and went back to sleep. Ruby had a headache, but it didn't bother as long as she laid still, so that's what she did. She could hear the others getting up and moving around after a while, but they were quiet and didn't disturb her. It was quite a while later that she heard one of the Jags close to the bed.

"Man, I never thought we'd find anyone as lazy as Timmy."

Ruby pulled the covers over her head.

"Get lost," she groaned.

Tim rolled over.

"Come on, guys. It ain't that late. Let us sleep."

"It's after noon."

"So? We didn't get in until four or something."

"We're going out. You coming?"

"We'll catch up to you later."

The other boy laughed, and after a while they were left alone again in a quiet apartment. Ruby drifted off to sleep again. She awoke a while later with Tim's arms around her. He stretched languorously.

"You are lazier than me," he breathed. Ruby turned to face him.

"Man, my head hurts."

"Hangover. You packed 'em away pretty good last night."

"Mmm."

Tim cuddled her close, kissing her gently. Ruby pushed some of her covers back, too warm in the midday heat.

"Am I interrupting?" a voice questioned. Ruby startled, and whipped the covers back over herself, turning to identify the voice. It was Harlan, standing in the doorway grinning. He shared Tim's room. Tim sat up, stretching.

"You got lousy timing, man."

Harlan just stood there grinning. Ruby tried to find her clothes and figure out how to get at them. She felt her face getting red. She knew that all of the guys must have been around when she'd undressed for bed, but she couldn't remember that.

"Give'er a break," Tim commented. "Let her get dressed."

Harlan stood there a minute longer, then shrugged and withdrew. Ruby quickly pulled on her clothes and stumbled to her feet. Tim got up, pulling on a pair of jeans, and followed her. In the living room/kitchen, Harlan smiled slyly at them. He motioned to the girl waiting for him, and they went into the bedroom and shut the door. Tim opened the fridge and looked inside.

"We should give them ten minutes and then bust in on them," Tim offered.

Ruby smiled her approval, and sat down at the table and held her pounding head.

Merrill slapped the top of his desk hard. The noise of the report echoed off of the walls like a gunshot. He took a deep breath before speaking into the phone receiver again.

"What do you mean, you lost her?" he demanded.

"She met up with a group of Jaguars last night. They all went to a club. The Jags got thrown out a while later, and we followed them. We realized a few blocks later that Ruby was no longer with them, and went back to the club. She wasn't there either. Gave us the slip. It may have been accidental or intentional."

"So how to you intend to find her again?"

"We'll keep an eye out at the usual places. But we can't put a lot of manpower on it."

"Do what you can. She could still be in danger."

Chuck glanced at the caller I.D. and picked up the phone with a stifled sigh.

"Hello."

"Mr. Samuels? It's Mrs. Winters."

"Hi. What's up?" he questioned, impatient for her to get to the point.

"I think Ruby's run away," Mrs. Winters said tentatively.

Chuck drummed his fingers on the desk.

"Well, has she or hasn't she?"

"She told me she was going to Marty's. But she wasn't there when I checked up."

"What did Marty say?"

"She said that Ruby didn't want to talk. But I'm sure Ruby wasn't there."

"Same as yesterday. I think Ruby's got a boyfriend at school that she stays with now and then. She'll probably come back after school."

"She isn't at school."

There was silence on the phone while Chuck considered that. He cleared his throat, and his voice was a tone lower than it had been before.

"I hesitate to take any steps right away. Ruby has been known to disappear for a day or two before. I don't know that there's much point getting the police involved, if she's just upset about something or testing her limits."

"I really don't feel comfortable doing nothing."

Chuck looked at his watch.

"Why don't you give me a call when school lets out? If Ruby doesn't come home then, we'll do some looking."

Mrs. Winters sighed.

"All right. I'll talk to you in a couple of hours, then."

Ruby didn't really start feeling like herself until late in the afternoon. Her head pounded and her stomach was queasy. She knew it was just a hangover, but she couldn't remember being that sick from drinking before. She often drank small amounts, but not like she had with Tim and Jack. Tim gave her some aspirin, but it didn't seem to help. They went out as the evening wore on, and met up with some of the other Jags. Jack was with them. He glanced at Ruby, seeming unimpressed by her presence.

"You coming out with us again?" he questioned.

"Yeah, I guess."

"Got your blade?"

Ruby nodded, touching it in her pocket.

"Why? What're we doing?"

"You never know."

His question made Ruby uneasy. Later on in the evening, Tim warned her that they were entering Terminator territory. Jack obviously had in mind a little turf war to pass the time. Ruby kept her hand in her pocket, around the knife. Even Tim was getting jumpy, though he tried to appear nonchalant. For the first little while, it looked as if they weren't going to run into any of the Terminators, and Ruby was starting to relax. But then she saw a large group of them up ahead. Ruby froze. Tim shoved her.

"What's the matter with you? Keep going."

She managed to keep her feet moving, although her mind was numb. She was trapped between the two gangs, and the last thing she wanted was to face the Terminators. She pulled the knife out of her pocket and opened it. Tim eyed her, but didn't say anything. When they reached the other gang, Ruby expected them to throw themselves at each other tooth and nail, but both sides seemed oddly calm.

"What're you doing here?" one of the Terminators demanded. A chill went through Ruby. She had heard that voice the night that Mike was killed. He had been there. The Terminator scanned the Jaguars there. Ruby didn't even hear Jack's answer. The Terminator's eyes stopped on Ruby.

"You recruiting girls now?" he questioned with a sneer. "We like to save our girls for after the fights."

Jack grinned, bouncing up and down on his heels.

"Then how come you brought all these girls with you?" Jack questioned, gesturing to the group of Terminators. There were growls of anger from the Terminators, and a few of them surged forward, but were held back.

"My girls can match your little boys any day," the Terminator leader said.

Both sides seemed to be heating up. Ruby saw, out of the corner of her eye, some of the Jaguars palming knives and brass knuckles.

"Get ready," Tim warned her.

Ruby couldn't take her eyes off of one of the Terminators in the middle of the group. He saw her watching him and grinned. There were a few more insults tossed back and forth between the gangs, and then the Terminators were on top of them. Ruby tried uncertainly to defend herself. She was too distracted by the two boys who had killed Mike. She tried to watch both of them at the same time as she tried to protect herself from the approaches of other Terminators. She felt like she was in a haze, and everything was happening in slow motion around her. She noticed that one of the younger Jags was trying to fight off two Terminators, and she pushed in beside him to help. He grinned his thanks without a word. The crowd engulfed them again. Ruby was grabbed from behind by two strong arms, and she squirmed around to face the Terminator who had killed Mike. He leered at her, pleased with himself. Ruby froze up for a minute, face to face with him, on the same level with him for the first time. Her stomach knotted up and she couldn't seem to pull away from him.

"How about you and me go somewhere quiet to get reacquainted," he suggested, oblivious to the chaos around them. Ruby shut her eyes and tried to block it all out. The world spun around her, and she felt like she was falling. Her mind went back to that night... Something suddenly blew the two of them apart. Ruby caught herself against a wall and opened her eyes. She righted herself and started back into the fight. After an eternity, she heard someone calling her.

"Ruby—come on, will you?"

She looked around, and Tim grabbed her by the arm.

"Come on! Get out of here!"

She realized there were only a couple of Jags left fighting around her. She was trying to stave off four Terminators, and had not even realized it. She turned and ran after Tim. He glanced back a couple of times to make sure that she was still with him. After a few blocks, they stopped running. Tim waited for Ruby to catch up, and they walked for a few minutes in silence. Another group of Jags was walking up ahead of them, just within sight and calling distance. Tim started to breathe more slowly, to relax a bit. He glanced at Ruby and didn't say anything. She tried to smile at him, but it was strained. Her heart was racing out of control still, and the world seemed eerily quiet. Someone in the group up ahead of them was coughing. Fog was gathering as the night got cooler. Ruby sped up her pace a little, trying to get closer to the main group. Tim stayed close to her. They went a few more blocks, and caught up to the other Jags. Jack turned as they walked up.

"You didn't do too badly," he commented. He had a good shiner and a cut lip.

"Are you kidding?" Harlan questioned, sounding like he had a cold. "She was great! Man, she was something out there."

"Saved my butt," one of the young Jags agreed.

Ruby shrugged modestly. She'd protected herself; that was all. If she'd done it well—she was lucky. Jack nodded.

"Not bad," he repeated, smiling. He touched her cheek briefly.

"You're bleeding, you know."

Ruby wiped her cheek with the back of her hand. It came away smeared with blood. She wiped it again with her palm, and wiped her hand on her jeans. She smiled slightly.

"Let's go celebrate," Harlan suggested. He dabbed at his nose tenderly with a rag, dabbing away a thin stream of blood.

"We lost, moron," Jack snapped.

Harlan considered.

"Then let's go anesthetize ourselves."

Ruby glanced around.

"I gotta go back to the apartment and get my stuff," Ruby commented.

"Aren't you going to stay around tonight?" Tim questioned in surprise.

"I got somewhere to be tonight," Ruby said firmly.

They eyed her speculatively. But she was more of an equal with them now, and if one of the Jags said that he had something to do or somewhere to be, who was going to challenge him? Ruby was one of them now. They said nothing when she separated to go back to the apartment. She picked up her knapsack, took out the latest business card, and caught a bus.

∼

Willhelm opened the apartment door, and then looked like he would shut it again. Ruby put her foot in the doorway so he couldn't close it if he tried.

"I need help," she told him.

"I can't help you, Ruby," he shook his head.

"I need somewhere safe! Please!"

He hesitated, and Ruby stepped up and pushed through the open door.

"Come in," Willhelm said belatedly. "I'll call the police."

"No, don't call them. If the gang sees me talking to another policeman..."

"Nobody's going to see. I assume you didn't tell anyone you were coming here," he seemed suddenly worried.

"No. Of course not. But if they followed me, or if they have someone on the inside..."

"Don't you think you're being a little melodramatic?"

"Does this look melodramatic?" Ruby demanded, gesturing to her face. She'd looked at it in the mirror at the apartment. Dark blood stood out along the cut on her cheek, with several streams of blood down her cheek, and soaked into the collar of her t-shirt. It looked ugly, although it was only a surface cut and didn't even hurt.

Willhelm looked a little sheepish.

"I'm not used to having clients burst into my house at all hours of the night," he explained.

Ruby looked around, and sat down in the corner of the couch, pulling her knees up to her chest and her chin resting on her knees. She rubbed the smooth skin of her calves and thighs.

"I'm cold," she said meditatively. "Could I maybe have a coffee or something?"

"Yeah, I'll put something on." Willhelm eyed her, buttoning up the top couple of buttons on the shirt he had obviously just thrown on when she rang the doorbell. He looked at her for a minute, then turned and went into the small kitchen.

Ruby looked around carefully, gleaning everything she could about Willhelm from her surroundings. He was a tidy person, but not obsessive like Chuck. There were magazines laying on the side table, and a book open on top of them. So he liked to read. It figured that a lawyer would like to read. He had a tie draped over the back of one of the chairs. A pop can on the other side table.

Willhelm returned with a cup of coffee.

"It's just instant," he warned, handing it to her. "You just take it black, right?"

Ruby couldn't remember how he would know that. She nodded and took it from him.

"Thanks."

She made sure he saw how her hands were shaking when she took it. He looked at her for a moment, then left the room again. He brought out a blanket for her. Ruby wrapped it close around her.

"I'm just a little shaky," she offered.

"What happened?"

Ruby shook her head.

"I don't know… it all happened so fast. I'm not sure what happened."

"Are you okay? Other than the cut on your face?"

"I think so."

"Once you've warmed up, we'd better clean that cut."

Ruby nodded. She sipped at the coffee, watching him steadily over the rim. Willhelm fidgeted under her gaze.

"You can stay the night," he said slowly, "but in the morning we'll make some phone calls and figure out some other arrangement."

"Okay. I'm sorry, I just didn't have anywhere to go…"

"Well… at least there was somewhere safe for you to come."

Ruby nodded and was quiet. She drank the coffee very slowly, trying to draw it out. Willhelm sat watching her. He was tired. His eyes were puffy and his eyelids kept sliding downward, but he was trying to give her his attention.

"I got you out of bed," Ruby observed.

He smiled wryly.

"It is two in the morning."

"Oh… sorry. I guess you want to go back to sleep. I'll just… sit out here a while."

"I could sleep on the couch and let you have the bed."

"No, no—you take the bed. I can sleep out here."

"Are you sure?"

"Yeah. I don't want to mess you up. You'll be tired for work if you try to sleep on this couch."

"Okay—do you need anything?"

"No, I got a blanket. I'll be fine."

Willhelm nodded. He really wanted to go back to sleep. He stood up.

"Let me know if you need anything."

"I'm fine."

He went back to bed. Ruby turned the TV on quiet, and sat up watching it for a while. There was no noise at all from the bedroom. After an hour or so, Ruby turned off the TV and slipped down the hall into the bedroom. Wilhelm had a queen bed. He was asleep right in the middle of it. Ruby squeezed in beside him, careful not to shake the bed or touch him and wake him up. After a few minutes, he shifted away from her without waking up. Ruby gathered the blanket around her and went to sleep.

∼

"What are you doing here?"

Ruby opened her eyes, squinting. It couldn't be very late in the morning yet. Willhelm was sitting up in bed, staring at her in what could only be described as horror.

"I got here last night," Ruby murmured, and turned over.

"You were on the couch."

"I got cold."

He didn't move or say anything. Ruby eventually turned around to look at him again.

"What's wrong?"

"Everything. This is wrong."

Ruby squinted at the clock.

"What time is it? Why are you awake?" she questioned.

"It's six o'clock. I have to get ready for work."

"Okay. Go ahead."

He stared at her, perplexed, and then got out of bed. She watched him go to the dresser and closet to get his clothes before going into the bathroom and turning on the shower. She lay there for a few minutes, dozing, before the running water reminded her of the drinks and coffee she had consumed not so many hours ago. She dragged herself out of bed and went into the bathroom.

"Hey, do you mind?" Willhelm growled.

"What?"

"Some privacy?"

She looked at the sliding doors on the shower in amusement. They were frosted glass, and she couldn't see anything more than his shadow unless she opened the doors.

"Sorry. Just be a minute."

"Couldn't you wait?"

"Nope. Hey, you want some company in there?"
She could see him turn suddenly towards her.
"No. Will you get out?" he demanded.
"Yeah, yeah."
Ruby washed her hands and left him alone. As soon as she was out the door, he turned off the shower. She imagined Willhelm was probably into his clothes before even drying off completely. She grinned and went into the kitchen. Ruby took off her shirt and ran hot water over the collar to see if she could get some of the blood out. It didn't seem to do much good. It was already stained. Willhelm walked up behind her.
"Now what are you doing?" he demanded, exasperated.
Ruby turned around.
"Just trying to clean off the blood," she explained, showing him the shirt.
"That won't come out."
"Yeah, so I discovered."
He was staring at her chest. Ruby shrugged and stepped towards him.
"Doesn't matter. I've got another one in my bag."
He stood there, frozen. Ruby grinned and walked by him, brushing against his arm as she passed. He turned and watched her go back into the living room and pick up her knapsack. The doorbell buzzed. Willhelm hit the button to release the front doors of the apartment building. He shrugged at Ruby.
"People buzz me because I'm first on the board."
"Yeah."
Ruby dumped her knapsack onto the couch to find her extra shirt. A key turned in Willhelm's door, and the door swung open.
"John, thanks for—"
A man walked in, and stopped, spotting Ruby standing there only half-dressed.
"Oh…"
He quickly averted his eyes, and turned his head away. He didn't seem to want to look at Willhelm either.
"Uh, come into the kitchen," Willhelm invited, his face flushed bright red. He glared at Ruby, and led his friend into the other room. Ruby pulled a shirt on, repacked her knapsack, and joined them in the kitchen.
"This is Ruby. She's a—uh—friend of the family. Needed somewhere to stay for the night."

The other man nodded awkwardly at Ruby.

"Sorry..."

"It's okay. I got nothin' to hide. So you're Johnny's...?"

"Darren's a friend of mine," Willhelm explained. Ruby nodded. Willhelm looked at his watch.

"I've got to get ready for work. Are you ready to go, Ruby?"

"Yeah, I guess," she said reluctantly.

"Good. You want to be dropped off somewhere?"

"No, that's okay. I can find my own way around."

Ruby walked along the street, thinking over the visit with Willhelm. She'd have to meet with him again soon. She had a feeling she could win him over with a little time together. She stopped at a coffee shop a few blocks away from Willhelm's apartment building. She sat down at the counter and ordered a coffee. Sitting at the counter with it, she gathered her tangled hair back with both hands, and holding it in place tied it with a rubber band. She picked up the coffee and sipped at it. She put it back down on the counter.

"What do you call that?" she demanded, her mouth twisting in disgust.

The counter boy turned around. His eyes flicked over her quickly. A far cry from her admirer in the cafe near Chuck's apartment, he scowled at her.

"What's the matter with it?"

"Is this supposed to be coffee or sewage?"

He shrugged.

"I don't hear anyone else complaining."

"Make a fresh pot."

"Not until this one is empty."

Ruby reached across the counter and picked up the nearly empty pot of coffee. She dumped the remaining dregs on the floor, and set the pot down.

"It's empty now."

He scowled at her. He ignored her as he mopped up the spilled coffee. He squeezed the rag soaked with coffee into her cup.

"There you go, blended just for you."

Ruby knocked the mug onto the floor and stood up. What a dump. She moved on towards the school. There was, at least, fresh coffee in the cafeteria. She'd surprise everyone by being there before classes even started.

The school was quiet. There were only a few teachers and students there. Ruby was used to being able to sleep in late into the morning. She was never up early, especially after a late night like she'd had with the gang. She sat down in the cafeteria with a Styrofoam cup of piping hot coffee. One of the guidance counselors saw her and came up to the table.

"Well, hello Ruby. This is a pleasant surprise."

"Morning, Mr. Kyle."

"You've been missing an awful lot of school lately," he observed.

"Uh-huh."

"Are you okay? How are things at home?"

Mr. Kyle sat down across the table from her, raising an eyebrow. She sipped her coffee. They'd talked before. She had talked with all of the guidance counselors at the school at one time or another, as they shunted her back and forth, hoping that she would "click" with someone. That someone new might be able to reach her.

"You know I'm not at home," Ruby reminded him.

"Your foster home, I mean. Are things going all right?"

"I'm here, aren't I?"

"Your foster mom called here the other day looking for you. She was pretty upset about you disappearing."

Ruby looked up at the clock on the wall.

"I guess I'll call her before class."

"You mean you haven't been back there?" his voice rose.

"I've been busy."

"The police were even looking for you," he expounded.

Ruby shrugged.

"It's no big deal. I'm all right."

"Well, I'm hoping you'll attend more than two classes today…" He cocked his head to the side and smiled, cajoling her.

"What difference does it make?" Ruby said, rolling her eyes.

"You can do it, if you put some effort into it."

Ruby shook her head.

"I've missed too much to ever catch up. There's no point."

"When you decide that maybe you do want to get an education, there are a lot of programs to help students like yourself get back on track. You just have to say the word."

"I don't care about school."

He shook his head, lips pursed.

"Make sure you at least let your foster mom know you're okay. You've created quite a bit of concern around here."

"Yeah, okay."

He got up and left her alone again. Ruby sat there, lost in thought. Marty and Kate spotted her a few minutes before the first bell. Kate was bouncing and hyped up about something. Marty frowned and sat down next to Ruby. She touched Ruby's cheek gently with her thumb.

"Who did that?"

Ruby pushed Marty's hand away. She held onto it briefly to show that she wasn't mad, and then let go.

"It was an accident." She shrugged.

"Uh-huh. What boy were you with this time?"

"I don't know where you find all these guys!" Kate interjected. Marty ignored her, staring steadily at Ruby. Ruby shifted.

"I wasn't with a boy."

"How'd you get cut?" Marty demanded.

"I was with the Jags."

Marty looked exasperated.

"The only thing worse for you than one boy is a whole gang. When are you going to figure it out, Ruby?"

"Guys aren't so bad," Kate said. "You just don't have a boyfriend, that's why you get so mad."

"Why would I want a boyfriend?" Marty questioned. "So I could end up shot or beaten up like Ruby?"

"A boyfriend might mellow you out a bit," Kate pointed out.

"No thanks. Ruby, you gotta get out of this life. You're really gonna get hurt."

"I'm all right."

"You won't be one of these days."

Ruby looked at the clock.

"I have to make a phone call."

She walked away from them. She put change in one of the pay phones inside the main doors of the school, and dialed the Winters' number. Mrs. Winters answered after a couple of rings.

"Hello?"

"Hi."

"Ruby? Where have you been? Are you okay?"

"I'm fine. I'm at the school."

"Where have you been? I've been worried sick."

"Yeah, I've just been with friends."

"You need to let me know if you're not going to be home. I have to know where you are and make sure that you're going to be safe."

Ruby was in no mood to listen to a lecture. However nice Mrs. Winters might try to be about it.

"I gotta go. I'll talk to you later."

She hung up the phone. Ruby didn't know where she was going to be after school, so there was no point in telling Mrs. Winters that she would be home when she might not. The bell rang, and Ruby went to her classes.

Ruby looked around at lunch for Brian, but couldn't find him. She used some more change to call Chuck.

"Hi, Chuck. Are we going to get together tonight?"

"If you want to make an appointment to see me, I have an opening at three," he told her evenly.

"What's the matter, someone listening to you?"

"No."

"Then come get me tonight," she invited.

"Sorry. That's over. Time for both of us to move on."

"You'll be sorry, you know that."

There was silence for a while.

"Did you want to make an appointment?" Chuck questioned finally.

"No. When can I see Ronnie?"

"You really messed things up there. I might be able to set something up, but you haven't made things easy for me. Are you back at the Winters now?"

"No. I'll meet Ronnie somewhere else."

"Not unsupervised, you won't. Will you meet at her foster family's?"

Ruby shook her head, staring up at the ceiling.

"I guess," she conceded.

"I'll look into it."

"What's their address?"

"I'll let you know after we get something set up."

"You can't call me," Ruby reminded him.

"You really should get a cell. Just call me later, and I'll let you know what we've arranged."

"Aren't you going to ask me where I'll be?"

There was no answer from Chuck for a few minutes. Ruby heard his suppressed sigh.

"Honestly, Ruby... you've been able to look after yourself up until now. I don't know what you're doing, and I don't want to hear. Okay? If you tell me, I'll put it on your file. Everything from now on goes on your file," he said sternly. There was a muffled thump, and she pictured him smacking his hand on top of her file for emphasis.

Ruby stood there with the phone to her ear, her mind blank. She didn't really believe that Chuck was serious about breaking up. She couldn't understand how he could suddenly be so cold toward her.

"Why put it on my file? It isn't like you want anyone to actually look at it," Ruby sneered.

Chuck hung up. Ruby didn't waste her money on another call. She went and found Marty.

"I'm not going to stick around this afternoon. You want to go somewhere?"

Marty hesitated.

"I have a test to write this afternoon. If I don't write it..."

Ruby rolled her eyes.

"Fine. Where's Kate?"

"Chasing boys."

"Junior high boys!" Ruby made a disgusted face.

Marty touched the cut on Ruby's face.

"That's what older boys do to you."

"Are you going to be around tonight? If I come over or something?"

"Yeah. I'll be home."

"Okay. I don't know. I might come over."

Marty nodded.

"If it's the Jags or me, come over, huh?"

Ruby shrugged. She left the school and went looking for the Jags.

There were a couple of black jackets in the arcade, but they weren't Jags, so Ruby didn't stick around. They might recognize her as having been at the fight the night before. She had to be more careful now about being seen alone. She went by the apartment and one of the boys let her in. Harlan was lying on the mattress in the front room watching a fuzzy picture on the TV. He turned slightly when she came in to look at her.

"Well, so you came back."

His nose was bandaged or something. The whole side of his face was bruised and swollen up. His words were unclear, sort of muffled. Ruby looked at him for a minute.

"How'd all that happen? You out with that punk girlfriend again?"

Harlan laughed loudly, wincing when the movement jarred his sensitive muscles.

"Yeah right," he snorted, his eye tearing a little. "Got it at the rumble last night."

"I don't remember you looking that bad last night."

"It hadn't bruised up yet. You don't look so great yourself."

Ruby knew her face was slightly bruised, and of course there was the cut on her cheek, but she didn't look nearly as bad as Harlan.

"I just need a hot shower. And some more sleep."

"Why, your boyfriend didn't let you sleep in?" he teased.

Ruby clenched her jaw, and looked for something flippant to say, but knew that she had failed to respond quickly enough. She ended up not saying anything, just smiling knowingly at him and going into the bedroom. Tim wasn't there. Ruby frowned and went into the bathroom to shower. The apartment was quiet aside from the noise of Harlan's TV and the occasional outburst from the other couple of gang members who had hung around. Ruby shut the door behind her, but it didn't even latch properly. The seat on the toilet was up, naturally, and the inside of the shower stall stunk of mold. Ruby stripped down quickly and stepped gingerly inside. At least there was hot water, even if there did seem to be a shortage of soap. Ruby opened the shower curtain and got a sliver of soap out of her knapsack. Always helped to be prepared. She let the steam fill the room and stood idly under the stream of hot water, letting it soak her hair and warm her body. Her muscles were stiff and sore after the fight. She hadn't realized what a workout it had been. She had plenty of minor bruises mottling her body. She massaged her skin gently, lathered a little soap over her body and hair, and rinsed off again. There was a cool draft when someone opened the bathroom door, and Ruby glanced at the shower door nervously. She remembered barging in on Willhelm that morning, and grinned. She waited a few moments, and then peeked out the corner of the curtain. Julian, one of the younger boys, was scraping his face with a dull razor.

"Need a hand?" Ruby questioned.

He started, cutting himself, and swore. He turned and looked at her, his neck flushing red.

"I didn't know it was you in here!" He cursed again, looking back at the mirror and the cut on his face. "Man, you can't do that when a guy's shaving!"

"Hand me a towel?" Ruby said politely.

He prodded the towels on the floor with his toe as Ruby shut off the water. He picked one up and handed it to her.

"I didn't know it was you in here," he repeated, embarrassed.

Ruby wrapped the towel around herself before opening the door.

"Can a person get some privacy around here?" she questioned. "Girl stuff, you know?"

Julian looked panicked.

"Yeah. Sorry. I'm going."

He hurried out of the room, pulling the door shut behind him. It stayed open a crack, but Ruby forced herself to take her time drying off and getting dressed. If they were going to spy on her, they would only be encouraged by modesty on her part. As long as she was casual, the thrill would quickly wear off, and she'd get more used to changing around them. Ruby ran her fingers through her hair, and put her knapsack over her shoulder. She walked back into the bedroom. Everyone was out in the front room. They were joking around with Julian, who was extremely red-faced, but trying to look cool and composed. Harlan cackled when he saw Ruby.

"What'd you do to poor Julian? Pull your knife on him? First chick I known who takes her knife in the shower."

Ruby just smiled.

"I think he slipped while shaving," she said innocently. Julian had apparently nicked himself pretty good. He was trying to stop the cut from bleeding, but kept pulling it around with his fingers and starting it bleeding again.

The door opened, and Tim walked in.

"Hey, what's up?" he questioned. He nodded at Ruby. "Hey."

"Hi. You doing anything?"

He shrugged.

"No."

"But I am," Jack said from the doorway. He had followed Tim in. "You're with me this afternoon."

Ruby looked at him.

"Why? What's up?"

"Come on."

Ruby looked around at the others. They were all waiting for her response. Ruby shrugged her shoulders, trying to look cool. Her stomach was tight and slightly nauseous. She held her arm out for Jack.

"Let's go, then."

He nodded approvingly and put his hand on her back to escort her out. She tried to relax, so that he wouldn't know she was nervous. She was finding it hard to breathe quietly, hard to get air. The door to the apartment shut behind them, and Jack rubbed her back soothingly.

"Hey, take it easy, baby. I just want to talk."

Ruby nodded as if she was unconcerned.

"Where are we going?"

"Over to my place."

"Where's that?"

"It's not far."

Ruby kept quiet. His apartment was a few blocks away from the others, pretty much the same type of place. Cheap subsidized housing projects, with thin walls and grungy halls. Jack let go of her while he unlocked the door, then pushed her in gently ahead of him. Ruby took a look around while he shut and locked the door again. Jack took a quick look around the apartment to make sure that they were alone. Then he went to the fridge and pulled out a couple of beers. He handed her one. Ruby nodded her thanks and pulled the tab.

"So what'd you think of the fight last night?" he questioned.

Ruby shrugged with one shoulder.

"We lost."

"Yeah. But that wasn't the point." His eyes were steely, intense. Ruby glanced away from him.

"Then what was?"

He took a drink of his beer, timing his answer.

"Which one killed Mike?"

Ruby took a deep breath. She'd wondered if he'd ever ask her, but she'd about decided that he didn't care and wasn't going to ask.

"Take all the time you like," Jack said evenly. "I got lots of time. You just take time to remember their faces, and tell me which ones were there."

Ruby tried not to remember. She tried to block it out of her mind.

"How do you know it was Terminators?" she questioned, ignoring the images trying to force their way into her brain.

"I've known from the start it was Terminators. That was obvious. I want to know which ones."

"I'm not feeling so good," Ruby said weakly, and went to find his bathroom. Jack didn't stop her. Ruby hadn't had anything to eat since coffee in the cafeteria, but she hung retching over the toilet anyway, her eyes tightly shut, trying not to remember those two nights. She'd rather do anything than let herself remember. It was a long time before she managed to settle her stomach down, and Ruby splashed cold water on her face, trying to chase away the nausea. She shut off the taps and went reluctantly back out to talk to Jack. He watched her walk in, and didn't say anything.

"I only saw one of them last night," Ruby lied.

"Okay. Which one?"

Ruby licked her dry lips.

"The one you were talking to. Their leader, I guess."

"Slash. Yeah, that doesn't surprise me. Was he the trigger?"

Ruby stared at Jack.

"Was he the one that shot Mike?" Jack prodded.

Ruby hesitated. She nodded her head slightly. Jack watched her closely and didn't believe it.

"Who pulled the trigger?" he repeated.

"He wasn't there last night."

Jack sat back and took another swig of his beer. He watched her thoughtfully.

"I think you're lying to me."

"He wasn't there."

"Describe him to me."

Ruby shook her head.

"It was dark. I couldn't see them. I just recognized—Slash's voice last night."

"No, I don't think so." Jack was silent for a few moments, drinking his beer and watching her. "Slash was there... and somebody else..." he mused. "It would have to be one of his lieutenants. Troy, Cash, or Laskin."

Ruby just looked at Jack. She didn't know his name. She knew him —his face, his voice, his hands... but she didn't know his name. It meant nothing to her. She took another drink, struggling to keep the memories deeply suppressed.

"Cash is handsome, the chicks love him. Nice face. Dark hair. Good build." He studied her face. "Laskin is more like Harlan. Big, broad. Pale face. Lot's'o' muscles. Dirty blond. No? Troy, then."

Ruby shook her head.

"I didn't see. They were shining lights in my eyes. I couldn't see them."

"Troy's just a little guy, but vicious. Crazy cat. Dark, greased hair. Bright blue eyes. Wiry, tough guy."

Ruby's stomach was doing gymnastics. She swallowed, trying to keep the beer down. His description was accurate, adding clarity to the flashbacks. Ruby tried to put down her beer, but couldn't reach the table. She tried to find something to steady her shaking legs. She thought she should try to get back to the bathroom, but the room was dissolving around her so that all she could see was the flashbacks.

"Steady there."

The images overwhelmed her. Hands closed over her arms, and Ruby fought loose.

"No—don't touch me—please…" the words caught in her throat, she felt like she was being strangled.

"Relax, honey. Just relax."

She fought off his hands with failing strength. The harder she tried to protect herself, the more paralyzed she felt. Paralyzed, just like that night. Unable to keep his hands off of her body. She felt him pick her up, but she could no longer fight back. She saw Troy's face clearly in her mind, his ugly leering smile. She could feel his gentle touch on her body. The gentle, soft strokes that sent waves of confusion and uncertainty over her. His voice filled her ears, quiet, soothing, like you talked to a baby or frightened puppy.

He was slapping her cheeks gently, steadily, talking to her in a low, steady, slightly angry tone. Ruby became slowly aware that it was Jack, not Troy, and that she was lying on his bed as he tried to bring her out of her flashback. Ruby moved her face away from his hands.

"Stop—stop it."

He studied her, his eyes piercing.

"What's the matter with you?"

"Nothing. Nothing, I'm okay." Ruby pushed herself up to a sitting position.

"I never figured you the fainting type."

"Did I faint?" Ruby questioned weakly.

Jack shrugged.

"I don't know what else you'd call it. Too many pills."

"No, I don't take pills."

"What did he do to you?"

"Who?"

"Troy."

"I never saw Troy."

"How stupid do you think I am? If Troy and Slash shot Mike, we're gonna kill them," he said it casually, as if it was nothing. "And if you'll tell me what he did to you, I'll make him suffer first. What'd he do, beat you up?"

"No—he didn't hurt me. He didn't do anything. I don't know if he was the one who shot Mike."

"He was. And we'll pay him back."

"No... it couldn't have been him. I remember when he was standing there—it was a big guy."

"Laskin? Are you sure?"

"No—it's all muddled up... they woke us up, and shone the lights in our eyes. It was really disorienting. And then everything happened so fast, and they were gone. I really don't know what happened."

"But you remember he was big."

"It seemed like it, yeah," Ruby lied desperately.

Jack nodded.

"Good. Then we'll take care of it."

CHAPTER
Seven

Ruby dialed Chuck from a pay phone down in front of Jack's building.

"Hello?" his voice sounded strange to her. Muffled, or as if his attention was on something other than the phone call.

"Chuck?"

"Ruby?" he growled. "What do you want?"

"Did you set something up with Ronnie?" she reminded him.

"Oh—you can go over there tomorrow during the day. The two of you can't be alone, and you can't stay there after dark. Okay?"

"Where do they live?"

Chuck gave her the address.

"I'm told the number 22 bus stops a block away."

"Just a sec, I have to write this down."

Ruby dug a piece of paper out of her bag and had him repeat it. She scribbled out the address.

"Good. It's been a long time since I saw her."

He answered her as a car came around the corner, moving very slowly while the driver looked for something. Their eyes met, and Ruby realized it was a cop. One of the ones who had been watching her. She swore. Chuck stopped talking on the other end, surprised.

"What?"

"I gotta go."

Ruby hung up. The car moved quickly on, the cop pretending it hadn't been her he was looking for. Ruby tried to figure out where to go. They were still on her. She picked up her bag and found Willhelm's card. Her fingers shaking, she managed to get through to him on the first try.

"Yes?"

"It's Ruby."

"What do you want?" he sighed.

"I want the cops to stop following me."

There were a few moments of silence.

"I thought you were mad at them for taking you off of surveillance before," he pointed out.

"I'm tired of being used for bait."

"They're protecting you."

"They didn't protect me last time. I want them off me," she insisted.

"I'll see what I can do for you—but are you sure that's what you want?" he questioned.

"Yeah. I know what I want."

"All right. I'll talk to the police about it."

"Thanks. I'll see you later."

She hung up the phone and decided to take Marty up on her offer for her to come over. She caught the bus and headed over. She got there before Marty was home from school and sat on the front steps waiting for her. It was an hour or more before Marty got there. She hugged Ruby briefly and unlocked the door for her. They both went in.

"You hungry?" Marty questioned.

Ruby shrugged.

"Not really."

"You had anything to eat today?" Marty studied Ruby's face.

"Coffee for breakfast, beer for lunch," Ruby said with a laugh.

Marty shook her head. She opened the fridge.

"I'll make something. You starve yourself. You gotta put on some weight."

"Yeah, I know. I just... haven't been up to eating much lately." Ruby shrugged.

"You're going to sleep here tonight, right? You're not going off with the Jags again?"

"Yeah, not tonight. I'll stay."

She was thinking about the police tail. If they were on her again, she would do best to stay places that would not look suspicious.

"Do you have to call your foster mom?"

"I guess." Ruby went to the phone and dialed up Mrs. Winters. "Hi, it's Ruby."

"I would like you home tonight," Mrs. Winters said firmly.

"I'm at Marty's."

"Let me talk to her mom."

"She's not here yet."

"Is Marty there?"

"Yeah, just a second."

She handed the receiver to Marty, who raised her eyebrows questioningly.

"Hi, Mrs. Winters… yeah, we're at home. I'll have her call when she gets in, I'm just making dinner… okay, bye."

She hung up.

"My mom has to call her when she gets here. I don't know, she doesn't sound too happy about it."

"Too bad. What's she going to do about it?"

Marty shrugged. Ruby went into the front room, and Marty heard the liquor cabinet open.

"I thought you had booze for lunch."

"Just beer."

"Don't let my mom catch you in there. Don't take enough for her to notice."

"I'm not." Ruby walked back into the kitchen with a glass of wine.

"You sleeping better now?" Marty questioned, as she mixed together some Hamburger Helper.

"As long as I'm not alone."

"I wish you'd just move in here."

Ruby looked at Marty for a moment.

"Your mom wouldn't like it," she said, looking away.

"She wouldn't care. We've talked about it before."

"You have?"

"Sure."

Ruby picked at the salad Marty had pulled out of the fridge. She sipped at the glass of wine, keeping her thoughts to herself. She'd never really been wanted anywhere. Foster families took her because that's what they did. Her own family hadn't wanted her from the start. Chuck had wanted her—but only sometimes, and only on his terms. She and Marty had been friends for a long time, but she'd never heard this invitation before. Marty continued to make dinner in silence. She'd never been one to waste words. She said what she thought needed to be said, and that was it. She glanced at Ruby, and put her hand on her shoulder briefly.

"I mean it. Live here."

"I'll think about it."

Marty nodded.

"How come you and Kate hang out together?" Ruby questioned, changing the subject.

"I don't know," Marty admitted with a shrug. "Just 'cause we always have, I guess."

"You're not alike at all."

"No. She wants to be part of the in crowd; she tries so hard to be cool."

"But you still like her," Ruby said.

"I've known her since kindergarten. I know her pretty good. No surprises."

"Why do you think she wants to be popular so much?"

"Some people just do. I think her mom was popular in school, and thinks that she should be too."

"Huh. Why don't you care about being popular?"

"Why don't you?" Marty countered.

"I don't know. Those people are so shallow. I don't care what people think. I don't want to have to be anything, just what I am."

Marty nodded.

"Yeah. You want to be part of that crowd, you have to be what they dictate. I don't do anything just because people think I should."

Ruby nodded.

They were watching TV when Marty's mom got home. She stopped to talk with them.

"Hi, honey. Hi, Ruby."

"Hi, Mom. Ruby's foster mom wants to talk to you to make sure Ruby can stay."

"Sure. What's the number?" She pulled out her cell phone.

Ruby told it to her. Marty's mom dialed it.

"Hi. It's Mrs. Rodger. Marty's mom. Ruby said you wanted me to call… no, I don't mind her staying here any time… they're no trouble… okay, bye."

She hung up the phone.

"You can stay. I think you'd better go home tomorrow, though. She sounds pretty worried."

"Yeah, maybe."

"Are you okay, Ruby?"

Ruby looked up from the TV, a little surprised.

"Sure."

"You're pretty pale. Did you guys get something good to eat?"

"Yeah, we ate," Marty assured her.

"You two are going to bed early. I don't want you getting sick while you're staying here."

The girls didn't bother arguing. She nodded and left them alone.

Ruby awoke when Marty started to move around restlessly. She untangled herself carefully from Marty's arms, and Marty woke up. She opened her eyes and looked at Ruby for a moment, then smiled.

"Hi. What time is it?"

Ruby shrugged. Marty stretched lazily, like a cat.

"I guess we don't have to get up. No school."

"I'm going over to see Ronnie today."

"Yeah? Right away?"

Ruby looked at the window, noting it was already bright outside.

"Pretty soon, I guess."

"Do you need to do laundry?"

Marty was always practical. Ruby nodded.

"Yeah. I suppose it's about time I did."

She slid her feet out of bed and picked up her bag. She pulled out the bundle of dirty clothes. She saw the stained t-shirt, and sighed.

"What gets blood out?" she questioned.

Marty looked at it.

"Nothing, when it's already dry. I'll give you one of my t-shirts."

"Thanks. I'll go put these in."

Marty got out of bed as Ruby left the room. She padded out to the kitchen to get coffee started. Marty's father was in the kitchen drinking beer, with his feet up on a chair.

"Hi, precious," he greeted. "How's it going?"

"Shouldn't you be sleeping?" Marty said neutrally, walking past him without meeting his eye.

"A man needs time to unwind after work. You're up pretty early for a Saturday morning, aren't you?"

"Yeah, a little," Marty agreed.

She went about preparing for breakfast, ignoring his presence. Ruby wandered into the kitchen a few minutes later, yawning.

"You got coffee on?" she questioned.

She finished the yawn and opened her eyes and saw Marty's dad there for the first time.

"Oh—hi."

"Mornin', Ruby."

She felt his eyes following her as she went over to the coffee pot. She was always uncomfortable when he was around. She felt herself flushing as she realized that the oversized t-shirt of Marty's that she'd slipped on as a night-shirt the night before just barely reached her thighs and was extremely thin and worn. If she hadn't just thrown all the clothes she owned in the washer, she would have gone and changed. She didn't like Marty's dad looking at her like that. It was quite obvious Ruby didn't have anything on underneath the t-shirt. Ruby took her cup of coffee over to the table and sat down at the opposite end of the table from Marty's dad, using the table as a shield from his eyes.

"So how's school going for the two of you?" he questioned.

"Pretty good," Marty answered, not turning around.

Ruby shrugged.

"Like always," she mumbled.

"What's your best subject?"

"I dunno. English."

"English was never one of my better subjects. But you're pretty good at it, aren't you pumpkin?" This was directed at Marty.

"Yes, Dad."

He grinned and gulped down the last of his beer.

"I get the picture," he said, "I'll leave the two of you alone."

He took his booted feet off of the chair and dropped them each with a thud on the floor. He heaved himself to his feet and exited the kitchen, headed for his own bedroom. Ruby breathed a sigh of relief.

"Why didn't you tell me he was here?" she demanded in a whisper.

"I didn't know. Usually he's in bed, if he's home at all. How was I supposed to know he'd be here?"

"Man, I walk in here practically naked...!"

"What exactly is it about my dad that prompts this modesty in you? Since when do you care who sees your body?"

"I do!" Ruby insisted.

"Uh-huh."

"Just 'cause there are a few guys I stay with, that doesn't mean I traipse around giving anyone a peek!"

"Why do you care if my dad sees you like that? I'm dressed the same way, and I got plenty more under here to hide. If I don't care, why should you? You got nothing under there."

Ruby shrugged.

"I don't like the way he looks at me."

"It's all in your mind. He doesn't look at you any differently than he looks at me."

"I know."

Marty heard Ruby's tone, and turned to look at Ruby, disbelief in her face.

"You think... ! You're crazy. I'm his daughter, that's all he sees. He doesn't look at my body."

Ruby was not convinced.

"Why don't you like him, then?"

"Why don't I like him? 'cause he's a deadbeat. He's a slob, he's crude, he spends more than he makes, and he's a jerk. But he's no... pervert." Marty shook her head. She went on making breakfast, not speaking. Ruby sipped the hot coffee, putting her feet up on her chair with her knees under the shirt. Mrs. Rodger shuffled into the kitchen wearing a tattered bathrobe and furry slippers.

"That's ladylike," she told Ruby. Ruby grinned at her. She went over and got a cup of coffee.

"Thanks Marty. This smells great."

"Dad wake you up?"

"Oh, I would have been up in a while anyway. Did you guys have a good sleep? Are you feeling better this morning, Ruby?"

"I'm fine."

"Good. You're still looking a little piqued. You take care of yourself. Are you staying around here today?"

"No, I have to go see my sister."

"Oh, well good for you. What's for breakfast, Marty?"

Marty gestured.

"Pancakes, fruit... you want anything else?"

"That will be great. I'll make juice."

Ruby watched them working side by side. She had never had that sort of rapport with her own mother. With anyone. But she'd always been thoroughly comfortable with Mrs. Rodger. She and Marty were both so open and straightforward. They weren't loud, didn't say more than they had to, but they were genuine.

"Are you going to come back here tonight?" Mrs. Rodger questioned as they were eating breakfast.

Ruby shrugged.

"I don't know yet."
"You're always welcome here."
She nodded.
"Thanks."

Ruby checked the house number on the big brick house on the corner lot before going up the cobbled path. She rang the doorbell, shifting back and forth impatiently. Ronnie's foster father answered the door and glowered at her disapprovingly. Ruby tried to look cool.

"Where's Ronnie?" she questioned.

"You're Ruby?"

"Yeah."

"You can stay for an hour."

"My social worker said I could stay as long as I wanted," Ruby protested.

"You can stay for an hour."

"It took me an hour and a half to get here on the bus."

His expression changed slightly, but Ruby couldn't tell whether he would change his tune or not. He stepped back to let her in. Ruby slipped past him, her stomach tight. She was led into the family room, where a number of children were watching cartoons on TV. Ronnie was with them. She turned around and saw Ruby.

"Oh—hi, Ruby."

Not nearly the excitement she'd shown before. The atmosphere of the room was thick with tension as everybody turned to look at her. They'd been telling stories about her. Ruby was sure of it. She squirmed under their curious stares.

"Hey, Ronnie. Uh—let's go where we can talk…"

"You'll stay in here to visit," Ronnie's foster dad told them firmly.

"We can't talk here."

"Sorry."

Ruby's face burned. She motioned to Ronnie.

"Come on. Please? You and me gotta talk."

Ronnie looked uncertainly at her foster father for direction. Ruby was not going to let him control the situation.

"I was your family long before these guys, Ronnie. I remember when you were born. I looked after you long before these guys even knew you existed."

Ronnie got to her feet and approached Ruby.

"We'll... we'll just go in the kitchen," she told her foster dad apologetically. Ruby put her arm around Ronnie's shoulder companionably, smiling. They went into the kitchen where they could have a little privacy.

"What's he been saying about me?" Ruby demanded.

"What?"

"You foster dad. What's he been telling you about me?"

Ronnie shrugged, looking down at the floor.

"He doesn't know anything about me—he's never even seen me before. And Chuck can't tell him anything about me, because that's confidential between me and him. So anything your foster dad's saying, he made up himself."

"He didn't say anything."

"I'll bet. How come no-one will let me talk to you? Can you tell me that?"

Ronnie shrugged.

"Mr. Samuels said I wasn't supposed to go over to see you before. With no-one there."

"My foster family was there. And it isn't like I did anything to hurt you."

Ronnie looked ready to cry.

"We weren't supposed to sleep together," she said, her voice breaking.

"Who told you that? There's nothing wrong with sisters sleeping together! I didn't do anything to hurt you, did I?"

"I don't know."

"What do you mean, you don't know? I never hurt you! It's no wonder I'm in trouble if you're making up stories!" Ruby said angrily.

Tears started to stream down Ronnie's cheeks. Ruby only stayed angry for a few minutes, then forced herself to recall that Ronnie was just mixed up by the stories they were telling her, by everyone saying that she'd done something shameful. She hugged Ronnie.

"It's okay. I'm sorry I got mad. It's not your fault."

"I didn't tell anyone," Ronnie sobbed, shaking all over.

"I know, I know. It wouldn't matter if you did. You should be able to tell anyone you like. It wasn't any big secret. You didn't do anything wrong, and neither did I."

Ronnie nodded, gulping. Ruby tried to brush away Ronnie's tears.

"It's okay. I'm sorry. It's your dad I'm mad at, not you," she explained.

Ronnie sniffled, trying to catch her breath.

"I miss Mom," she said, surprising Ruby.

"Yeah. You could go back there, you know."

Ronnie shook her head.

"I can't, 'cause of Daddy."

Ruby tensed.

"He didn't do anything really. It's just what they're telling you, isn't it? Like with me."

Ronnie didn't answer. She just stood there looking lost and confused. Ruby hugged her close, patting her back.

"Ronnie, he didn't hurt you. He couldn't have."

"Get away from her," Ronnie's foster dad growled from the doorway. Ruby jumped, and turned around. Ronnie pulled away from Ruby quickly.

"I wasn't doing anything wrong," Ruby told him, scowling.

"Just get away from my daughter," he said tightly. Ronnie moved further away from Ruby.

"She's not your daughter. You aren't related to her. I am. And I'd never hurt her."

"You've already hurt her—you and her father."

"Dad never did anything either."

The man shook his head in disgust. His mouth was a tight, angry line.

"Get out of this house," he snapped.

"I don't have to."

"You get out of here, or I'll call the police."

"No, you won't. What're you going to tell them? That I came over to visit my sister, and I gave her a hug so you want me thrown out? Come on."

"Ronnie, go on up to your room."

"Stay here, Ronnie," Ruby snapped, before Ronnie could begin to obey. Ronnie stood there looking at the two of them, not moving. Her foster father picked up the receiver of the kitchen wall phone and dialed. He turned his back and took a few steps out of the room to speak, and Ruby knew it was a bluff. She turned back to Ronnie, trying to look casual.

"He's just blowing hot air," she assured Ronnie nonchalantly. She went to the fridge and looked inside. Milk or juice. And there was no coffee maker or teakettle on the counter. She looked at Ronnie.

"Isn't there anything to drink?"

"There's juice."

"Yeah, well I guess you're still drinking that, aren't you." Ruby sighed, and poured a couple of glasses. They sat down at the table to drink them, and Ruby glanced up at the doorway, where Ruby's foster father was hovering again.

"Leave us alone."

"You two are not going to be alone. Ronnie, please go upstairs. I don't want you getting hurt."

Ronnie looked at him pleadingly. He didn't back down. Ronnie stood up and headed for the door. Ruby watched her go, trying to keep her anger under wraps. Ronnie disappeared from sight.

"You may as well leave now," Ronnie's foster dad observed.

"I came to see Ronnie. You can't make me leave," Ruby said stubbornly.

"Would you leave if your social worker told you to?"

"No."

"The police are on their way over. I'm giving you a chance to leave before they arrive."

"I'm not leaving," Ruby repeated.

He shook her head.

"Why are you doing this?"

"Why are you trying to keep me away from Ronnie? I'm not trying to take her away from you, you know. I don't care if you're trying to adopt her. I don't care if you keep her away from my folks. Why should I? I'm not there."

"I'm keeping you away from Ronnie because I don't want her hurt any more."

"I'm not hurting her. I just came to talk."

The doorbell rang. A few moments later, a timid looking woman led two uniforms into the room. Ronnie's foster dad motioned them in.

"Thank you for being so quick. I want this girl charged with assault and taken away from the house."

They stood looking at Ruby blankly.

"She assaulted my daughter a couple of weeks ago. She came here to do it again. I found them in this room in an embrace."

Ruby opened her mouth to object, looking for something to say.

"You liar! I was hugging her because she was crying!"

"She was crying because you were trying to harm her—again."

"No!"

The cops started to move towards her, starting to understand what was happening.

"Her father has already been charged with assault, and apparently Ruby here follows in Daddy's footsteps."

Ruby stepped towards him.

"Ronnie is not your daughter! She's my sister!"

"She's my foster daughter," he explained to the officers. "Since she was taken out of her parents' custody for her own protection."

"She was not; she asked to be removed, just like me," Ruby insisted.

"No, she didn't. She came here from the hospital after being assaulted."

Ruby couldn't believe that he was going to have her arrested.

"Talk to my foster family—" she started, but he cut her off.

"Arguing isn't going to get us anywhere. You can investigate after you get her out of here, can't you? I want her away from my daughter; this whole thing is just tearing her up..."

They closed in on her. Ruby just stood there, frozen, as they put the handcuffs over her wrists and escorted her gently out of the house. They warned her not to bump her head when they eased her into the back seat of the police car. They shut the door, locking her in, and went back into the house for further discussions. Ruby sat in the car, slumped back against the seat. She closed her eyes and tried to make sense of the whole mess.

It seemed like hours before the two officers come back out of the house, talking seriously with one another. One was holding her knapsack, and held it up as they got into the car.

"This is yours?"

"Yeah."

They pulled out from the curb.

"Did you talk to Ronnie?" Ruby questioned.

"Yes, we talked to her."

"So where are you taking me?"

"To the police station."

"Why? If you talked to Ronnie, you know I didn't do anything!"

"Ronnie couldn't confirm that," he said quietly.

"What do you mean, couldn't? He wouldn't let her talk? Was he there when you talked to her?"

"No, we talked to her alone."

"So what did she say?" Ruby demanded.

"Just sit back and relax. We'll go over everything when we get to the station."

"Come on! I didn't do anything."

"You'll get a chance to tell your side of the story," he soothed.

Ruby stopped arguing and sat back. She stared out the window, trying to keep her mind blank. They pulled up in front of the police station and one of them opened the door for her. Ruby was helped to her feet, and they took her up to the doors holding her arms gently. Ruby eventually found herself in a small office alone, waiting for the officers to come back.

Cisco sat down on the edge of a desk and looked at his partner.

"What are we going to do?"

"She's been charged. We have to investigate."

Cisco opened his notebook, sighing.

"I'll call the social worker."

Bentley nodded.

"I'll look into the charges against the father. Figure out what the history is here."

Cisco sat down at the desk and picked up the phone. He dialed the number Ronnie's foster father had given to him.

"Mr. Samuels?"

"Yes, speaking."

"My name is officer Cisco. I'd like to talk to you about Ruby and Ronnie Simpson."

The social worker's long exhale traveled down the wire.

"What's Ruby gotten herself into now?"

"Ronnie's foster family has charged her with assault."

Samuels swore.

"You've got to be kidding. What happened over there? I didn't even think Ruby would be there yet."

"You knew she was going over to see Ronnie today?"

"Sure, it was a scheduled visit. Ruby was allowed to go over there any time today to see Ronnie, with Ronnie's foster parents supervising. What happened over there?"

"Apparently Ruby was—er—touching Ronnie inappropriately," Cisco said delicately.

"How could she? They were being supervised!"

"Apparently, not closely enough."

Samuels swore again. Cisco rolled his eyes. The man wasn't being terribly informative.

"Is there anything in Ruby's past that would lead you to think that she might hurt Ronnie?" he suggested.

There was silence for a few minutes.

"Ruby and Ronnie come from the same home," Samuels said slowly, logically, his voice calm now. "If Ronnie was being abused, then it's not much of a stretch that Ruby might have been when she was home. They were both put into foster care at the same age. Abused children can be abusive themselves."

"So you think it's a possibility."

"Well, of course it's a possibility. That's why it was a supervised visit. But there's never been any indication—"

"Were there signs that Ruby was abused herself?"

"No. Well, except that Ruby is... er... pretty mature for her age."

"Does she have a boyfriend?"

"Not a steady boyfriend, I don't think, but she definitely gets around."

"You wouldn't be surprised if something happened between Ruby and Ronnie that wasn't quite right."

"I think something might have happened to make Ronnie feel threatened, but it was probably innocent on Ruby's part."

"Ronnie's foster father said something about Ruby assaulting Ronnie a couple of weeks ago, too."

"Well, nothing proven. Ronnie spent a couple of nights with Ruby. Ronnie won't talk about what happened. Ruby admits that they slept together, but not that there was any inappropriate contact."

"And she was allowed to go over there again today?"

"They weren't supposed to be left alone together. We can't verify what happened that night. Neither one will talk openly about it."

Cisco shook his head wearily, noting it with a sigh.

"Has Ruby been in any other trouble, Mr. Samuels?"

"What kind of trouble?"

Cisco pursed his lips, considering.

"Why was she put into foster care?"

"She was very rebellious. Her parents couldn't control her."

"There was no suspicion of abuse?"

"No, not back then. Ruby has problems with authority. She always has. Parents, teachers, social workers, anyone who makes the rules. She likes to run her own life."

"How about police?" Cisco suggested.

"She hasn't really had contact with the police until a couple of months ago. The occasional scrape for vagrancy or being in a bar underage, but she's never been arrested."

"What's happened in the last two months?"

"A boy she was sleeping with was murdered. She's had... a bit of contact with the police since then. But it's not because of anything she did wrong."

"I see. Is there anything else I should know?"

"I don't think so. Listen—don't tell her that I've given you any personal information about her, okay?"

"Why not?"

"I've spent years trying to build up a trusting relationship with Ruby. I would hate for that to all be destroyed by her thinking I'd passed on confidential information," Samuels coaxed.

"We'll try to be careful."

Bentley was still talking on the phone when Cisco hung up. Cisco waited for him to finish. Bentley hung up, and shrugged.

"Well, that was pretty uninformative."

"Likewise. What's the scoop on the dad?" Cisco questioned.

"There's not much to go on. Probably he would never be convicted, but if they keep this going long enough, they can keep her in foster care… and hope that after a while Ronnie will get up the courage to accuse him."

"She didn't accuse him?"

"Nope. She went to hospital. The hospital called child welfare. They investigated and charged the dad."

"Evidence?"

"No. Just suspicions. There's another girl between Ruby and Ronnie. Chloe. She denies everything emphatically. The next kids are five. They have no idea what's been going on."

"The mother?"

"Very close-mouthed. And Ronnie herself denies that daddy ever touched her."

"So there's no reason to suspect him, other than that nobody is pointing any fingers in any other direction."

"Right. How about the social worker? What did he have to say?"

"Like daddy like daughter. Maybe she did something, maybe she didn't. No evidence one way or the other. Ruby's word against the foster family's."

"Well, let's see how her story sounds."

They walked into the room where Ruby was waiting. Cisco sat down on the bare desk, and Bentley sat down in the chair behind it. Ruby was still sitting with her hands cuffed behind her back, looking uncomfortable.

"Sorry to keep you waiting for us, Ruby. How're you doing?" Cisco questioned.

Ruby studied him suspiciously, but took his friendly tone as an indication that he was ready to listen.

"Are you going to take these off me?" she glanced over her shoulder to indicate the cuffs.

Cisco didn't move.

"I'll get them for you in a minute. So what exactly happened over there?"

"Nothing! I didn't do anything. All I did was hug Ronnie. I can hug my sister!"

He nodded, considering.

"Where were your hands?"

"What?" Ruby frowned in consternation.

"Well, when you hugged Ronnie, where did you put your hands?" Cisco prompted.

Ruby stared at him for a moment, replaying the scene in her mind. She shifted uncomfortably.

"On her back," she said hesitantly, "her back—around her shoulders…"

"Where were Ronnie's hands?"

"On her face—or at her sides—I'm not sure."

"Ronnie didn't hug you back?"

Ruby could see that wouldn't sound good. She hesitated.

"Well, not at first… she was crying… but then she hugged me too," she claimed.

"Where did she put her hands?"

"Just behind my back."

"Above or below your waist?"

"Umm—above."

"How much taller are you than Ronnie?"

"A foot or something, I guess."

"How close did you hold Ronnie?"

"I don't know."

"Were your bodies touching?"

Ruby didn't like his phrasing of the question. She looked for a way to answer it so that it wouldn't sound wrong.

"I guess we were touching… I didn't notice." She shrugged.

"Did Ronnie hold you tight?"

"No."

"She was upset, but she wasn't holding you tight?"

"Well, not tight—she was holding me…"

"Did she lean her face against you?"

Ruby was tensing up. There were no more right answers. He was asking questions in such a way that it didn't matter what she said, it could be taking the wrong way.

"I didn't do anything wrong," Ruby repeated firmly. "I gave her a hug when she was crying. I was trying to make my sister feel better."

"Why was she crying?"

"Her foster dad made her upset… saying…"

Cisco waited.

"What did he say to upset Ronnie?" he prodded.

"I don't remember," Ruby said flatly.

"How long were you there?"

"For a few minutes… not a long time."

"And you don't remember what he said that made her cry?"

Ruby sat there and didn't say anything. Cisco got up and unlocked the handcuffs. Ruby looked down at her hands, rubbing her wrists.

"I don't know what their problem is," Ruby said to the silence in the room.

No-one said anything for a while. Ruby's gaze wandered restlessly around the room. But there was nothing to look at. The room was bare and cold. The walls were green, and Ruby didn't know if that was supposed to be calming, or if it just happened to be the bargain deal the day they last repainted it.

"Why don't you tell me about your family," Cisco suggested.

"I don't have a family."

"You have Ronnie."

"Yeah."

"Tell me about the rest of your family."

Ruby continued to stare down at her hands, and she didn't talk as though she was speaking to them.

"Mom, dad, me, Chloe, Ronnie, and the twins."

"What was it like when you were living at home?"

"Ronnie was just a baby… she must have been three when I left. Chloe's two years younger than me."

"How old were you when you left home?"

"Eight."

"The same age Ronnie is now."

"Yeah."

"Why did you leave?"

"I didn't like being trapped there. I wanted to control my own life."

"Why did you feel trapped?"

"I don't get along with my folks. I don't like school. I like to stay out however late I feel like and eat or drink what I feel like. I don't like being told what to do."

"Eight is pretty young to have that kind of freedom."

"I could handle it," Ruby proclaimed.

"Don't your foster families have rules?"

"I do what I want. If they won't let me do what I want, I leave."

Cisco was silent. He made a couple of notations in his notebook. He looked back at Ruby, meeting her gaze steadily.

"You said you don't get along with your parents?"

"Yeah."

"Why not?"

Ruby's stomach started to gurgle and tighten. She stared hard at her hands, thinking back through the veil of darkness that the last five years of wandering and freedom had created. What was on the other side of the veil was foggy, like it was another life. When she thought back, she felt the same way as she had back then—the tight, sick feeling in her stomach. Trapped, worried, an urgent feeling of impending doom. But she couldn't remember much of what had happened. The feelings were as clear as yesterday, but the memories were like they had happened to someone else.

"I can't remember," she said quietly.

"Did you get along with your dad?"

"He wasn't around much. I had fights with my mom."

Cisco sensed that she was trying to divert his attention.

"Over what?" he questioned.

"I don't know. Stupid things. I don't remember anymore."

"But you got along with your dad?" he returned to the former line of questioning.

"I—I guess so. It's a long time since I lived there."

"He never hurt you or touched you inappropriately?"

"No, never!" she insisted.

Cisco got up.

"We'll be back with you in a minute, Ruby."

Bentley got up to join him. He paused in the doorway.

"Can I get you something, Ruby?"

She looked up at him.

"I'd like some cigarettes."

Her voice, even to herself, sounded very young and quiet. She sat in the silence of the room after they left, wondering why this was happening to her.

∼

"What do you think?" Cisco questioned.

"She's lying."

"Yes, but what really happened? I'm not sure what she's hiding."

"Do you think she did anything to Ronnie?"

"Not today. From what everyone has said, she didn't have the opportunity. She was only there for a few minutes, and they were never really alone."

"You think something happened when she slept over?" Bentley suggested.

"I wonder. Ronnie is pretty upset and confused about something. And I don't think that the foster father would get this upset over nothing."

"What about their biological dad?"

"Something going on there," Cisco said with a nod.

"You think so?"

"I'm sure of it."

"So what does that mean?"

"It means that Ruby probably left home for the same reason as Ronnie. Which means that she's more likely to have hurt Ronnie."

Bentley nodded.

"Why don't you go back in, I'll get her some cigarettes."

"I can't believe how young these kids start smoking."

Cisco went back in to see Ruby. He sat down again and studied Ruby. She looked back at him, trying to keep her expression blank. She looked vulnerable, not like someone capable of what she had been accused of.

"There's one thing we haven't talked about yet," Cisco said.

Ruby was silent.

"What happened a couple of weeks ago when you saw Ronnie?"

"Nothing happened," she said, kicking the leg of the desk a couple of times. "Nothing."

"She came over to stay with you at your foster family's house," Cisco said.

"Yeah."

"And how did you spend your time?"

"TV. Talked a bit."

"And she slept over."

"Yeah, so?" her tone was challenging.

"Why is Ronnie's foster dad so upset about that?"

"'cause my social worker told him we should have been supervised."

"Why is that?"

"I don't know."

"So what did they think happened?"

Ruby flushed.

"Nothing happened!"

"I don't think you heard my question. I said what did they think happened?"

Ruby concentrated on her crampy, gurgling stomach, trying to make her muscles relax. The longer she sat in the room, she worse she felt. It must have been the green color of the walls.

"I gotta use the restroom."

Cisco nodded. He escorted her out of the room and down the hall, then waited outside the door for her. After ten minutes had passed, he knocked on the door.

"Ruby?" There was no answer. Cisco opened the door and walked in. Ruby stood in front of the sink, patting her face with a wet paper towel. She looked up at him when he came in, and didn't say anything. "Are you all right?" he questioned.

Ruby shrugged.

"Let's go," Cisco instructed. He took her by the arm, and led her out of the room. He took her down the hall, as Bentley came from the other direction. He followed them back into the small office for further questioning. Ruby sat down again. Bentley handed her a small pack of cigarettes, and tossed a book of matches down on the desk in front of her. Ruby tore the package open and pulled a cigarette out. She put it in her mouth, and stuck one in her mouth. She struck a match a few times before it lit. She held the flame to her cigarette with shaking hands. It took three matches to light. Cisco watched this unemotionally.

"You and Ronnie slept together," he said, when she finally got it lit.

"It wasn't like that," Ruby insisted.

"What, then?"

"I couldn't sleep. I can't sleep alone. I invited her over so I wouldn't have to sleep by myself. Not to hurt her. I never hurt her."

"Ronnie's not so sure."

"That's because everyone's telling her I did. She's only a kid, she believes what they tell her."

"Like you believed your dad when he said he wasn't doing anything wrong?" he suggested.

"My dad didn't do anything."

"I think he did. And I think you're just as confused about it as Ronnie. I think that you're trying to work it all out, in your own way."

"I'm not confused," Ruby said clearly, biting off each word. "And I know I never did anything to Ronnie. Why would I hurt my own sister?"

"Because you're mixed up."

Ruby shook her head. Cisco frowned, studying her.

"What did Ronnie wear to bed?" he questioned.

"A night-shirt."

"It came down to her knees?"

Ruby shook her head.

"Mid-thigh," she admitted.

"And what were you wearing?"

"A t-shirt."

"With…?"

"Nothing."

"Sweats, shorts, underthings?"

Ruby shook her head.

"But I was dressed…" she protested.

"How long was the t-shirt?"

"I don't know… almost as long as Ronnie's."

Cisco watched Ruby light another cigarette. Her hands were a little steadier now. He let her smoke for a couple of minutes in silence while he considered her answers. He sighed.

"Ruby. Whether or not you intentionally touched or hurt Ronnie, can't you see how she might be confused by you getting into bed with her almost naked? You would have touched in your sleep, you probably cuddled right up together. Skin against skin… you pulling her closer…"

Ruby started to blush. A deep red wave started at her throat and spread over her face. She wiped her forehead with the back of her hand. Sweat was breaking out over her whole face. She shook her head.

"I didn't do anything wrong," she insisted.

"What you did was inappropriate. You didn't think it through."

Ruby shifted uncomfortably.

"I want to go home."

"I don't think you realize you've been arrested."

"Where's my lawyer?" she demanded.

"You haven't called anyone."

"I want to call him."

Cisco picked up the phone on the desk and handed it to her. Ruby looked at it.

"I need his number. It's in my knapsack."

Cisco looked at Bentley.

"Bring it in."

Bentley disappeared for a few minutes and came back with the knapsack. They both watched carefully while Ruby went through it and found Wilhelm's number. She dialed his number and waited for an answer.

"It's Ruby... I've been arrested." He had obviously asked what for, and Ruby struggled for the words. "They—they think I did something to my sister. I'm at... the police station. I'll let you talk to the cops."

Cisco took the phone and gave Wilhelm instructions to find them.

Wilhelm seemed nervous around Ruby. Watching her out of the corner of his eye, he listened to the officers outline the situation, shaking his head. He spoke to Ruby lowly. The police officers were still present, observing.

"You admit to sleeping with her," he said.

"Sleeping in the same bed as someone isn't the same as sleeping with them," Ruby reminded him, forcing a teasing grin.

Wilhelm looked a little green. He nodded. He spoke to the officers.

"I admit that Ruby was imprudent, but she certainly intended no harm. Is this going to go to trial?"

"I suspect that Ronnie's foster parents would be satisfied with a promise that Ruby won't have any more contact with Ronnie."

"What?" Ruby broke in.

Wilhelm touched Ruby on the shoulder to quiet her.

"Ruby, do you want to go to court? And maybe to juvenile?"

"No."

"Then I think you'd better agree to stay away from Ronnie."

Ruby scowled, but kept quiet.

"Will you release her to me?" Wilhelm questioned.

"Yes. But if she goes near Ronnie again, this will definitely go to court."

Wilhelm took Ruby by the arm, picked up her bag, and escorted her out. Ruby let him take her to his car. They both sat down and were silent at first.

"Are you feeling okay?" he questioned, after a deep, calming breath.

"Yeah," Ruby said in a small voice.

"You look sick. You're sure you're okay?"

"Yeah. Thanks for coming."

He nodded.

"I'm sorta hungry... could we go somewhere to eat?" Ruby suggested.

"Uh, sure. You probably need to get some sugar in your blood. You're pale as a ghost."

Willhelm started the car, and took her to a restaurant. He didn't have much to say, and Ruby figured his mind must be on other things. People didn't normally take her to real restaurants like that. She went to fast-food places, diners, coffee shops—not real restaurants. But he probably took clients there all the time on an expense account and didn't even think about it. Ruby struggled to read the menu, half in cursive writing and half in French.

"What's good here?" she questioned, deciding to short-cut the problem.

He glanced at her.

"Oh... I think you'd like the chicken cordon bleu. You like chicken?"

"Sure."

He ordered it for her. Ruby ordered a diet coke to drink, knowing the look she'd get from him if she ordered wine. He acted bored with the place. He must have taken people there a lot. It was classy—somber colors, dim lighting, waiters in black suits, white tablecloths on the tables. Ruby relaxed, looking around and trying to take it all in, but at the same time trying not to look as if she was awed by it.

"So tell me about your family," Wilhelm suggested.

Ruby was startled. She shrugged.

"I dunno. They're just normal."

"You're the oldest?"

"Yeah."

"Why did you leave?"

"Why do I gotta tell this to everyone I meet?" Ruby demanded, peeved. "I just felt like it, okay? I found out I could leave if I wanted to, and Family Services would take care of me, so I asked them to take me away. It wasn't 'cause anything horrible was going on. It was just because I didn't want to be there anymore."

"I bet that was some shock to your parents."

"They didn't care." Ruby flapped her hand, waving it away.

"Eight is pretty young to lose a kid. Most parents expect to have them for another ten years."

"They had plenty of other kids. They had their hands full. I was disrupting the family so they were glad when I left."

"You must have been pretty disruptive, for them to feel that way."

Ruby nodded, smiling a little and puffing out her chest as if it was something to be proud of.

"I was in trouble all the time at school. And I didn't go home every night. Even got caught shoplifting a few times."

"A regular little terror."

"I was. Always fighting with my sister and my mom, too. They hated me."

"Do you see them any more?" he questioned.

"Now and then. I go back sometimes to sleep if I'm out real late or something and can't go anywhere else."

"And they don't mind?"

"I don't stay. Just have a coffee and hit the road again. I haven't had a real fight with my mom for a long time."

"What did you fight about back then?"

"Everything. Anything she said, and anything I said. We never got along on anything."

"Are you ever going to go back there to live?"

Ruby shook her head adamantly.

"No. I'd rather live in a cardboard box than go back there."

"Just because you and your mom used to fight?" He raised an eyebrow.

Ruby shrugged.

"I didn't like it there," she said flatly.

Willhelm stopped questioning her when they brought the food. Ruby prodded the chicken a bit, and decided it looked all right. She wasn't really hungry, that had mostly just been a ruse to spend some more time trying to bond with her cute lawyer.

"What are your sisters like?" Wilhelm questioned.

"Chloe and me always fought. The rest... they were too young. I don't really know them."

"Ronnie included?"

"Yeah. She was only three when I left. I haven't really talked to her much since then."

He nodded.

"What about you?" Ruby questioned, turning the tables. "What's your family like?"

"Not a big family like yours. I was an only child. My dad was a doctor, my mom stayed home."

"Nice life."

"I was expected to be a doctor too. So I rebelled and became a lawyer instead."

Ruby giggled.

"Oh, you rebel," she mocked.

He smiled.

"I never could stand blood. So I'm a disappointment to my dad, but my mom figured I turned out all right."

Ruby shook her head.

"My folks never wanted me to be anything. Just quiet."

They ate the rest of the meal in silence.

The door was locked and Ruby had to ring the doorbell. Mrs. Winters came to the door and let Ruby in.

"Ruby—where have you been?" she fussed. "Are you okay?"

Ruby remembered the cut on her cheek from the fight with the Terminators. She shrugged.

"It's nothing. I'm fine."

"Where have you been? I was so worried!"

"I called you," Ruby pointed out.

"Please come home at night. And don't tell me you're at Marty's when you're not."

Ruby shrugged and went upstairs to her room. She shut the door and put down her bag. She liked Mrs. Winters all right, but she wasn't going to start obeying a bunch of rules for her. Rules were what she had run away from in the first place. She stayed in her room until Mrs. Winters came to get her for supper. Mrs. Winters knocked on the door, waited for a moment for Ruby's answer, which never came, and then she opened the door.

"Ruby, come on down for supper," she invited.

Ruby followed her down the stairs without a word. She sat down at the table with Mr. and Mrs. Winters, feeling awkward, like they were watching her. She picked at the food Mrs. Winters had prepared without interest.

"I'm not that hungry," she said. "I don't feel good."

"Have you got the flu or something?"

"I guess. I dunno."

"You'll have to make sure you get to bed in good time."

Ruby nodded. She pushed the food around on her plate.

"Can I make some coffee?"

"Sure, go ahead."

Ruby got up and went over to the coffee maker. She fiddled with it while it percolated. The Winters watched her, but didn't seem to know what to say to her. She had a cup of coffee, and then went up to her bedroom again.

∼

It was late and pitch black. Ruby crept into the bedroom and slipped carefully under the covers beside Mrs. Winters. Mrs. Winters stirred, and a minute later woke up and groaned.

"Ruby. Go to your own bed."

"I don't feel good," Ruby protested, and didn't move.

"You can't sleep here. Let's go get you settled back into your own bed."

"If I move, I'm going to barf."

Mrs. Winters lay beside her, not sure how to react. Then she turned over and stroked Ruby's hair.

"Poor little one," she murmured.

Ruby snuggled up to her and tried to calm her stomach and go to sleep.

Ruby felt like she was awake all night. She finally fell asleep for a few hours, but awoke out of this heavy sleep to Mrs. Winters leaning over her, looking worried.

"Ruby? Are you feeling okay?" she questioned.

Ruby rolled over, then regretted it as nausea washed over her.

"I don't feel good," she moaned.

"You look rotten. Do you want me to take you to the doctor?"

"No."

"Are you sure?"

"Yeah."

"Can I get you anything?" Mrs. Winters offered.

"Maybe some tea."

"Sure. I'll get you some."

Mrs. Winters left to prepare it. Ruby lay there, still, and dozed until Mrs. Winters brought her the tea. Mrs. Winters sat on the edge of the bed to see how she was doing.

"Did you have your own kids?" Ruby questioned, sipping the tea slowly, propped up just enough that she wouldn't spill it down her front.

Mrs. Winters smiled.

"Yes. Two. A boy and a girl. They left home years ago. Your bedroom was Brenda's. A long time ago."

"Where are they now?"

"Brenda lives in Phoenix. Married a dentist. Mike lives here in town and we see him now and then on weekends."

"Do you wish they lived here?" Ruby wondered.

"I had a hard time when they left. But they're happy, and need to find their own independence. And we are never long without children."

"You like kids?"

"Sure we do. That's why you're here."

Ruby took a careful sip of the hot tea.

"But you get paid for me to be here."

Mrs. Winters nodded.

"Yes, we get some money. But that's not why I do it. I don't like the way my house feels when it's empty. As long as there are children here, I'll feel young."

"You're not that old," Ruby countered.

She smiled.

"To you, I'm ancient."

"No, I've had real old foster parents. Ones with white hair that could hardly walk by themselves."

"That must have been difficult for you."

Ruby readjusted her position slightly.

"I don't like the homes where you have to take care of the foster parents," she agreed.

"When it's supposed to be the other way around. Did they have other foster kids, or just you?"

"Couple others. Couldn't control them, though. They just did whatever they felt like."

"Did you have to take care of the other children too?"

"Not there. I'm not a good babysitter. They were older than me, though. A couple of boys."

"Hmm. Fun."

"Do you usually have more than one foster kid?" Ruby asked.

"Sometimes."

"You ever consider adopting any of them?"

Mrs. Winters felt Ruby's forehead, not answering right away.

"It's pretty hard to adopt foster kids, Ruby," she deflected.

"I know. Some foster parents do, though."
"We haven't ever adopted any of our kids."
They were both quiet for a while.
"Are you feeling any better?" Mrs. Winters questioned.
"I'm tired."
"Okay. Go to sleep again for a while. I'll check on you later."

Ruby was sick all that day, and the next. So wretchedly sick that she could not even roll over in bed without feeling nauseated. She spent half the day in bed and the other half in the bathroom. The day after that, Mrs. Winters insisted on taking her to the doctor. Ruby endured a rough ride in the car and dragged herself into the doctor's office. The doctor saw her after an hour's wait. He talked to her a bit, and ran a few tests. Ruby was so miserable, she hardly heard a word he was saying to her. He left her in the examination room alone for a long time. After a while he came back in. He pulled over a stool and sat down, looking at her thoughtfully.

"How old are you, Ruby?" he questioned.

"Thirteen."

"You have a boyfriend?"

"He just dumped me," Ruby said flatly, thinking of Chuck and his inexplicable abandonment of their relationship.

"Has anyone ever talked to you about birth control?"

"Yeah, I know all that stuff," Ruby waved a hand.

"But you don't use it?" he pressed.

Ruby stared at him.

"I always use it. Always."

"When was your last period?"

"I dunno. I've never been regular."

"Are you planning anything nine months from now?"

Ruby shook her head adamantly.

"I always use—"

"You're pregnant, Ruby."

"No, I'm not."

"The blood test was conclusive. Your HCG is very low, so I expect you're not very far along. Can you remember when your last period was?"

"No. I'm not pregnant."

"You're nauseated because of morning sickness. Since it's so severe, I'll give you something for it."

"Give me something for the nausea. But it's not morning sickness."

"I'm going to schedule a follow-up appointment with you. If you're going to have a healthy baby, you have to take care of yourself right now."

"I am not having a baby," Ruby insisted.

"We will talk about your options at your next appointment."

"Don't tell Mrs. Winters I'm pregnant."

"I'm not allowed to tell anyone without your consent," he admitted.

"You're not going to tell anyone that lie."

"It's not a lie. I'll see you in a couple of weeks."

"No, you won't."

He didn't argue with her. He just wrote out the prescription for her and handed it to her.

"That prescription will last you two weeks. Then if you want more, you'll have to come back here. I also want you to start taking prenatal vitamins."

"Thank you," Ruby said, taking the prescription from him. She went back out to the waiting room where Mrs. Winters was sitting. She handed Mrs. Winters the prescription, and went out to the car. Mrs. Winters lingered in the doctor's office for a moment, then followed her out.

"We'll go pick this up, so you can start feeling better."

Ruby nodded. She waited for Mrs. Winters to unlock the door for her, and sat in the car in silence. Mrs. Winters spoke to her a few times, but getting no response, she gave up.

CHAPTER Eight

Within a couple of days, Ruby was back on her feet again. Mrs. Winters commented that she was still pale, but definitely starting to look better. Ruby went to the arcade and found, instead of the Jags, Brian.

"Hey, Ruby! Long time since I've seen you. What're you up to?"

"Hi, Brian," she grinned, happy to see him. "Skipping school?"

"Sure. What do you think, you want to join me?"

Ruby nodded.

"Yeah, great. You want to go to a movie?"

He shrugged.

"Sounds good."

He put his arm around her and they walked to the door. A couple of the Jags stopped them in the doorway.

"Hey, Ruby—where are you going? Where have you been?"

Brian looked from one to the other, his face growing pale. Ruby shrugged.

"I've been sort of sick."

"Where are you going? You going to come by tonight?"

Ruby glanced at Brian and shook her head.

"I got plans right now, okay?"

The Jags eyed Brian, scowling. Ruby shoved past them.

"Come on, Bri'. I'll catch you guys later."

They watched Ruby and Brian leave without saying anything else. Brian looked at Ruby when they were a good distance away.

"How long have you been hanging around with them?"

"A while."

"Don't you think that's a little dangerous?"

"I know what's dangerous. I can take care of myself," she disagreed.

"I don't know. A gang? Why did you have to get involved with them?"

Ruby didn't answer. As she and Brian walked together, she watched for any of the Terminators. She hadn't really been worrying about them until Brian started talking about danger. That was where the danger would come from. Not the Jags, but the Terminators.

"Let's just go to the movie," she said, looking around carefully.

Brian gave her a strange look, and they went to the theaters. Ruby relaxed once they were sitting down, and she and Brian kissed until after the opening credits had rolled past.

They went back to Brian's house after the movie. His parents were both out, and Ruby and Brian snuggled on the couch in front of the TV until Brian's mom came home. She glared at Ruby, and Brian withdrew slightly. He put his arm casually over her shoulders. Ruby got up and went into the kitchen.

"Are you headed home?" Brian's mom questioned.

"I guess."

Brian was watching her over the back of the sofa.

"Ruby? Stick around a while, why don't you?" he coaxed.

Ruby rolled her eyes.

"Not much point staying here now."

"Come on. Mom won't mind. Will you, mom?"

She looked daggers at him.

"Not at all," she said grudgingly. Ruby helped herself to a beer in the fridge, and sauntered back over to where Brian was sitting. She slid up against him, not letting him move away when he shifted uncomfortably under his mother's icy gaze. She glared at them for a while, but eventually stormed off into her bedroom and shut the door. Brian relaxed more then.

"She sure doesn't like me," Ruby commented.

"It's not you. She thinks that you're too young for me. Afraid I'll corrupt you."

Ruby grinned.

"More like I'll corrupt you. She thinks I'm wild."

Brian kissed Ruby's forehead.

"You are."

He flipped through channels restlessly, then got up.

"I'm hungry. What do you want?"

"Another beer."

"What else?"

Ruby shrugged. Brian puttered in the kitchen for a few minutes, and came out with another beer for Ruby and some sandwiches. Ruby accepted both, but opened the beer without touching the sandwich. They stretched out together on the couch, watching TV.

Ruby next became aware of Brian's mother's face in front of hers.

"Get up! Come on, you little hussy, get up!"

Ruby looked around, her vision still fuzzy with sleep. It was dark. The TV was still droning on quietly. Brian shifted underneath her, starting to wake up too. Ruby propped herself up a little, trying to remember what had happened. Brian's mom grabbed her roughly by the wrist, trying to pull her to her feet. Brian shifted suddenly to a sitting position, nearly tumbling Ruby onto the floor. Ruby was trying to pull back away from the woman's grasp while getting her bearings. Brian held her around the waist, and pulled her arm back from his mother's grasp.

"Leave Ruby alone," he ordered. "She hasn't done anything."

"Get out of my house. And stay away from Brian!" she shrieked.

"Mom! Leave her alone!"

"I want her out of the house, and she's not coming back here."

"Mom, go back to bed. I'll see Ruby off."

"Uh-uh. She's out now!"

Ruby got to her feet. She rubbed her eyes.

"I'll see ya, Brian."

"You're not going out alone at this time of night. I'll drop you off somewhere."

Ruby shrugged.

"Don't bother."

"You're not going off someplace with her in your car," his mother snapped.

Brian shoved her.

"Leave her alone."

"I'll call Child Services," she threatened.

Brian looked at Ruby, uncertain. Ruby shook her head.

"I don't want any trouble, I'll go. See-ya around."

Ruby headed for the door. She paused dizzily with her hand on the wall, then she went on. Brian stood awkwardly at the front door watching her departure.

"Sorry about this."

"Whatever."

Ruby walked away down the sidewalk without looking back at him.

Ruby stopped by Tim's apartment, but no-one was there. The Jags were out. She considered staying there to wait for them, but she didn't think it would be good for her image if they came back to her hiding out there. She went out again to see if she could find them.

Ruby wasn't sure what time it was, but she knew it was late. She stuck pretty close to the apartment and kept her eyes peeled for Terminators. She wasn't sure where the gang's boundaries were or whether the Terminators would respect them. She kept her hand on her knife. Eventually Ruby stopped in at an all-night cafe with a pay phone, and got out her phone numbers. She flipped through her cards. She tried a couple of numbers before she had any luck.

She stood at the doors of the cafe until a police car drove up. She went out and got into the car.

"Hey, Brown," she greeted.

He studied her.

"What are you doing out so late, Ruby?" he questioned.

Ruby shrugged.

"I was staying with a friend. Got kicked out."

"You want me to take you home?"

"No. I can't go there. I got a friend who will let me stay."

"One that won't kick you out?" he questioned.

"Yeah."

"What kind of friend kicks you out at three o'clock in the morning?"

"Is it that late?"

"Sure is."

Ruby shook her head.

"I fell asleep at a guy's house. His mom doesn't like me, wouldn't let me stay."

"Where am I taking you?"

Ruby directed him toward Marty's neighborhood. He pulled away from the curb.

"I'm glad you called me."

"Yeah. Thanks for picking me up."

"We should see what we can do about getting you someplace that you could spend the nights regularly, rather than running around town all night."

"I have a foster family," Ruby offered.

"Is that where we're going?"

"No."

"Then what are we going to do about you?"

"I dunno. Marty said I could move in with them."

"Is that where we're going?"

"Yeah."

"Good. Why don't you move in there permanently?"

Ruby shivered with a sudden chill. She stared out the window, watching the empty streets they drove through and rubbing her arms.

"I don't like permanent. I like freedom."

"You wouldn't have freedom there?"

"It's not the same."

She told him where to turn, and in a few minutes they pulled up in front of Marty's house. Brown hesitated, looking at her.

"Will you be okay?" he checked.

"Yeah, no problem." Ruby got out of the car. "Thanks again."

He nodded and watched Ruby walk up to the house. He didn't pull back out right away, but sat there watching her in. Ruby grimaced and rang the doorbell. Marty's mom answered the door in her slippers and robe.

"Ruby! What's going on? Are you okay?" She saw the squad car against the curb and walked by Ruby without waiting for an answer. She went up to the car and leaned against it for a few minutes, talking to Brown. Ruby stood on the front step awkwardly, waiting for Mrs. Rodger to come back to the house. After a few minutes Mrs. Rodger nodded and came back up to the house as Brown pulled away. She motioned Ruby into the house.

"Come on. You need to go to bed. We'll talk in the morning. Do you need anything to eat before bed?"

"No."

"If you're worried about waking Marty up, you can sleep on the couch," she offered.

"I'll sleep with Marty."

"Okay. Don't stay up talking."

She locked the door and headed back to her bedroom. Ruby went in the other direction to Marty's room.

∼

Ruby awoke the next morning to the noise of Marty's mom getting ready for the day. Marty stirred beside her and sat up, stretching and smothering a yawn.

"Ruby… when did you get here?"

"At nearly four o'clock in the morning," Marty's mother informed her from the doorway.

"What guy were you out with?" Marty demanded.

Ruby shrugged.

"I was at Brian's house. Then his mom kicked me out."

"Why do you have to stay with all of these boys? Why can't you just stay with me?"

"I like boys," Ruby said, pulling down her t-shirt to her thighs as she slid out from under the covers.

"Ruby," Mrs. Rodger said quietly, in a serious voice. "I am worried about you. That policeman said it wasn't the first time that he's picked you up."

"Policeman?" Marty repeated, her tone going up to a squawk.

"I called him," Ruby snapped. "It was late. I wanted to get here safe, so I called Brown 'cause he's driven me before and been really cool about it."

"I'm still worried, Ruby. You're putting yourself in dangerous situations. You're going to end up hurt," the older woman persisted.

"You've already been hurt," Marty interjected.

Ruby looked from one to the other.

"Are you ganging up on me?"

Ruby's mom sat down on the edge of the bed.

"We're not ganging up on you, Ruby. I'm not going to try to force you to do anything. I just want to help you make some changes that will make you safer. I don't want to hear one day that you've been found dead in an alley somewhere. I want you to be safe and happy."

Ruby leaned back against Marty, feeling warm and comfortable. She closed her eyes.

"I know I'm safe here."

"Then why don't you stay here?" Marty pursued.

"I don't know. Social Services would never allow it."

"Why not?"

Ruby shrugged, feeling somewhat less comfortable under cross-examination.

"Lots of reasons. Look, I don't want to end up in another city somewhere."

"Why would you end up in another city?"

"So that Social Services could get me away from 'bad influences'. If I don't go back to my foster family sometimes, I'll get moved."

"Social Services wouldn't let us take care of you?"

Ruby didn't answer at first. Moving in with Marty... in ways it would be good, but she knew things would change if they made it a permanent arrangement. Things always changed once they were permanent. They would treat her differently. They would start putting restrictions on her, setting curfews, dictating who she could associate with. She liked Marty and her mom. She didn't want things to change.

"Social Services says you have to have money. And they have to interview both parents and all."

Ruby opened her eyes and looked at Marty's mom. Mrs. Rodger looked thoughtful.

"You don't want to move in here, do you?"

"They wouldn't let me," Ruby repeated firmly.

Marty put her arms around Ruby from behind. She bent over to talk quietly in Ruby's ear.

"Your social worker let you go without a foster family before."

Ruby started and turned to look at Marty.

"What?"

"You can hide it from some people, Ruby. But not from me. I knew you didn't have a foster family."

"Why didn't you say something?"

"You didn't want to tell me, so I kept quiet. Things were better when you didn't have a foster family. Things have been bad since you moved in with the Winters."

Ruby shook her head.

"Why can't you get him to do it again? Take you away from the Winters and not reassign you. Tell him that you will stay here."

"Chuck's mad at me. He won't take care of things anymore."

Mrs. Rodger gave Ruby a quick hug.

"Ruby, you're welcome here. You know that. You can come here any time—three-thirty in the morning, or whatever. I just want you to be safe."

Ruby nodded.

"I know," she agreed. She swallowed, finding her throat suddenly tight and hot.

"You don't have to stay here permanently. We don't have to make any particular arrangements. I just want you to be okay."

Ruby nodded wordlessly. Mrs. Rodger stood up.

"Let's get some breakfast. Will you give me a hand, Marty?"

"Yeah."

Ruby and Marty both climbed out of bed.

"Is he here?" Ruby questioned, stopping in the doorway.

They both turned and looked at her.

"Marty's dad's not home."

Ruby nodded and headed towards the bathroom.

"I'm going to have a shower."

When Ruby got out of the shower, she wrapped a towel around herself and went into the kitchen to get a cup of coffee.

"Does your foster mom need a phone call?" Marty's mom questioned.

Ruby poured her coffee, and went over to the phone. Balancing the receiver on her shoulder, she dialed the Winters.

"It's Ruby."

"Where are you, Ruby?" Mrs. Winters' anxiety was clear in her voice.

"At Marty's. I'm okay."

"Can I talk to her mom?"

Ruby handed the phone to Mrs. Rodger.

"Hi. Yes, Ruby's okay. I'm sorry she didn't call last night, she got in pretty late. I'll tell her. Bye-bye."

She hung up the phone.

"She wants you to stop by there sometime today. Okay?"

"I might."

She nodded.

"Sit down, and we'll have something to go with that coffee."

Ruby nodded, sipping at her coffee.

"I just have to get something on."

She went back into Marty's bedroom and pulled on a shirt and some pants. She swallowed a couple of nausea pills and went back out to the kitchen.

"Are you coming to school?" Marty questioned.

"No. I gotta see someone."

"Stay away from the Jags."

"How do you know it's the Jags?" she challenged, unable to suppress a grin.

"I know it's not your social worker."

"Yeah, I'm not seeing him anymore."

"Stay away from the Jags too."

"Don't worry about me."

Ruby sat down and nibbled on the toast that Marty gave her. When they finished breakfast, Ruby picked up her knapsack and said goodbye.

Ruby got out of the bus and walked up to Tim's apartment. She let herself in and nodded a greeting to the boys who were up and around. Tim was obviously still in bed. She took a couple of steps towards the bedroom.

"Is he alone?" she asked.

"Who, Tim?"

"Yeah. Tim. He's by himself, right?"

They all nodded. Ruby opened the door and went in. She shut it behind her and stripped off her pants and shirt. She lifted the covers on Tim's bed.

"Lemme alone," Tim groaned, pulling his pillow over his head. Ruby slid in beside him. He turned over and looked at her. "Ruby! Hey, what're you doing here?"

"I knew you'd still be sleeping."

"Yeah, come on in."

Ruby cuddled up to him, closing her eyes. She liked the warm, safe feeling of being enclosed in his arm. She took a few deep breaths, and went back to sleep again.

Tim woke her up after a few hours, kissing her and pulling her close. Ruby stretched, feeling warm and comfortable.

"Hi."

"Good morning. Where you been lately?" he questioned.

"Sick."

"Where'd you go last night?"

"With a friend," Ruby said firmly, discouraging further questions along this line. Tim considered her response, and then shrugged, deciding it was more important to keep her in a good mood.

"You going to stick around tonight?" he questioned.

"Sure. Anything happening?"

"Jack's been asking about you. He wants you for something."

Ruby sat up. Her stomach tied in knots.

"Jack is? What did he say?"

"Lie down. I don't know, you can ask him tonight."

Ruby put her feet over the edge of the bed.

"When was he looking for me?"

"Aw, Ruby—come on..."

"I gotta go find him."

Tim lay there and watched her dress.

"You don't have to run every time he calls," he protested.

"I'm not. I have to see what he wanted me about."

Ruby headed for the door. Frustrated, Tim got out of bed and followed her. Ruby picked up her bag and walked out of the bedroom and to the front door.

"Don't you even want something to eat?" Tim questioned.

"I'm not hungry."

Ruby left. Tim looked around at the other guys angrily.

"Well, what're you looking at?" he challenged.

Ruby headed over to Jack's apartment, wondering what he had been looking for her about. Her mind went reluctantly back to Mike. It was strange not having him around anymore. She hadn't seen him very often, but it had been a long time now, and she felt like he should be showing up again soon. Ruby had seen him killed, yet she couldn't believe that it had really happened. She had tried as hard as she could to forget all the details of that day. She had not really thought about Mike and what had happened to him. She said the words, but she couldn't believe that it had really happened.

She got up to Jack's apartment and knocked on the door. She stood at his door knocking for a few minutes before turning away to leave. She was two steps away when the door opened. Ruby turned and looked at Jack. He stepped back, opening the door wide to invite her in. Ruby stepped into his apartment, her stomach tightening, nausea returning. Jack looked her up and down. He rubbed his unshaven chin.

"Where've you been?" he questioned thickly.

He was drunk. She'd seen Jack gulp down tequilas without a grimace before, and remain steady as a rock. He must have had a lot to drink. Ruby looked around. There was a collection of bottles on the table.

"I was sick," Ruby told him.

"Sick. How convenient. I've been looking for you."

"Tim just told me. I came right over. What did you want me for?"

"You and me are going over to see some boys," he said.

"Who? When?"

"Right now. Put down your bag, and we'll go."

Ruby put down her knapsack slowly. Jack finished off one of one of the bottles on the table.

"Are you sure you're okay...?" Ruby questioned tentatively.

He stared at her, and then grinned, showing his teeth.

"You just leave everything to me, Ruby. I'm in fine form."

Ruby flushed hotly. She opened the door again and he followed her out. He put his arm around her, staggering very slightly.

"You got your blade with you?" he questioned, his warm, beery breath in her face.

Ruby swallowed.

"Yeah. Where are we going?"

Jack reached behind his back, under his jacket, and she felt him push something hard into her waistband. Ruby's heart raced. A gun. Her knife wasn't going to be enough this time, he was giving her a gun.

"I don't care if you know how to use it or not," Jack said. "I want you to have it handy anyway."

Ruby tried to swallow the lump growing in her throat. Her mouth was dry and sticky. She licked dry lips to no avail. Jack kept his hand behind her back, swaggering beside her with a scowl on his face. Ruby was finding it difficult even to breathe. Whatever was on Jack's mind, it was dangerous. She wished he'd brought one of the bottles along with him, or offered her something in the apartment. She could really use something to steady her nerves now.

They ended up entering an alleyway half an hour later. Ruby started to ask Jack what was going on, and he silenced her with a quick movement. She moved the way his firm hand directed. His swagger was gone, and so was the drunken slackness that had been in his face. He guided her into the alleyway, to come face-to-face with Slasher and a big fellow at his shoulder—Laskin, she assumed. Ruby felt weak-kneed. He had brought her to witness a killing. Another shooting. Jack's right hand was behind Ruby's back. With his left, he produced a gun, pointing it towards Slasher and Laskin before they could react to his presence.

"What are you doing here?" Slasher demanded. His voice cut through Ruby like a knife. It pierced her heart, and she was certain she was going to black out. Memories of the night that Mike was killed came flooding back. Jack's right hand stayed firm on Ruby's back, willing her to keep her feet and be a witness to what was going to happen.

"You were expecting someone else?" Jack taunted. Steel entered his voice. "Not a muscle, Laskin, or I'll blow off your kneecap."

Laskin froze. Slasher studied Jack and Ruby with sharp eyes.

"What is this, Jack?"

"I think you know what this is about," Jack answered. He smiled, watching them sweat as they tried to figure out how to get away unharmed.

Everyone was silent for a few minutes.

"You're not going to do anything," Slasher challenged.

"I don't bluff," Jack said flatly. "Are you going to ask for it to be quick?"

Slasher dove to the side, scrabbling for his gun. Jack let go of Ruby, firing at Slasher and then aiming a couple of shots towards Laskin. Ruby whipped the gun out of her waistband, and nailed Slasher as he pulled his piece, aiming unsteadily at Jack. Jack held his gun steady on Laskin and glanced at Ruby.

"You were the trigger man, Laskin."

"No, Jack. I swear, it wasn't me," the big boy's voice was high.

"It was you, Laskin. You left a witness."

Laskin shook his head, staring pale-faced at the gun. Ruby watched, frozen. Her voice was gone; she couldn't tell Jack that it wasn't Laskin. She would have to tell him who it was, then. And she would have to admit that she had lied to him before. He might decide to shoot her.

Jack pulled the trigger. Ruby saw Laskin go down without being sure where he was hit. Jack walked over to where Slasher had fallen and kicked him. He walked back to Ruby, shoving the gun back down behind his back. Ruby looked down at the gun in her hand. It was warm. She hadn't even looked at it when she pulled it out. She tried to put it back in her waistband, but her hands were shaking too much. Jack helped her to tuck it away.

"Why didn't you tell me you could shoot?" he demanded.

Ruby gulped.

"I never shot a gun before in my life."

He studied her for a moment.

"Let's scram. Before someone calls in the shots."

Ruby followed Jack's lead. They got a few blocks away, and he pulled her into a bar. He sat her down and ordered a few drinks. He pressed one firmly into her hand.

"You need this."

Ruby took the drink. It warmed her up; taking away the chill she had caught in the alley. Jack slid in beside her and put his arm around her shoulders. He sipped at his own drink, but obviously didn't need it like Ruby did. He held her close. Ruby leaned against him, closing her eyes. She saw Troy's face before her eyes. Ruby opened her eyes quickly. She had just seen two hoods executed, and she was still seeing Troy's face. Jack looked down at her.

"What?"

"Nothing. Would you get me another...?"

He waved down a waitress, and ordered more drinks. Ruby drank another, and breathed out slowly, relaxing her tense muscles. Jack bent down and kissed her, but his eyes were foggy and his mind obviously wasn't on her. He ordered a couple more drinks and they sat together, each lost in their own thoughts.

Ruby opened the door and stumbled into the room. She aimed for the stairs and tripped, falling to her knees. She crawled to the stairs and climbed to her feet, using the handrail to pull herself up. Mrs. Winters hurried over.

"Ruby? Are you okay? Where have you been?"

Mrs. Winters' hands helped Ruby stabilize herself.

"Are you hurt?" Mrs. Winters questioned urgently.

She put her arm around Ruby, and gasped.

"You're drunk!"

"As a sailor," Ruby agreed, holding onto Mrs. Winters for support.

"Whew! I'm amazed you managed to get home. Let's get you to bed."

She helped Ruby get up the stairs, one clumsy, halting step at a time.

"I'm going to be sick," Ruby informed her.

Mrs. Winters hustled Ruby into the bathroom barely in time. She left Ruby hanging over the toilet while she turned on the faucet to fill the tub.

"Let's get you out of those clothes. I'm guessing it's not the first time you've been sick tonight."

Ruby groaned weakly.

"You're right," she agreed.

Mrs. Winters shut the bathroom door.

"Are you okay for a few minutes?" she questioned, when Ruby stopped heaving.

Ruby nodded.

"I'm done."

Mrs. Winters hoisted Ruby to her feet, and grasped her shirt.

"Arms up."

Ruby obeyed unsteadily. Mrs. Winters stripped the shirt off and threw it on the floor. She pushed Ruby's fumbling fingers out of the way to unbutton Ruby's jeans, and pulled them down to Ruby's ankles.

"Let's get you in the tub," she ordered. Ruby stepped out of the jeans and slipped on the porcelain tiles. Mrs. Winters tried to catch her and lower her slowly, but Ruby still landed hard. She didn't appear to even feel it. Mrs. Winters helped Ruby up and steadied her to step into the tub. "Sit down," she ordered. Ruby obeyed. Mrs. Winters shut off the water. "Okay, wash up."

Ruby splashed around a little in the water. Mrs. Winters sat on the edge of the tub watching Ruby to make sure she didn't drown herself. After a while, Ruby started to shiver.

"Time to get out," Mrs. Winters advised.

"I'm cold."

"I know you are. You'll warm up after you're dry. Come on."

Ruby climbed out of the tub and Mrs. Winters wrapped a towel around her. She took Ruby into the bedroom, and took an unworn nightgown out of the drawer of the dresser. Ruby lay on the bed wrapped in the towel, not moving. Mrs. Winters made her sit up again, dried her off the best she could, and pulled the nightgown on. She tucked Ruby in and left her to sleep it off. She made two phone calls before going to bed herself. One to Mr. Samuels to inform him of Ruby's condition. The second call was to Marty's house.

"Uh—Ruby's not here," Marty told her hesitantly. "Did she tell you she was coming?"

"No. She's here. I appreciate when you let me know that she's okay, and I thought you might like to know that she's safe tonight too."

"Oh. Thanks Mrs. Winters."

"You're welcome. Talk to you again."

Ruby was not ready to wake up when Mrs. Winters shook her in the morning. She snuggled down further under her covers, trying to block out the interruption.

"Come on Ruby. Time for school."

"Ohhh... I'm sick," Ruby protested.

"You're hung over. Get out of bed."

"I can't. I don't feel good."

"That's not going to work today. If you didn't want to be hung over, you shouldn't have had anything to drink."

Ruby tried to remember the night before, but it was mostly a blank. She remembered going out with Jack. They must have tied it on pretty good. And he had been drunk before she even started. Whenever she tried to remember what had happened with Slasher and Laskin, all that surfaced in her memory was Troy's face. No matter how hard she tried to block him out, and replace it with the images of Slasher and Laskin, the only thing she could think of was his hands on her body, quelling her protests. Ruby sat up as Mrs. Winters pulled away the blankets and took her by the arm. Her stomach churned violently as Mrs. Winters escorted her firmly down the hallway to the bathroom.

"I'm gonna..."

"Not until you're in the bathroom, you're not."

Ruby was pushed into the bathroom, and the door was shut behind her. She stood there looking at herself in the mirror. She didn't look any different. She had caused an innocent man to be killed, but she didn't look any different. She had shot a man, and she still looked the same. Ruby hunched over the toilet and threw up.

It was a while before there was a knock on the door, and Mrs. Winters called her through the door.

"Are you ready to go to school, Ruby?"

Ruby didn't answer.

"Can I come in, Ruby?"

Ruby got up and washed her face, still not answering. Mrs. Winters opened the door and came in.

"Are you going to shower before school?"

Ruby shook her head.

"I don't feel good. I can't go," she said.

Mrs. Winters leaned against the counter.

"Do you want to tell me why you drank so much last night?" she questioned.

Ruby shook her head. She started to turn away from Mrs. Winters, catching the edges of her nightgown to take it off and shower. She stopped and looked at it. Suddenly, she felt nauseated again. She stared at the nightgown, feeling the lace along the short sleeves. Mrs. Winters touched her arm.

"Ruby? What's wrong?"

Ruby jerked away from Mrs. Winters' touch. Out of the thick fog of the night before, she remembered Mrs. Winters' fingers unbuttoning her pants. Ruby stepped back from Mrs. Winters, confusion filling her mind. Her stomach was tied in tight, hard knots.

"Don't touch me," she warned. "Keep your hands off of me!"

Mrs. Winters raised her brows questioningly.

"Be ready for school in half an hour. We'll get you some breakfast and I'll drop you off so you can still make it in time."

Mrs. Winters stepped out and closed the door. Ruby had a two minute shower and went back to her bedroom wrapped in a towel. Her heart pounded in her ears. She felt the bump on the side of her head, trying to remember how she got it. Ruby looked at the rumpled bed for a minute, dressed, and picked up her knapsack. She went down the stairs to the front door. She ignored Mrs. Winters' call from the kitchen and ran from the house.

CHAPTER Nine

Chuck looked up at his secretary, who had been hovering over him for several minutes, waiting for him to look up.
"Hi."
"Ruby Simpson is here to see you."
"She doesn't have an appointment." Chuck frowned.
"She seems pretty upset," the woman persisted.
Chuck pursed his lips.
"How upset?"
She shrugged in exasperation.
"I think you should see her."
"All right," Chuck sighed, "send her in."
Ruby walked in a couple of minutes later. Chuck noted that his secretary was right. Ruby did look upset. She was white as a sheet, her mouth in a pronounced frown, and she moved jerkily, looking around as if she thought she was being chased. Chuck motioned for her to sit down. Ruby plunked into the chair.
"I want to be moved," she said immediately.
"Moved away from the Winters?" Chuck said.
"I'm not going back there!" she asserted.
"What happened?" Chuck questioned, keeping his voice low and calming.
"I want to be moved," Ruby repeated.
"You've never asked to move to a different family before. Is that what you're asking?"
Ruby nodded.

"I'm not going back there," she said forcefully.

"Okay. Relax. I'm not going to take you back there. We'll move you to a new family." He let it sink in for a few moments. "Now. Are you okay?"

Ruby breathed out slowly. Chuck watched her hands gradually release the arms of the chair.

"Are you okay now, Ruby?" he repeated.

"Yeah."

"I will need to make a report on why you want to be moved. For your file."

"I just don't like it there."

"What don't you like? The Winters are experienced foster parents."

Ruby swallowed strenuously. She rubbed her hands along the arms of the chair.

"I just... feel closed in."

Chuck studied Ruby, frowning. Ruby never said that. The only time that she talked about being closed in was when she was talking about her own family.

"What made you feel closed in? I thought you and the Winters were getting along all right."

"What do you know?" she challenged.

"I know Mrs. Winters called me last night to tell me that you came home drunk out of your mind," Chuck suggested.

Ruby shrugged.

"So what could possibly have happened between Mrs. Winters putting you to bed and you getting here this morning?"

"Nothing. I just don't like it there."

Chuck shrugged.

"I'll have to talk to the Winters too."

"Go ahead."

"If you'll go sit in the waiting room, I'll get something arranged for you. Okay?"

"I want to talk to Ronnie. Can I talk to her on the phone?"

"You know you're not allowed to talk to Ronnie."

Ruby shook her head and walked out of his office. Chuck called Mrs. Winters.

"Hi. Samuels."

"Mr. Samuels. Hi, what's up?"

"I guess you know Ruby's asked to be taken out of your care," he said delicately.

"What?" Mrs. Winters' voice was shocked. "No—she walked out of here this morning without a word. I had no idea…"

"Did something happen this morning?"

"No… she woke up with a hangover. We talked for a minute in the bathroom. Then she got all jumpy."

"What made her jumpy?"

"I don't know for sure. She told me to get away from her. I don't know what happened to upset her."

"Okay. See if you can remember anything. I think something happened that made her think of her family. I'd like to figure out what it was."

"I'll let you know if I can think of anything."

"I'd appreciate it."

Chuck made a few phone calls to potential foster families, wrote some notes on Ruby's file, and went out to the waiting room to see her. He looked around, but she wasn't in any of the chairs waiting for him. He started to walk back to his office, but the receptionist waved him to a stop as he walked by her. She covered up the mouthpiece of the phone, interrupting her call.

"Looking for Ruby? She's at the phone."

Chuck turned and looked around. There were pay phones between the double doors, and Ruby stood at one of them talking. He went over to see who she was talking to. Ruby was talking urgently into the mouthpiece, visibly agitated. She saw Chuck coming up on her, and quickly cut off the connection. She hung up the receiver clumsily.

"Who're you talking to?" Chuck questioned casually.

"Never mind," she growled.

"You're not trying to get Ronnie, are you?"

"No."

"Who?"

"None of your business."

"Well, let's get you to your next foster family."

Ruby nodded, picking up her knapsack. Chuck motioned for Ruby to go ahead of him, and Ruby led the way to his car.

When Chuck got back to his office after dropping Ruby off, he found messages on his desk from Ronnie's foster mom and from Mrs. Simpson, Ruby and Ronnie's mother. He sat down and opened Ruby's file up again. He called Ronnie's foster mom.

"Hi. It's Mr. Samuels."

"Oh. Thanks for calling me back. I thought I should let you know that Ruby's trying to talk to Ronnie again."

"I suspected as much," Chuck admitted. "Something is going on with Ruby, but I don't know what it is yet. I don't think she should be allowed to talk to Ronnie… but if this goes on for long, it might be the only way to find out what's on Ruby's mind."

"You don't think she's going to come here again, do you?"

"I don't think she will. Let me know if she shows up, though."

Ronnie's foster mom agreed. Chuck hung up and called Ruby's mother.

"Hi, Mrs. Simpson. Did you get a call from Ruby this morning?"

"What's this all about? Why is she calling here?"

"I'm not sure. I was hoping that you could tell me what it was about."

"I don't know. She wanted to know where Chloe was, and if she was okay. Why wouldn't Chloe be okay?" she demanded.

"I'm not sure what's going on with Ruby today, Mrs. Simpson. She asked to be taken out of her foster home. I think something has happened that worried her. Is that all Ruby asked?"

"Yes. That's all. She hung up suddenly."

"Ah. I interrupted her. Let me know if she calls you or shows up there again, okay?"

When he hung up, he pulled out Ronnie's file. He turned back to the back pages of the file, the reports on Ronnie's visit to the hospital. He read through it slowly, thoughtful. Chuck walked by his secretary's desk.

"I want to know if Chloe Simpson, Ruby's sister, has ever been taken to emergency. I'm going over to talk to the Winters."

She nodded.

"Okay."

Sitting in the living room, Chuck put the file on the coffee table and slid it across to Mrs. Winters.

"Let me tell you my thinking here. When Ruby came into foster care, we had no indication that she was abused. She never said anything to lead us to believe that she was leaving for any other reason than what she said. She said she felt trapped, closed in, restricted. She fought constantly with her mom. It wasn't until the hospital called us about Ronnie being admitted to emergency that we started to wonder. Both girls were the same age when they came to us. No-one in the family will admit that there is anything going on. This morning, when Ruby asked to be moved, she said that she felt closed in. I think something happened to remind her of her experience at home."

"And this?" Mrs. Winters indicated the file.

"I want you to read through the hospital and police reports of Ronnie's condition when we took her into foster care. I think that what happened to Ronnie happened to Ruby. And something happened last night that reminded Ruby of that. I want to know what connections you can make between these reports and what happened last night."

"You don't think that Ruby was assaulted last night?"

"I don't know. Don't get me wrong, I am not accusing you or your husband of anything. Whatever happened may have been before she even got back here."

Mrs. Winters opened up the file. She read through the file silently. She looked up after a few minutes, brows drawn down.

"Ronnie had alcohol in her blood."

Chuck nodded and didn't comment. That had jumped out at him too. Mrs. Winters looked back down at the file again. She frowned after a while.

"What does it mean that all forensic evidence had been eliminated?" she queried.

Chuck raised his eyebrows.

"She had a bath after she was assaulted. Cleaned up to eliminate any forensic evidence that would have proven it was her father."

Mrs. Winters pursed her lips.

"I gave Ruby a bath last night. She reeked of drink and vomit."

Chuck nodded and wrote it down.

"That's two things."

Mrs. Winters went reluctantly back to the file, not wanting to read any more. She sighed.

"All Ronnie was wearing was a nightgown."

"And Ruby?"

"I bought her some nightgowns when she came here. She usually just put on big t-shirts. Last night, after I bathed her, I put a nightie on her."

Chuck nodded.

"Okay. So those three things together—too much to drink, someone bathing her, and waking up in the morning in a nightgown—that was enough to remind her of what had happened to her at home. Enough to scare her off."

Mrs. Winters nodded.

"I think that's everything. I don't see anything else."

"Well, it's a start. I don't know if it will be enough to get one of the girls to talk about it, but it's a start. If they were that drunk at the time of the assaults—it at least explains why they are so confused."

Ruby was not going to like it at the Skinners. They had a full house, four other foster kids. Ruby was sharing a room with a seventeen year old. She left her knapsack on the bed and took advantage of the fact that Marilyn was at school and went through her drawers and closet. Then she went outside without telling Josie Skinner where she was going, and walked to the closest bus stop.

Ruby's timing was not good, arriving at the elementary school between recess and lunch. She walked around in the silent schoolyard for an hour before they let out. It was another half-hour before she spotted Ronnie. Ruby still wasn't used to those cutesy dresses and braids the foster family dressed her in. Ronnie looked surprised to see her.

"Ruby?"

"Yeah. How's it going, Ron'?"

Ronnie shrugged, looking around as if she expected someone to break them up. Ruby put her arm over Ronnie's shoulders and walked partway out to the soccer field with her.

"Ronnie... what happened at home?" she asked.

"What do you mean?"

"I don't remember much of what it was like. Did mom or dad—hurt you?"

Ronnie shook her head emphatically.

"What happened when you went to the hospital? It was somebody else that hurt you?"

Ronnie nodded.

"Uh-huh." Her voice was small.

"Your foster family doesn't do nothing to you, do they? They don't try to touch you or anything?" Ruby pressed.

"No. They're nice," Ronnie assured her.

Ruby breathed out slowly.

"Good. You gotta watch out, though. Sometimes folks who seem nice aren't really," she warned. "They're just waiting for a chance."

"Not my foster family. They really are nice."

"Okay." Ruby started to walk away, then turned back. "Ronnie—mom and dad never hurt Chloe neither, did they?"

Ronnie shook her head wordlessly.

"Okay. Good."

Ruby was aware that she had stepped off of the bus a couple of stops early, but her mind was whirling with uncertainty and doubt. She needed to walk, to breathe, and she wasn't concentrating on where she was going. Feelings had surfaced in her that she hadn't felt for years. Other than a couple of flashes of memory, the night before was a black hole, a complete blank. But what she did remember stirred up unwelcome and painful emotions. She couldn't sort through them.

Lost in thought, she didn't realize she was in the no-man's-land between the Jags' and the Terminators' territories. Before she knew what was happening, Troy had her arm twisted up behind her back, and his arm pulling hard around her throat. He jerked her head up towards him, grinning at her.

"Don't you know you shouldn't be walking in this part of the woods alone, little girl?"

Ruby tried to say something, but the words were stuck in her throat. She couldn't get her voice to work. He was pleased with her submissive reaction.

"You've been a good little girl, haven't you? You've helped me get right where I wanted to be." He chuckled. "You just remember how to keep your mouth shut, won't you?"

He slowly released his tight hold on her. He turned her around and pulled her close. He cupped the back of her head and kissed her hard. Ruby wanted to pull away from him, but was paralyzed. Her muscles were frozen. Her skin crawled when he touched her. She felt sick. Troy pressed her into the wall and continued to kiss and grope her. It seemed like eternity before he released her and backed off. He grinned at her, licked his lips, laughed, and walked away. Ruby hit the ground on her knees and threw up.

Chuck was sick and tired of hearing about Ruby when Merrill called.

"I want to ask Ruby Simpson some more questions. But her foster mom says she's been moved."

"I thought that stuff was all cleared up now," Chuck said in exasperation.

"We've run into some complications. Two of our suspects in the murder were killed yesterday."

Chuck shook his head.

"I don't believe it. I'll get you her new number, but she is probably at school."

"You yourself admitted she doesn't spend much time there. We already checked the school. She's not there."

Chuck opened Ruby's file again, muttering under his breath.

"I can't believe one kid could cause so much trouble in one day."

"Having some trouble with her today?" Merrill inquired.

"That's an understatement. Okay, here's the new number." Chuck read it off to Merrill.

"Thanks," Merrill said, writing it in his notepad.

Chuck hung up the phone, and his secretary hovered close by.

"Another call from Ronnie's foster mom," she informed Chuck when he looked up. "Something about Ruby showing up at the school."

Chuck swore.

"And you asked about Chloe Simpson's hospital records. She was admitted through emergency three years ago. Apparently she is allergic to wine."

Chuck stared at her.

"What's her date of birth?"

She looked down at the file in her hands, and calculated it mentally.

"She's eleven."

"She was eight when she was admitted."

"Yes."

"Was Ruby ever admitted before she came into foster care?"

"Nothing on her file. I'll have to check with the hospitals."

"Do that next," Chuck instructed.

"Sure."

Tim was looking off into the distance, thinking. He watched the girl huddled against the wall for a couple of minutes before he focused in and realized that it was Ruby. He cut his conversation short and jogged over to her.

"Ruby? What's the matter, Ruby? Are you hurt?"

He sat her up, looking for injuries. There was no blood. He pulled up her shirt, but there were no bruises or broken ribs.

"What's the matter, Ruby? Come on. Let's get you out of here before someone sees us."

He pulled her to her feet, and half-dragged her a few blocks away until they were on safe ground. Tim stopped and hugged her, holding her face in his shoulder.

"Settle down. It's okay, Ruby."

Ruby started to sob, her body shaking. Tim held her tightly, rubbing her back and stroking her hair. He murmured comfort to her. She eventually started to settle down.

"What happened?" Tim questioned when she was more relaxed and had stopped crying. Ruby shook her head in response. Tim took her back to the apartment.

"Are you going to be okay?"

Ruby looked around uncertainly. She saw that Tim had picked up her knapsack on the street, and took it from him.

"I have to shower," she said quietly, and she went to the bathroom.

She stripped down and stepped into the shower and turned the water on hot. She relaxed under the steam, withdrawing into herself and erasing all the memories. The shower door creaked open, and Ruby jumped. Tim smiled reassuringly.

"It's okay, relax. I thought you might like this."

He handed her a drink. Ruby took it, nodding.

"Thanks." She looked down at the liquid in the glass, at the drops from the shower hitting the surface, and giggled. Somehow she found it funny. She took a soothing drink. Pretty soon it would all be gone. She wouldn't remember anything. She would succeed in blocking it out.

Ruby spent the evening with the Jags. Mostly it was uneventful.

"Who's leader of the Terminators now that Slash is dead?" Ruby asked Tim.

"A hood called Troy. He's pretty twisted, but he'll keep a good grip on the gang."

Ruby nodded. She had feared as much. Not only had she gotten Laskin killed for his involvement in a murder he didn't commit, but she had rewarded the one who really did pull the trigger. She dreaded what would happen next.

RUBY, BETWEEN THE CRACKS

∽

Ruby went to school the next afternoon, but was distant and uninterested in both classes and friends. Marty asked her a few times what was wrong, and Kate pestered her to find out what she'd been doing. Ruby kept to herself and stared up at the boards blankly. Her mind was on so many other things, she couldn't even be bothered to laugh at Kate's desperate flirting with all of the boys. It just didn't interest her. After school, she went back to her foster home instead of going over to the high school to look for Brian or one of the other boys she knew.

Josie came up to Ruby's room a few minutes after she walked into the house.

"Where were you last night, Ruby?"

"I stayed over with a friend."

"You can't stay with friends on school nights. I expect you here after school, unless you call me to tell me where you are and get permission. And you'll have a curfew of nine o'clock. You have to be back here by then each night. Okay?"

"Okay," Ruby agreed with a shrug.

Josie looked awkward, having expected a fight. She didn't say anything for a moment.

"We're having dinner in an hour. Do you have homework?"

"No."

Josie nodded.

"Okay."

Josie went back downstairs. It wasn't until after dinner that Josie told her that Merrill and Banks were on their way to see her. Ruby tried to decide whether to leave, or stay and answer their questions. She decided she was too tired to bother taking off, and stuck around. Merrill and Banks showed up just at the time that Josie was giving directions as to who was to do the various evening chores. Ruby was excused to go talk to them.

"Have you remembered anything about the night Mike was shot?" Merrill questioned sarcastically.

Ruby shook her head.

"Figures. Well, we've had some interesting developments on Mike's murder. What do you think about that?"

Ruby shrugged.

"What do you think has happened?" he prodded.

"How do I know?"

"I think you know. You've been hanging around with the Jaguars lately."

"So?"

"What happened to the Terminators who killed Mike?"

Ruby suddenly knew what they were after her about. What they didn't know—couldn't possibly know—was that she had been there. Her face got hot.

"How do I know?"

"I think you know."

Ruby looked at him, keeping her eyes steady, and didn't say anything.

"Two of the Terminators we suspected of being involved in the murder have been killed."

"So?"

"Who did it?" he questioned.

What would he say if he realized he was talking to one of the shooters?

"How do I know?" Ruby shrugged.

"I think you know."

"I don't know anything about it."

"You've been hanging around with the Jags a lot. One of them must have said something to you."

In fact, they had said a lot. There had been little else discussed by the Jags the previous evening.

"No-one said anything to me," Ruby lied.

"Did you ever meet either of the boys who were killed?"

"No—I don't know who was killed."

"Oh, yeah. Well, I guess we'd better take you down to the morgue to find out if they were the boys who killed Mike."

Ruby gritted her teeth and looked around the living room, thinking it through. She couldn't very well argue it. She'd been there when Mike was killed. She said she didn't know what had happened to the boys. What could she say?

"I don't want to go."

"Well, it's not a fun job, but we need to know if we can close this case."

"You'll leave me alone if I go down there?"

Merrill nodded slowly.

"If you can identify that these boys were the ones who killed Mike, and fill in the details, we can close the file."

"I'll go, then," Ruby sighed in agreement.

"Good. Tell your mom, and we'll go."

"She's not my mom," Ruby reminded him. She got up and told Josie that she was going out with the officers. They took her out to the car, and Ruby sat uncomfortably in the back for the ride to the police station. They went into the room where two bodies were laid out under two tables under sheets. Ruby stood between the tables, making her face expressionless and looked straight ahead, waiting for them to show her the bodies.

Merrill pulled back both sheets to reveal their faces. Ruby stared at the faces without seeing them. She focused on the air a few inches above their faces.

"Is it them?" Merrill questioned.

Ruby nodded.

"Yeah. It's them."

He stared at her, and Ruby grew uncomfortable under his gaze.

"What?" she demanded.

"You told us you never saw their faces."

Ruby's mind whirled. It seemed like such a long time since she had talked to them. It seemed like another lifetime, before everything else had happened.

"I said I didn't remember anything," she told him. "Their faces jogged my memory."

"Their pictures didn't jog your memory."

"Then they must have been bad pictures," Ruby snapped. Merrill didn't argue it. They all stood around for a few minutes longer. "Well, you said if I identified them you would leave me alone."

"I know this has been hard on you," Merrill said gently, trying to meet her eyes.

"Tell that to Chuck," Ruby muttered, thinking about how he had dumped her when it all started.

"What?"

"I said tell it to my social worker."

Merrill nodded slowly.

"I'll let him know you've been helpful," he agreed.

Ruby shrugged.

"Can I go now?"

"I'll drive you home."

Ruby shook her head.

"No... I don't want to go back there."

"Where do you want to go, then?"

"I have a friend."

"Do you want us to drop you off?"

Ruby would have said yes, but the last time she had gone to Marty's she had been dropped off by a cop, and she didn't think she'd better make a habit of it.

"No. I'll take the bus."

"Is this another boyfriend?" Merrill questioned.

"That's not any of your business."

"It is if he's in a gang."

"It's not a boyfriend," Ruby said. "She's a girlfriend I stay with sometimes."

"Good. We probably won't see you again, so you take care of yourself."

Ruby nodded, and Merrill walked her out of the building.

When Marty opened the door and saw Ruby there, she was surprised at how pale and tired Ruby looked. She opened the door the rest of the way and held out her arms. Ruby stepped in and held onto Marty tightly. She didn't cry, didn't collapse, didn't do anything but stand there holding Marty. After a few minutes, Marty withdrew and reached around Ruby to pull the outside door shut. With one arm still around Ruby, she guided her friend into the bedroom. They sat down on the bed. Ruby stretched out on the bed face-down. Marty rubbed Ruby's back and stroked her long, fine hair.

"What happened, sweetie?" she questioned after a while.

"I don't know," Ruby said into the pillow. "I'm all mixed up."

"Did you sleep last night?"

"No."

"You look beat. And at school today... you sure you can't tell me what's wrong?" she coaxed.

"I don't know what's going on," Ruby mumbled through the pillow.

"Is it the Jags? What did they do?"

"No, not the Jags. Mrs. Winters."

"What did she do?" Marty prodded.

"I don't know. I can't remember anything."

"You remember something."

Ruby felt nauseous. She rolled over.

"There's some pills in my bag. I need them."

Marty went through the knapsack and took them out.

"Are you okay?"

Ruby nodded, taking one of them.

"I need a drink."

"I'll get you some water for that," Marty agreed.

"No, a drink."

"Pills and booze don't mix."

Ruby sighed. She lay there, waiting for the nausea to pass. Thinking about Mrs. Winters, but trying not to. Marty sat on the bed next to her, brushing Ruby's hair back from her face.

"Why don't you tell me what you remember," Marty suggested.

Ruby propped herself up onto her elbows, frowning.

"Marty... did you know me five years ago?"

"When you first went into foster care? I knew who you were. I didn't really get to know you right away."

"Did I ever say anything to you? About home?"

"You've never talked about home. All I know I've guessed."

Ruby looked at her and didn't say anything. Marty looked a little sad. She cocked her head to the side, looking into Ruby's eyes.

"You never talk about your dad," Marty elaborated. "But I guess whatever he did to you was pretty bad. Most nine-year-olds don't run into the arms of the first man they meet. You want comfort from anyone but people like my dad." Ruby didn't say anything, not quite believing what she was hearing. "Ruby, sleeping with these guys now is one thing," Marty said. "it's not good for you, and you'll only get hurt. But sleeping with them before you were ten? That means something."

"Why wouldn't I remember, if something happened?" Ruby challenged.

"I don't know. Because you didn't want to. You blocked it out. What did Mrs. Winters do?"

Ruby didn't answer the question directly.

"I don't remember fighting with my dad—just my mom," she said.

"Whatever he did—she had to have known. Maybe you were mad at her for ignoring what was going on."

Ruby thought about it.

"Why would she let anyone hurt me?" she questioned, brows drawn down in concentration.

"Ronnie got hurt, right?"

Ruby nodded. She'd mentioned it to Marty weeks before.

"Yeah, but she said it wasn't our dad."

"Who was it, then?"

"I don't know," Ruby shrugged. "She didn't tell me."

"Why not?"

Ruby swallowed.

"Because she didn't want him to get in trouble?" Marty suggested. "She knows who it is, right?"

"She knows who it is... but she said it isn't him."

"Then it's because she has feelings towards him, is afraid to tell anyone who it was."

"I need a drink," Ruby said, looking around.

"You just took a pill. You can't have a drink."

"I really need a drink," Ruby insisted, voice raised.

"You drink too much. It's not good for you."

Ruby got up and left the bedroom. She went to the liquor cabinet in the front room and poured a drink. Marty's mother happened to walk by her into the kitchen.

"Stay out of the liquor, Ruby," she said, without raising her voice.

"I really need a drink."

"There are better ways to deal with your problems. Come talk to me."

Ruby joined Marty's mom in the kitchen with a glass in her hand. Mrs. Rodger pointed to the table.

"Put it down and tell me why you need it so badly."

"If you don't believe in drinking, why do you have booze in the house?"

"That's not what we're here to discuss. Tell me what's going on, Ruby. What's the matter?"

Ruby sat down at the table and put her tumbler down. She stared at it.

"I don't know what happened... I was drunk."

"Well, that's a good reason not to get drunk again. What do you think happened?"

Ruby put her face in her hands, swearing.

"Something bad. Something bad happened. Something happened to Ronnie. And something happened to Chloe. And something happened..."

"To you?"

Ruby nodded. She rubbed her burning eyes with her fists.

"I need a shower. I can't think. I need to have a shower."

She stood up. Mrs. Rodger put her hand gently on Ruby's arm, stopping her.

"Ruby..."

"What?"

"If you've been hurt, you shouldn't have a shower. Not until you've been to the hospital."

Ruby looked up at Mrs. Rodger's face, and saw her concern.

"It's way too late for that," she said, and she went into the bathroom to shower.

Marty went into the kitchen and saw the drink still sitting on the table. She poured it down the sink.

"Do you think she's okay?" she asked her mother.

"Ruby's tough. She'll work her way through this eventually. She's staying the night?"

Marty looked at her watch.

"I think so."

"I'll call her foster mom."

Marty shook her head.

"No. She hurt Ruby. She's not going back there."

"I can't say I'm disappointed she's left. Things have been pretty disrupted since Ruby moved in there."

Marty shook her head.

"I can't believe Mrs. Winters could do anything to hurt her. You think you're safe with a foster mom."

Merrill watched Samuels' apartment building. He'd been there quite a while and hadn't seen anything. He hoped he wouldn't see anything. It was getting quite late when he saw Samuels pull into the underground parking in a white sports car. And there was a passenger in the car. Merrill called his partner and gave Samuels and his company lots of time to get up to the apartment and get settled in. Banks pulled up beside Merrill, and they went up to Samuels' unit together. Merrill knocked on the door. Samuels didn't answer. Merrill continued to knock, and eventually the door was opened, Samuels looking irritated. He was disconcerted to see Merrill and Banks there.

"Merrill? What's wrong? Is Ruby okay?"

"We have a warrant to search your apartment."

"Now?" The social worker went sheet white.

"Now, Mr. Samuels."

He didn't stop them from pushing their way into the apartment. Merrill looked around and headed for the bedroom. Samuels just stood there looking like he was going to faint. Merrill found Samuels' young lady friend lying on the bed in a man's housecoat. When Merrill walked in, her mouth dropped open, and she swore.

"Cops?" she questioned weakly.

"That's right, honey. You're going to have to get dressed again. How old are you?"

"Eighteen."

"Got any I.D.?"

She shook her head. Merrill picked up her purse.

"Is this yours?"

She nodded wordlessly.

"Can I take a look?"

She shrugged. Merrill found her I.D. inside. She was seventeen.

"Are you in foster care, Julie?" he questioned, looking over her I.D.

"Yeah."

"And Mr. Samuels is your social worker?"

"Yeah."

"How long have you been seeing him?"

She gathered the robe closer to herself.

"Not long... just a few times. He's on the rebound. Just broke up with his old girlfriend."

"Has he told you anything about Ruby?"

"No, not really. He misses her. But he doesn't really talk about her."

"How long were they together?"

She shrugged, shaking her head.

"I dunno. A couple years, I think."

"Do you know how old she was?"

Julie shook her head silently.

"She's thirteen now."

She stared at him, eyes wide.

"Thirteen?" she repeated.

"Thirteen. Also one of his wards."

"That's..." she couldn't find the appropriate words. Merrill nodded.

"Yeah. I'm going to need you to come down to the police station with us."

She motioned to her clothes. Merrill left her alone to get dressed. He nodded to Samuels.

"You're under arrest."

Samuels just stood there, eyes wide and horrified.

∼

Merrill splashed cold water on his face in the bathroom and went back to talk to Chuck, who had been booked on a number of charges and was looking very gray.

"I want to talk to you about the assault on Ruby after Mike was killed."

Chuck frowned.

"What would I know about that?"

"I am told you were there that night."

Chuck's jaw dropped.

"What?"

"We have witnesses that put you in the area," Merrill told him.

"I didn't get there until after the police had arrived!" Chuck insisted.

"What did you see?"

"Nothing. I saw the flashing lights, and I saw Ruby being loaded into the ambulance. I left."

"Why did you leave?"

"I didn't want to be seen in that neighborhood."

"I think Ruby was assaulted by someone she knew," Merrill told him.

"I never hurt Ruby!"

"I sure hope not."

"I would never do anything to harm her."

Merrill rolled his eyes, and Chuck shifted uncomfortably.

"Other than sleeping with her," Merrill amended.

Chuck put his face in his hands.

"And abusing a position of trust," Merrill reminded him.

"You don't know how it was," Chuck protested.

"Let me see if I can guess. She needed more attention than you could give her at work. You started meeting her after work. You got close. You realized she was so much more mature than her age. It just happened so naturally. It felt so natural."

Chuck shook his head, speechless. Merrill studied him, disgusted.

"How many other girls?" he questioned.

"Just Ruby."

"And Julie."

"Yeah. But... I knew it wouldn't work."

"You don't seem to realize how serious this is."

"I didn't pursue this. It was Ruby's idea, and she kept it going. I ended it when things got out of hand."

"When things got out of hand? How long did that take?"

Chuck looked uncertain. Merrill waited.

"A couple of months."

Merrill shook his head.

"Closer to a year, maybe," Chuck amended.

Merrill shook his head again. Chuck was silent.

"Ruby is very mature," he said finally, "and very pushy. She's manipulative and a flirt, and when she puts her mind to it…"

"You are an adult. She is not. It was your responsibility to make sure nothing happened."

"You don't understand what she's like."

"I understand she is a thirteen year old. And I understand that two years ago she was eleven. Eleven years old!"

Chuck put his face in his hands again.

"I know," his voice cracked and he started to sob.

Ruby stood under the shower spray for a long time. Until the water turned ice cold. She felt gross, like she was sweaty and grubby and she had to get clean. She stayed in the shower until the water was too cold to stand it anymore. She shut off the water and got out of the tub. Drying off, she rubbed her arms hard to warm up. Ruby wrapped the towel around herself and went to Marty's bedroom. Marty was busy doing homework. She looked at her watch as Ruby walked in.

"That was some shower," she said. "You'd better be sparkling clean now."

Ruby shrugged.

"Feeling better?" Marty questioned.

"A little."

"You'd better get some sleep tonight."

Ruby looked through Marty's closet for something to wear. She was shivering violently, her teeth almost chattering.

"You silly kid," Marty told Ruby, moving her out of the way. She pawed through the clothes on the shelf, "You'll catch cold." She handed Ruby a fuzzy fleece night-shirt, and kicked her slippers out of the closet. When Ruby had the night-shirt on, Marty handed her a housecoat. "There, wrap up. And go sit on the bed."

Ruby wrapped the housecoat around her and went over to the bed to snuggle under the warm blankets. Almost before she laid down, she was asleep.

For a while, things seemed to just sort of be in limbo. Ruby went to school and came home with Marty. She wasn't sure how much time passed, whether it was weeks or months. She couldn't face foster care, or Brian, or the Jags. She just felt like the world was too complex. Marty took care of her, made her comfortable and didn't push her to talk about it.

Eventually, though, Ruby started to feel like getting out again. She started to wonder what was happening with her old acquaintances. She went to find Brian at lunch one day. He hugged her and kissed her on the forehead, smiling broadly.

"What's up, Ruby? It's been ages since I saw you!"

"Yeah. I haven't been around much."

"Well, I hope that's going to change. I thought—maybe you were mad at me."

"Mad about what?" Ruby said blankly.

"When you were at the house before…"

Ruby thought back, and remembered the incident at Brian's house.

"Oh, that. I forgot." She shrugged.

"Good. I was worried you were upset about my mom…"

Ruby shrugged.

"Parents are like that. They think they gotta protect us."

Brian gave her a squeeze.

"You're so cool about it all. I was so mad at her for throwing you out like that! I still am."

"So why don't you leave?" Ruby questioned.

"I don't know. It's pretty easy where I am. You know—other than her not liking you."

"Is she home now?"

"No, she's at work."

"Let's go over there, then."

Brian shook his head.

"I have a test to write this afternoon. But another day."

"I guess."

"So what are you doing this afternoon—going back to school?" he questioned.

"No. I'll go find some friends."

Brian nodded. Ruby pulled away from him to leave.

"Ruby…"

"Uh-huh?"

"Not that gang, right?"

Ruby looked back at him.

"What if it is?"

"I just don't want you to get hurt."

"I won't."

She left Brian, and went to look for the Jags. She went by Tim's apartment to find him. Tim and some of the others were sprawled in front of the TV, engrossed in some afternoon soap. Ruby slammed the door shut behind her, and they jumped and looked around. Ruby grinned. Tim saw her and whooped.

"Ruby! Man, I thought you got busted or something. Where you been? You gonna stick around a while this time?"

Ruby laughed.

"For a while. What's new?"

"Hey, you don't know yet, do you…?" he said eagerly.

"Know what?"

"About the treaty with the Terminators."

Ruby felt sick.

"Treaty?" she repeated faintly.

"Yeah, it turns out that Jack and Troy were buddies years and years ago. They got together last week and decided that if we combined forces, we could wipe out all of the other gangs."

"No."

Tim shrugged.

"We've all gotten used to the idea by now. I wasn't too keen on it myself to begin with, but… it makes us stronger."

"Not the Terminators," she protested.

"As good as any."

Ruby shook her head.

"I can't believe it."

"It's stupid," Harlan agreed explosively. "We're Jags, not filthy Termites!"

"Shut up, you idiot!" one of the others snapped. "You don't know what you're talking about."

"You may all be scared of Jack," Harlan blustered, "but I'm not! It ain't right for Jags to join up with that trash."

Ruby nodded.

"Yeah, that's right."

Tim glared at her.

"You don't know what you're saying, Ruby. Just keep your mouth shut. Got it?"

Ruby was surprised at the anger in his eyes. And the fear. She looked around at the other boys. They all were nervous about her and Harlan's vocal protests.

"Keep your mouth shut," Tim repeated warningly.

Harlan took Ruby's arm.

"Let's get out of here, Ruby."

Ruby hesitated, and then nodded. They left the others at the apartment. Harlan was fuming.

"At least someone else sees how stupid this is! The rest of them are just too scared to stand up for themselves!"

"So what are you going to do?"

He looked irritated.

"I don't know. All I know is, I'm not joining up with any Terminators."

"So why don't the others just refuse too?" Ruby questioned.

He looked at her.

"Because it's treason. And there's only one sentence for treason."

Ruby looked at Harlan blankly.

"You go against Jack," Harlan said baldly. "You're looking to get killed."

No wonder Tim had told Ruby to keep her mouth shut. She stared at Harlan.

"So we're not going back to the Jags."

"That would be suicide. Nope, we're on our own now, with Jack's order out on us."

Ruby shook her head.

"We're gonna get killed."

"If we're not careful."

"How can we not get killed?" her voice rose. "How are we going to protect ourselves?"

"I got a piece. We'll figure something out."

"Where are we going to stay tonight?" Ruby demanded, irritated with him for having no plan.

"We?" he questioned. "Yeah, I guess we gotta find somewhere to hang out for a few days, until we figure out which way the wind is going to blow."

"And then what?"

"It depends on what the gang decides they're gonna do. They may come over with us."

"Where do we go tonight?"

Harlan shrugged.

"We'll go to a motel or shelter or something, until we decide what to do."

That night, Ruby stayed with Harlan. But she found him too rough for her liking. She woke up early in the morning, stiff and aching all over. Ruby slipped out of bed as slowly and quietly as she could to avoid disturbing Harlan. He didn't even stir. She sneaked into the bathroom and looked at herself in the scratched mirror. She had a black eye that certainly wasn't going to be disguised by a little foundation. She was going to bear the marks of their late-night activities for some time. As quickly as Ruby could, she pulled on the rest of her clothes. She picked up her shoes and tiptoed out of the suite barefoot. She didn't bother to shut the door tightly behind her. She slipped on her shoes when she got out into the hallway.

She was a few steps away from the lobby of the motel when she heard the gunshot. She saw the desk clerk drop behind his desk, and Ruby flattened herself against the wall, not breathing. No-one came through the lobby. There was no movement. Eventually, the desk clerk stood up slowly, looking around. Ruby watched him without stirring. He picked up the phone and dialed, whispered into the receiver, and then hung up. Looking around, he saw Ruby standing there. Ruby peeled herself away from the wall and took a deep breath. She nodded at the desk clerk and slunk out of the lobby.

CHAPTER
Ten

Ruby had gone the only place she could think of. Back to Marty's. She awoke the next day to Marty staring at her. Ruby withdrew slightly.

"What?" she questioned.

Marty reached out and touched Ruby's bare stomach. Her nightshirt was riding up from moving around in her sleep. Ruby stared at Marty, trying to read the expression on her face. Marty seemed stunned. Ruby touched her belly self-consciously and pushed Marty's hand away.

"Stop it—what's wrong?"

"Ruby… are you pregnant?"

Ruby pulled her shirt down with both hands to cover her stomach. Marty put her hand flat on Ruby's stomach. Ruby pulled away. Marty wouldn't let her back away.

"Ruby, I can feel the baby move! How far along are you?"

"I'm not pregnant." Ruby tried again to push Marty's hand away. "Leave me alone. It's just gas."

"You think I'm stupid? Ruby, I thought you protected yourself," Marty accused.

"I do. I told you I'm not pregnant," Ruby said firmly.

"I think we should take you to a doctor."

"I've seen a doctor."

"What did he say? Why didn't you tell me about this?"

"He said… it's indigestion."

"When are you due, Ruby?" Marty persisted.

"I'm not."

Ruby climbed out of the bed, angry with Marty. She went into the bathroom and turned on the shower before using the toilet and stripping down. She climbed into the shower and closed her eyes. Ruby massaged her body with both hands. She stopped and opened her eyes with her hands both on her stomach. She looked down, feeling her belly with both hands. Then she closed her eyes again, letting the steam rise around her and the warm water run through her hair and over her face.

Marty went into her mother's room and sat down on the edge of the bed. Her mother stirred and awakened. She rolled over to look at Marty.

"Morning, sweetie."

Marty didn't say anything right away.

"What's up?" her mother questioned softly.

"I think Ruby's pregnant."

"Oh, no."

Marty nodded.

"Did she tell you?"

"No, she said she's not. But… she's showing. And I could feel the baby move."

"She's quite a ways along, then. Maybe we should call her social worker."

Marty shook her head.

"I don't think that's a good idea."

"What is she going to do, then?"

"I don't know. We'll have to wait and see."

The shower went off, and Marty got up.

"I don't even know how to talk to her about it, when she denies that she's even pregnant."

"We'll figure something out. Maybe she just needs some time to get used to the idea."

"After this long, I don't think she's going to get used to it."

Ruby applied foundation around her still-black eye, wondering whether she should go back to the Jags again. She was scared to death that what had happened to Harlan would happen to her. And if it didn't, she'd be going back to a gang composed of Jags and Terminators. Jack and Troy. Jack she could face, if he decided to let her off the hook. But Troy—she couldn't face him. She didn't know what to do about it. But the longer she left it—it wasn't going to get any better. Her stomach writhed with nausea.

Marty and her mom were quiet for breakfast. Not unusual. They talked if they had something to say, and if they didn't, they were comfortable with silence. Ruby had a quick glass of juice and piece of toast, and picked up her bag.

"Coming to school?" Marty suggested.

"No, I gotta go see someone."

Marty nodded and didn't pursue it. It seemed to Ruby that Marty had something else on her mind.

She was afraid that Jack would be out with some of the other boys already. But she didn't need to worry; he was still at his apartment. She knocked quietly on the door, and he opened it, and then leaned against the door frame with his elbow, looking at her.

"Well, well, well. Look what we've got here."

Ruby didn't say anything, biting her lip and shifting her knapsack uncertainly. He stood there studying her.

"What made you come back here?" he questioned.

Ruby hesitated.

"I didn't know what else to do."

"Well, you were stupid to come here," he growled.

Ruby shifted back and forth.

"What am I going to do, run away?"

"That's one thought."

"I made a mistake."

"Yeah."

"Are you going to let me in?"

Jack looked at her for a minute, then opened the door the rest of the way to let her in. Ruby walked in, and when he shut the door again, she saw the gun in his other hand. It had been behind the door where she couldn't see it. Ruby was shaken. She sat down quickly at his table, her knees weak.

"What are you going to do?" she questioned.

"I don't know yet. I can't figure out why you're here."

"I didn't want you to think… that I was against you."

"You've changed your mind?"

"I was never against you."

"You voiced your opinion quite clearly. I've heard it from several sources."

Jack straddled a chair backward and sat looking at her.

"I was taken off guard," Ruby said. "I wasn't around when this was going on."

"Doesn't matter."

Ruby tried to explain.

"I'm not against the Jags and Terminators getting together."

Jack frowned, looking at her. He fiddled with the gun, tapping it on the table next to him.

"It's not the Terminators. It's not you."

He waited for her to finish. Ruby couldn't go any further. The words stuck in her throat.

"It's Troy," Jack said, finally getting it.

Ruby closed her eyes. She saw Troy's face in front of her. She opened her eyes again. Jack had leaned in closer to her.

"You don't like slimy little Troy, is that it?"

She shrugged. Jack laughed.

"You ought to learn when to talk and when to keep your mouth shut," he advised.

"I was stupid... I didn't listen to Tim when he told me to shut up."

"You're new at this. When you're new, you listen, or you don't survive."

Ruby nodded.

"You don't have to love Troy," Jack told her, "but you're gonna have to put up with having him around for a while."

"I will," she agreed.

"You don't have a choice. I'm telling you you will, or you won't be around."

Ruby nodded. She knew. She understood now. She would do as she was told. Jack was sliding his gun back into his waistband. The door opened and Troy walked boldly in. Jack had the gun half out again, and then saw who it was.

"You're lookin' to get plugged, Troy!" he growled.

Troy glanced around the apartment idly and saw Ruby.

"Well, look who's here. Hi, sweet thing."

Ruby swallowed, her stomach gurgling and lurching. She sat there frozen as Troy approached her. He cupped her face with one hand, stroking her fine blond hair with the other. He moved in close, holding her tighter.

"Back off," Jack ordered.

Troy looked at Jack, raising his eyebrows questioningly.

"Keep your paws off of Ruby," Jack warned.

"What, you like this pretty young thing for yourself? I've never known you to be partial to little kids."

"You're sick, you know that? And if I tell you to keep your paws off, you keep your paws off. I don't need to give you a reason."

Troy smirked, and winked at Ruby as if they shared a special secret. He released her slowly, but didn't let her go completely before brashly kissing her on the lips. Then he pushed her away from himself, grinning at his own private joke. Jack felt anger rising in his chest, just barely under control. He couldn't do much about Troy's behavior, because if he did the Terminators would split off again. But seeing Troy scorn his warning like that made him furious. Ruby's face was pinched and white, and she looked like she was going to fall off her seat or faint dead away. She was more afraid of Troy's approach than she'd been when she saw Jack's gun pointed at her. No wonder she'd been so upset about hearing of the alliance between the Jags and the Terminators.

"Ruby, get lost. Troy and I got to make some plans."

Ruby nodded quickly, and got up. She made her way unsteadily to the door, and was gone. Troy grinned at Jack, nodding.

"She's a fresh little bundle, isn't she?"

When Ruby walked in, Tim's mouth dropped open, and he stared at her as if he'd seen a ghost.

"What's wrong?" she questioned.

"Ruby?"

"Yeah... why are you so surprised?"

He reached out hesitantly and touched her. He ran his hand along her arm, and then touched her face disbelievingly.

"I thought you were dead."

In a flash, Ruby understood. Harlan had been shot. She was with him. Things had been taken care of... everybody had assumed that she'd been killed too. Ruby shook her head.

"No... I wasn't there. I'm okay."

"Are you... does Jack know...?" he stammered.

"I just came from there. It's okay."

"Are you sure?"

Ruby nodded.

"I should have listened to you," she said quietly, without meeting his eyes.

"Darn right you should have," Tim agreed. He embraced her and pulled her close, his breaths shallow and quavering slightly. "I thought I'd lost you for good," he whispered, pressing his face into her hair. Ruby snuggled up close to him, feeling warm and safe.

"Mmm, don't let go," Ruby murmured.

"I won't."

Merrill motioned for the other officer to sit down. Coates looked a little uncomfortable.

"As you know, I'm handling the Samuels case."

"Sure. How can I help you?"

"We've reached the point where we need to talk to Ruby Simpson about what went on."

"You haven't talked to her before now?" Merrill said, surprised. "You've had the case for months."

"No, we didn't really get to that point in our investigation until now. But we've run into some problems."

"What problems?"

"Ruby's disappeared."

"I can see how that might be a problem. She's not with her foster family?"

"Hasn't been since Samuels was arrested."

Merrill nodded thoughtfully.

"I was hoping that you'd be able to tell us where Ruby hung out," Coates suggested.

"Have you checked out the school?"

"It's been weeks since she showed up for a class."

"I gather she hasn't been too big on school," Merrill agreed.

"So can you help me? Know where she might be?"

Merrill got up and went to his files.

"We had her under surveillance for quite a while..." He pulled out a folder and flipped through it. "I can give you the addresses that she spent time at regularly."

"That would be great."

Brian opened the door, and his stomach tightened when he saw the uniformed officer.

"Yes?"

"I'm looking for Ruby Simpson."

Brian shook his head.

"She's not here."

"Can you tell me when the last time you saw her was?"

Brian considered it.

"I don't know. It's been a long time. A couple months."

"Can you tell me where I might find her?"

"I don't know. I think she's been staying with Marty. Or the gang. I don't know for sure. She hasn't been around."

"Marty? Do you have his address?"

"Her. Her address. No, I don't."

"And the gang?"

"I don't know which one, or where she would be staying if she was with them. Sorry. I haven't seen her for a long time."

"Okay. Thanks for your help."

Coates rang the doorbell, and waited. After a few minutes, a young woman with wildly curly hair answered the door. The smells of tomato sauce and garlic wafted through the open door. She looked at him and raised her eyebrows.

"I'm looking for Ruby Simpson," he told her.

"I'll get her. What's up?"

"I just want to talk to her."

She motioned for Coates to come in, and he sat down on the couch.

"You're Marty?" Coates questioned.

"Yeah."

Marty went to the back of the house. A few minutes later, Ruby came out. She glanced down at Coates.

"Hi."

Coates surveyed Ruby thoughtfully, frowning at her slightly bulging tummy.

"Hi, Ruby. I've had an interesting time trying to track you down."

"What do you want?"

"I want to talk to you about your former social worker, Charles Samuels."

"*Former* social worker?"

Coates heard the emphasis on "former".

"You weren't aware that Samuels was arrested?"

"Arrested?" Ruby's voice was surprised. "For what?"

"For—er—his involvement with you."

Ruby shrugged.

"I never charged him."

"You didn't have to. You're a minor under government care."

Ruby motioned him into the living room, and slid into the easy chair, stiffly putting her feet up. Coates sat across from her.

"So what do you need me for?" Ruby questioned.

"I need to hear your side of the story."

"What's to tell?"

"You're pregnant?" Coates observed.

Ruby glared at him.

"No."

"Is Samuels the father?"

"What are you talking about?"

Coates frowned. He tried to proceed like Ruby wasn't pregnant.

"How long were you and Samuels involved?"

"I don't remember. A couple years, I guess."

"How old were you when it started?"

Ruby grinned.

"Chuck's been my social worker from the time I first went into foster care. I was eight then."

"But how old were you when the two of you... started keeping company?"

She shrugged, pursing her lips.

"Uhh... ten or eleven."

"Can you tell me who initiated it?"

"Who initiated it?" Ruby repeated. "Who cares? We spent some nights together. We started sleeping together. It's not like he tied me to the bedposts or something!"

"Why were you spending nights with him?"

"Because he was cute," she laughed.

"Did Samuels realize how serious it was? Did you?"

"He knew he'd get in trouble if anyone found out. He knew he'd lose his job."

"He's going to do more than lose his job. Didn't you realize he would go to jail for what he was doing?"

Ruby shook her head.

"He didn't force me to do anything. I wanted to sleep with him."

"It's still against the law."

"But there's nothing wrong with it."

Coates was taken aback. He felt his face get hot and fumbled for a reply.

"Nothing wrong with it? There certainly is something wrong with it! What Samuels did was completely wrong and immoral!"

Ruby shook her head.

"I didn't do anything wrong."

"No, you didn't. Samuels did."

She laughed in disbelief.

"Chuck did something wrong, but I didn't? Sort of hard when we were both doing the same thing!"

Ruby sat there, shaking her head. Coates was at a loss to get through to her.

"Do you know of any other girls that Samuels was seeing?"

"No. If he was seeing someone else, he was careful not to let on."

"We have evidence that he was also seeing other girls under his supervision."

"I wondered sometimes. Well, I don't know any other foster kids under him. Other than Ronnie."

"Ronnie is…?"

"My sister. But he wouldn't…" Ruby stopped, cutting herself off. She paled. "If Chuck laid a finger on Ronnie, I'll kill him!"

"How old is Ronnie?"

"She's eight."

"Well, we're dealing with each of Samuel's files individually. I'll make sure we put Ronnie near the top of the list."

"She won't talk to you. She's too shy."

"I'll have a woman officer talk to her, if you think it would help."

Ruby sighed.

"I don't know. I don't think she'll talk to anyone."

"Why not?"

"Ronnie doesn't talk to people. She keeps it inside."

"Which do you do? Talk it out or keep it inside?"

Ruby shrugged.

"I don't know… I just try to forget about it, I guess."

"Is that why you don't want to talk about Samuels?" Coates suggested.

"I talked to you about him. He dumped me ages ago, why should I care about him anymore?"

"How long ago did you break up?"

Ruby rolled her eyes, counting on her fingers. She counted it out three times before answering.

"I think seven months ago or something. Winter... it was cold out. Maybe February or something."

"And you're due when?"

"I told you I'm not pregnant," she repeated firmly.

Coates decided to terminate the interview.

"I'm going to get back to you with some more questions after we've progressed in our investigation a little more."

Ruby shrugged.

"You'll be staying here?"

"Yeah, probably. Mostly."

"Maybe I could get the address and phone number from your friend," Coates suggested, hoping for an opportunity to talk to Marty privately for a moment. Ruby rattled off the phone number.

"And you've already got the address," Ruby pointed out.

"I guess I do."

"What was all that about?" Marty questioned after Coates was gone.

"Nothing. Some stuff about my social worker." Ruby shrugged.

"Is everything all right?"

"I guess." Ruby went over to the liquor cabinet, and moved around several empty decanters. "I need a drink. Where's the booze?"

"You know you can't drink right now, Ruby," Marty said.

"I just want a small drink. There's nothing wrong with that."

"We've gone through this before."

Ruby glanced at Marty, shaking her head.

"I'm going out, then."

"You can't buy alcohol."

"Someone will buy for me," Ruby said with assurance.

"I really don't think you should, Ruby," Marty said firmly.

Ruby shrugged.

"I'll be back later."

Ruby slipped on a pair of sandals and walked out. Marty shook her head. She turned to go do her homework, and saw her father standing in the doorway of his bedroom.

"What?" Marty demanded.

"How long is she going to stay here?"

"Ruby lives here. She'll stay here as long as she likes."

"What are you going to do when she has the baby?"

"Just stay out of it, all right? Mom and I will take care of things."

"Babies cost money," he growled.

"Babies get government benefits, too."

He looked thoughtful.

"Yeah, they do, don't they?" he mused.

Ruby hung around the bar, looking for someone safe to talk to. A young man or woman just old enough to drink. No-one too tough. No-one who looked dangerous, but on the other hand someone who would not question her about her decision to drink, lecture her, or call Social Services on her. A couple of young men headed towards her, and Ruby looked at them for a moment before realizing that one of them was Tim. She turned quickly to walk off, but he had already noticed her. It had been quite a while since Ruby had seen him or any of the other Jags.

"Ruby! Hey, where are you going, come here!" Tim called, grinning.

Ruby turned reluctantly.

"Oh... Hi, Tim."

"Ruby, I don't get you! You'll be around for a while and then you disappear for weeks! Where have you been?"

Ruby shrugged.

"I... just haven't been feeling so good lately. Got some bug or something..."

She avoided his eyes, looking around as if she had somewhere else to go. Tim was staring at her intently. He took her by the arm.

"Let's go in, huh? We'll have a drink..."

"The bouncers..."

"Oh, they'll let you in with us. Come on."

He guided her towards the door. Ruby let him take her in. She had come looking for a drink, after all. They found a table and ordered a round of drinks. Tim's friend was impatient with them.

"So are you going to introduce us, man?"

"Oh, yeah. Rich, this is Ruby. She hangs around with the Jags sometimes. Rich is one of the old Terminators."

"Oh, you're *the* Ruby?" Rich questioned, with the emphasis on "the". Ruby shrugged. So they'd been talking about her behind her back. And who knows what they'd said about her.

Tim was unusually quiet. They had a few beers, and Rich got up to put the moves on a chick up at the bar. Tim moved closer to Ruby, putting his arm around her and nuzzling her hair.

"Uh, Ruby...?" he said softly.

"What."

"This—er—'bug' you've got... is everything okay?"

"Yeah, fine."

"Are you sure? I mean, if you need anything... I'll take care of it."

"Nothing you can do," Ruby said.

"Are you sure? 'cause really, I'll help you with whatever you need. Really."

"I don't need anything."

"Okay. I won't bug you about it, then. I just... you know, I look after my own."

Marty roused herself to Ruby's knocking on the door. She got up and opened the door. Ruby had problems getting both feet up the half-step into the house. Marty steadied Ruby and helped guide her in. Once into the house, Ruby walked pretty steadily, not like she was drunk. But the smell of alcohol was definitely on her breath.

"How much did you have to drink?" Marty questioned.

"I had a couple beers. Maybe three. That's all."

Marty listened to her words carefully. But there was no slurring.

"I'm just clumsy," Ruby told her, discerning her thoughts, "I don't know why—I just keep running into things and dropping things lately."

Marty yawned.

"I think that's pretty normal. Come on. Let's get to bed."

Ruby nodded. She followed Marty to the bedroom and sat down to undress. She held her stomach, wincing.

"You okay, Ruby?"

"Yeah. The beer must have bothered my stomach..."

"I told you not to drink."

"Yeah, I should have listened to you," Ruby agreed.

Marty nodded.

"Climb in."

Ruby slipped in and cuddled up with Marty. She was asleep in minutes. Marty lay awake, having trouble settling down again after being awakened so abruptly. Ruby's breathing was slow and even. Marty started to relax and drift off, though still partly aware of her surroundings. She was aware that Ruby was moving around every now and then, but Marty stayed in a dozy state of sleep for what seemed like a long time. Then she managed to rouse herself. Ruby was curled up in a ball, her face slick with sweat. She was pale as a ghost. Marty sat up quickly and touched Ruby.

"Ruby? Ruby, are you okay?"

Ruby's fists were both pressed against her stomach, and she opened her eyes, looking up at Marty with a frightened expression.

"It hurts…"

"It's okay. It's okay. How long has it been hurting?"

Marty shifted for a more comfortable position and landed on wet sheets. She gasped and took Ruby's hand.

"It's okay. How far apart are the pains?" she questioned.

"They don't go away…"

"Oh, no. I'll be right back, I just have to see if mom's home."

Marty dashed down the hallway and shook her mom awake.

"It's Ruby."

"Uh-oh. Let me get dressed, and we'll go. You'd better get something on too."

"Okay. I think—I think she's pretty far along. She said the pain doesn't stop."

"For some people it doesn't."

"Okay. Hurry."

Marty ran back to Ruby's side.

"It's okay, honey," she comforted, holding Ruby's hand briefly.

"Why won't it stop?" Ruby moaned.

"It's okay. Hang on while I dress. Just be a second."

Ruby groaned, pushing her hands into her stomach. Marty quickly pulled on a pair of pants and some shoes. She sat down on the edge of the bed, stroking Ruby's hair. Tears sprang up in Ruby's eyes. She didn't speak any more, just laid there curled up, quietly sobbing.

"It's okay. It's all right…"

Marty's mother came in, with her jacket on.

"Okay, Ruby. Let's see how you're doing."

She bent over Ruby, looking at her face and putting a hand gently on her stomach. She turned and looked at Marty, who was watching anxiously.

"Why don't you call an ambulance," she suggested calmly.

"Okay."

Marty left. Mrs. Rodger pulled back the sheets and pulled up Ruby's night-shirt. She shifted Ruby's position slightly.

"Why don't you move a bit, Ruby. Here, like this."

Ruby moved uncomfortably, letting Mrs. Rodger guide her into the new position.

"There, now you've got it. Now take a deep breath. No, nice and deep. There, that's good. Relax some more. It'll be okay. Nothing to it."

She held Ruby's hand, encouraging her quietly. Marty was engaged in talking to the 911 operator until the ambulance got there. Standing by the phone, trying to keep herself calm and answer the operator's questions clearly, she heard a high, thin cry from the bedroom. The receiver dropped from her hand and she ran into the room. Her mom looked up.

"I guess this makes you an auntie," she said.

Marty stared down at the wet, red baby in amazement.

"It's so little," she breathed.

"She. And yes, she is. Too tiny yet. The ambulance is on the way?"

"Yes. Oh, I left the phone." Ruby ran back out to the kitchen and picked up the dangling receiver. "It's a girl," she announced, "and she's really tiny."

"The ambulance is almost there," the operator reassured her. "Hang in there. Is the baby breathing?"

"Yes."

"Someone will be right there. Why don't you go turn on the porch light and open the front door."

"Okay. Just a minute."

Marty did as she was instructed. She popped back in to check on her new charge. Ruby laid motionlessly on her back, her eyes shut. She seemed totally uninterested in the new baby. They were quiet, waiting for the ambulance. Marty brought the medics into the room, and they wrapped the baby up and took Ruby out to where they had a stretcher waiting. Ruby just kept her eyes closed and didn't move.

Ruby was a little shaky, but happy to be out again and free to go wherever she liked. She had been staying inside for what seemed like a long time, but now she could go wherever she liked, see whoever she pleased. And the first stop was by the school to see if she could find Brian. She hung around the school at lunchtime, and didn't see him until he came back from his house. He saw her, and stopped. Ruby went up to him, wondering why he didn't come over to greet her.

"Ruby," he greeted lowly.

"Hi."

"I didn't expect to see you here."

"Why not?" she smiled at him, lowering her eyelids flirtatiously.

"Well, because... Marty told me..." Brian trailed off.

"Marty told you what?"

"She asked me if the baby was mine."

"Why would it be yours?" Ruby questioned carelessly.

"Well, because... but you and me always used..." he looked uncomfortable and didn't finish.

Ruby shrugged.

"So why're you worried?" she prompted.

"Well, it's just that... sometimes... stuff happens."

"So don't worry about it."

Brian looked relieved. He breathed out a pent-up breath.

"Good. My mom would kill me..."

"Yeah, no kidding," Ruby agreed. Brian sighed.

"Good," he repeated.

"So you want to do something?" Ruby questioned.

"Uh... yeah, I guess. What do you want to do? Arcade?"

"No. I don't want to run into the gang yet."

"Oh, I guess not. Go watch a video?"

"Sure."

Brian tentatively put his arm out for her, and Ruby took it and walked beside him.

It had been a long time since Ruby had passed the time with Brian, and she enjoyed it. He was good for her, kind and gentle with her and pretty much obeyed the law; not like the Jags. She didn't mind the Jags so much when she really needed company, but an afternoon with Brian was like a refreshing drink of water.

They watched a couple of movies together and made popcorn. There were a few beers in the fridge, which they shared between them. After a while, they turned the TV off and, lounging side by side on the floor in front of the couch, cuddled and held each other, just enjoying being together again.

"I forgot how much I like this," Brian sighed.

"Yeah. Been too long. I like to be held."

He tightened his grip on her and stroked her cheek.

"You're so pretty, Ruby. I wish we could be together all the time, like this."

"Me too."

Ruby was back to Marty's in time for supper. Ruby left Brian's before his mother could get home. Neither of them wanted another scene with Brian's mom. Marty was stretched out in bed feeding the baby her bottle. Ruby looked around.

"What's for supper?" she questioned.

"Whatever you make," Marty sighed. "There's leftovers in the fridge, or you could make some spaghetti or something."

"I thought you said you were going to make supper."

"I was. But Stella's been fussy all day and I haven't had a chance to get anything started. If you want something, you make it."

"What do you want me to make you?"

Marty looked up at Ruby, her expression softening.

"Anything you feel like making, sweetie. I'll eat anything I don't have to make."

"Okay. Your mom home for supper?"

"No, I don't think so. Make a little extra and put it in the fridge in case she hasn't eaten when she gets home."

"Okay," Ruby agreed.

"And Ruby?"

"Yeah?"

"Could you mix a couple more bottles for Stella and put them in the fridge?"

Ruby frowned, considering.

"I dunno... how do I make them?"

"Read the instructions on the side of the can. Follow it exactly."

"Okay."

Ruby went back into the kitchen and started on macaroni and cheese. While the pasta was boiling, she picked up the can of dry formula and looked at the instructions. She went back into the bedroom, where Marty was lying down watching the baby sleep.

"Marty...?"

"Uh-huh?"

"Can you tell me the instructions?"

"You can read them," Marty encouraged.

"Yeah, but I don't understand them."

"Hand it to me."

Marty read the instructions aloud to Ruby. Ruby listened to her, and nodded.

"Okay. I get it."

"Make it just like it says."

"I will."

Ruby mixed the bottles carefully and put them in the fridge. After draining the pasta and adding the milk and cheese packet, she cut some tomatoes into the macaroni the way Marty liked it, and let it simmer a while longer. She filled a bowl for Marty and took it in to her. Marty smiled tiredly.

"Thanks. That's perfect. Will you put Stella in her crib?"

Ruby looked down at the tiny baby, and shook her head.

"No, I'll drop it."

"Her, she's a girl. Your daughter."

"I'll hurt her."

"I'll show you how to do it. You won't hurt her or drop her."

"No. I don't want to," Ruby insisted, backing away.

"Come on."

"No. I don't want to touch it."

Marty got up gently and slowly so as not to disturb the baby, and shook her head.

"You have to admit it sooner or later, Ruby."

"I don't want to pick her up."

"I need your help now and then."

"I did. I made supper for you."

Marty put the baby into her crib, and took the bowl from Ruby.

"Thanks. It looks great."

Ruby nodded and went to the kitchen to get her own. She put a few spoons full in the bowl, and went to talk to Marty while she ate.

"You need to eat more than that," Marty told her, looking at the bowl.

Ruby put her hand over her stomach, frowning.

"I have to lose this weight. It's gross."

"You'd lose it in a minute if you nursed Stella. Even if you won't, though, you'll lose it on your own. You don't look fat."

"I do too."

"You look just great. No-one would guess you had a baby a few weeks ago."

Ruby turned her head away.

"I didn't."

Chuck opened the door and saw Coates. He looked slightly embarrassed, dropping his eyes.

"Hi. Come in."

Coates nodded and entered.

"How have you been managing?" Coates questioned neutrally.

"Pretty good... considering the way people look at me now."

"Uh-huh. Well, you'll be happy to know that you have a healthy little girl."

"What?" Chuck said blankly.

"Your little girl..."

"You mean Ruby?"

"I mean Ruby's baby."

Chuck stared at Coates.

"Ruby's baby?" he repeated.

"I take it she didn't tell you she was pregnant?"

"No... she didn't tell me that."

"I take it she's been pretty quiet about the whole thing. I thought she might have called you about it, though."

"It can't be my baby... did she tell you it was my baby? Did she tell you I got her pregnant?"

"No, but the timing's about right. And you can't exactly convince me that the two of you weren't involved."

"Ruby always uses birth control."

"Birth control isn't one hundred percent effective," Coates pointed out.

"Did she tell you the baby was mine?" Chuck questioned.

"She told me she wasn't pregnant."

"I wasn't the only one she was seeing, you know."

"Well, you're the only one we know about. Can you tell me who else she was seeing?"

"She had a few friends... What about the boy who was murdered? What about him?"

"When was that? Shortly before the two of you broke up?"

"Yes. If it could have been me, it could have been him."

"Well, I guess when the time is right, we'll have to run some paternity tests."

"Ruby wouldn't—"

"Ruby doesn't have to. She's a ward of the state. You know that."

"It couldn't be my baby," Chuck maintained.

Coates shook his head.
"Right."

Marty got up to feed and try to settle Stella again. Ruby moved around, then sat up sleepily as Marty sat down on the bed with the baby.

"Why does it have to cry so much?" she said irritably.

Marty scowled.

"Because you drank when you were pregnant. She has plenty of problems because you couldn't stop drinking for a few months."

Ruby lay down again.

"She's ugly, too. I thought babies were supposed to be cute."

Marty cuddled Stella close while she gave her a bottle.

"She's not ugly. Maybe she looks like her daddy."

She waited, but Ruby didn't give her any clue as to the baby's parentage.

"Why did you tell Brian he was her daddy?" Ruby demanded.

"I didn't tell him he was. I asked him if he was. You won't tell me."

"Well, you didn't need to tell Brian that."

"I didn't tell him anything. Stella deserves to at least have one of her parents admit that she exists."

Ruby turned over and closed her eyes, trying to go back to sleep. A long time later, when she was close to sleep, Marty had put Stella back in the crib and cuddled up to Ruby to sleep. Ruby sighed.

"Marty...?"

"Umm?"

"We're best friends, right?"

"Sure."

Ruby hugged Marty.

"Is that all we are?"

Marty was silent for a minute. Then she turned over to look at Ruby.

"What do you mean, sweetie?"

Ruby found it difficult to answer. She touched Marty on the cheek, as Marty often stroked hers, looking into her eyes. Marty pulled Ruby's face against her chest, kissing her on the forehead.

"Of course we're more than friends," she agreed.

Ruby held onto Marty tightly, her eyes burning. She buried her face in Marty's neck, and eventually fell asleep again.

Marty slept soundly until eight, and then woke with a start, jumped up and dashed over to Stella's crib. The baby was sleeping quietly, her breathing even. Marty breathed out in relief. She looked around for Ruby, but the bed was empty. Marty went out to the kitchen and put the coffee on. She turned when her mother came in.

"Mom, is Ruby here?"

"I don't think so."

"Did she feed Stella?"

"No, I knew you were up late last night, so I got her up and fed her before she could wake you."

"I thought maybe Ruby had..."

"No."

They both were quiet for a while.

"She's still not paying any attention to Stella, huh?" Mrs. Rodger questioned.

"No. Do you think she ever will?"

"I think she needs time. Eventually... I hope so."

"She acts like Stella doesn't exist... like she was never pregnant and still doesn't have any responsibility."

"Ruby's had some tough experiences to work through. It's not an excuse, but it's understandable. I hope she'll eventually get to the point so that she can accept this."

"Meanwhile, that baby's going to grow up."

"Are you doing okay with your correspondence work?"

"Yeah. It makes me so mad that I quit school to take care of her baby, while she's off running around like nothing ever happened."

"And it's worse because you love her."

Marty nodded, and didn't meet her eyes.

"Uh-huh. And she acts like it doesn't mean anything to her. Last night, I thought..." She shook the idea off. "And then today she runs away."

"Ruby wants to be loved so much. But she's afraid of it, too."

Tim was happy to see Ruby again, but he kept glancing at her surreptitiously, as if he was trying to figure something out.

"So... how're you feeling?" he questioned, looking away from her.

"Good. Better now."

"Yeah? Good to hear it. So everything is cool now, huh? You're going to be around more often now?"

"Sure."

"Troy's been wanting you for something."

Ruby swallowed. Her heart raced.

"What for?"

"He never says. Just wants to know where you are."

"I don't want to talk to him."

Tim nodded.

"He's a creep," Tim admitted. "No-one likes him."

"I don't want to talk to him," Ruby repeated firmly. "I don't want to see him."

"Okay, I get you. I'll keep an eye out for you."

Ruby breathed deeply, trying to erase Troy's face from before her. But his face was always before her, even now, months later.

"Let's go find the others," she suggested.

"Yeah."

Marty answered the door, and it was Brian. She opened the door and motioned for him to come in.

"I should've called," he said awkwardly.

"Ruby's not here," Marty informed him.

"I didn't figure she would be. I—uh—wanted to see the baby."

"What did Ruby tell you?"

"She said it wasn't mine. I just—wanted to be sure."

"You think you're going to be able to tell by looking at her?" Marty questioned.

Brian held up an envelope.

"I brought my baby pictures. I hoped that…"

"That might help. Come on in. She's just sleeping."

Brian followed her into the bedroom, and looked down at the baby in the crib.

"Can we get her up?"

"I guess."

Marty bent over and picked Stella up. The baby stirred, but didn't completely waken. Marty held her cradled so that Brian could see her.

"What do you think?"

"I don't know. She doesn't look like my pictures."

"Let's see."

Brian took the pictures out of the envelope. He showed them to Marty, and Marty shook her head.

"I don't see any resemblance."

"That's a big relief."

Marty sighed, smiling.

"Too bad, I was hoping it would be someone responsible, someone who would be interested."

"You don't have any idea who it would be?"

"A couple, but I don't like the choices. I know you would have taken care of things."

"Yeah. I hope you get it figured out."

Marty nodded.

"I certainly didn't expect to be a mommy at this point of my life."

"Yeah. I can't imagine... not even at my age now. I'm glad Ruby's got you as a friend."

"I hate to think of what might have happened to this baby if I wasn't there when she was born."

"Why?"

"She would have ended up dead in a trash can."

"Do you really think so? Ruby wouldn't do that, even if she didn't want the baby."

"She would have had the baby and left. She won't even admit that Stella's hers."

After being out all night with the Jags, Ruby expected to sleep soundly until the afternoon. She was restless trying to sleep, though. She cuddled up close to Tim, but couldn't seem to relax. She slept lightly and restlessly. She hardly realized that she was asleep when she awoke from a nightmare. She was sitting up in bed, and Tim was holding onto her.

"Shh, shhh... it's okay, Ruby. Hush..."

Ruby put her hands over his for comfort. She looked around the dim room, disoriented.

"What happened? Where's Mike?"

"Ruby. You're dreaming. It's just a dream, Ruby."

She looked at him, still confused.

"Mike's okay?"

Tim studied her, frowning and shaking his head.

"Mike was offed months ago."

"He was?"
"He was. You were there, Ruby."
Ruby put her hands up to her face.
"Where's Troy?"
"Troy doesn't stay here. He's got his own place."
"Are you okay?"
"I'm okay. Are you?"
Ruby wiped the tears from her face and laid down again.
"Tim?"
"Yeah, what is it, baby?"
"Hold me."
He put his arms around her, and Ruby laid against his warm chest, listening to his slow, steady heartbeat.

Stella had an infection and a fever. After a long day and many tears from both of them, Marty rocked in the front room with Stella, watching TV. Ruby walked into the house and went to the kitchen without even saying hello to Marty. Marty swallowed her anger and continued to rock Stella. After a while, Ruby walked back out of the front room licking her fingers. She saw Marty there with the baby.
"I didn't see you—I thought you'd be in bed," she whispered.
"Didn't you hear the TV?"
Ruby looked at it.
"Oh… I guess so. I didn't notice. Why are you still up?"
"Stella's sick. There's no way I'll get to sleep tonight."
"Oh."
Ruby looked awkward. She stood there for a moment.
"Where have you been the last few days, Ruby?" Marty questioned.
"Here and there."
"I need you here some of the time. I need your help."
"Yeah, I know."
"You've been off with the Jags?"
Ruby looked up, eyebrows raised.
"How'd you know?"
"Because your face is bruised."
Ruby touched her cheek.
"Bar-room brawl. We weren't involved, I just got in the way."
"Doesn't sound like a smart place to be."
"I guess not."

Ruby stood there watching Marty try to keep Stella quiet.

"Aren't you going to come to bed?" she questioned, cocking her head in invitation.

"I told you I have to stay up with Stella. She's sick."

Ruby shifted her feet.

"Is your mom home?"

"Yes, but she has to go to work in the morning. She's in bed."

"Do you think she'd mind if I slept with her?"

"You might keep her awake."

"I can't sleep by myself," Ruby protested, "and it's too late to find somewhere else."

Marty shrugged impatiently.

"You can see if she minds, Ruby, but if she does, you can sleep by yourself for one night. She has responsibilities tomorrow, you don't. If you don't sleep tonight, you won't lose your job in the morning."

"I don't have a job," Ruby murmured, going to find Mrs. Rodger. Marty rolled her eyes, and listened for her mother's voice. Everything was quiet, and Ruby didn't come back out. Marty closed her eyes and rocked the baby.

CHAPTER Eleven

Mrs. Rodger awoke with Ruby's arms entwined around hers. Frowning, she worked herself out of Ruby's grasp, and looked down at her. Ruby's baby fat had disappeared quickly, and she was as slim and slight as ever. When she had pulled away from Ruby, the girl curled up tightly, with her fists in front of her face, as if she was a boxer. Mrs. Rodger stroked Ruby's hair.

"Ruby... Ruby, it's time to get up."

Ruby's face twitched slightly, but she didn't surface.

"Come on Ruby, wakey wakey..."

Ruby started and her eyes flew open.

"What is it?" she questioned worriedly.

"Shh, nothing. It's time to get up."

Ruby sat up, looking around her uncertainly.

"When did I get here?" she questioned, uncurling.

"Some time last night. I don't know for sure."

"Was I drunk?"

"You didn't seem to be."

Ruby rubbed her eyes.

"I don't remember."

"Well, I'm having a coffee and a shower. I'll see you later. Go check to see if Marty is up, and if not, give the baby a bottle before she wakes Marty up."

Ruby opened her mouth to protest, but Mrs. Rodger had already left the room. Ruby got up and went to Marty's bedroom. Marty was lying in bed with her clothes still on. The baby was in the crib asleep. Ruby went into the kitchen and found a bottle in the fridge. She went back into the bedroom and put the nipple to the baby's mouth. Stella started to suck, still mostly asleep, and woke up slowly and stared up at Ruby. Ruby had expected the baby to hold onto the bottle herself, and stood there impatiently, looking for a way to prop the bottle up and go make some coffee. She looked into the baby's staring eyes, waiting for Stella to finish the bottle.

"Ruby?"

Ruby jumped, and she turned around to face Marty.

"Oh, you're up. Here."

Ruby held the bottle towards her. Marty didn't move to take it. Stella started to whimper in the crib, and Ruby turned back around to plug the nipple back in her mouth again to stop the noise.

"Your mom said to give her a bottle before you woke up."

"Thanks," Marty stretched tiredly. "That was nice. I could use a break."

Ruby stared at the baby.

"She has blue eyes."

"Sure, so do you."

"Not that color. They're really blue."

Stella started to turn away from the bottle. Ruby pulled it back.

"There. She's done."

"She's not done. She just needs to be burped."

"I don't want her spitting up on me," Ruby protested.

"You use a cloth so she doesn't. I'll show you."

"No."

Ruby gave Marty the bottle firmly, and went out to make coffee.

"Didn't you warm it up?" Marty called out, looked down at the bottle in her hand.

"No."

"She doesn't usually take it cold."

Ruby poured water into the coffee machine.

Marty picked Stella up and held her over her shoulder to burp her.

"Did your mommy feed you?" she said softly to the baby, "Did you know that's your mommy? Did you see her?"

She jiggled and patted the baby's back. "You were real good for her, weren't you?" She felt Stella's head. "Fever's gone today, huh? You're feeling better now." She nuzzled Stella's fuzzy head and sighed. She went into the kitchen to talk to Ruby.

Ruby was sitting at the table, sipping a cup of coffee, staring off into space with a far-away look in her eye.

"Penny for your thoughts?" Marty offered. Ruby came back down to earth.

"Oh, I made coffee. Want some?"

"Yeah, thanks."

Marty got Stella to burp and plunked Stella down in Ruby's lap. Ruby caught hold of Stella awkwardly, looking terrified that she might drop the baby.

"No, Marty..." she objected.

"You can give her the rest of her bottle now," Marty said calmly.

"I'm gonna drop her!"

"Relax your arms. Here, hold still." She tried to get Stella settled more comfortably in Ruby's arms. Ruby tried to hand the baby back to her, but Marty refused to take her. "Hold on. There. Hold her with that arm, and then take the bottle in the other hand."

"No."

"There you go."

Ruby was forced to hang onto the baby and feed her. She sat there rigidly for a few minutes, but then started to relax a little. Mrs. Rodger came into the room.

"What's for breakfast?"

She ignored the fact that Ruby was feeding the baby, and went about just as usual.

"What's this?" Clive questioned. Naomi looked at the memo he held.

"Back when Ruby Simpson left her last foster home, Chuck asked me to find out if she'd ever been to hospital. There were parallels between Ruby and Ronnie's histories, and he wanted to find out if she'd ever been to emergency."

"But she hadn't."

"Broken bones, infections, stitches... no sexual assault or alcohol problems."

"So she doesn't have the same history," Clive observed.

"If she does, she was never hospitalized as a result."

"Okay. Put this on her file."

Naomi took it from him. She hesitated.

"I still think Ruby was abused too," she urged.

"She ran away from her last foster home, didn't she?" Clive questioned.

"Yes."

"And no sign of her since?"

"No."

"Then let's concentrate on the kids we've got contact with."

"We could probably track her down, if we tried."

"And then she'd run again. Let's worry about the kids who are willing to be helped."

Naomi nodded and went to file the memo. Clive continued to work through the layers of paper on his desk.

∼

Ruby sat on the bus looking out the window, lost in thought. Someone sat down next to her. Ruby didn't look to see who it was.

"Hi there," a male voice greeted.

Ruby turned her head to look at him. The bus was almost empty. There were plenty of free seats, but he had chosen to sit beside her. He was probably college-age, and very good looking. Ruby smiled at the boy, liking his looks.

"Hi."

"I'm Jamie."

"Ruby."

"A girl of few words. On your way to school?" he queried.

"No, I don't go to school."

"Ahh. So you're just enjoying the sun?"

"Uh-huh."

"You want to join me for a cappuccino in the park?"

Ruby looked him over, and nodded eagerly.

"Sure," she agreed.

"Great. My treat. I like to go to the park to study in the mornings when it's like this. It's nice and peaceful."

Ruby nodded. Whatever he liked. She always thought it was pretty boring in the morning, but she wasn't going to argue with a man willing to treat her to a coffee in the park.

He went on talking about school and his interests, and Ruby listened politely, nodding occasionally. They got off at his stop and he got her a drink at the little coffee stand at the front of the park. They sat down in the sun, and Jamie pulled out a few books so that it would look as if he really was there to study.

"I've seen you on the bus before," he confessed, "but I never had the guts to come sit by you before."

She couldn't remember having seen him on the bus before, but that didn't mean he hadn't been there. She stretched out in the sun, closing her eyes and letting it shine on her face. It made her slightly sleepy, in spite of the coffee she had drunk, and she found herself dozing a little as he talked to her. He stopped talking, and Ruby came abruptly out of her doze when he kissed her. She jumped, panicked, seeing Troy's face vividly in her mind.

"Sorry," Jamie apologized, smiling down at her. "You just looked so pretty lying there in the sun."

"It's okay," Ruby blew out her breath, trying to slow her racing heart. "I just sort of drifted off for a minute." She smiled at him.

"I've been talking about myself, hardly letting you get a word in edgewise."

"No, it's fine. Mmm, come here," she pulled him closer to kiss again. He grinned and stretched out beside her to embrace and kissed her again.

They ended up at his apartment, which was conveniently close.

Ruby lay lazily in bed listening to him shower in the next room. After a while he came back in, wrapped in a blue robe.

"You want some more coffee?" he questioned.

Ruby shook her head.

"I've had lots today. You have juice or something?"

"Sure, I'll make some orange juice."

He rattled around in the kitchen for a while, and returned with a glass of orange juice for her and another coffee for himself. He sat down beside her.

"So tell me about you," he commented. "You know all about me now."

Ruby didn't answer at first. She sat up and sipped at the juice.

"I have a baby," she said finally.

He looked surprised.

"A baby? Really?"

"Yeah. My friend takes care of her."

"Her? A little girl? How old is she?"

"Just a few months. I don't… I don't really have anything to do with her. But I fed her this morning. For the first time."

"Cool. I bet you'd make a good mother," he approved.

"No. I don't really even like her," Ruby confessed.

"Why not? Babies are fun. Can I come over and see her sometime?"

"I guess."

"Let's go over now," he proposed.

Ruby shrugged.

"If you really want to…"

"Yeah, I want to see your kid. Come on. I like babies."

"All right," Ruby shrugged, "whatever you want."

Marty was sleeping while Stella napped in her crib. She awoke to voices, and found that Ruby had brought home some boy with her. Marty rubbed her eyes and sat up.

"Ruby?"

"This is Jamie," Ruby gestured. "He wanted to see the baby."

Ruby led him by the hand over to the crib and pointed to Stella. "There."

Jamie gave Marty a brief wave, grinning, and bent over and picked Stella up, awakening her. He jiggled her to keep her quiet.

"Wow, she doesn't look anything like you, does she?"

"No. She's ugly."

Jamie studied the baby's face, and didn't deny it.

"Well, they say ugly babies grow up to be beautiful ladies," he said.

"She looks like a monkey," Ruby said flatly.

Marty got up off the bed slowly, still feeling a little disoriented.

"Ruby, can we talk?"

Ruby shrugged and let Marty take her out of the room. Marty led her into the kitchen.

"Who is this guy, Ruby?" she questioned in a whisper.

"His name's Jamie." Ruby shrugged.

"I heard that part. Just how much do you know about this guy?"

"He's nice."

"How long have you known him? I've never heard you mention him before."

"I just met him this morning."

"You met him today and you brought him home to see Stella? You never even touched Stella before today!"

"Well, you said you want me to pay attention to her, don't you? So I told him I had a baby."

"How old is Jamie?"

"I don't know. In college."

"And what does some college boy want with you? He shouldn't be interested in a thirteen year old girl!"

"Why not? Give him a chance, you'll like him. He wanted to see the baby."

"What does he want with a baby? Come on, Ruby, this guy doesn't make sense. I don't get a good feeling about him."

Ruby opened her mouth to argue, and Jamie came out of the bedroom with Stella.

"What's up? Anything wrong?" he inquired.

"Stella should be sleeping," Marty said. "I wish you hadn't gotten her up."

Jamie studied Marty, looking friendly.

"You're Ruby's friend who's taking care of the baby?"

"Marty."

"Hi, I'm Jamie. I think we got you up too, didn't we?"

"Yeah, I was having a nap while she slept. Stella's been sick lately."

"Well, why don't Ruby and I take her for the afternoon and give you a break. Huh, Ruby?"

Ruby hesitated. Marty shook her head forcefully.

"Ruby doesn't know how to take care of Stella. She's not ready to take her out by herself."

"Oh, I've taken care of babies before. Come on, Ruby. Let's take Stella to the zoo or something."

Ruby hesitated. She was interested in Jamie, not in the baby.

"I don't know…"

"Come on; let's go spend some more time together. But if you don't want to go back out…"

"No, no—I want to go. Let's go," Ruby jumped in, not willing to let him get away just yet. He was too different, too new.

"Then it's settled," Jamie said with a smile. "Let's get a diaper bag together and we'll go to the zoo."

Ruby nodded and looked around.

"Do we have a stroller or something?" she asked Marty.

Marty nodded.

"In the closet. But you're not taking Stella out alone."

"She's my baby. You said you wanted me to take care of her."

"You don't know anything about taking care of babies."

"I'm taking her anyway," Ruby said with an uncaring shrug.

Stella was good enough to sleep through most of the zoo trip. That gave Jamie and Ruby plenty of time to linger under the trees to kiss and to walk arm in arm down the quieter pathways. Stella was really too small yet to pay any attention to the animals.

Ruby went back to Jamie's apartment after the outing, and they left Stella to sleep in the stroller while they spent the evening. When Stella got hungry, Ruby lay her down on the floor with a pillow propping up the bottle so that she could spend time uninterrupted with Jamie. Jamie even changed Stella's diaper when Ruby refused to touch it.

Ruby sort of liked the feeling of being a family. Her and Jamie and Stella. Just their own little family, like Ruby had never really been a part of herself. And taking care of a baby wasn't as hard as Marty made it out to be. They didn't need that much attention.

∽

When Stella woke them up with her screams in the middle of the night, Ruby groaned and covered up her head. After a while Jamie nudged her.

"Aren't you going to look after the baby?" he suggested.

"No."

"She needs a bottle or something."

"She doesn't get a bottle at night anymore," Ruby disagreed.

"Well then, she needs to be changed," he suggested.

"She can just go back to sleep."

"Don't you think you should check on her?"

"No. Are you going to?"

"No."

"Then go back to sleep."

Eventually Stella's cries did settle down, and they all drifted off back to sleep. In the morning when Stella awoke again, it was Jamie who got up to look after her.

∽

Marty spent a restless night worrying about Stella. It was a long time before she managed to find a troubled sleep. She was up early in the morning, and was sitting up with a coffee when her mother got up.

"No sign of Ruby?" Mrs. Rodger questioned.

"No. Do you think we should call the police or Child Services or something?"

"If we had guardianship of Stella, I would. But she's Ruby's baby, and if we report her and get Stella taken away from her, we may never see her again."

"I wish I'd known this was going to happen... you could have got guardianship or something."

"What was it that prompted Ruby to take Stella with her? She hadn't ever even touched her before yesterday morning."

"That boy, Jamie. I don't know what he wants with Ruby or Stella, but I don't like him. Why would a college boy want to play daddy like that?" Marty shook her head, brows drawn down in frustration.

"Who knows? At least with the two of them looking after Stella together, she'll be all right."

"As long as they don't get bored with her and ditch her somewhere," Marty mumbled.

"They won't."

Marty drank her coffee, not satisfied with her mother's assurances.

Ruby and Jamie were transferring buses down near the arcade, walking down the street to the next bus-stop to get them back to Marty's house again. Ruby was a little nervous, not really wanting any of the Jags to see her with a baby. It was hard enough to get the respect of the gang without having some motherly rep to deal with. That was the last thing she wanted the Jags to think of her as. But it turned out that it wasn't one of the Jags she ran into, it was one of the Terminators. Troy.

He sauntered up to them to torment Ruby. Ruby froze where she was, holding the stroller still. Jamie looked around and saw Troy.

"Just keep going. He won't bother us."

Ruby shook her head, and looked for a way out. There was no easy avenue of retreat. Troy walked right up to them, smoking, his eyes bright with interest.

"Well, aren't we just the cutest family," he sneered. "I never pictured you as the baby kind, Ruby. Who's this, your brother?"

"Just ignore him," Jamie advised, taking control of the stroller and pushing it forwards. Troy stopped it with his foot.

"Aren't you going to introduce the baby to his uncle Troy?" he demanded. He pulled the blanket away from the baby's face to get a look at her. He stopped, staring at her. Ruby couldn't take her eyes off of Troy's face. His electric blue eyes, his dark hair, his small features. She felt sick to her stomach. Ruby had blocked out as much as she could about that night last year when he'd attacked her in the warehouse. She had tried to forget the things he had said and done to her, but she just couldn't.

"Stay away from my baby," Ruby warned Troy, feeling for her knife. Mike's knife. The knife that Mike should have used to protect her last winter.

"Your baby?" Troy repeated. "It looks more like my baby to me."

He tried to undo the straps that held Stella firmly in place, his fingers clumsy. Ruby got the knife out and switched it open.

"Get away from her, or I'll split you!"

He looked up at her; a smile on his face, but when he saw her expression, his smile disappeared.

"So kitten has claws after all," he said with a short laugh.

He stepped back a bit, considering his options. Jamie was an unknown factor, someone who might be tough or might run at the next sign of trouble. For now, anyway, he was standing up pretty well. Troy could go for his gun and threaten to blow them all to the next county, but Jamie, his hand loosely in one pocket of his jacket, could be armed and just waiting for an excuse to use his piece. At any rate, Ruby had her knife out, and she was definitely ready to use it. He'd seen her rumble before. She might be inexperienced, but she wasn't unskilled. Troy looked down at that strange little baby in the stroller, frowning. He knew it was his baby. There was no doubt in his mind.

"Get back," Ruby snapped, her heart thumping hard in her chest.

Troy chuckled.

"I'll get you alone again one of these days, Ruby. Count on it, 'cause I'll be looking forward to it."

He backed off and left them alone. Jamie looked at Ruby and didn't say anything. Ruby gave him no explanation. She was weak-kneed as they walked away. She was glad that she was holding onto the stroller, because it kept her on her feet. She put the knife back in her pocket and kept going.

As soon as they walked in the door, Marty was unbuckling Stella from the stroller and picked her up.

"Where have you guys been? Why didn't you bring her back yesterday?" she questioned, almost frantic. "I'm the one looking after this baby; you can't do this to me! She needs to be changed, couldn't you even do that?"

"Whoa," Ruby protested. "We changed her. We took good care of her. And she's my baby, not yours."

"Well, I have to go," Jamie offered, not wanting to get in between their argument. "I'll see you around, okay Ruby?"

"Yeah. I'll see you."

He kissed her briefly, and left. Marty took Stella into the bedroom to change her and feed her. Ruby followed her.

"I thought you wanted me to take care of her," she complained.

"I do. But I want you to take it slowly, let me show you what to do. You can't just jump into this."

"I did it last night. I did okay."

"Come here, beside me."

Ruby crouched down beside Marty, gagging at the dirty diaper. She watched Marty carefully clean the baby's skin.

"If you don't clean her up really good when you change her diaper, or let her sit in a dirty diaper, she'll get sores and a rash."

"I didn't change her. Jamie did."

"Well, you need to know how to do it."

Ruby shook her head.

"I don't like babies."

Marty blew her breath out in frustration.

"No, not unless there's a boy hanging over your shoulder ogling her," she agreed.

Ruby didn't respond.

Jack swore, looking around. Ruby glanced around at the dark street.

"What is it?" she questioned lowly.

"That old geezer tripped a silent alarm."

"How do you know?"

"Shut up. Keep your head down."

Ruby was still, watching and listening, trying to figure out what it was that Jack had seen. She saw a dark car go slowly down the street, and tried not to move. She wanted to run. Jack was tense beside her, and she could hear his breathing rasping loudly in the darkness. The car rolled to a stop across the street from them. A spotlight cut through the blackness and illuminated them and the pile of trash they had ducked down behind. The doors of the car started to open.

"Run!" Jack ordered, and he jumped up and took off. Ruby followed him. "Split up!" he told her, as she caught up to him. Ruby veered off down an adjoining street. There were shouts behind them, and Ruby hoped that they would follow Jack, the dangerous looking hood, and not the slight figure slipping down another street.

Ruby took a wrong turn and ended up faced with an eight foot chain-link fence. She could back up or go over the fence. She could hear one of the cops chasing after her, getting close. Ruby jumped and caught the fence up high with both hands, and scrambled to get over it. The cop was behind her as she got over the top. Ruby jumped down quickly, and rolled her ankle on the other side. She tried to keep going, but the pain prevented her from getting away very quickly. The cop was more careful how he landed coming over the fence, and he caught up to her easily.

"Hands up," he ordered from behind her, and as Ruby raised her hands, he grabbed the back of her collar. He swung her around against the concrete wall of the building they were beside. Ruby's leg buckled as he pushed her against the wall.

"Easy," he warned her. "Stay still. Keep those hands up! Don't move."

He frisked her, found her knife, and checked her pockets carefully. They were both breathing heavily. He pulled her away from the wall again.

"Back over the fence," he ordered.

"I can't," Ruby protested breathlessly.

"It's the only way out. There's another fence just as tall at the other end of the alley."

"I hurt my ankle."

"Take it slow, then. It's the only way out."

Ruby limped over to the fence with him holding onto her arm, and looked up at the fence.

"I can't. Couldn't you…"

"Up and over. It's the only way."

Another cop came down the alley on the other side of the fence.

"Get him? I lost the other one."

"Got *her*. She's coming back over the fence."

"I can't," Ruby protested again.

"You'll climb back over by yourself, or I'll drag you over. Go ahead, your choice."

Ruby put her hands into the links on the fence. She put her good foot into the links to raise herself up, but couldn't hold her weight on the other. The cop gave her a boost from behind, and Ruby got another step further. He climbed up behind her, pushing her up whenever she needed to shift her weight. Eventually, they got to the top, and Ruby carefully climbed over the top. The cop also climbed over, and as she searched for a toe-hold on the other side, his movements shook the fence and she lost her footing. She landed with a crash on the other side. The second cop helped her to her feet.

"Let that be a lesson for you," he chuckled. "Don't jump fences when you're being chased."

He pulled her arms behind her back and cuffed them. The first cop landed beside her, and they walked back slowly to the unmarked car. By the time they got to the car, Ruby's ankle was so tender she couldn't put any weight on it and even trying to hop on the other foot with the support of the two officers jarred it painfully. They helped her into the car and shut the door. Neither one said anything to her as they drove to the police station. When they got there, one of the cops went into the station while Ruby sat in the car with the other officer. The first came back out a while later with a pair of crutches. They released her from her handcuffs so that she could use the crutches. No-one said anything to her.

"We need you to participate in a line-up," a cop told her after she'd been sitting in a room for an hour or so. Ruby was allowed to enter the room ahead of the other girls, and then the crutches were taken away from her. Ruby nervously watched the mirrored glass on the wall. The other girls were around her age, all blond. Ruby stood there waiting. Eventually, they were instructed to leave, and an officer came in and gave her crutches back.

"You're under arrest for armed robbery," the officer informed her, and she was taken back to the room that she had spent the hour waiting in. One of the officers who had chased her over the fence came in to talk to her. His name bar said 'Blackstein.'

"Well, Ruby. You're in some trouble now," he observed.

Ruby shrugged and didn't say anything.

"Now, you've got a pretty good record, so if you will help us out here, we can probably let you off without a lot of trouble. But if you won't cooperate... can I count on you?"

"It's my first arrest," Ruby told him.

"Well, that's not what our record shows. Another arrest for assaulting a young girl."

"That wasn't true! The charge was dropped."

"It's still there on your record. Why don't you tell me what happened tonight?" Blackstein urged.

"Nothing happened."

"Give us the name of the boy who was with you when your guys robbed the convenience store. That's all we need from you."

"You've got the wrong person. It wasn't me."

"You were identified in the lineup. The store owner didn't even hesitate. He recognized you easily. And we've got him looking through mug shots for your accomplice right now. It won't be long before we have a name, but if you can give it to us first, we can work out a deal with you."

Ruby thought through what had happened that night.

"I was at the convenience store tonight," she told him. "It's one that I go to all the time. My face would be familiar to the owner."

"What were you at the store for?"

"Formula for my baby."

"Did you buy it?"

Ruby shook her head.

"Why not?"

"That guy came in with his gun, and robbed the place."

"You're saying you weren't with him."

"Yes."

"Why did you run from us, then?"

"I thought you were his friends. You weren't in a marked car; I thought you were his friends and if I didn't get away..."

"Why did you leave with him?"

"He had a gun. He told me to come with him. I thought he'd let me go as soon as we were out of the store," Ruby invented.

"Your story doesn't ring true. Describe the boy who robbed the store."

Ruby stared up at the ceiling.

"Taller than me. Dark hair. I don't know. Average."

"What was he wearing?" the cop prodded.

"Blue jeans. Black shirt. Black jacket. A gang jacket."

"Which gang?"

"I don't know... everything happened so fast," Ruby claimed, shaking her head.

"Jags?" Blackstein suggested.

"I don't think so."

"Terminators?"

"Maybe... I don't think so. They're usually in twos."

"You seem pretty familiar with the gangs," he observed, his tone cynical.

"Not really... I've just seen them around."

"Who was it, then? Rippers?"

"Yeah… I think so. I'm not sure, but I think so. I don't know."

"Wait for a second."

He left the room, and then came back a few minutes later. Ruby wondered if he really believed her, or if he was just playing along with her.

"Why don't you describe for me what happened at the store?"

Ruby did her best, trying to throw in just enough detail for them to believe her, spinning it as if she had been an innocent bystander instead of being the one that Jack had sent in to scope the store out ahead of time.

"How old is your baby?" he questioned, after asking for more details of the robbery. Ruby was startled by the segue.

"A couple months."

"Boy or girl?"

"Girl."

"Where is she right now?"

"At home, my friend's watching her for me."

"You're a little young to be a mom, aren't you?"

"I guess," Ruby admitted.

"Is the baby's father in one of the gangs?" he questioned, eyes sharp and quick.

"No. He's in college."

"What's his name?"

Ruby gave him Jamie's name. Her ankle was throbbing and Ruby tried to put it up on the empty chair across from her. The cop shoved the chair a little closer so she could.

"What's the name of the boy you were with?" he sighed.

"I don't know," Ruby said evenly.

"Why did you guys pick that store?"

"I go to that store 'cause it's on my way, by the bus route. I don't know why he robbed it."

"Isn't it a little late for you to be out all by yourself in that neighborhood?"

"I guess."

"A little dangerous, isn't it? For someone your age?"

"I had my knife with me."

"Doesn't help if you meet up with someone with a gun, does it?" his eyebrows quirked up.

"No. But who's going to give me a gun permit?"

He smiled. Ruby rubbed her bruised elbows.

"My ankle really hurts," she complained.

"Well, you shouldn't go around jumping fences."

"Can I at least get an Aspirin or something?"

He sighed, nodding.

"I'll take you down to the station doctor. He can tape it up for you."

Ruby nodded. The cop handed her the crutches and they walked down the long halls together. Ruby was glad to get off of her foot again when they reached the doctor's office. The doctor felt it and moved it around gently.

"A bad sprain," he admitted. "It's pretty swollen. You should get it x-rayed tomorrow to make sure there's no fracture. I'll tape it up for tonight."

"Can you give me something?" Ruby questioned. Her face was pale, her head spinning after his careful manipulations.

The doctor nodded.

"I'll give you codeine." He turned his attention to the cop. "But you shouldn't question her when she's on codeine."

Blackstein sighed and rolled his eyes.

"Well then, I guess we're going to have to put you in a cell for the night. Do you want us to call anyone for you?"

"No."

"Parents, your friend who's taking care of your baby?"

"No."

"Okay."

Once he had Ruby settled for the night, Blackstein went back to the crime scene to see if it jived with Ruby's story. He didn't believe for a minute that she hadn't been involved in this herself, but he still had to investigate it thoroughly.

He walked up and down the aisles, talking to the old man who owned the store, who had returned after identifying Ruby in the line-up.

"Had you ever seen the girl before tonight?" he questioned.

"I recognize her face. She's been here before."

"So, she's a regular customer?"

"She's been here before," the man repeated carefully.

"How about the boy?"

"I haven't seen him before." The old man shook his head.

"So they're never together when she comes."

"No. I've never seen him before."

"But the girl was easy to pick out of a lineup, because you've seen her before."

"Yes."

Blackstein thought about that for a few moments, letting his eyes travel around the interior features of the store. Windows, lighting—a bit dim, product shelves, front counter. Considering all of the angles and viewlines.

"How long was the girl here casing it out before the boy came in?"

"Just for a minute."

"What aisle was she in?"

"Number three, at the back."

Blackstein walked to the back corner of the store. Just where you would go if you wanted to make sure the store was truly empty. There was a can of infant formula on the floor. Blackstein looked around. If she had been standing there when the boy came in and wasn't his lookout, why not just duck down? Why head towards the door, all the way on the other side of the store?

"Did the two of them speak to each other?" he questioned, walking slowly back up to the counter. "Call each other by name?"

"No. He just told her 'come on' when he had the money," the old man said with a shrug of his hands.

"Did *she* threaten you at all?"

"No, she didn't say anything. Just the boy."

Blackstein tapped his fingers on the counter.

"Were they definitely together, or could the girl just have been a bystander?"

The old man looked taken aback. He frowned, a crease appearing in the middle of his forehead.

"They were together. I told you that."

"Yeah, well, the girl's singing a different song."

The old man shook his head, his lips pursed together.

"I'm sure they were together. She came in to case out my place."

"As long as you're sure. You didn't come across the boy in the mug shots?"

"I don't think so. I didn't get a really good look at him."

"The girl said he was wearing a gang jacket. Did you notice which gang he was from?"

"I didn't see the picture… he didn't turn his back until he got to the door, and then I couldn't see… I'm a little short-sighted."

Blackstein looked at the man sharply.

"Exactly how short-sighted?" he challenged.

"I saw them both, I just couldn't make out his jacket," he insisted.

"Okay. I'll be talking to you again, let you know how things are going."

～

Jamie opened the door to find a policeman waiting on the other side. He looked worried and anxious about the unexpected visit. But he took a deep, slow breath, and forced a smile.

"Uh—yeah?"

"My name is Blackstein. Could I talk to you for a few minutes?"

"Yeah, come in."

Jamie opened the door the rest of the way and let Blackstein in. He was wearing only a pair of blue jeans that he had obviously pulled on in order to answer the door. He motioned for Blackstein to sit down on the couch. Blackstein opened his notepad.

"I'm sorry to disturb you at this time of night. I need to ask you some questions about a girl named Ruby Simpson."

"Ruby?" his eyebrows went up. "Okay... what do you need to know?"

"You and Ruby are pretty close? You know quite a bit about her?"

Jamie shook his head.

"No."

"No? It sounded to me like you knew each other pretty well."

"Uh-uh. I haven't known her very long."

"She said you were her baby's father."

Jamie laughed.

"Her father? I didn't even meet Ruby until a couple of weeks ago!"

"I see." Blackstein leaned back. "Do you know who the father is?"

"Nope. Although we ran into this one guy..."

"Who?"

"A guy from a gang, I guess. We were out for a walk with the baby when we ran into him. He said he thought the baby looked like him. Might just have been talk, though." Jamie gave a wry smile, and looked away.

"Do you know which gang he was in?"

"No. But they weren't on good terms. Ruby held him off with a knife. Wouldn't let him close to the baby."

"You didn't see the emblazon on his jacket?"

Jamie frowned.

"I was sort of shook up. I knew he was from one of the gangs, I didn't know which one—I don't think I ever saw the logo on his jacket."

"Can you describe him?"

"Short and wiry. Blue eyes and dark hair, like the baby."

"Did Ruby mention his name?"

"No, I don't think so."

"You think he was really the father?"

"I don't know. I've only known Ruby for a little while."

"You don't know of any involvement she might have with any of the gangs?"

"No."

There was a light on in the back of the house when Blackstein approached. He knocked quietly on the door rather than ringing the doorbell. A girl about Ruby's age holding a crying baby opened the door.

"Where's Ruby? Is she okay?" she questioned immediately.

"Ruby's fine. But she is in a bit of trouble. Can I ask you a few questions?"

She nodded, but didn't invite him in.

"You're Marty?"

"Yes."

"And this is Ruby's baby?"

"Yeah, this is Stella, Ruby's daughter." Marty held her at an angle that Blackstein could see her face for a moment, then cuddled her to her shoulder and tried to calm her, patting her back.

"Ruby was in a convenience store that was robbed this evening. She says that she was there to pick up baby formula."

Marty raised her eyebrows.

"Really. I did tell her yesterday that we needed more, we're getting low."

"So she might have been telling the truth."

"Sure."

"Have you known her to have any interaction with any of the youth gangs?"

Marty rolled her eyes and sighed.

"The Jaguars."

Blackstein shook his head.

"The Jags. Figures. Well, up until now her story was starting to look like it might be true. But if she is with the Jags…"

Marty frowned suddenly.

"You think Ruby *robbed* the store? With one of the Jags?"

"That's the idea."

"Oh, boy." Marty shook her head.

"You don't think she could be involved?" Blackstein said.

"I sure hope not. She hasn't done anything criminal before."

"They all start somewhere. If she's been hanging around with the Jags, she'll get there eventually."

"Will she be coming home tonight? Where is she?"

"She's in a cell at the station. She'll probably be home tomorrow morning. We'll need to question her some more."

"Don't be too hard on her… she's not a bad kid, just mixed up," Marty said. "She's been in a lot of different foster homes."

"She hasn't been real cooperative, but she hasn't been too bad."

Ruby slept restlessly through the night. She didn't think she would sleep at all, but the codeine must have made her sleep. Her ankle was stiff and swollen when she awoke. She sat on the bed, her back against the wall and her feet up on the bed in front of her. She couldn't believe she was actually in jail. But she had to stick with Jack and the Jags, she had to do what the guys wanted her to, or she would lose their protection.

The robbery was nothing after seeing Laskin and Slash shot. There was no violence, no blood. She hadn't even been nervous about it. She figured it would go off all right. But it hadn't.

The door opened and an officer stood there. He stood there for a moment without saying anything.

"Well, come on," he said impatiently.

Ruby got up and limped over to him. They had taken away her crutches. He motioned for her to turn around, and handcuffed her. He didn't have anything to say to her. He escorted her in to where Blackstein had questioned her the day before. She sat and waited in the empty room for another hour waiting for someone to come talk to her. Then Blackstein came in. He looked tired. Ruby scowled at him.

"When are you going to let me go?" she demanded.

"Take it easy. I have some more questions for you."

"I've been waiting here for an hour."

"You're exaggerating. Let's get back to business, and you can go home."

"When's breakfast around here?"

Blackstein glanced at his watch.

"Already passed. Didn't you get anything?"

"I've been sitting in here staring at the wall."

"I'll get you a coffee. How do you like it?"

"Black."

"Sugar?"

"No."

"Okay. I'll be right back."

He left again, and it was another half hour before he got back. Ruby's stomach was growling and she was getting irritated with all the waiting. He finally got back, and handed her a Styrofoam cup of light-colored coffee. Ruby looked down at it and didn't remind him she had ordered it black.

"It's about time," she grumbled. She picked it up and took a sip. It was cold and sweet. She put it back down. "I want my lawyer," she said flatly.

Blackstein raised his brows.

"What?"

"I'm tired of you jerking me around. I want my lawyer."

"Hey, sorry I took so long. I got sidetracked," he apologized.

Ruby glared at him for another minute.

"So are you going to ask me those questions or what?" she said grumpily.

"Who was the Jag you were with last night?"

"I don't know who he was. I didn't think he was a Jaguar, though. One of the other gangs."

"You know the Jags pretty well."

"Who told you that?"

"I asked around," he said with a shrug.

"I want to get out of here."

"Admit that you know the Jags."

"I know some of them," she agreed.

"Admit that you were there last night to case out the convenience store."

"I was buying formula for my baby," Ruby maintained.

"Admit that you got mixed up in something that was over your head."

"I got in the middle of a hold-up. It wasn't my fault."

"I'll need you to sign a statement about what you told me. Then you can go home. As long as you stay with your friend so we can reach you again when this goes to trial."

"I'll sign whatever you want."

"Good girl. You stay here. I won't be long this time."

Ruby sat back to wait.

"Can you get me more pills too?"

He hesitated, and then nodded.

"I'll see what I can do. What happened to your crutches?"

"They took them away. Thought I'd use them as a weapon, I guess."

He shook his head and walked out again.

CHAPTER
Twelve

Ruby knew they'd be watching her. They'd be watching to see if she went straight to the gang. But she wasn't going to give them a chance. She went to Jamie's apartment instead. He wasn't around, but the lock on the door was a simple spring lock, and Ruby had learned from the Jags how to get by those. She let herself in and looked around his apartment. She'd been there before, but not alone. She hadn't had a real chance to check it out by herself and see what kind of a person he really was.

Jamie was a tidy person. Everything was in place, like a homemakers magazine picture. He must have had a woman's touch in his apartment sometime, because everything seemed to be coordinated. Nothing looked expensive, but at the same time, you know it wasn't cheap. He hadn't just picked stuff up at the flea market. And he was either very clean or had a maid come in.

Ruby opened the fridge and cupboards, and helped herself to a sandwich. She sat down in front of the TV and waited for Jamie to get home. He started when he saw her sitting there.

"Ruby—you surprised me. How did you get in?"

"The door was open. Sorry, I didn't think you would mind."

"No, I don't mind." He stood there with one hand on the door frame, looking at her thoughtfully. "There was a policeman here last night."

"Yeah, sorry about that."

"Why did you tell them I was Stella's dad?"

Ruby shrugged.

"She doesn't have a dad. You were the first one that came to mind."

"I'm flattered. But we don't know each other really well, so... don't push it, all right?"

"Guess it was stupid, huh?"

He shook his head.

"I like you, and I like Stella. But I'm not ready to be anyone's dad quite yet. You have to give me some time for that one."

"Okay."

Jamie stood there, not saying anything. Ruby turned her attention back to the TV. After a few minutes, Jamie came over and sat down beside her on the couch, putting his arms around her.

Blackstein sat in his car in front of the apartment building, watching for Ruby to come back out. She had gone to the boyfriend instead of to her baby. Her loyalties appeared to be a bit backwards. If she cared more about seeing her boyfriend after a night in jail than she cared about seeing her baby, then what were the chances that she'd actually been at the store to buy baby formula? He knew Ruby had been in on the robbery, but it bothered him that she had a good back-up story and that the store owner couldn't identify the boy. It should have been the other way around. He should have been able to identify the one with the gun, and not the accomplice who had cased out the store. The Jag had been standing closer and had been the focus of attention. The owner had admitted to being nearsighted enough not to make out the emblazon on the jacket when the boy was still only a few feet away at the door. But he had identified Ruby easily in the lineup. He should have been able to pick out the Jag's mug shot from the pictures they had shown him.

Blackstein wished Ruby had just gone home. He knew that they would never convict her without the boy, even though she was guilty. She should have gone home to her baby. She hadn't even read the statement he gave her to sign. Ruby had said she would sign anything he gave her, and she meant it. He could have given her a statement that said she had murdered the old man, and she would have signed it. That bothered him too, because it meant that the statement would never stand up in court. Not that she had admitted to anything more than being in the store and leaving with the Jag, but it would have been nice to at least use her statement on those points. He could just hear the legal aid attorney questioning him in court.

"Did she read the statement before she signed it? Didn't she say she would sign anything you gave her? Why did she say that?"

He didn't know why she had said it. She shouldn't have. She should have said that she'd sign it only if he got it right. She should have protested having to sign anything, the guilty ones did.

When Ruby got home, she had Jamie with her again. He played with Stella in the bedroom while Marty talked to Ruby.

"Are you okay? I was so worried about you," Marty touched Ruby's cheek, brushing a loose strand of hair back, gazing into her eyes.

"Other than my foot, I'm okay," Ruby said, shrugging.

"How did you do that?"

"Jumping over a fence."

Marty shook her head, smiling a bit at that.

"But they were good to you? They didn't hurt you?"

"No."

"Were you in jail with other people? They didn't put you in with weirdoes, did they?"

"No. They put me in solitary."

"Good."

"Do you have some Aspirin or something? For my ankle?"

"Yeah, in the bathroom."

Ruby limped to the bathroom to get some. The pain after walking and taking the bus from Jamie's apartment was almost unbearable. Marty watched her go into the bathroom and shut the door. Marty went into the bedroom where Jamie was cooing to the baby. Jamie looked up when Marty came in. Neither of them said anything for a moment. Jamie looked back down at Stella.

"You don't approve of me, do you?"

Marty stood looking down at him.

"Why would I?"

"Why wouldn't you? I haven't hurt Ruby or Stella."

"What interest do you have in Ruby? What exactly attracts you to a thirteen year old girl and a baby?"

"I like Ruby. She's cute and she's fun to be around."

"She's a kid."

"She's mature. A lot more mature than most of the girls I know. And she's not thirteen. She's fourteen."

Marty looked startled, and then shrugged.

"So she's fourteen. The reason you think she's mature is because she's been hurt. She's had to grow up and be independent."

"She hasn't been hurt by me."

"You're sleeping with her."

Jamie didn't disagree.

"I wouldn't hurt Ruby."

"You *are* hurting her. Just like all the other boys in her life."

"I don't know anything about any other boys. All I know is that I haven't done anything to hurt her."

Ruby came back down the hallway to the bedroom.

"What's up?" she questioned, looking at the two of them.

Marty shook her head, scowling.

"Let's go out," Jamie suggested.

Ruby shook her head.

"I have to keep off my foot a while," she said. She was pale, her face drawn and tired. "I can't go out."

"Mind if I stick around here for a while, then?"

Ruby looked at Marty.

"Is it okay?" she coaxed. "Just for a little while?"

"For a bit, but you need to get some sleep. You look wiped out."

"Yeah."

"Watch some TV?" Jamie suggested.

Ruby nodded.

"Yeah, sure."

They went out to the living room and sat down in front of the TV, Jamie with one arm around Ruby and Stella cradled in his other arm. Ruby rested her head on Jamie's shoulder, her leg propped up to relieve the pressure on her ankle. Marty sat down on the easy chair to keep her eye on them, and especially on Stella. They had hardly been watching ten minutes, and Ruby was asleep. Stella fell asleep as well, and Jamie sat there with the two of them, grinning.

"Good company, huh?"

"Ruby's not feeling well," Marty pointed out.

"The two of you are pretty close," he observed.

"Yeah. That's right."

"That's cool. I'm not trying to get between you two. I think it's good that she has a girlfriend."

Marty frowned and looked suspicious. She walked over and took Stella from him.

"You should leave. Let Ruby sleep."

Jamie didn't like it, but he shrugged and got up, careful not to wake Ruby up. She didn't stir.

"I'll see you around," Jamie told Marty.

She didn't say anything to him, and he let himself out. Marty sat down next to Ruby, watching her sleep.

Ruby awoke suddenly and sat up. The room was dark and empty. She wasn't sure where she was. She stood up quickly, looking around and trying to make our shapes in the dimness. She took two steps away from the couch before she felt the pain of her sprain, and her leg buckled so she hit the floor with a crash. Ruby lay still, holding her foot. Tears were starting in her eyes and she lay there frozen, listening for movements. A door opened somewhere, and she heard a voice call out "Marty?" softly. There were footsteps nearby, and a light went on.

"Ruby," Marty's mom rushed over to her and took her by the hand.

"I didn't know where I was," Ruby whispered, sitting up and hugging her tightly.

"It's okay. You're all right now. Get up, and we'll put you in bed with Marty."

"I can't. My foot."

"I'll help you. Let's see."

She looked at Ruby's ankle, and realized it was swollen to twice its normal size.

"Just don't stand on it," she suggested. "Hop on the other foot. I'll hold you up."

She helped Ruby get to her feet. The hopping jarred Ruby's ankle too much. She leaned her weight on Mrs. Rodger, gasping.

"I can't."

She was sheet white, and Mrs. Rodger was worried that if they went any further, Ruby would faint. She propped Ruby up against the wall.

"Wait right there. Don't move. I'll get help."

She went back to her bedroom, and Ruby leaned woozily against the wall waiting for her to get back. Then she realized that Mrs. Rodger had gone to enlist help from her husband. She heard him grumbling as he got up, about having to take care of everybody else's kids. Ruby tried to get down the hallway on her own, but collapsed again. Marty's parents hurried out of the bedroom towards her.

"Don't touch me," Ruby protested when he reached towards her. But he ignored her protest and scooped her up in his arms like a child.

He was used to carrying far heavier loads. Ruby froze in his arms, the tears brimming up in her eyes and running down her cheeks. He put her down gently in Marty's bed, pushing Marty away from the edge with one hand. Ruby lay still, and he looked at her foot.

"It's broken," he deduced, "take her to the doctor and have it set tomorrow."

"Are you sure it's broken?" Mrs. Rodger questioned. "Ruby said it was just sprained."

"You can never tell with ankles. But I bet it's broken."

"Should we take her to emergency tonight?"

"Tomorrow. Let her sleep tonight, if she can."

"Will you be okay tonight?" Mrs. Rodger questioned Ruby. "Will you be okay if we wait?"

She carefully removed Ruby's tight shoes and socks. When she reached for the waist of Ruby's pants to help her undress for sleep, Ruby stopped her.

"No—leave it," she looked towards Marty's dad.

"Oh, I'm sorry, Ruby. Thanks for your help," she told her husband. He got the hint.

"Yeah, whatever," he muttered, and left the room. "Night, Pumpkin."

Pumpkin was what he called Marty. But Marty wasn't even awake. Ruby let Mrs. Rodger unsnap her blue jeans and take them off, and Ruby pulled the edges of her t-shirt down to cover herself. Mrs. Rodger tugged a blanket over her.

"There. You'll be okay?"

"Yeah."

"Okay. See you in the morning."

Mrs. Rodger left again. The light in the hall went out. Ruby snuggled up to Marty and tried to ignore the throbbing in her foot and go to sleep.

The next day the doctor took x-rays and confirmed what Marty's dad had suspected. The ankle was broken. Ruby waited patiently while the doctor set it and gave her instructions on taking care of it. She picked up her crutches again, nodding.

"You'll give me some pills."

"Yes. But I don't want you to take any more than you have to, okay?"

Ruby nodded. He motioned to the baby that Marty was holding.

"Are you nursing her?"

"What?"

"Breastfeeding?"

"No."

"Because if you do, you're going to have to stop while you're taking the painkillers."

"I'm not."

"Okay. Try to keep off of that ankle, okay? Keep it elevated."

"I will."

Mrs. Rodger wanted to take Ruby back home, but Ruby shook her head.

"I got other things to do."

"Don't get in trouble."

Ruby didn't answer. She turned and went down the street on her crutches, heading for the bus stop. Marty rocked Stella, shaking her head.

"She's going to the Jags."

"I hope not."

"She is."

Ruby got to Tim's apartment, and went straight to the kitchen to wash some pills down with a beer. Tim watched her.

"What happened to you?" he questioned.

Ruby shrugged.

"Broke my ankle."

"How'd you do that?"

"Jumping over a fence trying to outrun a cop." Ruby grimaced.

Tim grinned.

"Well, that was pretty dumb," he observed.

"Yeah, I know. Seemed like a good idea at a time. Jack got back all right?"

"Yeah. He knew better than to jump any fences."

"I didn't know the alley; I didn't know it was a dead end, okay?"

Tim grinned.

"Uh-huh. How's it feel?"

Ruby rolled her eyes.

"These pills don't work."

"I'll bet. What'd they give you, Tylenol?"

"I guess."

"I'll get you something better," Tim promised.

Ruby was sleeping when the gang went out for the night. The pills that Tim had given her made her dopey. She couldn't go out anyway, she would slow them down. Ruby drifted in and out of consciousness. She hated to sleep alone, but she was too woozy to go anywhere else. Nightmares plagued her constantly, waking her up in a hazy cold sweat. But the drugs were too much and she would fall right back into restless dreams.

Ruby awoke to Troy's face before her. She blinked a few times, trying to get rid of the image, but it didn't fade or go away this time. He was really there this time. He grinned at her.

"Hello sweetheart, you miss me?"

Ruby struggled to sit up. Troy sat down on the bed, casually pinning down her free leg. The cast made it too difficult to move the other.

But he had made a mistake this time. He was too sure of himself. Before he'd had a gun. Both times he'd kept her still with his gun. But this time, it was still in his pocket or waistband because he thought she was an easy target. And Ruby had her knife in her pocket. Mike's knife. The one Mike should have had in his hand to protect her the night they held a gun to her head. The knife she should have used when Troy had grabbed her off the street. The knife that had convinced Troy to back off when he was threatening the baby.

It seemed like it took forever to get her hand to her knife without him realizing what she was doing. But the room was dim, lit only by a bulb shining in from the other room, and he couldn't see her well enough.

Troy heard it snick open, and froze. Whether he realized what she was doing or not, Ruby didn't know, but he didn't move until she shoved the knife into his belly, and then he quivered when she struck.

He fell across her. Skinny though he was, he was too heavy for Ruby to move. One leg was already immobilized by the cast. She could hardly even move her arms with him across her.

Ruby was still dopey and disoriented by the drugs that Tim had given her. She struggled for a few minutes to get him off of her, but when she couldn't, she eventually dropped back off to sleep.

Jack and Tim and the others got back in the early hours of the morning. Tim went to get a beer from the fridge. Johnson walked by the bedroom, and raised his eyebrows.

"Ruby's got company," he said.

Tim looked startled.

"Who's with Ruby? I thought everyone else was with us."

Johnson shrugged.

"Someone's in with her."

Jack glanced around the apartment, and nodded at the cap lying on the table.

"Troy."

"Ruby doesn't like Troy," Tim said, frowning. "She said…" he trailed off.

He went to the door of the bedroom where Johnson was standing, and looked at the vague shapes in the darkness.

"Ruby?"

Tim hesitated, and then flipped the light switch. He looked at them for a couple of minutes before he could take it all in. He swore and walked over to the bed. The blankets were drenched with blood. Johnson was motioning violently for the others to all come see. Jack approached, a snide comment on his lips, but it died away and he didn't say anything.

"Ruby," Tim said softly, and he caught hold of Troy's jacket and tried to pull him off. Troy was a dead weight. Jack came over silently and helped Tim to pull the body off from Ruby. Tim cupped his hand over Ruby's cheek.

"She's hot," he said.

Jack nodded. He turned over Troy's body with his foot, his eyes sharp.

"Johnson, and the rest of you, get rid of this. And good. I don't want the cops turning it up in a couple of days. Tim…"

"I'm not leaving Ruby."

"No." Jack looked Ruby over. "Wake her up, and get her cleaned up and changed. We'll burn her clothes and the sheets. I don't want her saying anything."

He stooped down and pulled the knife out of Troy's belly.

"She did the right job, that's for sure. Come on, you guys. The cops will smell the blood a block away. Get it out of here."

He closed the knife and put it in his pocket. Johnson and the other boys carried Troy out of the room, and Jack went over and shut the door. He nodded to Tim. Tim shook Ruby, trying to waken her. She didn't stir.

"She stoned?" Jack questioned.

"Yeah."

"She told me she didn't do drugs."

"She needed something for the broken ankle."

Jack went into the bathroom and soaked a cloth with cold water. He came back and wiped Ruby's face and neck with it. Ruby started to surface, but didn't open her eyes. Jack slapped her cheeks lightly with his hand, and Ruby started to move to avoid it.

"Ruby. Open your eyes. Time to get up. Open your eyes."

She reluctantly opened her eyes and looked foggily at the two of them.

"Get up," Jack told her.

Ruby shook her head.

"I'm tired," she moaned.

"I don't care. Get up."

They both forced Ruby into a sitting position, though she was still unsteady. Ruby looked down at the blood soaking her shirt and breathed in sharply.

"Oh, man... Oh, no... oh, man..."

She swore and rubbed the front of her shirt between two hands as if she could get it out.

"Come on," Jack urged, sliding her legs over the edge of the bed. "Stand up."

"I don't feel good."

"Get moving. Come on."

They got her up between them and took her into the bathroom. Ruby collapsed on the floor when they released her. She managed to stay sitting up, and she plucked at the blood-soaked shirt, disoriented. Jack grasped the bottom edge of the shirt with both hands and pulled it off over Ruby's head. He threw it on the floor.

"Get her pants off," he told Tim, looking disgusted. All of Ruby's clothes were soaked with blood. "And get her in the shower and cleaned and sobered up."

Tim struggled to get Ruby's pants unbuttoned. He was biting his lip, trying to keep his emotions under control. He slapped Ruby's cheeks to try to keep her awake and aware. He left bloody fingerprints on her face. Ruby rubbed her eyes, pushing Tim's hands away.

"Don't touch me."

"Come on, Ruby. Don't do that."

She pushed his hands away when he tried to work on her buttons again.

"Don't touch me," she insisted more vehemently. "Keep your hands off me or I'll kill you!"

"Ruby, it's Tim. It's okay."

Ruby fended him off, swearing. Jack grew impatient.

"Get her in the shower," he advised, grabbing one of Ruby's arms. Tim caught her by the other arm, and together they dragged her, struggling, to the shower and dumped her into the shower stall. Jack turned on the cold water. Ruby shrieked and sputtered. The water running over the tiles was tinged pink. Ruby struggled to get up or escape the cold water from the shower. After a few minutes her shouts turned to whimpers. Jack turned off the tap.

"Tim… give me a hand…" Ruby started. He stooped over and gave her his hands and helped her to her feet. Ruby held her head for a few minutes once on her feet. She sat down on the toilet.

"What happened?"

"Why don't you tell us?" Jack suggested.

Ruby looked at him and picked up a towel to wrap around herself. She shook her head.

"Man, have I got a headache."

"I'll bet. What happened?"

Ruby held her head.

"Troy—is he here?"

"We're taking care of him."

"Did I kill him?"

"Cold as ice," Jack confirmed.

Ruby looked relieved.

"He wouldn't leave me alone. He just wouldn't leave me alone."

Jack lit a cigarette, watching Ruby.

"Troy wasn't a great guy, but this is going to cause us some real problems."

"Sorry I wasn't thinking of gang politics," Ruby sneered sarcastically.

"Maybe you should have been. When the Terminators hear that you iced their leader, you're really gonna have to watch your back."

"As long as Troy's not there."

"There's worse guys than Troy."

Ruby shook her head.

"No, there's not," she said flatly.

Jack shook his head and lit a cigarette.

"You got other clothes with you?" he questioned.

Ruby nodded.

"In my knapsack." She rubbed at the bloodstains on her jeans. "This isn't going to come out."

"We'll burn them."

"What?"

"Cops can test blood, figure out where it came from. There isn't going to be any evidence for them to find if we burn it."

"Oh."

"So get out of that stuff and we'll get rid of it," Jack urged.

Ruby struggled for a moment with the button of her fly, and got it undone.

"Are you going to stand there watching?" she demanded.

Jack smiled.

"You don't have anything I haven't seen."

Ruby started to unzip and wriggle out of her jeans. Jack nodded and walked out. Ruby stood up unsteadily and Tim helped her out of the jeans and back into the shower, warm this time. He picked up the bloody clothes and left Ruby to shower off.

Johnson and Erwin walked out of the building with Troy between them. They kept a sharp lookout for anyone who might notice them. They got about halfway down the block and Johnson noticed the two figures getting out of the car parked in front of the apartment building. Johnson picked up his pace.

"Watch them," he warned.

The two men started to trail them. Johnson swore.

"Around the corner, and we dump him and split," he instructed lowly. Erwin nodded in agreement. The continued at the same pace until they rounded the corner at the end of the block. They dropped the body and fled. By the time the cops got around the corner, Johnson and Erwin were too far away for pursuit. They crouched over Troy's body.

"He's cold," Smith said. Gerald nodded.

"I'll get a crew over. Once they're here, we can go find the Jags the girl is staying with."

They didn't know which apartment Ruby was in, but they asked questions at a few doors and were quickly pointed in the right direction. There was no answer at Tim's apartment, and they kicked in the door with guns drawn. Smith held the Jags in the front room under gunpoint while Gerald checked out the rest of the apartment. The rooms were blue with smoke. Gerald checked out the bedroom. The blankets had been stripped off of one of the beds, but the mattress itself was stained with blood. The shower was running, and Gerald pushed the door open with his toe, gun ready. He pushed back the shower curtain.

Ruby yelped and tried to cover herself up.

"Get out," Gerald told her.

Ruby had problems stepping over the edge of the shower with the cast on her foot. He offered one hand, keeping the gun on her with the other. Ruby grabbed a grimy towel and wrapped it around herself. She looked around awkwardly.

"Where's your clothes?"

"In my bag, the other room."

He motioned her with the gun, and Ruby walked out into the bedroom, swaying on her feet. Obviously drunk or stoned. She could hardly stand up. She found her bag and picked it up. Gerald took it away from her and dumped it on the floor, moving stuff around on his floor so that he could make sure she wasn't going to pull a weapon on him. It wouldn't be a smart thing to do in her condition, but it wouldn't be the first time a gang member did something stupid. Ruby picked up her clothes slowly, pulling on a shirt and pants, struggling to get the blue jeans on over her cast and damp skin.

Gerald took her out to the front room where the others were waiting. He left Ruby with Smith and took another walk through the apartment. The smoke was more than just cigarette smoke. There was a heap of ashes out on the fire escape. Unrecognizable, but Gerald knew it was the sheets from off of the bed.

"Let's frisk'em," he said to Smith, and holstered his gun. Smith held his gun on the Jags while Gerald frisked them one at a time. They handcuffed each of the gang members and called for more units to help bring everybody in and bring homicide up to the apartment.

Ruby sat in the squad car beside Andrew, She didn't have a jacket on, and she was shivering in the cool night air. Andrew scowled at her and didn't say anything. Ruby turned her face away from him and leaned against the window of the car. She closed her eyes and let herself drift. She'd hardly been able to stay awake since Tim and Jack had wakened her. Now sitting in the moving car with the drone of the engine, it was easy to fall asleep.

∽

When Gerald got out of the car, He saw that Ruby had fallen asleep. Smith got Andrew out of the car, and Gerald opened Ruby's door. Ruby nearly fell out of the car. Gerald caught her and pulled her to her feet. He had to practically drag her into the police station. He put her into one of the interrogation rooms, depositing her into a folding chair. Ruby put her head down on the table in front of her, and was immediately unconscious. Gerald shook his head in disgust and left the room to see if Smith needed a hand with Andrew.

When he got back to Ruby, she was still fast asleep on the table. A stream of saliva was running down her chin. He left and got a coffee, and brought it back with him. He shook Ruby hard to waken her, and put the coffee in her hand.

"Drink up; it's going to be a long night."

"I don't feel good," Ruby mumbled.

"What are you on?"

"Just pain pills for my ankle," she gestured to the cast, in case he didn't understand.

"Drink the coffee."

She sipped at it obediently.

"What happened tonight?" Gerald questioned.

"Nothing. I wasn't feeling good. I went to bed."

"Uh-huh. Why don't you tell me who killed the boy?"

"What boy?"

"The Terminator your boys dropped down on the sidewalk."

"I don't know what you're talking about."

"How old are you, Ruby?"

"Fourteen."

"You want to know what juvie is like for fourteen year old girls?"

"Don't threaten me," she muttered.

"I'm not threatening you, I'm telling you like it is. You ever been in prison before?"

"I'm not going to prison."

"What do you think happens when you're accessory to a murder?" he questioned, leaning forward on the table.

"I don't know what happened," she protested. "I was sleeping, I didn't see anything."

"Don't lie to me."

"I'm not."

"You done that coffee? I'll get you another one."

Ruby nodded. Gerald ducked out to get a second cup, and got back as she was starting to doze off again.

"There you go. I can keep them coming just as long as you need them to keep awake. You going to be okay for a while now?"

"Yeah."

"So tell me about what happened."

"I can't. I don't know."

Gerald slapped Ruby. Her eyes went wide, and she leaned back in her chair, moving further away.

"That waken you up a little more?" Gerald demanded. "Maybe you can remember a little bit better now."

"You're not allowed to touch me," Ruby protested.

"You're not in much of a position to argue."

Ruby didn't answer. She sat there looking at him with wide eyes.

"Are you ready to tell me what happened now?" Gerald repeated.

"Nothing happened."

He slapped her again, but Ruby saw it coming this time and avoided the full brunt of the blow. She swallowed, staring at him. He saw her hands clench, but there was nothing she could do. If she decided to try to fight him, in spite of the difference in size, he could put her in cuffs.

"I want my lawyer," Ruby said.

"I don't think so."

"I got the right to have my lawyer here."

"If you're going to call your lawyer, I'm not going to help you."

"I want my lawyer," she insisted.

"What good do you think a legal aid lawyer would be for you now? You've got yourself in the middle of something pretty serious this time."

"I got the right!"

He slapped her again. Ruby pushed her chair back and got up, moving out of his reach. Gerald walked around the table, grabbed her, and pushed her back into the chair.

"Shall we start again?"

"Get away from me."

Smith came in and stood in the doorway. Gerald went out into the hallway with him and shut the door behind him.

"What's up?"

"I thought you might want some details."

"Go ahead."

"Preliminary report is that he's been dead about three hours. He's been lying face down since then. Stabbed to death. They turned up a knife at the scene with blood on it."

"Fingerprints?"

"Two sets. Hers and one of the Jags."

"Okay. Let's book the both of them. Any of those kids talking?"

"Not yet."

"Someone will. We'll play them off each other."

He went back into the room and motioned to Ruby to stand up. He took her by the arm and escorted her out to be fingerprinted and booked. He watched as Ruby was stripped down to change into a jail uniform. Ruby kept her eyes down. Gerald walked up to her.

"You got your cast wet," he commented. Ruby didn't look at him.

"I was in the shower," she said flatly.

"Looks like you got blood on it."

Ruby looked down at her cast. The rim of it was stained brownish-red.

"Let's see your hands," Gerald ordered.

Ruby clenched her fists and didn't let him see them. The heavy-set matron who was attending to her change of clothes grasped one of her hands firmly and forced it open for Gerald to see. He examined her nails for blood, but couldn't spot any. The matron released Ruby and briskly finished changing her. Gerald took her back to an interrogation room.

"So your fingerprints are on the murder weapon too," he commented.

Ruby didn't say anything. She rubbed the fabric of her uniform.

"It will be better if you just tell me what happened, Ruby."

"Nothing happened."

"Don't start that again."

"It's the truth."

"Tell me what it was that happened. I'm sure there's a good explanation," he pressed.

"I want my lawyer."

Gerald pushed the table violently out of the way and slapped her harder this time, making her head snap back.

"What happened, huh? What did he do? Did he try to hurt you or were you just in a bad mood?" his voice grew louder with each question, "Did you do it in cold blood? Was it an initiation to the Jags? What was a Terminator even doing there? Someone bring him in? Tell me what happened!"

Tears sprang to Ruby's eyes, but Gerald couldn't tell whether she was upset or angry. She stood up, and Gerald caught the automatic movement of her hand to her pocket before she remembered that she was not wearing her own clothes and was not armed. She was prepared to defend herself, but there wasn't much she could do without a weapon.

"Sit down."

"No."

He caught her by the shoulder to sit her down, and she pulled away. Gerald grabbed her arm tightly and forced her to sit down. Ruby swore at him angrily. He ignored her protests.

"What happened tonight?" he pressed.

"Nothing happened."

"A boy is dead. Murdered. That's not nothing. You were there, you did it."

"No, I didn't."

"How did your fingerprints get on the murder weapon?"

"I don't know."

"How did blood get on your cast?" Gerald raised an eyebrow.

"I don't know."

"Don't know much, do you?"

Ruby shrugged, eying him warily.

"Do you know what's going to happen to you?"

"I'm going to go home."

"No, you're not. You're spending the night in a cell here, and then you're going to be transferred to juvenile. You'll go to court, you'll get convicted, and you'll go back to juvenile for a few more years. Maybe we'll be able to convince a judge that you're a dangerous offender and get you tried as an adult."

"I'm not going to jail."

Gerald shook his head. He walked out to find out how the others were doing. Smith was working at a desk and saw him.

"Any luck?"

"So far she's denying that anything ever happened. She's pretty sure of herself, but I think that will wear off with the drugs."

"She's high?"

"Pain pills, she says. Uh-huh. They're not prescription, I'll tell you that. Any progress with the others?"

"One says he doesn't know what happened, but he's sure it was the girl. Seems he's more worried about how the Terminators will react than about the cops. They've identified the boy as the newest leader of the Terminators. Killing the other gang's boss is not good for PR."

"How did the leader of the Terminators end up in the bedroom of a Jag's apartment?" Gerald questioned, frowning.

"Vice says that the Jaguars and Terminators have been working together lately. They had formed some sort of alliance against the other gangs."

"Well, this will certainly improve that relationship, won't it?"

"I don't think so."

"Neither do I. Who should I talk to in there if I want to play them for some more information?"

Smith looked down at his paperwork.

"Guy in number three. Tim Nietz. He's pretty jumpy, but he hasn't said anything yet."

"Great."

Gerald went into interrogation room three. Tim was sitting in a chair trying to put on his toughest face, but his underlying nervousness was clear.

"Well, Tim," Gerald said, interrupting the other officer who was there questioning him. "Your friend Ruby has certainly been saying some interesting things."

Tim turned to him, scowling.

"You don't know anything."

"On the contrary. I've learned quite a bit about what happened there tonight. Ruby's pretty shaken up."

"She's just stoned," Tim sneered, trying to hide his concern, "She doesn't have a clue what happened."

"Drugs have a funny effect on people. Some people they make quiet, some people get talkative…"

"Ruby gets tired. You think I don't know? She's been out of it all night. A bomb could'a' gone off in the room and she wouldn't have known the difference."

"She's tired," Gerald conceded, "But she does seem to have moments of clarity. So why don't you help yourself and tell us what happened, so we don't have to take this any further."

"I'm not talking about it."

"I think you'll change your mind. I think you should reconsider, seeing as there's only so many people that Ruby could point the finger at."

Tim leaned back in his seat.

"Ruby would never point the finger at me, even if I had done something. But I didn't."

"You may think so, but it's different when a person's scared, when they know they're going down. They reach out for someone to drag down with them. And whoever's closest… she probably thinks that you would understand. That you wouldn't mind going down for her."

"I'm not going down. I wasn't there," he shrugged.
"Can you prove it? You have an alibi?"
"I was out with the rest of the guys. They'll tell you that."
"And I suppose Ruby was out with you too."
"Ruby was sleeping."
"And this Terminator just walked into the apartment, stabbed himself, and died there."
Tim grinned.
"Now you got it, man," he agreed, running a hand through his hair.
"Why don't I believe that?"
"If you believe what Ruby says when she's stoned, you'll believe anything."
"Not when what she's saying makes sense."
A flash of doubt crossed Tim's face, and then was gone. He smirked, looking self-assured.
"Well, I'm glad something about this makes sense," he commented, tipping his chair back on two legs. Gerald turned and walked out. He went back to Smith.
"Which one had his fingerprints on the knife?"
"Number six. Jack Wilson, leader of the gang."
"So you think the leader of the Jags killed the leader of the Terminators? I guess it's a distinct possibility."
"Yeah."
Gerald glanced in at Ruby before going on to talk to Jack. She had managed to stay awake since he'd left her. She was sitting on the chair, fidgeting with her empty coffee cup. Caffeine was kicking in and the drugs were wearing off. He went on to interrogation room six. He planned on just listening to what the other officer was saying to Jack, but when he entered, Jack looked up at him and demanded to know who he was.
"I've just been in talking to your girlfriend."
He snorted.
"Ruby's not my girlfriend. She was Mikey's girlfriend; we've just been looking after her since he was offed."
"And that includes killing Terminators for her?"
"Why would I kill a Terminator? We have an arrangement with them."
"So you're going to let Ruby take the fall for this one."
"What're you talking about? She's not going to take any heat for this."
"Only two sets of prints on the murder weapon."

"So we both touched it since it was used. Big deal. I took it out of Troy's guts."

"And Ruby?"

He shrugged.

"I guess she looked at it after I put it down."

"Why didn't you call the police when you just happened to find a Terminator dead in your apartment?"

"It ain't my apartment."

"Why didn't you call the police?"

"Because I didn't want to attract any heat, okay? I didn't want this," he gestured to his surroundings. "So we thought we'd just get rid of the evidence. So are you going to charge us with obstruction? Because I want to go home."

"Tell me what you found when you got to the apartment."

"We found a stiff. It wouldn't be the first time, right? Someone got sloppy and didn't clean up after himself."

"Where was Troy?"

"On the bed."

"Where was Ruby?"

"I didn't notice."

"Tim said she was out with you fellows," Gerald suggested.

"Well, then she must have been there."

"Ruby said she was sleeping at the apartment."

"Then I guess they'd better get their stories straight, huh?" Jack shrugged.

"Why was Troy killed?"

"Guess he got in someone's way."

"Why wasn't he out with his own gang?"

"Maybe he was. Maybe they were *all* at the apartment."

"I think you know that didn't happen," Gerald said.

"What do I know? I wasn't there."

"But Ruby was."

"Ask Ruby."

"Was Ruby the only one there?"

"I don't know."

Gerald rolled his eyes.

"Come on Jack. We both know that you know what happened there tonight."

"I wasn't there. I don't know anything."

"You know what happened."

"I wasn't there," Jack repeated. "I don't know."

"Can you prove you were somewhere else?"

"Can you prove I was there?"

"I don't need to. The jury will take one look at you and know that you were there. We've got your fingerprints on the knife. We don't need anything else to get a conviction."

"So convict me," Jack said, shrugging.

Gerald nodded his head.

"We will, boy. You can count on it."

Jack laughed at him. Gerald walked back out and went to talk to Ruby again. She was still awake.

"You ready to tell me what happened now?"

"No."

"I've been talking to some of the Jaguars. It sounds as if you were the only one at the apartment, huh?"

Ruby didn't answer.

"You were the only one there when he was killed, and your fingerprints are all over the weapon. What do you think that adds up to in court?"

"You don't know what happened."

"So tell me."

Ruby shook her head. Gerald got fed up with her stubbornness.

"Fine. We'll see how many days in jail it takes before you're ready to talk. Come on."

He motioned for her to stand up. Ruby got up slowly, and he took her by the arm.

"Let's go."

She was slow and unsteady on her feet. As soon as they got out where other people were, Ruby started to make a fuss about not being allowed to see her lawyer.

"All right, you can call him," Gerald said quickly. He led her to a phone.

"Where's my bag?" Ruby questioned.

"Still back at the apartment. It's evidence."

"His number's in my bag."

"Look it up in the phone book, then."

Ruby looked at the big phone book by the phone.

"I don't know how to spell it."

"What's his name?"

"Willhelm."

He took the phone book from her impatiently, and flipped through it.

"J. Willhelm?"

"Yeah, John."

Gerald read the number to Ruby, and she dialed it carefully. A male voice answered the phone.

"Uh—Johnny?"

There was silence for a moment.

"No, this is Darren. Who's this?"

Ruby frowned.

"It's Ruby. Aren't you..." she trailed off, confused.

"Just a sec," he said, and passed the phone to Wilhelm, saying something to him.

"Who is this?" Willhelm questioned.

"Ruby Simpson," she swallowed. "I'm in a bit of trouble."

"Where are you?"

"Police station."

"What for?"

"Murder," Ruby said, her voice small.

"Yikes. I'll come down. Don't talk to anyone."

"Okay."

"I'll be right down."

"Thanks."

Ruby hung up the phone slowly. Gerald was waiting for her impatiently.

"All right? Let's get you down for the night."

"My lawyer's coming. Right now."

"Well, he can pick you up from the cell block."

He escorted her to the jail cells. Ruby stopped as he walked her by some of the other Jags who had already been incarcerated.

"I want to be with the others."

"We don't mix the sexes in the cells. Boys and girls are separate."

"I don't want to be in with the women."

"Too bad."

He had the jailer put her in a cell with a few women. Ruby hobbled over to one of the bunks and sat down. The women looked at her and didn't say anything.

Willhelm walked along the row of cells, wondering what Ruby had managed to get herself into this time. He saw her sitting forlornly on one of the bunks, looking very small and scared. The officer who had introduced himself as Smith had the guard unlock the door. Ruby looked up to see what was going on, and brightened a little when she saw Willhelm. She looked exhausted. She got up slowly and Willhelm noticed the cast on her leg. She didn't have any crutches. She limped over, and hugged Willhelm. He patted her comfortingly on the back, awkward. He tried to detach her tactfully. After a moment she withdrew. Tears had started down her cheeks.

"Johnny…"

"Wait until we're alone, Ruby."

She sniffled and she hung onto his arm for support as they walked down the hall. The guard wanted to handcuff her, but Smith shook his head.

"She's all right."

Smith showed them into an interrogation room, and stood at the door for a minute watching through the skinny window. Ruby embraced Willhelm again, sobbing. Willhelm looked up and saw Smith still watching them. Their eyes met, and Smith backed up and left. Willhelm rubbed Ruby's back.

"It's okay. Settle down Ruby, and tell me what happened." He sat her down, and sat down across from her. "Just take a breath and tell me what happened."

Gerald looked up when Smith opened the door. Smith stood there waiting for him. Gerald joined him in the hallway.

"Ruby's lawyer got here."

"Uh-huh."

"She broke down. She's talking to him."

"She's coming off her high. She's not feeling so good about herself any more. I bet the lawyer will be in here to plea within the hour."

Smith nodded.

Ruby wiped at the tears on her face, trying to slow them down. She was embarrassed by her show of emotion, but couldn't seem to shut the tears off.

"I'm sorry," she apologized.

"You've had a pretty rough night. It's okay."

"I had to stop Troy!" she insisted.

"It's self-defense. They can't put you in jail when it was self-defense."

"He wouldn't leave me alone."

"We'll work it out. Don't you worry about it," he soothed again.

Ruby nodded, choking on her sobs. Smith and Gerald walked into the room.

"So, what's up?" Gerald questioned.

"Ruby's pleading self-defense," Willhelm advised.

"Let's hear her story."

"Ruby was attacked. This boy has been terrorizing Ruby for months. He attacked her while she was sleeping and she defended herself the only way she could."

"Why didn't Ruby tell us that when she was arrested? Because she needed time to think up a story?"

"Because she wanted to talk to her lawyer."

"She could have requested counsel at any time. She was just high and too confused to think of anything."

"Ruby told me that you hit her."

"Ruby's a little liar," Gerald snapped.

"Ruby's a young girl in police custody with a bruised face," Willhelm countered.

"Ruby was arrested last week for armed robbery and this week for murder. Tell her she should start keeping better company."

Ruby covered her face with her hands as another flood of tears washed over her cheeks.

"I want to go home," she choked out.

"You're not keeping her here tonight," Willhelm told Gerald.

"Ruby's staying in our custody until a court says otherwise."

"Release her to me. I'll make sure she gets to court."

"Can't do that. Ruby's a dangerous offender."

"I'd like to talk to your supervisor."

Gerald shrugged.

"I'll get him. But he is going to tell you the same thing."

Gerald and Smith left. Willhelm looked at Ruby.

"You know I'm not going to be able to get you home tonight."

"Yeah," she sniffled.

"You'll be free to go tomorrow."

"Okay."

"Don't worry. It'll be okay. You didn't do anything wrong. You just defended yourself."

Ruby nodded.

"Now what's this about armed robbery?" Willhelm questioned.

"Nothing. I was there when it happened."

"What's up with that?"

"It's going to go to court too."

"Well, you've been leading an exciting life, haven't you? Why don't you cool it for a while?"

Ruby nodded.

"Okay," she said in a small voice.

"Okay. I'm going to take you back so you can get some sleep tonight. Then I'll talk to the police a bit more before I have to go to the office. You get lots of sleep tonight and in the morning, and we'll get your hearing out of the way in no time."

"Yeah."

Ruby stood up and followed him to the door.

"Johnny?"

He glanced at her, shaking his head slightly.

"Don't call me Johnny, okay? John or Willhelm. Not Johnny. What is it?"

"Darren—he's the guy I met at your place, right?"

"Yeah, you did."

"Are you and him…?" Ruby trailed off.

Willhelm raised his brows questioningly.

"I know you said he was your friend," Ruby said awkwardly. "But he has a key to your apartment and answers your phone at four in the morning. You guys are…" she hesitated, "roommates?"

"Yes."

"Oh."

Ruby thought back to his reaction to finding her in bed with him, to her being in the bathroom when he was showering, and his confusion on coming into the kitchen and finding her shirtless, and then Darren coming in and seeing her there. She started to grin, thinking about how brazenly she had flirted with him, all the while thinking she was so close to breaking down his defenses. Willhelm smiled back, obviously thinking about the same thing.

"Now you understand why things were so… awkward," he said.

"Yeah, I get it now. Why didn't you tell me?"

"I honestly didn't know whether you were consciously trying to… interest me… or if it was unconscious."

Ruby shook her head.

"Next time maybe I'll figure it out sooner."

He smiled.

"Let's get you to bed."

They couldn't find any evidence that it wasn't self-defense. All of the Jags backed up the story that Ruby was left alone in the apartment sleeping, if they said anything. When Ruby's lawyer mentioned to them she was pleading self-defense, a couple of them volunteered the story of coming back to the apartment to find Troy dead in Ruby's bed. As much as Gerald tried to discredit their stories, the details were fairly consistent. The more they dug, the more genuine the story seemed to be. Gerald was eventually told to drop the charges and let Ruby go. There was no hearing to be held, Ruby was simply to be set free. The rest of the Jags were warned about destroying evidence, obstructing justice, etcetera, and they were also let go. If there was no murder, there were no accessories, and nobody wanted to deal with the paperwork.

"Coming back to my place?" Tim questioned Ruby.

"No... not yet. In a day or two. I don't feel like going back there yet."

Tim shrugged, understanding.

"Don't be long in coming back, okay?"

"I won't. Be there tomorrow or next day."

"Okay."

He gave her a quick kiss.

"See you later."

Ruby went to the bus stop.

When Ruby got to Marty's house, she was ready to crash. She'd only gotten a couple of hours sleep. Marty was in the living room watching TV, and Stella was on the floor on a blanket. Marty looked up.

"Are you okay?"

"Yeah."

"You look horrible."

"Thanks."

Ruby went to the bedroom and lay down. Marty followed her into the bedroom, handing her a stack of papers and a pen.

"Sign these where the red tags are," she instructed.

Ruby looked at the documents blankly.

"What's this?"

"Papers giving Mom joint guardianship of Stella."

"Why?"

"So that we can legally take care of her when you take off. And when you're here, for that matter."

"Why your mom?" Ruby questioned. "Why not you?"

"I'm not old enough."

Ruby stared down at the papers.

"What if I want to take her somewhere?"

"You're still her guardian too. Both of you would be."

Ruby considered it, then shrugged and signed all of the tagged pages.

"I'm going to sleep," she said, handing them back.

"Okay."

Marty's mom got in. She greeted Marty with a smile, and took her jacket off. Marty motioned to the papers.

"She signed them."

"Good. Is she still here?"

"Yeah. Her face is bruised up. She just wanted to go to bed."

"I worry about her," Mrs. Rodger sighed.

"Me too."

Ruby woke up when Marty and Stella got up from their nap. She sat up and watched Marty play with Stella. Marty heard the bedsprings creak and turned over.

"Hi."

"Hi." Ruby rubbed her eyes.

"Are you going to tell me what happened to you?" Marty questioned

Ruby shook her head.

"No."

"Why not?"

"You'll get mad."

"Why would I get mad?"

Ruby rolled her eyes.

"Trust me, you would."

"Who hit you?"

Ruby shook her head.

"I got in trouble. You don't want to know."

"What kind of trouble? More police trouble?"

"Yeah. But they let me go. They dropped the charges."

"Stay away from the Jags and you'll stop getting into that kind of trouble," Marty advised.

"It wasn't the Jags."

"You weren't with the Jags yesterday?"

"Yeah, but it wasn't because of them."

"Just tell me what happened," Marty said in exasperation.

"No."

Ruby got up and left the room. Marty shook her head and changed Stella's diaper.

CHAPTER
Thirteen

Ruby stayed up watching TV until Marty's dad came home from work. He saw her sitting there.

"Well, hi there. What are you still doing up?" he questioned.

Ruby tried to decide whether to get up and retreat or whether to sink into the couch and pray he left her alone. She stayed frozen where she was.

"I couldn't sleep," she muttered.

"What? Speak up so I can hear you."

"Leave me alone."

"I'm not doing anything to hurt you," he snapped, leaning over the couch to look at her.

Ruby cringed away from him.

"Stay away from me."

He stroked her cheek and neck. Ruby closed her eyes, her throat closing up. Her stomach tied itself in knots. He touched her hair gently, pushing it back from her face. Ruby reached up to push his hand back. He caught her hand and cradled her face in his other big, rough hand. His hands were huge, they covered her whole face. He moved around the couch to move closer to her.

"Get away," Ruby whispered, unable to find her voice.

"You don't want me to go away. You think I haven't seen you making eyes at me? I see you watching me all the time. I know."

Ruby shook her head. He held her still and kissed her. Ruby didn't fight him, paralyzed. He put his arms around her and pulled her close.

"No!"

Ruby sat up, looking around wildly. Marty put her hand on Ruby's leg.

"It's okay Ruby. You're dreaming," she comforted.

"Where's Daddy?" Ruby demanded.

"Whoa. Daddy? He's not here, Ruby. You haven't seen him in a long time," Marty soothed.

"Are you sure?"

"I'm sure. It's okay."

Ruby laid back down slowly, rubbing her hands on the front of her shirt.

"Can you get it off? It's stained."

"There's nothing on your shirt, Ruby. It was just a dream. Go back to sleep."

Ruby was unconvinced. She rubbed it harder.

"I have to take a shower."

"It's the middle of the night. You can shower in the morning."

"I have to shower now," Ruby insisted, climbing out of bed.

"Ruby..."

It was too late. Ruby was out the door. And a few minutes later, the shower went on. Marty shook her head and let herself doze off again. She awoke to Ruby getting back into bed again.

"Okay now, Ruby?" she questioned softly.

"Hold me."

Marty turned over and hugged Ruby. They both fell back asleep.

Ruby walked into the kitchen, yawning and stretching. She made no mention of her nightmare.

"I'm taking the baby out today."

"I'd rather you stayed around here with her," Marty countered.

"She's my baby," Ruby challenged.

"You going to see Jamie today, or something?"

"Yeah."

"Don't keep her away all day, okay? She doesn't know you. And don't keep her overnight."

Ruby shrugged and didn't agree or disagree.

"I'll get the stroller. You're going to change her before we go, right?"

Marty smiled.

"I think you should change her."

"No way."

"It's not hard."

"Not for you. No way, you change her."

Marty did. She got Stella ready to go, knowing there was no point in arguing about it. All she could do was hope that Ruby would bring her back after a few hours. Ruby took a few minutes to get Stella buckled in properly, and left for Jamie's place.

Jamie worked on homework while Ruby watched TV. Stella squirmed around on the floor, jamming her fists in her mouth and slobbering. She occasionally squawked at Ruby, but Ruby ignored her. After a while she approached Jamie and looked over his shoulder.

"Are you almost done?"

"Pretty near. Play with Stella a while, then I'll be done."

"I'm bored," Ruby complained.

"Well, find something to do. Give Stella a bath or something."

"Why would I want to do that?"

"Ruby, leave me alone. You know I've got work to do."

Ruby withdrew.

"I don't know what you want to go to college for anyway," she muttered, flopping down on the couch.

He looked at her over his shoulder.

"You can get a better job if you go to college."

"Your daddy's going to give you a job anyway, why bother?"

Jamie shrugged.

"Well, he's paying for college. What do I care?"

Ruby got up again and wandered around the room restlessly.

"Isn't it boring? I hate school."

"Well, it's not high school."

"I'm not in high school."

"Yeah, I keep forgetting. Just be quiet for a few minutes while I finish this off."

"Yeah."

Ruby sat and watched a mind-blowingly boring daytime soap. It was another half hour before Jamie finished his work and closed his books. He came over to where Ruby was sitting.

"Sorry, hon'. I was as quick as I could be," he apologized contritely.

Ruby looked sullen.

"I came to be with you."

"You know I have to keep up with school. Sometimes it's going to interfere with things."

He put his arm around Ruby. Ruby pulled away, still angry. Stella started to cry, and when Ruby didn't move to look at her, Jamie bent over and picked her up.

"She needs to be changed."

"Go ahead."

Jamie shook his head and took Stella to the bathroom where there was a changing pad on the bathroom counter. Ruby listened to him babbling to Stella while he changed her. He sure did like babies.

He brought her back out a few minutes later, talking in his high, baby talk voice.

"There, mommy, all clean and sweet again. Tell mommy it's time to eat, Stella."

Stella burbled and smiled at Ruby.

"Come on, Ruby, let's feed her."

Ruby got up from her seat. Jamie had gotten a high chair since they'd been there last. Jamie put Stella into the seat and got a jar of baby food out of the fridge. Ruby sat down at the table and watched him feed Stella strained carrots. That was how daddies should be. He was so patient with her. He actually liked her. He liked to feed her, liked to change her, liked to hold her and rock her to sleep.

But feeding Stella was tedious and took a long time. Ruby got a beer out of the fridge and sat drinking it, waiting for Jamie's attention to turn back to her. Although Ruby was happy to provide something that interested Jamie, she was jealous of all of the attention Stella got from him. Jamie should have been paying attention to Ruby.

Stella was asleep in her food by the time she finished the carrots. Jamie put her down in the stroller to sleep.

"Now we can spend some time together," he announced.

"James... do you have some Aspirin or something for my ankle? The pain is killing me."

He looked at her and saw how pale she was.

"Yeah, I have some pills that work great. I'll get some for you."

"Thanks."

The pills the doctor gave her just didn't work. Ruby needed something stronger, like Tim had given her. Jamie brought her out some prescription pills, and Ruby swallowed them.

Her ankle took a long time to heal. She was still taking pain pills after the doctor took the cast off. Some she got from the doctor, although those weren't very potent, some she got from the gang or from Jamie. Marty never had anything strong enough to make a difference to Ruby. Stella was starting to toddle by the time Ruby got the cast off. The hearing for the armed robbery kept getting put off further, and Willhelm told Ruby that he didn't think it would go to court. The witness was too unreliable, and had never been able to finger the trigger man.

It was hard going back to the gang after what happened with Troy. Ruby had nightmares there. Not that she didn't have them at Marty's house too, but at Tim's there were always more people around to hear her cry out in the night. No-one ever said anything, but Ruby knew she often woke the others up. The alliance between the Terminators and the Jaguars dissolved with the news that Ruby had killed Troy. The fighting between the two gangs was fiercer than ever, and Ruby had to be especially careful of where she went. She was a target any time she got close to Terminator territory, and had to make sure that she was never alone. She had to be with Jack, Tim, or one of the others any time she even got close to the edges of their territory. But Ruby was a good fighter, and they didn't complain too much about having to babysit her.

The sickness hit her suddenly. At first Ruby thought it was the pills. They often made her nauseous in the morning. But they didn't make her throw up or so sick she could hardly move. The first couple of days she was at Tim's apartment. After two wretched days of hardly being able to move, Ruby managed to get one of the guys to drive her to Marty's house. He helped Ruby up the sidewalk, and she walked into the house with shaky knees and a churning stomach.

The house was empty. Marty must have gone out with Stella somewhere. Stella was big enough now that Marty had a little bit of freedom to get out of the house with her. Marty was always telling her what new thing Stella had done—or worrying about what things she hadn't. Not that Ruby encouraged this. She was glad that Stella hadn't started talking yet. She went into the bedroom and lay down.

Marty was chattering away to Stella when she got in. For someone who had never had much to say, Marty was always talking to the baby.

"Oh, hi, Ruby. You okay?"

"I don't feel good."

"I hear there's a wicked flu going around. But we haven't got it yet, have we Stella?"

Stella smiled a gummy grin and squealed. Ruby groaned.

"I haven't been this sick in a long time... I think I was with the Winters last time I felt like this."

"Well, it will pass in a day or two. You've just picked up some bug."

Ruby would have nodded in agreement, but it would just make her feel worse. She closed her eyes and drifted off to sleep.

Marty made coffee, ignoring her father sitting at the table. He would go to bed before too long as long as she didn't encourage him to talk to her. They were both studiously ignoring the sounds of Ruby around the corner in the bathroom throwing up.

"She's not pregnant again, is she?" Marty's dad demanded.

"No, she's just got the flu."

"We can't afford another brat running around here."

"She's just sick. She wouldn't be dumb enough to get pregnant again."

He grunted and didn't pursue it. But Marty watched the coffee percolate, wondering if it was true. She hadn't even considered the possibility that Ruby was pregnant again. Stella was not quite a year old. It didn't make sense that Ruby would let it happen again. Marty was sure Ruby couldn't be pregnant again.

Stella was playing on the floor beside Ruby's bed. Ruby was lying in bed and was supposed to be keeping an eye on her. Marty came back in.

"How's she been?"

"Good."

"You don't do much with her," Marty said. Not really a complaint. Mostly an observation.

"No, so what?" Ruby shrugged.

"You wouldn't get pregnant again, would you?"

"No."

"I mean, with Stella, it was just an accident, right?" Mary persisted.

"Uh-huh."

"You always use..."

"Look, I'm careful," Ruby said hotly. "Getting pregnant before wasn't my fault!"

"Have you ever told her dad?"

"He's dead."

Marty was surprised.

"What?"

Ruby shrugged and nodded.

"He's dead," she repeated.

"When did this happen? You never told me that before."

"A while ago."

"How? What happened?"

Ruby shook her head and didn't answer. Marty played with Stella.

"So how're you feeling?"

Ruby groaned.

"Ruby..." Marty started hesitantly.

"Uh-huh?"

"Is this how you felt before you had Stella? When you went to the doctor and he told you it was morning sickness?"

Ruby nodded.

"This is what you felt like then?" Marty repeated.

"Uh-huh."

"Then you're pregnant again."

Ruby shook her head.

"Can't be."

Marty shrugged and picked up Stella.

"If you have another baby, I'm not taking care of it. I'll call Social Services."

"I'm not having another baby."

Brian snuggled under the warm blankets of the bed with Ruby.

"It's been a long time since we saw each other, huh Ruby?"

Ruby nodded.

"I been sick, and with the gang... and Jamie—but all he's interested in is the baby."

Brian frowned.

"I like to be with you, and you can stay with Marty. I don't know why you want to be with anyone else."

Ruby traced a circle on the bed sheet with her finger.

"I don't know why," she said slowly. "I'm scared not to be with the gang... they're protection. And Jamie... he's like a family or something. You know—daddy, mommy, baby... like a real family instead of just me by myself."

"Why don't you go visit your family or something? How long has it been since you saw any of them?"

"I dunno... seems like a couple of years now... I was at Winters when I saw Ronnie. The others, it's been longer than that."

"Why don't you go see them?"

"Nah... I don't really want to see my parents. I'd like to see Chloe and Ronnie. But..."

"But what? Why don't you see them, then?"

"I'm not allowed to."

"Oh."

They were silent for a while.

"And I don't like to be at Marty's if her dad's home," Ruby said.

"Marty doesn't get along with him real well either, I don't think. But it's better than anywhere else you could stay."

Ruby nodded.

"At least you're not bouncing around to different foster families anymore."

"Yeah," she agreed.

"I need money," Ruby told Jamie, out of the blue, as they ate a fast-food dinner. He looked at her.

"Money? What for?"

"I got a... I got a problem I gotta take care of."

"A problem? What are you talking about? What kind of problem?"

"I have to see a doctor."

"Social Services pays for your medical bills, don't they?"

"Yeah, usually. But not this time."

"Why not? What do you need done?"

Ruby shrugged.

"Nothing. It's personal. Besides, I don't exactly want to let them know where I'm living. I'm sort of... under the radar."

"How much do you need?"

"A few hundred."

Jamie frowned.

"What are you getting done?"
Ruby shook her head.
"I don't want to talk about it."
"Are you sick? I thought you were feeling better."
"I have some pills… but…"
"Are you okay?"
Ruby shook her head.
"I don't want to talk about it."

Marty opened the door and saw Jamie standing there. Marty looked over her shoulder at Stella, and stood toe to toe with Jamie so that he couldn't get in.
"Ruby's not here."
"That's okay. I wanted to talk to you about her."
Marty frowned.
"What about her?"
"She's been asking about money… for some medical procedure."
"What medical procedure?"
"She wouldn't say. I got the feeling… maybe it was for an abortion."
Marty felt sick. She swallowed and shook her head.
"An abortion? Did she say that?"
"No. She said she's been sick… she said it would be a few hundred dollars… she didn't want to talk about it."
"Oh, no. That's just great. Well, I told her I wouldn't take care of another baby."
"I would take care of it."
Marty looked at him.
"You would? What about school?"
"I could get a sitter when I was out."
Marty shrugged.
"Well, you'd better tell her that, then."
"I will, when she comes back. So is she pregnant for sure?"
"I think so. She says no, but she did the first time too."
"Why?"
"I don't know. She just can't seem to handle it. Are you the father?"
Jamie laughed explosively.
"You're not subtle, are you? No, I couldn't be. We were always careful."

"That's what Ruby always says, but she's not careful enough. Careful doesn't get you two pregnancies."

Jamie jumped to Ruby's defense.

"I don't think the first time was her fault. I met the guy who said Stella was his. He was pretty... nasty."

"Ruby said he's dead."

"Did she? Well, he was in one of the gangs, so I guess that happens."

"What do you mean it wasn't Ruby's fault? Unless he..."

Jamie nodded.

"I don't think it was consensual."

"How do you know?"

He shrugged widely.

"You didn't see them together. She pulled her knife on him. Pretty good sign that they weren't on good terms."

Marty sighed.

"Well, that's something, at least. But that can't be what happened this time, too."

"But Ruby's always careful."

"Birth control fails. Even if you're careful."

Jamie looked uncomfortable with her statement.

"I don't know who the father is... but I don't want her to get an abortion."

Marty nodded.

"I'll tell her when I see her."

"Tell her I'll take care of the baby. I don't care whose it is."

Marty nodded again.

"Okay. I'll tell her."

It was Tim who brought Ruby home. She was leaning on his arm and was very pale. Marty had never met Tim before. He seemed a little embarrassed, helping Ruby into the house, ducking his head in a quick greeting, flushing red at the throat.

"What happened?" Marty questioned. "Are you okay?"

"She's okay," Tim said. "Just a little shaky."

"Ruby... you had an abortion?"

Ruby looked up at Marty, eyes surprised.

"Yeah."

"Are you okay?"

"Yeah. I'm okay."

Marty put her arm around Ruby.

"You'd better get some rest."

Ruby nodded. Tim stood in the doorway for a few moments.

"I'll see you around, okay Ruby?"

"Thanks, Tim."

"Yeah, no problem."

Marty took Ruby into the bedroom and helped ease her into bed.

"You should have stuck around here. Jamie was looking for you—didn't want you to have an abortion."

"I'm not having a baby," Ruby said flatly.

"Jamie said he'd take care of the baby, if you kept it."

Ruby shrugged.

"I don't ever want another baby."

"Then you stop putting yourself in risky situations," Marty insisted.

"I just want to go to sleep, Marty," Ruby begged.

"Okay, sweetie. You go to sleep."

Ruby nodded and curled up. Marty left her alone.

Marty walked into the bathroom to bathe when Ruby was washing down a couple pills with a glass of water. Marty frowned.

"Are you still taking those morning sickness pills?"

Ruby glanced at her.

"I still feel sick."

"Maybe you should see the doctor again. You shouldn't need them anymore."

Ruby shook her head.

"It'll go away. I'll just finish the bottle."

"You should see the doctor if you're still sick," Marty insisted.

"I'm okay."

"You look better today. Are you still depressed?"

"Feeling a bit better."

"Good. Are you going out?"

Ruby nodded.

"Yeah."

"If you want to go to the doctor tomorrow, I'm taking Stella in. You could come along."

"What for?"

Marty hesitated.

"She's not meeting milestones. She's not developing like she's supposed to."

"She's slow."

"She's more than slow."

Ruby shrugged.

"Whatever. I don't want to go to the doctor tomorrow."

"Okay."

Tim watched Ruby as she slept. She looked peaceful when she slept, like she never did when she was awake. Awake, she always looked restless and unhappy. She smiled sometimes when she was having a good time, but it wasn't a really happy smile. She'd been depressed since the abortion, too. The doctor said that was a normal reaction. But Tim hadn't thought that Ruby would be. She was tough, she could handle it. Besides, she really hadn't wanted the baby. So why be depressed by the abortion?

He stroked Ruby's cheek, and she started to wake up. She frowned, and a few minutes later, opened her eyes.

"Hey," she said softly.

"Hi, Ruby. You ready to get up?"

"Why?" she rolled over and looked around. "What's happening?"

"We're gonna go over and shoot some pool."

Ruby stretched.

"Okay."

"You want to shower? It's free."

"Yeah."

Ruby looked like there was something she wanted to say. Tim waited for her to continue. Ruby shrugged and didn't say anything.

"What is it?" he prompted.

Ruby was hesitant.

"Those pills you gave me before... do you have something that would make me feel better...? Not so bad...?"

"Yeah, sure—I can get you some uppers. You'll feel better."

Ruby nodded.

"Good. I just can't... I can't keep on feeling like this."

"It'll make you feel better. I promise."

"Okay."

Ruby was hyper all night. Her heart raced, and her palms sweated so much that she could hardly even hold a pool cue. But she definitely felt better. She went up for another beer, and Tim followed her.

"Careful how much you drink," he warned. "The pills will make you drunk faster."

Ruby smiled.

"I think I might be drunk already," she admitted.

"Then don't get a drink."

"I'm thirsty."

She ordered a beer, and Tim didn't stop her from taking it.

"Just be careful," he warned.

They made Ruby jumpy too. Although she felt better than she had when depressed, she felt like she was on edge all night. She was sure the Terminators were going to show up at any minute and bring the place down around her ears. She watched the door when anyone came in to make sure it wasn't the Terminators.

"You hopped up?" Jack demanded, scowling at her.

Ruby shrugged.

"Timmy gave me something."

"Just settle down. You're gonna make all the boys jumpy."

"I can't settle down. I'm too hyped." Ruby sidled up to him flirtily. "How come you want me to settle down? You not getting enough attention?"

Jack pushed her away.

"Get off of me," he said disgustedly. "I don't need you slobbering all over me."

"How come you don't have a girlfriend, Jack?" she questioned.

"I have lots of girls."

"But no-one special."

"You let your head be turned by some girl, you get in trouble."

"What girl ever got you in trouble, Jackie?" she teased.

"Don't call me Jackie, sweetheart. Now go play with Timmy, he's all by himself over there just waiting for you. Go on, go cheer him up."

He physically turned her around to face in Tim's direction. Ruby focused her attention on Tim and walked up to him.

"What's the matter, Timmy?"

She put her arms around his neck and drew up close to him.

"You miss me?" she questioned.

Tim smiled.

"You are *so* smashed, Ruby."

"Uh-huh," she agreed.

She tilted her head up to kiss him, but started when the door opened and turned to see who it was.

"It's okay," Tim said. "Just relax."

She turned back towards him and kissed him.

CHAPTER
Fourteen

Tim walked slowly down the street with Ruby. Her feet hurt. She was sore and tired and walked slowly. Tim didn't say anything for a while, though his thoughts were heavy.

"Ruby..."

"Uh-huh?"

"That doctor I took you to before... for the abortion?"

She looked at him with a frown.

"What about him?"

"I went back to talk to him yesterday."

"Why?"

"I didn't get to talk to him, actually. He wasn't there. So I talked to one of the other doctors at the clinic instead."

"What about?"

"About you," Tim said impatiently. "I know you're still pregnant. So do you."

"I can't be," Ruby objected. "You were there; I didn't chicken out of it. They did the abortion."

Tim nodded.

"I know. That's why I talked to the doctor. It's really rare, see. You must have been carrying twins, and he only aborted one." Tim said it all in one breath.

Ruby looked at him and didn't say anything. She couldn't think of anything to say. It seemed like it didn't matter what she did, she couldn't avoid having babies. She just looked at Tim, trying to fathom it.

"They said you should go see a doctor," Tim said quietly, trying to break it to her gently, "because the baby could be... badly damaged."

Ruby stopped walking and just hung onto her stomach, going green. She leaned against the wall.

"What if I get an abortion now?" she said finally.

"You can't, Ruby. That was months ago. It's too late now."

"I don't want a baby."

"I know."

"Neither does Marty. She's got her hands full with Stella."

Tim just nodded. There was nothing he could say.

"Why didn't they get it right the first time?" Ruby demanded angrily.

Tim didn't say anything. Ruby staggered into the alley and threw up. She leaned against the side of the building between heaves.

"Sorry," Tim told her, when she came back.

She walked along slowly, trying to work it out in her mind. She changed her mind about going back to the apartment and seeing the other Jags. She decided to go back and see Marty instead. She and Tim separated.

Ruby took the bus, and was exhausted by the time she got home. She sat down on one of the kitchen chairs, putting her feet up on another. She rubbed her ankles, closing her eyes. She just sat there, thinking. Eventually Marty's mom got home. Marty and Stella were out somewhere.

"You're looking pretty serious," Mrs. Rodger commented, seeing Ruby there.

"I have a problem," Ruby agreed.

"Do you want to talk about it?"

Ruby nodded, but didn't know how to start. Mrs. Rodger waited without saying anything. She sat down. Ruby moved her hands over her stomach.

"I guess I'm pregnant."

"Again?"

"Yeah. But there's something wrong."

"You saw a doctor?"

Ruby bit her lip. She shook her head.

"I didn't know. I—I had an abortion. But..." she broke off, and tears started down her face. Ruby swiped at them angrily. "The doctor screwed it up," she finished hollowly, "because I'm still pregnant."

"Oh, boy."

Ruby tried to dry the tears from her face and keep up a tough front. Mrs. Rodger took one of her hands.

"It's okay, Ruby. We'll get it worked out. How far along are you?"

"I don't know."

"You know the baby may be handicapped."

"Yeah."

"Have you talked to the father about this?"

Ruby stared at her, and then shook her head.

"Don't you think you should? This is something you should be deciding together."

"No."

"It takes two people to make a baby, Ruby."

Ruby shook her head.

"No. I don't want nothing to do with him!"

"You two are not on good terms?"

"Uh-uh."

"Well, the first thing to do is get you to a doctor. So we can get some more information about when you're due and what kind of damage the baby has."

"What'm I going to do? I don't want this baby."

"We'll talk to the doctor about your options. Okay? It's going to be all right, Ruby."

Ruby swallowed and nodded.

"Okay."

Marty's mom noted that the lab tech didn't bother to warm up the gel before squirting it on Ruby's belly. Ruby jumped when it hit her. A lab tech who didn't like teen moms, Mrs. Rodger guessed. Chewing gum, he put the transponder to Ruby's stomach and moved it around to get a good picture. Mrs. Rodger immediately picked up the sound of the baby's heartbeat, strong and steady. Ruby stared straight up at the ceiling and didn't glance at the monitor. Mrs. Rodger tried to make out details on the screen. She watched the masses of light, trying to make shapes out of them. The technician studied the monitor.

"I'd say you're about four weeks from delivery," he informed Ruby. Ruby didn't acknowledge him.

"That is what you wanted to know, isn't it?" he questioned Mrs. Rodger. "The age of the fetus?"

"Yes, that and the condition of the baby."

"Strong heartbeat. Fully developed spine and brain. I'll bring the doctor in to take a look, but everything looks normal to me."

He put down the transponder and went to find the doctor. Mrs. Rodger looked at Ruby.

"Everything will be fine," she assured Ruby.

Ruby didn't answer. The doctor came in after another half hour of waiting. He took the wand and checked Ruby over. The sound of the heartbeat filled the room again. He turned it down, smiling.

"Well, mommy, looks like you have a good healthy baby there."

Mrs. Rodger moved closer when Ruby didn't answer.

"This pregnancy is the result of an unsuccessful abortion," she explained.

The doctor raised his eyebrows.

"Well then, this is something you only see once in a lifetime. You've got quite the miracle baby here, mommy. Not only did she survive an abortion attempt, but she doesn't appear to have suffered any serious handicaps."

Ruby looked at the doctor for the first time.

"It's not deformed?"

"Not that I can tell from the ultrasound. All organs appear to be fully formed and functioning. We can't tell anything for sure before you deliver, but everything looks normal from here."

Ruby rubbed her eyes and looked at the monitor.

"I'll just give it to Jamie, then."

"Is Jamie the father?" Mrs. Rodger questioned.

"No."

"You're sure?"

She shrugged.

"Are you sure he'll want to take care of a baby that's not his own?"

"Yeah. He said he would. He loves babies."

Mrs. Rodger studied Ruby's uncovered stomach. With Stella, Ruby had put on some weight. She hadn't looked ready to deliver, but she had looked pregnant. This time, even with her gown up, it was hard to tell. You could see her ribs, and her stomach bulged a little, but not much.

"How big is the baby?" she asked the doctor.

"She's small. Not unusual for teen moms. Especially ones who smoke," he said pointedly, glaring at Ruby.

Ruby didn't respond.

"She? It's another girl?" Mrs. Rodger questioned.

"Yes."

She held Ruby's hand.

"I'm sorry we can't take care of her for you, Ruby. But we've already got our hands full with Stella."

"I know. I don't care. Jamie wants a baby."

"Has he ever tried to convince you to get pregnant? With his baby?"

"Yeah… a couple times," Ruby admitted.

"Well, I'm glad you stood up to him."

Ruby scowled.

"I'd rather be carrying his baby than this thing."

"Whose baby is this, Ruby?"

Ruby didn't answer.

Ruby lay in bed beside Marty, with her hands over her stomach. She felt like she was being punished for something, but she didn't know what. She didn't know why she had to keep going through this. She did everything she could to avoid having babies, but here she was again. She didn't know why she was being punished. She knew that most people wouldn't agree with the way she led her life, but it hadn't all been planned, it hadn't all been her fault. It was just the way things had happened. Why should she be punished for something out of her control?

She rolled over onto her side and put her arm around Marty. Throughout everything, Marty was always there, taking care of things. Ruby thought herself mature, but when you looked at Marty, she had so much more responsibility. She took care of a baby not even her own, looked after every need of a baby who wasn't healthy or normal. She could have just turned Stella over to Social Services at any time. She didn't have to do what she did.

Ruby closed her eyes and tried to ignore the constant cramps and go back to sleep.

Ruby had been giggling when she went to bed. She was high as a kite on her pills and booze. She had been a lot lately. Tim had trouble putting her to bed. She struggled with him when he tried to help her undress, and he eventually pushed her into bed still half-clothed. When he climbed in beside her, she wouldn't leave him alone. Tim put his arms around her and held her wrists tightly. She struggled for a while, protesting, but eventually she tired herself out and lay still. Tim fell asleep with his arms around her.

When she awoke in the night he moved away from her, one of his arms numb from lack of circulation. Ruby groaned, and he sleepily rubbed her back to settled her down again. Ruby rolled over and grabbed his arm in a vice-like grip. Tim tried to pry her hand off.

"Ruby, let go. Come on."

Ruby didn't relax her grip. She groaned again, and Tim propped himself up on one elbow, rubbing his eyes.

"Are you okay, Ruby?"

She put her hand over her stomach and released his arm. Tim lay back down and drifted off back to sleep. He slept restlessly, waking and dreaming. When he woke up, Ruby was tossing and turning, almost frantic. Tim put his arm around her.

"Relax, baby. Go to sleep."

She pushed him away. It was starting to get light out, and Tim could see her dimly, her face lined in a grimace.

"Ruby... are you okay? Are you all right?"

She shook her head, eyes screwed shut. Tim sat up.

"What is it, sweetie?"

Someone else muttered at Tim to shut up. Tim brushed the hair out of Ruby's eyes and felt her forehead. She was sweating. Her arms were rigid, her hands clenched into fists.

"The baby," Ruby said through clenched teeth.

Tim's heart raced. He swore.

"I'll take you to the hospital," he promised. He got out of bed and pulled on his shirt and jeans.

"Okay?" he questioned nervously. "You gonna be okay?"

"What's going on?" one of the other boys demanded.

"Ruby's in labor," Tim snapped.

There was dead silence in the room. Although Tim had known about Ruby's condition almost as long as she had, most of the gang didn't have a clue about her pregnancy. Tim looked at Ruby. She made no movement to get up.

"Ruby."

She didn't move. Tim pulled back the blankets to encourage her to get up. They were soaked with blood and water. Tim stood there just staring. He hadn't even felt the wet sheets when he was lying in them. He took Ruby's hand.

"Come on, baby. Let's get you to a doctor."

"I can't."

"You can, come on."

"No."

Someone turned the light on. Ruby covered her eyes. The other boys sat up, rubbing their eyes. A couple pulled their blankets over their heads.

"Should I call an ambulance?" Tim questioned.

Ruby shook her head.

"No."

"What do you want me to do?"

"Nothing," Ruby said through clenched teeth. "Don't do nothing."

Tim stood there staring at her awkwardly. Ruby held both arms crossed over her stomach, her face taut and pale. Tim sat uncomfortably on the very edge of the bed.

"Ruby... you're going to have this baby. Tell me what to do. What if there's something wrong?"

"Then the baby will die," Ruby said flatly.

Tim suddenly understood. He got up.

"I'm getting an ambulance," he told her.

Ruby tried to protest, but Tim didn't listen. He stepped into the front room and flipped open his phone to call the emergency dispatcher. A couple of the other Jags milled around, eyes wide, expressions curious, and sort of sheepish. They didn't know what to say to Tim. Tim handed the phone to one of them.

"Give them directions."

He went back into the bedroom. There were tears on Ruby's cheeks. Her hands were clenched into fists. Tim rolled one of the other Jags out of bed.

"Get out of here, you guys. Get out."

The rest of the boys who had remained quickly left the room. Tim bent over Ruby.

"Are you okay?"

Ruby nodded. She shifted onto her back and closed her eyes.

"Oh, man, it hurts, Tim."

"I know, baby. The ambulance is coming."

"I don't want this baby!" she protested.

"I know. I know. You don't have to do anything. It'll be okay."

He held her hand. Ruby gripped him tightly and lay there tense and stiff with tears running down her face. Tim stroked Ruby's hair with his other hand, trying to get her to relax. When the emergency medics got there, Ruby was sobbing and gasping for breath. Tim was ordered from the room while they examined Ruby.

Marty sat beside Ruby's bed, bouncing Stella on her knee.

"So did they say the baby was okay?" she questioned.

Ruby shrugged.

"They didn't say anything."

"It was another girl, like the ultrasound said?"

"Yeah. A girl," Ruby said curtly.

"Are they going to bring her in?"

"I hope not. I told them I didn't want to see her."

"Is Jamie coming to pick her up?"

"I haven't called him yet."

"Do you want me to call him?" Marty offered.

"No. Not yet."

Marty rolled her eyes.

"You're being so difficult. So are you going to get your tubes tied?"

Ruby looked at Marty, frowning.

"What?"

"Get your tubes tied. So you can't get pregnant a third time."

"What do you mean?"

Marty cocked her head to the side.

"You know; your fallopian tubes. It's an operation that keeps you from getting pregnant. Ever. But you can't get it reversed later, if you decide you want kids when you're thirty or something."

"How come you never told me about that before?" Ruby demanded, leaning toward Marty.

"I thought you knew all about it. And I didn't think you were going to get pregnant again after Stella."

"Well, I didn't plan on it," Ruby muttered. She lay still and didn't say anything else, eyes brooding.

Marty's mom came in.

"Hi, girls," she greeted with a smile, and she sat on the other side of the bed from Marty. A few minutes later, a nurse came in with the new baby. She handed the baby to Ruby.

"Baby's hungry, mom. Time to feed her."

Ruby tried to hand her back.

"Give her a bottle."

"She needs to nurse. Nothing's as good as mother's milk."

Ruby shook her head.

"I don't do that."

The nurse opened Ruby's robe, exposing her chest. Ruby reddened and clutched it shut, trying to handle the baby and keep the nurse back.

Mrs. Rodger stood up.

"Why don't you just let Ruby get comfortable with the baby first," she suggested.

The nurse frowned, but left the room. Ruby sat there awkwardly with the baby.

"Do you want to hold it?" she questioned Marty.

Marty nodded. Her mom took Stella, and Ruby handed the new baby to Marty. Marty beamed, holding the newborn on her lap.

"Oh, she's precious," Marty murmured. "She's so tiny. I forget that Stella was ever so small."

Marty unswaddled the baby, stroking her skin. The baby stared up at her placidly. Ruby watched the TV in the corner of the room rather than the baby. She smoothed out her hospital gown carefully.

"Hey, Mom," Marty said. "Did you see she has webbed toes?"

"Does she? That's funny. It runs in your father's family. I was surprised that you didn't, actually."

"Come look at her, Mom. She's so sweet."

Mrs. Rodger got up and stood over Marty's shoulder, looking on.

"She looks just like you did when you were born," she breathed, "just exactly the same."

"She sure doesn't look like Stella. I don't see any resemblance."

"No. Neither one takes after Ruby."

"Must look like daddy," Marty agreed. Her mom nodded slowly.

Jamie took the baby from Ruby once they got out of the hospital. He looked down at her, marveling.

"Oh, she's just beautiful," he cooed.

"She's yours."

"Well, you can come by any time to see her."

"Marty's mom knows some lawyer who does guardianship and stuff. Whatever you want, I'll sign it."

"Okay. I'll talk to her about it," Jamie agreed, looking at her.

"Yeah."

"You're still going to come over, right?" Jamie checked. "You're not going to stop just because I've got the baby?"

"Yeah, I'll come over sometime. You get tired of her, just call Social Services."

"I won't get tired of her," Jamie said irritably. "You know I love babies."

Ruby shrugged.

"Whatever."

Marty was sitting in the front room watching TV while looking after Stella. Her mom was in the bedroom. Her father walked in the front door and acknowledged Marty and went into the bedroom where her mother was. Marty muted the TV and listened to them.

"What're you doing?" her father questioned.

"Looking through Marty's baby pictures."

"Why?"

"She was such a cute baby, wasn't she?"

"Sure."

"But she never looked like me—she always looked like your side of the family."

He grunted.

"Strong genes."

"Ruby's baby looks just like Marty did when she was a baby."

"Yeah?"

"She could be Marty's sister, they look so much alike."

There was silence. Neither of them said anything. Marty looked down at Stella, her stomach tightening. Ruby had always been paranoid about Marty's dad. She'd always been worried about the way that he looked at her; she wouldn't stay in the same room with him. Marty had never believed that he would ever touch Ruby. She had thought that Ruby was just being paranoid. She tried to decide whether to get up and join the conversation. But she couldn't think of what to say.

"What're you saying?" her father said finally.

"Tell me you're not the father of Ruby's baby."

Again there was a period of silence. After a while, her father spoke.

"I don't think that the baby could be mine."

"But you don't know for sure."

"No, I couldn't say for sure."

"How could you do that? You know how confused Ruby is. She's vulnerable. You can't take advantage of her like that!"

He said nothing. Marty went to her bedroom to get Stella's stroller and went out for a walk.

∼

Ruby was a little nervous going back to the gang after having the baby. Especially after going into labor right there in Tim's apartment. This time she was going to talk to the doctor about what Marty had said—about getting her tubes tied so that she couldn't get pregnant again. Whatever happened, she did not want to end up getting pregnant again. She was never going to get married and decide to have kids when she was thirty. Someone should have told her about that before she got pregnant with Stella.

Ruby walked into the arcade, looking around carefully for any gang members other than Jags. Ruby plugged change into one of the games and played half-heartedly for a while. Her mind wasn't really on the game.

"Looking for some action?" someone said from behind her. Ruby turned, recognizing Jack's voice.

"Sure. What's up?"

"Nothing yet. I'm sure we could stir something up."

"Sure."

"Let's go get a drink."

Ruby nodded and went with him. He put his arm through hers as he always did when he was taking her somewhere. Ruby always thought it odd that Tim or one of the other boys would put his arm around Ruby's waist, or in her back pocket, or around her neck, but Jack escorted her like a gentleman, his arm through hers or his hand lightly on her back. He had been taught, sometime, how to treat a girl. The rest of his training had disappeared. He was rough and cold and rude. He was mean and vicious. He was rarely gentle or kind. But he still took her by the arm instead of around the waist, and she had once heard him call an old woman "ma'am," though he'd never met her before. Ruby walked with Jack to a pub that was open all day.

∼

It was the first time that Marty had even considered not going home. Finding out about Ruby and her dad was just too much. He knew how much Ruby had gone through, the struggles that she had with her life, the way she always got entangled with boys. He had heard all about it —he definitely knew about Ruby having Stella! There was no way he could say that he didn't think it was wrong. But he'd done it. And Marty knew that Ruby would never have gotten involved with him willingly. Ruby was afraid of him, paranoid about even being in the same room with him. She wouldn't be left alone in a room if she knew he was in the house. She wouldn't shower if she knew that he was around, and Ruby was fanatical about her showers. How long had something been going on?

When it started to get dark, Marty knew she had to figure out whether she was going home or not. She had Stella with her, and she really wasn't sure about going to a shelter or something. She finally sat down in a mall with Stella and thought. She opened her phone and did a 411 search.

An hour later she was at Jamie's apartment. They both walked around on eggshells, extremely awkward.

"Thanks for letting me come," Marty said. "I couldn't go home and I didn't know what to do—with Stella."

"Why not?"

Marty bit her lip.

"I really can't talk about it. I have to sort things out for a bit. But thank you."

"Aw, no trouble. The couch is a hide-a-bed. Just pull it out and you and Stella can share it, I have to get to bed, because Sheree just got off to sleep and she'll have me up in a few hours."

Marty nodded.

"I remember what that's like. Thanks again."

Jamie nodded, and went to bed. Marty laid in the hide-a-bed wide awake, thinking about her father and Ruby, and thinking about Jamie sleeping in the other room and what he must think about her. She didn't trust him and didn't like him, yet he was the only one she could think to call when she needed something.

In the morning, Marty sat with the baby, Sheree. Ruby's second baby. Maybe her half-sister. She studied Sheree's features, looking for similarities, for familiar nuances. As a child, she'd always dreamt about having a baby sister. She'd imagined a baby, imagined what she would look at, poured over her own baby pictures for hours. The doctors had removed the webbing between Sheree's toes, but there was that too. Her mother had not doubted that Sheree was Marty's father's baby.

"Umm, are you staying?" Jamie questioned.

Marty tried to think of what to do.

"Uh—no. I'll find somewhere else to go. It's okay."

"You're still not going home?"

"No."

"Why don't you stay here, then?"

"Are you sure you wouldn't mind?"

"Not at all. In fact, if you want to take care of Sheree, I'll pay you to stay."

"I'll take care of her. You don't have to pay me anything."

CHAPTER Fifteen

Ruby was dancing when the police crashed the party. Not dancing with Jack—he was at a booth in the corner still drinking. She was dancing with a young man that had approached her while she was up by the bar. Ruby had checked to make sure that Jack couldn't see her from the corner, and agreed. Jack wasn't the jealous type, but he was possessive. If she was out with him, he wanted her to be with him. So she danced with the new boy, keeping an eye on Jack's corner booth in case he got up looking for her.

When the cops came into the pub, Ruby stopped dancing for a moment, then continued, ignoring them. She watched the police come in and start putting people in handcuffs. A couple of cops stood with their guns out, watching for anyone to make the wrong move. A couple of dopes tried to get out the back way, but Ruby knew they'd have men and a car out the back too. There was no point in fighting them. Ruby's dance partner had stopped dancing, but she ignored this fact and kept moving until somebody killed the juke.

"Party's over," one of the cops told her, putting handcuffs on her wrists and giving her a little shove towards the door. Ruby looked around for Jack to see where he was. The cop pushed her harder. "Come on. No dawdling. Out the door to the wagon."

Ruby headed for the door. One of the cops at the door frisked her while another eyed her appreciatively. Ruby lowered her eyes and swung her hips as she went by him. He grinned and slapped her lightly on the butt as she passed. Ruby went out the door and another cop guided her into the waiting van and shut the door. Ruby glanced at the other occupants of the van. Jack wasn't one of them. She sat back and waited.

∼

She had to wait at the police station while everyone was processed and sorted out. Eventually one of the police officers came into the waiting room to talk to her. Ruby saw it was the officer that she had flirted with at the bar, and smiled. He returned the grin and sat down on a backwards chair in front of her.

"Ruby, right?"

"Uh-huh."

"What were you doing at the pub?"

"Drinking."

He flashed another handsome smile.

"You're too young to even be allowed into a bar, let alone sold drinks," he pointed out.

Ruby shrugged.

"I'm old enough."

"You're fourteen."

"I've had two babies. Doesn't that make me old enough?"

He looked at her for a moment, one eyebrow raised.

"No, it just makes you promiscuous."

Ruby felt her face get hot. He shook his head.

"They served you drinks?"

"Sure."

"How much did you have today?"

"A few beers."

"Anything else?"

"What else would I get there?"

He was still smiling.

"Don't play with me, doll. I'm not going to get on your case if you can give me straight answers. But I'll make your life miserable if you get cagey on me."

Ruby didn't say anything. He studied her seriously.

"We're going to do a blood test on you. What are we going to find in it?"

Ruby searched his eyes.

"Are you really going to do a blood test?"

He nodded.

"We do a drug bust, we run a blood test on everyone who was there. Now what are we going to find?"

Ruby shook her head, not trusting him.

"I don't believe you."

He didn't say anything for a few minutes, looking at her with his lips pursed.

"Okay. Well then, let's get that blood test. Stand up."

Ruby stood up, and he took her down to the station doctor. Ruby watched the doctor put a tourniquet on her arm to raise a vein. She looked away when he took out a needle and jabbed her.

"Don't like needles?" the doctor questioned.

Ruby shook her head, pale. The doctor finished up and labeled the vial.

"So what are we going to find?" the officer questioned.

"What's your name?" Ruby asked him.

"Charlie. What's your blood test going to show?"

"Charlie, that's nice. I like it."

"I said no games, Ruby," he warned.

"I guess maybe I'm a little drunk."

"I guess so. What else will we find?"

Ruby rubbed the arm of the chair with one finger.

"I've been taking some painkillers..."

"What painkillers?"

"Oxy."

He shook his head.

"So we'll find narcotics. How long have you been taking those?"

Ruby shrugged.

"Since I broke my ankle."

"How long ago was that?" he questioned.

"A few months."

"How many months?"

"I dunno. Ten or eleven."

"So you got yourself hooked on them, huh?"

"No. I just need them because it still hurts."

"After a year it doesn't still hurt. You're addicted to the painkillers. Do you get them by prescription?"

"No."

He nodded.

"Why not?"

"The guys get them for me."

Charlie nodded.

"Is that all we're going to find in your blood?"

Ruby nodded. Charlie studied her closely. He didn't believe that she was telling the truth.

"What else?"

Ruby thought about her answer. If she lied, he would find it in the blood test and know it.

"I get depressed," she started uncomfortably.

"So what do you take? Prozac or something?"

Ruby shook her head.

"What do you take when you get depressed, Ruby? Speed? Uppers?"

Ruby nodded. Charlie nodded as well.

"So you had alcohol, narcotics, and amphetamines tonight. That's a great combination."

Ruby didn't say anything. The doctor interrupted.

"You can't mix drugs and alcohol. You could end up killing yourself. At your age, you shouldn't even be touching alcohol or these sorts of drugs."

Charlie nodded.

"Uh, let's go back and talk some more, okay?"

He led Ruby back to the interrogation room and they sat down again.

"Okay, sweetie. Is that all we're going to find?"

"Yeah."

"No crack? No coke? Nothing else?"

"No."

"Good. Did you buy the drugs at the pub?"

Ruby bit her lip.

"No."

"Where, then?"

"I got them earlier from one of the guys."

"From who?"

Ruby shook her head.

"I don't have to tell you."

"It would be to your benefit if you did."

"No."

"I can't help you if you won't talk to me," he coaxed. "If you want to help yourself, you help me. If you don't want to help yourself, fine. You just tell me that."

"I don't want any help."

"Okay. I guess you and me are pretty well done, then. I'll call your folks to talk things over."

"I don't live with my parents."
"Where do you live?"
"With friends." Ruby shrugged.
"Do you have a social worker or something?"
"I did, but he got put in jail," Ruby said.
Charlie laughed.
"You're joking."
"No."
"What for?"
Ruby shrugged and didn't explain.
"Well, we'll find out who your new social worker is."

The door opened, and Ruby looked up, expecting to see the guard with lunch or something. But it was a man in a suit that she didn't know.

"Who're you?" she demanded.
"Mr. Clive, your social worker."
Ruby studied him with pursed lips.
"Well, you aren't nearly as cute as Chuck."
She was hung over, and it made her in a bad mood.
"I didn't come here to exchange insults." He put down his briefcase. "Are you interested in being assigned to a new foster family?"
"No."
"We could help you get straightened out, put you back on the right track."
"I don't do foster families anymore."
"Do you know what the alternative is?"
Ruby shrugged.
"I don't care. I don't like living with foster families. I haven't done that since I was eleven."
"So you don't want any help from Social Services."
"No."
"Fine, then. I have plenty of kids to look after who do want to be helped."
"Then go help them."
He shrugged and turned to leave. Ruby had a thought, and stopped him.
"Hey—are you Ronnie's social worker? My sister?"
"That's confidential."
"If you are, would you tell her I miss her?"

He nodded.

"Is she still with the same foster family she was before?"

"That's confidential."

"Did you know they want to adopt her?"

He shook his head slowly. He waited.

"Is that everything?" he prodded.

Ruby shrugged.

"Yeah, that's all."

He left. Ruby got her lunch a few minutes later. After eating, she lay back down to go to sleep. She slept most of the afternoon and was wakened by the door opening again. This time it was Charlie. He smiled at her.

"Hi, darling. How're you feeling this fine afternoon?" he said cheerily.

Ruby winced at his volume.

"Hi."

"Ready to move on?"

"Are you releasing me?"

"Releasing you? No, not today, sweetie. But you're off to some new quarters."

Ruby stretched and massaged her temples tenderly.

"Where to?"

"Drug rehab."

"What?" Ruby's voice rose. "I'm no junkie!" she protested.

"You certainly are if you've been taking narcotics and amphetamines in the amounts they were in your blood last night for very long," he pointed out.

"Oh, come on. I was partying last night. I had a bit too much. I don't usually. I just had a bit much last night."

"Don't tell me, baby. Tell the counselors in rehab. Come on. I'll take you over now."

Ruby shook her head.

"You can't make me go to rehab if I don't want to."

"We can if your guardians approve it."

"I don't have any guardians."

"Your Social Worker made the decision that you would do best in rehab."

Ruby opened her mouth to argue, but there was nothing to say. She'd refused to go to a family. She'd refused Clive's help, so he'd left her to go to rehab. Ruby got up, rolling her eyes a little at Charlie to make him chuckle.

"Well, it's better than here, huh?"

Charlie nodded.

"You got it, baby. At least you'll have some company."

Ruby nodded.

"I don't like to be alone."

"You don't strike me as a girl who likes to be alone."

Ruby took his hand.

"I especially don't like to sleep alone," she told him slyly, giving his hand a squeeze.

"I don't think they allow that in rehab," he snickered. He gave her shoulders a squeeze and turned her around to handcuff her wrists. He escorted her out to his car. Ruby sat in the front seat with him, and looked out the window.

"What's it like?"

"What?"

"Drug rehab."

"Better than jail, and better than juvie hall."

"How long will I be there?"

"At least a couple of months. And then we'll put you back in foster care and try to keep you on the right track."

"I don't want another foster family."

"Well, a halfway house maybe. Let's work on getting you straightened out first. Get you dried out."

Ruby rolled her eyes, and was quiet. He patted her on the shoulder.

"Sorry, sunshine. Got to do my job."

They drove across town and pulled up to the rehab center. It was right on the edge of town, away from everything else. Charlie turned off the engine and put his arm around her shoulders. He leaned over and kissed her firmly on the lips. Smiling, he got out of the car. He opened her door for her, and escorted her into the imposing looking building. Ruby grasped his hand as they walked up to the admitting area, her stomach tying itself in knots and her heart thumping hard. He squeezed her hand reassuringly and walked her up to the desk.

"This is Ruby Simpson. We called her in."

"Come around to the back," she ordered, opening a gate for them. Charlie took Ruby around to a bare room in the back of the admitting area.

"Tell me about her," the matron ordered.

"Ruby was picked up last night in a drug bust. She had high levels of alcohol, narcotics and amphetamines in her blood. She said last night she's been using narcotics for almost a year. She's fourteen. She's been in foster care since she was eight. She has arrests for assault, armed robbery and murder."

The woman nodded.

"Okay, honey. Strip."

"What?"

"We do a full search to make sure you can't smuggle anything in. So that we know you're dry from the minute you come in. We'll take your clothes. You'll be wearing a uniform while you're here."

Ruby looked at Charlie. He unlocked the handcuffs and patted her butt.

"Just take it easy and follow instructions. You'll be settled in before you know it. I'll come back to check up on you in a few days. Okay?"

Ruby nodded, her arms folded across her chest protectively. Charlie nodded to the woman and left the room. Ruby swallowed hard and tried to blank her mind. She started to undress under the woman's steady gaze.

Ruby's "processing" was completed as the evening drew on. A couple of counselors told her that she would receive her "orientation" in the morning. In the meantime, she was introduced to her new bunkie. She was to share quarters with a big, masculine looking girl. Her name was Lynn Carole, and her head was shaved short like an army buzz-cut. She regarded Ruby without much interest, looking her over casually. Ruby watched TV from the back of the common room until lock-up time. People ignored her—no-one bothered to introduce themselves. A few people looked at her, but didn't say anything. Ruby looked for Carole at lights-out, but didn't see her. One of the counselors directed her to her room. Carole was already there undressing for bed. She motioned to the bunk-beds.

"You get the top," she said curtly.

"Okay."

They were both tucked into bed when the lights went off. Ruby lay there listening to Carole breathe for a while.

"Lynn?"

"Shut up and go to sleep."

Ruby lay still for a while, then climbed out of bed. She sat down on the edge of Carole's bunk. Carole startled from sleep and looked at her.

"Can I sleep with you?" Ruby whispered.

Carole laughed huskily.

"Usually I have to bust heads to get some company," she said, and she held up the blankets for Ruby to crawl in. Ruby cuddled up close to her on the narrow bed. Carole encircled her with both arms and kissed her full on the lips. Ruby closed her eyes and put her face against Carole's neck and tried to pretend that she was back home with Marty.

In the morning Ruby stuck close to Carole, trying to follow her lead and figure out the rules of the place. She didn't get the formal orientation she'd been promised. The counselors seemed to have pretty much forgotten about her. Carole told her where she was supposed to go when. She showed Ruby where the group session for the beginners was, and Ruby joined the other nervous-looking teens in the conference room and tried to look cool. Mostly they just got lectured, and Ruby managed to avoid talking to the counselor about her "problem". Once the group session was finished, she looked around for Carole again.

"Well, if it ain't Lynnie's new sweetheart," a dark, tough-looking girl commented, sizing Ruby up. Ruby tensed up and looked quickly around, trying to figure out what she was going to do. Her first decision was never to be caught unarmed again. She knew from the Jags' talk about prison and rehab that you could make your own weapon, and had better do so the first chance you got. Everyone else who was tough would have one, and it wouldn't do to be left unprotected.

"And not even so much as a black eye," another chimed in. "Usually Lynn's bunkies are pretty roughed up for the first few weeks."

Ruby eyed the two of them warily. Two she could handle—but only if they were both unarmed. Any more than that and she was going to be in trouble.

"It would be a shame to see such a pretty face messed up. She is pretty, isn't she?"

Ruby stepped towards the first speaker determinedly, shoving her hands deep into her uniform pockets, trying to look confident and threatening, like she was sure of herself and her ability to handle whatever they dished out.

The gathering crowd suddenly dissipated and everybody went their different directions. Carole came up on Ruby's shoulder.

"They giving you grief?" she demanded.

"I can handle it."

"You're going to handle it, little girl? Most of them are twice your size, and experienced too. You let me take care of things for you."

Ruby shook her head.

"I have to get a knife or something. You're not going to be here all the time."

"They know me. They wouldn't dare do anything."

Ruby was stubborn. She didn't give in. Carole grinned.

"You think you're one tough little cookie, don't you? Well, don't you worry. I'll look after you."

She motioned for Ruby to follow her and they went into the common room, where some of the girls were watching TV and others were settling in to play cards.

Glenning watched Carole take Simpson back to their quarters with a casual arm around her shoulders. They went inside and the door shut behind them. Glenning shook his head. He walked down the hallway and stopped at their door. He stood there for a moment looking in through the narrow window. It was one-way glass, so that he could see in but they could not see him watching them. They were talking on the bottom bunk, Carole with one hand on Simpson's cheek, but Simpson seemed entirely comfortable with the physical contact. She didn't pull away or argue. Quite the contrary, after a few minutes she put her hand on Carole's thigh, fingering the fabric of her jumper. Glenning withdrew and continued on down the hallway. He stopped in the staff room to light up a cigarette.

"Anybody know anything about Simpson, Carole's new bunkmate?"

One of the counselors swiveled to face him.

"She was pretty quiet in group."

"Why was she put with Carole?"

"Only place to put her. We're pretty much full up."

"You're keeping an eye on her, aren't you?" Matron Black questioned.

"Yeah. She and Carole are getting pretty close."

"How close? The last thing we need is a lawsuit because she's getting beaten up."

"Real close. But I don't foresee any lawsuits."

Black looked at Glenning for a moment in puzzlement. Then she nodded, frowning.

"Keep an eye on them. And I'll sign her up for a consult with Dr. Rivers in case she needs to talk to someone."

Glenning nodded.

"I'll keep an eye on them."

Marty took a deep breath and opened the door. She pushed the stroller in and bent over to unbuckle Stella.

"Marty?"

Her mother came out to the front room, and hugged her.

"Marty, you scared me. Where were you? Why didn't you tell me where you went?"

Marty hugged her back tightly.

"I didn't know what to do."

Her mom stroked her hair gently.

"I'm sorry, honey. I'm sorry."

"It wasn't you. I just... I couldn't believe Dad would..."

"He's gone," her mother interrupted. "He won't be coming back."

"What did he say?"

"He really didn't have anything to say. What could he say?"

"How could he do that...?"

"I couldn't have been more shocked. When I looked at Ruby's baby, and saw your face... and her webbed toes... I just couldn't believe it was possible."

"Sheree."

"What?"

"That's what Jamie named the baby. That's where I was."

"Are you okay?"

"Yeah. I'm glad I don't have two babies to look after all the time."

"Were you looking after Sheree?"

"Yes. She's a high-needs baby too, like Stella. Not the same, but... I would be worn right out if I had to look after both of them."

"Well, it's a good thing Jamie wanted a baby so bad."

Ruby rubbed the thin blade against the metal supports of the bunk bed. Carole lay on the bed watching her.

"You don't have to do that."

Ruby didn't answer. Carole touched Ruby's arm.

"Come on, Ruby. Don't you have better things to do?"

"Nope."

"You're a persistent little thing, I'll say that for you."

"I'm not walking around here unarmed."

Ruby tested the edge of the knife. She slid it into the homemade sheath on her arm.

"Done?" Carole questioned.

Ruby nodded.

"Yeah. Let's go out."

Ruby looked up at the counselor that approached her as she sat playing cards with Carole and a couple of other girls.

"You've got a visitor, Simpson."

"What?"

"A visitor. A cop."

"Oh." Ruby left her game and went to the visiting area, wondering what cop wanted to see her. She got there and looked around and saw Charlie. He grinned at her.

"I told you I'd come check up on you."

"I didn't think you would."

He took her hands and sat down with her.

"I keep my promises. How are you doing?"

"Okay."

"Yeah? Feeling okay?"

Ruby rolled her eyes.

"I feel like a drink."

"I bet. Pretty tough quitting, isn't it?"

"How would you know?"

"I've helped a lot of kids through rehab. I know how tough it can be."

"Oh. So you come see lots of kids here, huh?" Ruby heard the resentment enter her voice, even though she hadn't intended to give her feelings away.

Charlie cocked his head at her.

"Is that jealousy, Ruby? I see lots of kids, but none as special as you. Come on. Would I take an interest like this in just anyone?"

When he held her gaze, a wave of warmth went over Ruby. She looked away, smiling and trying to hide the blush.

"Okay."

"So have you made some friends here?"

Ruby shook her head.

"Might be nice if there were some guys around."

"Well, they like to deal with one problem at a time here. You told me you've had two babies?"

"Yeah."

"If you were in a co-ed program, you're telling me you wouldn't be pregnant again in a month?"

"I want to get an operation so I can't get pregnant."

Charlie cocked his head.

"Why don't you just abstain?"

"What?" Ruby frowned.

"No boys, no babies."

Ruby shook her head.

"No way. And don't tell me to use birth control, because it doesn't work!"

Charlie shook his head and tactfully changed the subject.

"What's your roommate like?"

"You wouldn't like her."

"Why not?"

"Trust me. She's not your type."

"Do you get along with her?" he persisted.

"Yeah, all right."

"Good. You getting to know anyone else here?"

"No."

"Well... I can't stay too long. I'll be back in a few days to see how you're doing. Maybe then we can talk then about what's going to happen after rehab."

Ruby shrugged.

"You don't have to come back. I can look after myself."

"I'll come back to look in on you again," he promised, and stood up. Ruby hesitated, then stood up and kissed him. Charlie smiled.

"Okay, cutie. See you in a couple of days. Take care of yourself, okay?"

"Okay."

He gave her a friendly hug. He paused, his hand over the sheath on her arm. Their eyes met, and Ruby's mouth went dry, knowing he was going to turn her in.

"How am I supposed to protect myself?" she questioned.

He released her slowly.

"I don't want to hear you've been hurt."

"You won't."

"Or that you've hurt someone else."

"Only if I have to defend myself."

Even then, he hesitated. Finally he sighed and nodded.

"I'm trying to look out for you."

"You're not stuck in here. I am."

Charlie nodded and went on his way. Ruby watched him until he was out of sight. When she turned to leave the visitors room, Carole was standing in the doorway scowling at her.

"You and Kojak are a little familiar, aren't you?"

Ruby approached Carole with a bit of a provocative swing.

"His name is Charlie, and he's going to get me out of here," she said firmly. Carole studied her, and backed off.

"Okay, whatever. I just don't like to see you wasting yourself on something like that."

Ruby shrugged.

"You and Marty would sure get on great."

"Who's he?" Carole questioned suspiciously.

"She's a friend of mine. She's always getting after me for the guys I see."

"I don't know what you see in boys."

"Yeah, you sound just like her."

Black approached the two girls. She frowned at Carole, but spoke to Ruby.

"You're scheduled to see Dr. Rivers."

"Who's he?"

"Prison shrink," Carole informed Ruby. "Have fun. And be careful what you tell him."

"Whatever you tell him will be privileged," Black corrected, "You don't need to worry about it being repeated to anyone."

Ruby rolled her eyes at Carole, letting Black escort her off to her appointment.

"You should stay away from Lynn Carole," Black advised her lowly, when they were out of Carole's earshot.

"Pretty hard to do that when she's my bunkie," Ruby countered.

"Do you want to be moved?"

"No."

"You two shouldn't spend all your time together."

"I thought I could spend free time with whoever I want."

"Well, for a newbie, you're certainly well-versed in all the rules, aren't you? There's rules, Simpson, and then there's smarts. I'm telling you how to be smart."

"If it's not a rule, I don't have to do it."

"I'm telling you for your own good. People who spend a lot of time with Carole have a habit of getting themselves hurt."

"Then why did you put me with her?" Ruby demanded.

"Carole usually takes a while to get warmed up to someone. We don't usually see the warning signs until after a few weeks. But you and Carole seem to have warmed right up to each other. So I'm warning you—she's dangerous. You're going to get hurt if you spend too much time with her."

Ruby said nothing. She let Black lead her to the shrink's office. She sat down in the chair in front of the huge desk. Black murmured a greeting, and disappeared. Ruby sat there and studied the psychiatrist. He was an older man, with a round face and a graying mustache.

"Hello, Miss Simpson," he greeted.

"Ruby."

"Okay, Ruby. I am Dr. Rivers."

"Yeah, I figured. What's your first name?"

"Doctor," he said firmly.

Ruby rolled her eyes.

"Are you not comfortable with that?" he questioned.

Ruby shrugged.

"I don't care. I like to know people's first names."

"You aren't happy just having something to call people by?"

"Whatever."

"So what would you like to talk about today?"

"I don't know."

"Are you getting settled in here?"

"Yeah, I'm fine."

"Little bit scary, huh?" he sympathized.

"No. I'm not scared."

"You're surrounded by addicts, people you don't know. Some of them with violent pasts. I would find that scary."

"They're just regular people."

"You're used to having people like that around?"

"Not junkies, no. But… tough guys—I'm used to that."

"How do you deal with it?"

Ruby shrugged uncomfortably.

"I don't 'deal' with it. That's just the way it is. I don't control it, I just…"

"Go with the flow?" he suggested.

Ruby frowned.

"Yeah, sort of."

"Tell me about your friends."

"What friends?"

"You friends on the outside. People you spend time with."

Ruby leaned back in her chair and thought about what to tell him.

Ruby sat on the couch with Carole, watching TV and rubbing her temples.

"What's the matter?" Carole questioned.

"I got a headache."

"It's withdrawal. I'll get you some Tylenol."

Ruby nodded. Carole got up and walked away. Ruby felt the atmosphere of the room change immediately. She glanced around and saw that there were no counselors or guards hanging around. She folded her arms, letting the tips of her fingers rest under her sleeve on her knife. She pretended that she didn't see the other girls looking at her and watched the TV.

"Are you sitting all by yourself?" Kimberley questioned.

Ruby looked at her and smiled, her lips tight and unnatural.

"Well, I'm not sitting with you," she sneered.

"Oh yeah?" Kimberley questioned, moving closer.

Ruby was aware that she looked like an easy target. She was younger than a lot of the others, and definitely smaller in build. But they didn't know that she'd been with the Jags, that she knew how to take care of herself in a tough situation.

"Stay away from me, Kimberley," she warned.

"Or what? Lynnie took off and left you all alone. Who's going to look after you now?"

"I can look after myself."

"Oh yeah? I dunno, little girl. You might think you're grown up, but you ain't been around long."

"I been around," Ruby countered, putting her fingers around the handmade knife's hilt. She slowly moved into a position where she could stand up without making herself vulnerable.

"You know the talk. But I don't think you know the walk, kiddo."

Ruby took a step towards Kimberley, inching the knife out of its sheath.

"I think you're the one that better watch your step."

Two other girls moved in to flanking positions. Ruby eyed them and decided it was time to move before anyone became too comfortable. She pulled the knife the rest of the way out of the sheath and held it low as she moved in. By the time the girls saw it, it was too late. Ruby had disposed of Kimberley and was turning towards the others before they connected with the thought that she was armed. They tried to pincer her between them, but Ruby forced one of them back and didn't let herself get caught between them. Kimberley was on the floor, moaning and swearing and holding bloody hands over her stomach. Ruby kicked her without dropping her eyes, and both of the girls looked down when Kimberley cried out. Ruby took advantage of that split-second to move in on one of the girls, holding the point of the knife against her stomach.

"If you don't want to be split wide open, you'd better call off your friend," she said.

"Marsha—back off," the girl said with a gasp, frozen in position. Ruby watched Marsha warily, but both girls had decided that they'd had enough

There was a shout:

"Simpson, drop the weapon and put up your hands!"

Ruby looked around and saw Glenning. He had his holster unsnapped and his hand on the butt of his gun. He looked pretty jittery. Ruby saw Carole come up behind him, her jaw dropping when she saw what was happening. Ruby made the girl gasp by pushing the knife in slightly.

"Drop it!" Glenning shouted, the gun jumping halfway out of his holster. Ruby stepped back and let the knife fall to the floor with a clatter. She put her hands up. Glenning handcuffed her, closing the bracelets tightly over Ruby's wrists. He snapped his holster back up, and took out his walkie-talkie to call for medical aid for Kimberley. Carole watched Glenning escort Ruby away, looking stunned.

"Why couldn't Rivers tell us Simpson was ticking?" Glenning demanded. "That's the kind of thing he's supposed to find out for us."

"Dr. Rivers only had one session with her," Black protested. "He can't know everything."

"We should have been told that she might be violent."

"Her record should have told you that she was violent," Black snapped. "Considering that she has arrests for assault, armed robbery and murder. What were you doing leaving her in the common room with no guard?"

"She was only unguarded for one minute."

"One minute too long."

"Are we going to charge her?"

"Well, we have to charge her, but I doubt if it will stand. Not when she's claiming self-defense."

"She made a weapon," Glenning pointed out the obvious.

"Is she the only one in the center with a weapon? Because if you can find anyone else who's carried a weapon, she can still claim it was for self-defense."

Glenning didn't argue it. They found weapons all too often for him to make any kind of claim about the center being clean on this count.

"How's Kimberley Cox? Is she going to be okay?"

"Yes, she'll be up and around in a day or two. It looked a lot worse than it really was. Just tissue damage—no vital organs."

"She could just as easily have been killed."

"Good thing for you that she wasn't."

Ruby looked up when the door to her current accommodations opened. It was Charlie. He looked considerably less cheerful than usual. He glanced around the dim, bare isolation cell.

"Hi there," Ruby said.

"Well, I guess I should have known better than to let you hang onto that shiv."

"I needed it," Ruby asserted.

"I thought you said you wouldn't use it."

"Would you rather I was in the infirmary? Or the morgue?"

"Did you really have to use it?" he questioned, sitting down on the narrow bed beside her.

"It was three against one. I needed it."

"Three against one?" Charlie repeated.

"Yeah. Cox and two of her buddies. I wasn't going to wait until they had me pinned down."

"I'm glad you didn't get hurt. But you know this is just going to get you in more trouble."

"What're you going to do about it? I have a right to protect myself."

"It's not up to me. But I'd like to help you get out of here and go straight. If you go getting into more trouble, I can't necessarily help you out."

Ruby grimaced.

"Yeah, okay. But I have to take care of myself. You're not here to look after me. No-one is. I look after myself."

"Well, hopefully after this incident people will decide to leave you alone. But I'm not counting on it. Sometimes things just keep escalating—until someone gets killed."

"I won't get killed," Ruby promised.

"I hope nothing happens to you. But back off, try to stay away from trouble. Whatever you have to do."

"I'm not scared of anyone here."

He smiled.

"You talk tough, Ruby, but..."

His words sounded just like Kimberley's. Ruby felt her face tighten, and she scowled at him.

"I know the walk too," she snapped, "I thought I just proved that to everyone!"

Charlie looked taken aback.

"Whoa, where's that coming from, sweetie? I didn't mean you can't handle yourself. What I mean is... it's okay to be afraid. And it's okay to admit it to me. Just because you're tough doesn't mean that someone couldn't get the better of you. Look, I'm tough too. But I get scared out there sometimes... someone could pull a gun on me when I write a traffic ticket. Or when we raid a bar. Or anything. You have to be scared of what you can't control."

"Well, I'm not scared," Ruby said stubbornly.

Charlie cocked his head.

"Okay. You're not scared."

Ruby nodded.

"So how are you doing other than this?" his gesture encompassed the isolation cell.

"Okay."

"How's it feel to be dry?"

"It's okay... but I could really do with a drink. Just a small one."

Charlie laughed.

"You don't need it."

"No, I just really want it."

"You're doing pretty good. You handle this, and you'll be able to get out of here in a few weeks."

Ruby nodded.

"Yeah. Did you tell Marty I was here?"

"Marty? No. Who's that?"

"The girl I live with."

"Oh, sure. Give me her details, and I'll let her know for you."

Ruby gave him the information. He wrote it down in his notepad, and stood up.

"Can't stay and visit today, darling. I'd better be getting to work."

Ruby got up and hugged him. He patted her on the back.

"I'll see you next week."

"Okay."

"Keep yourself out of trouble, now."

"I will."

He squeezed her and let her go. He knocked on the door and the guard let him out and shut the door again.

Outside the isolation cell, Charlie watched a girl arguing with a guard. As he walked by them, he heard the girl mention Ruby's name. He turned and looked at her. She was an older teen or young adult— and twice Ruby's size. She had a hard face, with angular features.

"Are you Ruby's roommate?" he questioned curiously.

She hadn't seen him as he went by. She scowled at him.

"When she's not in iso, yeah. What're you doing here again?"

"Just visiting."

"Why don't you just stay away from her?"

"Ruby wants to see me. She needs someone looking after her."

"I look after her."

"That doesn't give me great comfort. I'll handle this my own way."

"She doesn't want you here. She just sees you because she thinks you can get her out."

Charlie studied her.

"Are you jealous of her or of me?" he questioned.

The guard caught Carole as she tried to hit Charlie. Her face was flushed dark with anger, and the guard had a hard time holding her back.

"I think you'd better go," he advised.

Charlie nodded and left, grinning.

The house seemed quiet and empty. Marty was restless and didn't know what to do. She had the radio on whenever her mom was out, for company. She'd often been alone in the house before, just her and

Stella, but it was different now. Her dad was gone and wouldn't be back. And Ruby had never stayed away for so long before. Marty was worried that something had happened her. She hadn't been to Jamie's or Brian's. Marty wasn't about to ask the Jags if she'd been staying with them, and she really couldn't go to the police. Marty didn't know whether something was wrong or whether Ruby just wanted to stay away from Marty's dad.

It was evening when the doorbell rang, and Marty was expecting her mom to be home any minute. She answered the door to a uniformed cop.

"Hi. Are you Marty?"

"Yes." Marty didn't say anything at first, just looking at him. He wanted to be invited in, but Marty didn't ask him. "Is it Ruby? Is she okay?"

"Ruby's fine. She asked me to stop by and talk to you to let you know she's okay."

"Is she in jail or what?"

"Drug rehab."

Marty breathed out.

"Good. I was afraid something happened."

"No, I picked her up in a raid. She was charged with illegal drug use, but it'll be dropped if she completes the rehab program."

"If?"

"Well," he grinned, "she doesn't have a choice. Social services put her in a closed care facility."

"Do you think it will help?"

"Initially. But not if she goes back to her old drinking buddies. I would recommend that social services put her in another city when she gets out, but she would just come back here, so there's not much point."

"Well, I'll try to help out, but Ruby likes action. She won't just stay around here. She'll be off looking for boys and action."

"It's up to Ruby. She'll need help, but staying clean has to be her own decision. We can't force her."

"Can I go see her?"

"Normally yes. But not this week, she's in some trouble."

Marty rolled her eyes.

"What did she do?"

"Got into a fight. Apparently self-defense, but she was carrying a hand-made weapon. So she's in isolation for a while."

"But she's okay?" Marty questioned.

"She's just fine."

"How long before she gets out?"

"Out of isolation or out of rehab?"

Marty shrugged.

"She'll be out of isolation next week, I think. It'll be a few weeks or a couple of months until she's out of rehab."

"Thanks for coming to let me know."

He nodded.

"No problem. Ruby asked me to let you know, and I said I would."

Marty closed the door slowly, and the cop stepped back and walked down the sidewalk. Marty sighed and sat down, relieved to know that Ruby was all right.

Ruby found when she got out things were different. The other girls looked at her differently. Ruby looked for a chance to fashion another knife, but the guards watched her closely, and frisked her down several times a day. But the other inmates still looked at her as if she was dangerous, instead of the little girl that they had seen her as before. They didn't sneer at her and stand close to her like they did before. Their voices were respectful instead of sneering and goading. Ruby ignored them, though some of them tried to make friends for her. There were a couple that she talked to, but mostly she kept to herself. She sat in the common room watching TV or spent time with Carole.

She'd been out of isolation for a few days when Marty came by to see her. Marty brought Stella and was waiting for her. Ruby gave Marty a quick hug, checking over her shoulder to make sure that Carole wasn't close by. She motioned for Marty to sit down. Stella sat on Marty's lap sucking a fist and looking around. Ruby grinned.

"Did Charlie come see you?" she questioned.

"Charlie?"

"The cop."

"Oh, sure. He didn't tell me his name."

There was silence for a few moments.

"I'll be out in a few weeks," she offered.

"Are you doing okay?" Marty questioned, looking her in the eye.

"Yeah. It's not so bad. Other than having no boys and no booze."

"Any more fights?" Marty questioned.

"Did Charlie tell you about that? He shouldn't have. It wasn't anything."

"What happened?"

"Couple girls thought they'd gang up on me. I cut one of them."

"How bad was she hurt?"

"Not so bad. She's still in the infirmary. But she didn't have to go to the hospital."

"I wish you didn't have to do that," Marty said with a repressed shudder.

"I don't care. I protect myself if I have to."

"So are you going to stay away from the drugs after this?" Marty raised her eyebrows.

"No."

Marty shook her head.

"Why not? You know it's not good for you."

"Yeah."

"So why not give it up?"

"Listen, I get enough lectures around here without yours. I only take what I need to keep going."

"What do you mean, what you need? You don't need drugs."

"Maybe you don't, but I do." Ruby pressed her lips together. "You haven't been through the same stuff as me."

Marty's expression changed. She pretended for a minute to fuss over Stella, straightening her dress and hair. Ruby studied her, puzzled.

"What's the matter?" she questioned.

Marty usually said exactly what she meant, straight out and unvarnished. But she hesitated, not looking at Ruby and speaking up.

"Marty? What's the matter? What'd I do?"

"It's not you, honey. It's my dad."

Marty looked up at Ruby, and was surprised by Ruby's expression of hate and fury.

"What'd he do to you? I'll kill him if he touched you!" she snarled.

"No," Marty said quickly. "No, it's not anything he did to me. It's what he did to you. Why didn't you tell me?"

"Oh." Ruby's eyes wandered away. She looked down, unable to meet Marty's gaze.

"He's Sheree's father, isn't he?" Marty pressed.

Ruby shrugged, looking down.

"Yeah, I guess," she admitted.

"I'm so sorry. I can't believe he would touch you…"

"It doesn't matter. He ain't going to touch me again," Ruby blustered.

"Mom kicked him out," Marty reassured her. "He won't be there when you come back."

Ruby looked up, surprised.

"Why would she do that?"

"Because she knew that Sheree was dad's daughter. As soon as she saw her. She knew that you wouldn't go to my dad, that you didn't let him—do that."

Ruby bit her lip.

"I don't want to talk about this." She shifted uncomfortably, scratching behind her ear. "I don't want to think about it."

Marty nodded.

"I know... but I had to talk to you about it. I had to let you know that mom and me—we'd never have let it happen, if we knew."

Ruby shrugged, staring at the blank wall behind Marty. She swallowed and said nothing.

"Ruby... the first time you got pregnant... what happened?"

Ruby's stomach tied in knots. She shook her head.

"I can't talk about it, Marty."

"It wasn't your social worker." Ruby shook her head. "And it wasn't Brian." Ruby continued to shake her head. "And it wasn't Mike or one of the other Jags."

Ruby covered up her face.

"Shut-up, Marty. Just shut-up." Her voice was tight, her face white.

"Was it your foster dad?" Marty persisted.

"No."

"Who?"

Ruby got up from the table and headed for the door. Marty stood up to stop her, but she didn't know what to say. Ruby got to the door, and in the hallway she stepped into the arms of another girl. Carole held onto Ruby when she tried to pull away, held her close and tight. Ruby sobbed and let Carole hold her. Marty stood in the visitor's area watching for a few moments, but Carole stared at her with hate-filled eyes, and Marty decided it was time to go.

Glenning saw Carole and Ruby and headed towards them to see what was going on.

"Break it up," he told Carole, touching her on the shoulder with his billy. Carole stroked Ruby's hair but didn't release her.

"Leave her alone."

"What's the matter?" Glenning questioned, figuring out that Ruby was crying. "Is she hurt?"

"She's okay. Now leave her alone. Just leave us alone."

"Let her go. Just let me see her, make sure."

Carole released Ruby, and Glenning frisked Ruby down and looked her over. He pushed her back to Carole.

"Take her back to your room until she settles down."

Carole nodded and put her arm around Ruby to take her down the hall. Glenning made a mental note to let Black know about the incident and set up another psychiatric appointment for Ruby.

Carole shut the door behind them and sat down on the bottom bunk. She hugged Ruby to her.

"What is it? What did she do to you?"

Ruby shook her head.

"Marty didn't do anything," she sobbed, choking for breath.

"Oh, that was Marty."

"Uh-huh."

"What's the matter, Ruby? Come on, don't cry…"

Ruby wiped at her eyes.

"I'm not," she protested.

Carole brushed away the tears on Ruby's cheeks and pushed her hair back.

"You're okay. Nobody's gonna hurt you. What's the matter?"

"Nothing."

"You're pale as a ghost. What did she say to you?"

Ruby shook her head.

"I don't want to talk about it."

"And what's with the baby, anyhow? Little slut…"

"It was my baby," Ruby said flatly, stopping Carole. Carole looked at her, startled.

"Your baby?" she repeated.

"My first one."

"Your first… how many…?"

"Two."

Carole opened her mouth, and Ruby shook her head.

"I don't want to talk about it."

Carole looked at Ruby with a frown, not liking this new development. Ruby was getting her composure back. She cleared her throat and rubbed her eyes.

"I'm just tired," she said. "My headache's back."

Carole nodded.

"Why don't you take a nap?"

Ruby lay down and Carole left her alone to sleep.

Dr. Rivers studied Ruby. She sat uncomfortably, re-crossing her legs and licking her lips several times.

"So, why are you here today?" he questioned.

"I dunno."

"I guess you've had a few ups and downs lately," he suggested, laying down a conversational path for her to follow.

Ruby shrugged and said nothing.

"Can you tell me what's on your mind?"

"No. Nothing bothering me," she said crisply.

"I can't help you if you won't talk to me."

"I'm not looking for help," Ruby pointed out.

"You don't think you need any help?"

"No."

"Why not?"

"I don't need anything."

"You think you're pretty self-sufficient, do you?" Dr. Rivers said.

"Sure."

"Everyone needs help sometimes."

Ruby shook her head.

"You take care of yourself by carrying a weapon?" he prodded.

"I don't have anything." She spread her arms wide in a shrug, then pushed up both of her sleeves to show she had nothing hidden.

"Not today."

Ruby didn't say anything.

"I hear you were upset about something yesterday."

Ruby shook her head.

"No, you weren't upset, or no you don't want to talk about it?"

She rolled her eyes.

"I don't want to talk about it."

"Your counselors are concerned that you're not getting much out of the program here."

"They're probably right."

"You don't think this is beneficial to you?"

"No."

"Why is that?"

"Because it's stupid. How's this going to keep me from going to a bar as soon as I walk out the door?"

"Well, hopefully you realize by now what it does to your body."

"So what?"

"You don't care that it's killing you?"

Ruby shrugged.

"Why don't you care?" he pressed.

"I don't know. I just don't really care. I like the way it makes me feel, I like how it takes the pressure off. So what if it's not good for me? Neither are a lot of things."

"Do you realize just how bad it is for you?"

Ruby looked pointedly at Rivers' clock.

"How long is this going to last?"

"If you keep it up, you could kill yourself within a year."

She rolled her eyes.

"I know plenty of guys who take a lot more than I do, and they're older than me."

Rivers sat back and studied her.

CHAPTER Sixteen

It had been more than a week since Ruby had seen Charlie, so she wasn't surprised when Glenning told her she had a visitor. She knew that it would be Charlie rather than Marty. Marty had just been there to see her. Carole tensed up at Glenning's announcement.

"For someone without a family, you sure get a lot of visitors," she griped.

"Yeah, so? I got friends."

"I don't like your friends."

Ruby shrugged.

"You don't have to visit them."

"Who is it, your girlfriend again?"

Ruby looked at Glenning.

"No, probably Charlie."

Glenning nodded.

"So are you coming?" he demanded.

"Yeah, I'm coming."

Carole grabbed Ruby by the arm as she started to leave.

"If it's that cop, you're not seeing him again."

Ruby shook her off.

"I'll see who I like. And I like Charlie."

"He's bad news. If you keep seeing him, you're just going to get hurt."

The way she said it, Ruby knew it was a threat. Glenning put his hand on Ruby's back to hurry her along.

"All right, you two. You can have your lovers' quarrel after the visit. If you don't come, I'll tell him you don't want to see him."

Ruby turned her back on Carole and went with Glenning to the visitor's room. She knew that Carole was following them. Carole wasn't allowed to come into the room, but she hung around the doorway watching. Ruby greeted Charlie lowly, but not with the hug or kiss that she usually did. Charlie caught Ruby's quick glance back at the door, and saw Carole.

"Your bunkmate, right?" he said.

Ruby nodded.

"Yeah. She's being a pain."

"Oh? How come?"

"I dunno. She doesn't like me talking to you."

He nodded.

"I saw her when you were in iso. She tried to hit me."

"She did?" Ruby rolled her eyes. "I hate guys who're jealous."

"Guys?" Charlie repeated, with one eyebrow lifted.

"Well, you know what I mean. She might as well be."

"I thought she seemed sort of possessive, but I thought maybe she just didn't like you getting the attention."

"No. She doesn't like me being friendly with anyone else."

"I see... Just how involved are you two?" he probed.

"None of your business," Ruby growled.

Charlie was taken aback.

"Okay. Just tell me to back off if I'm prying." He changed the subject. "How's your counseling going?"

"I don't like to talk to them."

"You and I talk okay. What's the difference?"

"You don't lecture me. If I say anything to them, they go into the spiel."

"Like?"

"Oh, they have them all memorized. About how drugs hurt your body. They don't make you feel good. They don't make your problems go away. They mess up your brain, they kill you, all that. I don't do hard drugs. I just take what I need to get by."

"And they don't get it."

"They don't get anything. You'd think they'd understand—I mean, it's their job, right?"

"Have you ever thought about going to a regular doctor with this stuff instead of illicit drugs? When you're on the outside, I mean."

"What's a doctor going to do?"

"Well, you take speed because you're down, because you're depressed."

"Yeah. Ever since the abortion."

Charlie's eyes widened slightly.

"You've had two babies and an abortion?"

Her glare convinced him not to pursue it.

"Sorry. You told me before not to get on your case about birth control. So you take speed because you're down. There are drugs that the doctor can give you by prescription that aren't illegal and aren't like amphetamines. They don't hype you up, they just take care of the blues."

"Yeah?"

"Yeah. And as far as the narcotics go, if you're still taking them because you're in pain, not because you're hooked, then maybe there's something wrong that the doctor could fix."

"Could you get me some of that stuff? Instead of uppers?" she inquired.

"Have you bothered to tell your psychiatrist that you're depressed?"

"No."

"Well, that's what he's there for, doll. You talk to him about it. He'll get you straightened out."

"You think he'd give me those drugs? He lectures about how bad they are for you too."

"These are a different kind of drugs. He'll give you Prozac."

"Okay," Ruby nodded.

"Speaking of doctors… how's your friend Kimberley?"

"Still in the infirmary."

"Really? I was under the impression that she would be out by now."

"Yeah, well, I guess she got pneumonia."

"Ouch. Any problems with anyone else?"

"No. They leave me alone now."

"Good. And you're not carrying any more weapons?"

He touched both of her arms where the sheath had been. Ruby shook her head.

"No. The guards watch me too close. No chance."

"So other than your bunkie, things are working out?"

"She's not so bad," Ruby said with a shrug, "just possessive."

"When does she get out of here?"

Ruby hadn't thought about it before. Everyone talked like Carole had been there for years and would never leave. But it was only a short term treatment program. Ruby shook her head.

"I don't know. I think she's been here a few times before."

"So, probably for a while."

"Yeah, I guess."

"Too bad. It would be nice to have her out of your hair."

Ruby shrugged.

"Then I'd just have another roomie."

"Well, you're dry, and have been for a while, so it probably won't be too long until they release you."

"Then what?"

"Then what. Probably some sort of halfway house. You ever lived in one?"

"No."

"Might not be too bad for you. It wouldn't be a family, like a foster family. It would be more like a boarding house."

"Social Services wouldn't make me go back to a foster family?"

"They might try working towards it, but once a kid gets to be your age, it's harder and harder to do. They know that."

"I just don't like foster families. None of them ever worked out for me."

"Uh-huh. Why did you get placed in the first place?"

"I didn't want to stay with my family anymore. So I got Social Services to take me away."

"Things must have gotten pretty rough. How old were you?"

"Eight."

"Old enough to know what you were getting yourself into. So what happened? No chance at reunification?"

"I didn't want to go back to them, and I didn't want to be adopted. Too old, anyway."

"So you just stayed in limbo."

"After a while, me and my social worker got involved. I sort of stayed with him part of the time. That's when I got out of foster homes. Then I didn't want to go back."

"When did you get involved with the gang?"

Ruby was surprised. She'd never said a word to him about the Jags. Charlie chuckled.

"You don't think I would do some checking up of my own? Your arrest record shows you've been involved with them. I didn't have to do much snooping to figure that out."

"Oh. Well, I went with Mike for a while. Then he got killed, and I started hanging around with the other Jaguars for protection."

"You've led a wild sort of life, haven't you? How long ago was that?"

"Two years ago, I guess. I was thirteen when Mike got killed."

Charlie shook his head.

"About time for you to be settling down."

Ruby thought back.

"It was a long time ago, now. I didn't realize how long ago… sometimes it seems like it just happened, and sometimes it feels like it happened to someone else."

Charlie nodded. He glanced at his watch.

"I'll talk to your social worker about looking around at some of the halfway house programs. Make sure we have a space for you somewhere when you get out of here. I've got to go today."

"Okay. You'll be back in a few days?"

"You bet. Take care of yourself."

Ruby nodded and got up. She looked at the door and saw that Carole was still there watching her.

"Man, she just doesn't give up."

"Good luck handling her."

Ruby shook her head and headed towards her friend.

"You didn't have to wait," she said sweetly. Carole looked angry.

"You just can't wait to get out of here and into bed with that cop, can you?"

Ruby eyed her coolly.

"It isn't like I plan on staying here forever."

"I told you you should stay away from him," Carole growled.

"What's your problem?" Ruby demanded impatiently. Carole moved suddenly, grabbing her by the front of her jumpsuit and throwing her into the wall.

"You're asking for it. You're really asking for it, you little sneak! Don't you get it?" She pounded Ruby back against the wall. "You're mine, baby. For as long as you're here, you're mine and you do what I tell you!"

Ruby struck out at her, not managing to hit anything solid the first couple of swings, but then getting into a position where she could struggle to free herself from Carole's grip. She fought blindly, not sure who had the upper hand. Carole was bigger and more experienced, but Ruby had her inborn skill, and desperation was on her side. She knew from what other inmates had said and from the warnings of the staff that when Carole flipped out, people got hurt. Ruby just saw red. She didn't know how often she was hitting Carole and how often she was being hit. When everything returned to normal, Ruby realized that she was being held back by strong arms.

Two guards were holding Carole and trying to get her handcuffed and subdued. Ruby stopped struggling and breathed deeply, trying to get everything back into the proper perspective. Carole had a bloodied nose and a split lip. Ruby couldn't even remember hitting her in the face. As the small group of guards took Carole away, Ruby felt handcuffs close over her own wrists. She jerked away involuntarily, a reflex.

"Hold still," Glenning told her. Ruby tried to.

"I didn't start it. I was just defending myself," Ruby told him.

"I know that. Everyone knows that. We'll take you to the doctor, and then you can go back to your bunk. Just take it easy and don't fight us."

Ruby looked over her shoulder to see who else was there with Glenning, which other guard had helped to separate Ruby and Carole.

"Oh, hi, Charlie."

"Remind me never to tangle with you. You're quite the wildcat there."

He gave her hand a quick squeeze. Ruby took another deep breath, trying to calm her rapidly beating heart. Glenning nodded to Charlie.

"Thanks for your help. I can take it from here."

Charlie nodded.

"See you in a few days, sweetheart. Don't put anyone else in the infirmary in the meantime."

Ruby grinned. Glenning escorted her down to the infirmary, where a doctor checked out her scratched and bruised face and body.

"You'll be sore tomorrow," he said after a bit, "but there's no lasting damage. You came out of that scrape pretty well."

Ruby waited while he finished cleaning the cuts, and then Glenning took her back to her room.

"Just spend some time cooling down, all right?" he advised.

Ruby sat down on the bunk and nodded.

"I'm going to lock this. I know it wasn't your fault, it's just protocol. We have to make sure everyone is secure while we go through the proper channels, all right? We have to make a routine inquiry, that's all."

He reached for the doorknob, but Ruby didn't want him to go yet. She was shaken and didn't want to be alone. Iso had almost driven her crazy after the fight with Kimberley.

"Glenning...?"

He turned back towards her.

"Uh-huh?"

"What's going to happen now?"

He gestured at the doorknob, thinking about what he had just said.

"No, I mean... is Lynn going to bunk with me still?"

"No, no. We'll make sure you two are separated."

"Then who's going to room with me?"

"You'll probably be alone for a few days. We'll reshuffle everyone else, and then the next admittee will be assigned to you."

"I don't want to be by myself."

"Enjoy the privacy. It won't last long."

"No," Ruby shook her head, "you don't get it. I don't want to be alone even one night. I want to be put in with someone else. I can't stand sleeping by myself—in a room by myself."

Glenning pursed his lips.

"Well, it's sort of unusual. Usually we move the instigator if there's problems between bunkies. I'll talk to someone about it."

Ruby stood up and stepped a little closer to him.

"How late do you stay here?"

"Why?"

"Well, if I'm by myself... I thought maybe you could check in on me tonight... to make sure I was okay."

She moved right up to him as she spoke. He took a step back and put his hands out to stop her from moving closer.

"No, I don't think so. I'll be gone at supper time."

"You could cover somebody's shift or something, couldn't you? If they happened to get sick?"

"Nobody's going to get sick tonight. Now, I told you I'd talk to someone about you getting a new bunkie tonight. Leave it alone."

Ruby got the message and backed off. She went back to her bunk.

"Most guys would jump at the chance," she commented.

"Well, I'm not most guys. And I'm not putting my job in jeopardy. I make a good living here."

Ruby said nothing, and he left.

Black sighed, looking down at her list of inmates.

"Well, I'll do some more shuffling then, and see if we can get her into another room tonight."

"Good. She was quite insistent that she not be left alone."

"All right. I'll do what I can."

Glenning took it as his dismissal, and started to turn around.

"One more thing."

He turned back.

"Jackson's called in sick. Can you take his late shift?" Glenning stared at her, startled. Had she somehow listened in on the interchange between him and Simpson? "I know it's short notice," Black apologized, "but I've been trying to get somebody else to come in, and no-one can swing it."

"Uh—yeah. I can take his shift. I'll need someone to take my morning shift, though."

"No problem. I'll get it lined up. Thanks."

When Ruby saw him still working after supper, Glenning hoped that she would just take it in stride and not say anything. But she stared at him when she saw him patrolling the common room, and then she approached him.

"I see you changed your mind," she said. Her voice was just a little bit too loud, and people turned and looked at them. Glenning made a motion for her to quiet down.

"We're working on getting you a new bunkmate," he informed her neutrally, trying not to look at her directly.

"Well, isn't that sweet of you."

If they had been anywhere other than where they were, Glenning would have thought she was drunk. Her voice had an uncontrolled quality to it, and even her walk seemed a little unsteady.

Glenning studied the TV on the far wall intently, hoping that she would get the message and leave him alone. But she walked right up to him, and he had to hold her at arm's length to avoid a sloppy embrace.

"Okay, Simpson. Cool it. Back off. Go watch TV."

"You pretend not to care, but I know your type. It's all just an act."

She strained against his hand to get closer. Glenning looked helplessly at the other guards patrolling the room, not knowing how to handle this.

"Simpson..."

"Ruby."

"Simpson, just..." he tried to turn her around and point her in the other direction. But Ruby foiled him and squirmed out of his grasp, ending up closer to him than before. Close enough to put her arms around him and press herself against him. Glenning felt her hand on his holster and he grabbed her hand and pried her fingers away. With the other hand, he tried to get his handcuffs.

"I know how you feel," Ruby insisted. "I can see it in your eyes."

Focusing on her eyes, he noticed that one pupil was widely dilated, the other normal in size.

"Simpson, are you okay?"

Their eyes met for an instant, and then her body stiffened. He found himself trying to catch her before she hit the ground in a full-blown seizure. One of the other guards whipped out his radio and ran over, calling for help.

"What happened? What did you do?"

"I didn't do anything. She and Carole mixed it up this afternoon. She must have gotten hit on the head or something."

The both knelt over her violently convulsing body, trying to keep her still and assess her condition.

Ruby awoke hazily, trying to open her eyes, but finding them sticky and heavy. She turned her head to look around. There was the murmur of voices around her, footsteps up and down the hall. There was a steady beeping beside her somewhere. The walls and ceiling were white. She was in a metal frame bed, and her limbs were heavy and immobile. Ruby swallowed, her throat dry and sore. She tried to blink her eyes to clear the dark spots and see more clearly.

"Are you awake, Ruby?"

She turned her head towards the voice and tried to focus on the speaker. It was Mrs. Winters. Ruby tried to speak, but her throat was swollen and her mouth wouldn't move to form the words. A small sound came out.

"It's okay. Don't try to talk. They just took the tube out a little while ago. Just try to rest."

Ruby closed her eyes and drifted back off.

The doctor examined Ruby. He glanced at Mrs. Winters.

"Has she said anything?"

"No. She's surfaced a few times. But she hasn't been able to talk."

He looked at Ruby's eyes and tested her reflexes.

"Well, only time will tell how much damage there's been."

"Do you think she will be okay?"

"No way to tell. We can only wait and see."

Mrs. Winters nodded. The doctor finished up his examination and left. Mrs. Winters left the room to call Ruby's new social worker, Mr. Clive, the one who had called her to see if she would sit with Ruby through her initial recovery. He must be a good social worker. When he was called by the rehabilitation center and told of Ruby's condition, he checked her file and started calling her most recent foster families to see if anyone would sit with her as she went through this ordeal. He didn't have to do that. He could have just let her lie in the hospital room all by herself.

She went back to Ruby's room and sat down on the chair beside her bed. She rubbed Ruby's shoulder.

Marty stood uncertainly in the doorway until Mrs. Winters looked up. They'd never met face to face, but Mrs. Winters knew immediately who she was.

"Marty? Come in."

Marty came in, and looked down at Ruby.

"How is she?"

"Better than when I got here."

Marty caught Mrs. Winters' eyes on Stella.

"Ruby's baby," she explained.

"Oh. How old is she?"

"Almost two."

Mrs. Winters frowned, but didn't say what she was thinking. She motioned to Ruby.

"When I first got here, she was on a respirator. She's been breathing on her own today."

"Has she been awake?"

"Only for a few seconds at a time. She'll open her eyes and then drift off again. The doctor says she's improving, but we won't know how much brain damage there is for a while."

Marty set Stella down on the bed and watched to make sure she wasn't going to crawl away. She could walk, but mostly she still crawled. She only walked a few steps if you stood her up.

"Was Ruby pregnant when I had her?" Mrs. Winters questioned, looking at Stella again.

Marty nodded.

"Poor kid. She had so many problems. I wish we could have done something for her."

Marty sat down on the edge of the bed beside Ruby and Stella.

"You helped keep her off the streets for a while. That's as much as you could do. And you're here now, but you didn't have to."

Mrs. Winters nodded, watching Ruby sleep.

Ruby woke up looking at Stella playing on her legs. She frowned, trying to remember where she was and make sense of it.

"M-marty...?"

"Ruby? Are you okay?"

Ruby turned her head to find Marty.

"W-wa-w-wa..." she couldn't quite get the word out.

Marty followed her gaze and picked up the glass of water and held the straw to Ruby's lips. Ruby sipped it carefully. Marty wiped away the dribble down Ruby's chin.

"Better?"

Ruby nodded.

"How do you feel?"

Ruby licked her dry lips.

"W-what...?"

Marty stroked Ruby's hair gently.

"You had a fight with someone at the rehab center, do you remember that?"

Ruby nodded.

"Well, the doctor figures you got a blood clot in your brain... and had a stroke or something."

Ruby looked at the water, and Marty gave her another drink. Mrs. Winters came back in. She looked at Marty and Ruby.

"She's awake. How're you feeling, Ruby?"

"S-s-scared."

"I'll bet you are. I'd be terrified. Do you want to sit up?"

Ruby nodded. Mrs. Winters raised the head of the bed. Ruby tried to move her arms. She looked down and saw that they were strapped in place.

"I'm sure the doctor will take those off. You were having seizures, so... I'll see if I can find him and make sure."

The doctor was happy to see that Ruby was awake.

"How's she doing?" he asked Marty and Mrs. Winters.

"She's a little confused," Marty said, "and she's having trouble talking."

"That's expected. She will probably need some physical therapy.

Hopefully there will be no lasting damage." He swiftly unbuckled the straps holding Ruby's arms, and took her hand. "Give me a squeeze, honey."

Ruby's fingers moved uncertainly.

"Good girl. How about the other hand? And can you wiggle your toes for me? All right. You still need to get as much rest as you can. Don't stay up gabbing."

Ruby nodded. The doctor patted her on the shoulder.

"You'll be just fine, honey," he promised.

Drug rehab was not as hard as the rehab Ruby found herself having to go through after the stroke. Walking was difficult. Talking was even harder. Ruby could manage one or two words at a time coherently, but after that her speech dissolved into unintelligible gibberish. Ruby found herself easily angered. She got furious when her feet wouldn't move the right way or she couldn't make herself understood. The doctor said that it was a mild stroke and she was lucky to have gotten through it with so little damage. Suddenly, instead of being surrounded by other addicts and hard cases, Ruby found herself surrounded by cripples and sick people, and they did scare her.

Her therapist was a young man, a tall sturdy fellow named Dickenson. He was tough, never letting her slack off at all. He pushed her to the point of collapse, and further if he could. He just laughed when she swore at him, and egged her on when she fought him. Ruby was strong, but her coordination was shot. When she tried to hit him, she had about a fifty-fifty chance of hitting her target. If she missed, Dickenson laughed at her and told her to try again. He made Ruby furious.

Marty was patient when she came to visit Ruby, listening to her carefully and giving her lots of time to speak.

"You get a good sleep last night?"

Ruby shook her head. Sleeping was the hardest thing. And not only was she alone, but there was a constant din of voices and phones and footsteps in the hallway and at the nurses' station. Nurses came in to check her vital signs every couple of hours. She'd had a couple of episodes since awakening that she stopped breathing, so at night she was always hooked up to monitors to warn the staff of any complications. The doctor said that her brain was rewiring itself, and after a while the incidents would stop.

"N-no. Had d-d-dreams."

"It's so strange not having you at home," Marty commented. "I was so used to you being there at least some of the time. The house seems empty."

Ruby nodded. Marty picked up Stella and put her back on the blanket in the corner where her toys were. She saw a writing pad on the table under the window, and picked it up.

"Are you practicing your writing?" she questioned.

Ruby nodded.

"H-hard."

Marty studied the page. It was illegible, but it was obvious that Ruby had labored for a long time over it. Ruby's fine motor skills were at the level of a two year old. Marty had watched Stella perform tasks that Ruby now had difficulty with.

Dickenson walked into the room.

"Morning, Ruby. Hi, Marty."

"Hello Mr. Dickenson," Marty greeted.

"Hi," Ruby managed.

"How're you today?"

"F-fine."

"Ready to get to work?"

Ruby nodded. Dickenson slid Ruby's feet off the side of the bed and gave her a hand standing up. He grabbed the walker that was sitting a few feet away and handed it to her. Ruby slid her feet carefully one after the other to move forwards into the hallway.

"Pick up your feet," Dickenson ordered sharply.

Ruby did for a couple of steps, and then started to shuffle again.

"I'm not putting you on sticks until you learn to pick up your feet."

Ruby turned her head and swore at him. Dickenson just laughed.

"You're figuring out how to walk and talk at the same time now, huh?"

Ruby concentrated on raising her feet off the floor to walk normally. After a few steps she slammed her hand down on the walker.

"I c-can't!"

He steadied the walker.

"You do that, you're going to fall flat on your face, Simpson. And I'm not going to catch you. Just take it easy," he warned.

Ruby shoved the walker away furiously.

"I—c-can't!"

She tottered, trying to get her balance without the walker there to steady her. She tried to grab onto Dickenson, but missed and fell down. Dickenson looked down at her and didn't move to help her up.

"What did I tell you?"

Ruby got to a kneeling position and held out her hand for him to help her up. He didn't move.

"You're too impatient, Ruby. You have to learn that it's not all going to happen in a day. It takes time and lots of hard work. I've rehabilitated plenty harder cases then yours, but you have to work with me."

"H-help m-m-me!"

Dickenson retrieved the walker and brought it over to her. He talked her through the steps to get back up, repositioning a hand or foot for her, but not picking her up himself. Ruby finally got back up into an upright position, sweat dripping from her face.

"Now are you going to do that again?"

"N-no."

"Good. Let's walk down to the elevator and go to the rehab room."

Ruby walked up and down between the parallel bars countless times, until her legs refused to hold her any longer. Dickenson stood her up several times, but Ruby's legs only buckled. He shouted at her to work harder, and Ruby managed to stay up for a second before collapsing. He finally conceded and carried her over to one of the gymnastics mats, where he laid her down and rubbed her feet and legs to stimulate the nerves.

"You're making progress," he encouraged. "Last week there's no way you could have gone for so long. It won't be much longer before you can throw away that walker."

"Umm."

"Don't get lazy on me, Simpson. A short "yes sir" will do."

"Y-y-yess-ssir."
"Yes sir."
"Y-yes s-s-sir."
"Good. We're going to have to work on "Mr. Dickenson"."
"F-f-firs n-n-n…"
"Mr. Dickenson."
Ruby shook her head.
"F-firsst n-name."
"No short-cuts, Simpson. As far as you are concerned, I have no first name. Mr. Dickenson."

Ruby rolled her eyes. She grunted when he pushed her knee up to her chest.

"M-m-mis-s-ster D-d-d…" the word dissolved into something unrecognizable. Dickenson laughed.

"Dickenson," he pronounced, and brought her other knee up to her chest.

"D-dick!" Ruby said strongly.

He grinned.

"You'll get there," he promised. He relaxed her legs and pulled her into a sitting position. Ruby leaned forward with her hands on the mat between her wide-spread legs, and stayed balanced. Dickenson went over to the colorful shelves on the other side of the room, and got out a shapes activity board. He removed the puzzle pieces and put the pieces and board in front of Ruby. He picked up the stopwatch on a string around his neck.

"Go."

Ruby didn't move.

"D-don' t-t-time."

"Clock's ticking. You'd better get started."

"N-no," she insisted.

"Why not?"

"P-p-prac-t-t-tice."

"You want to do a practice run first?"

Ruby nodded.

"Okay."

Ruby slowly picked up each of the pieces and maneuvered them into the matching holes. A couple of times she used both hands to get them into place, but she didn't drop any of them. Dickenson nodded.

"Good job."

He dumped the pieces back out, and started the stopwatch. Ruby dropped the first one she picked up. She cornered it and fit it awkwardly into place. The next one she dropped three times.

"Slow down," Dickenson advised.

Ruby threw one at him.

"Sh-sh-shut-up!"

He chuckled, and waited. Ruby fit the next three into place, but couldn't get the last one properly settled into the hole. She struggled with it for a minute, and then threw the whole thing over, dumping out the pieces. Dickenson raised an eyebrow, looking at his stopwatch.

"This is going to be the longest one yet."

Ruby stared at him, not moving. He waited, watching the clock. Ruby set the board upright again, and slowly picked up each of the pieces. A few minutes later, they were all in place. Dickenson stopped the clock, grinning.

"Ten minutes. I would only have been six if you'd kept at that piece instead of having a temper tantrum."

Ruby swore.

"Those words seem to come easy to you, don't they?" Dickenson commented. "Why do you think that is?"

Ruby considered it for a moment.

"Sh-short."

"Maybe."

Ruby touched the board.

"N-n-no m-more."

"You want to do something else?"

Ruby nodded.

"Umm."

"Yes Mr. Dickenson," he prompted.

"Y-yes-s s-s-sir."

"There you go."

He picked up the board and went over to the shelves to find another activity.

Charlie hung around Ruby's room awkwardly, waiting for her to get back. The nurses said that she would be done her therapy in a few minutes. Charlie sat down on the bed, looking around the room.

Ruby came back in using a walker and supported by her young occupational therapist. Ruby looked worn out. Dickenson helped her onto the bed and settled. He looked at Charlie.

"She needs her rest. Now's not a good time for visitors."
Ruby put her hand on Dickenson's arm.
"N-n-no. H-he s-s-stays."
"Don't wear yourself out," he warned.
"N-no s-s-sir."
Dickenson grinned.
"See you tomorrow, Ruby."
He left them alone. Charlie looked at Ruby and shrugged.
"So how are you, sunshine?"
"F-fine." Ruby said, a little embarrassed. "G-get-t-ting b-b-bet-t-ter."
"Sorry I didn't come sooner. I uh, don't like hospitals…"
"M-m-me n-n-nei-neither." Ruby motioned for him to come closer. Charlie sat down on the edge of the bed, and took Ruby's hand. "L-l-lonely."
"Not a great place to be for a person who doesn't like to sleep alone, hey, baby?"
Ruby shook her head.
"I couldn't believe it when the center told me what happened. I was just there—you were okay after the fight. I thought only old people had strokes."
"M-m-me t-too."
"You look okay, though. I was afraid half your face would be frozen and you'd be drooling or something."
Ruby faked a slack-jawed, cross-eyed, drooling face. Charlie laughed and relaxed a bit. He was ill at ease seeing her like that. Jails and rehab, he was familiar with, and they didn't bother him. But hospitals were different. He was thoroughly uncomfortable there. He shifted and looked around.
"You need some flowers or something, huh? This place looks like… like a hospital room."
Ruby nodded. She squeezed his hand.
"P-p-pee-peet-t-ah."
Charlie looked at her, perplexed.
"What?"
Ruby concentrated, looking straight into his eyes, as if she could make him read her thoughts.
"P-p-pizz-ah."
"Pizza?" he brightened suddenly. "Hey, you want me to order a pizza? Tired of the hospital food?"
Ruby nodded, grinning.

"Is it allowed?"

She shrugged.

"Can I call from here? Will this phone dial out?"

Ruby shook her head and motioned to the hallway.

"Okay. I'll go find one, since I'm supposed to have my cell phone turned off. What kind do you want me to order?"

Ruby gulped. What kind? She wasn't even going to attempt "pepperoni" or "Hawaiian". She shrugged. Any kind would be better than more instant potatoes.

"Doesn't matter? Okay. I'll be right back."

Ruby closed her eyes and relaxed. She must have fallen asleep, because the next thing she knew, Charlie was shaking her gently.

"Hey, sweetie. Supper's here."

The pizza smelled heavenly. Ruby breathed it in deeply, stretching her tired limbs. She rubbed her eyes.

"S-sorry."

"For falling asleep? That's okay. I guess my scintillating conversation just isn't quite enough to keep you interested today."

"N-no," Ruby protested.

Charlie wheeled the table over to Ruby's bed so that she could eat over it. He put a couple of slices down on it, and Ruby painstakingly picked one up. She raised it to her mouth very slowly, trying not to make a mess. The first couple of bites were successful. Then she raised it too quickly and it collided with her chin and cheek.

"Whoa, hang on," Charlie grabbed one of the napkins and wiped the worst of the mess off of Ruby's face. Ruby felt herself flushing.

"I'm-m m-m-mes-s-ssy."

"No problem," Charlie raised his pizza as if to take a bite, and smeared tomato sauce on his nose. "So am I."

Ruby giggled, and picked up a napkin in her fist and aimed for his nose. She got some of the sauce, and laughed again. They both continued to eat their dinner, Charlie occasionally smearing pizza on his face, and once or twice intentionally getting extra sauce on Ruby's face. A nurse came in with Ruby's regular dinner, and looked at them. Ruby held her hand up to cover her mouth, and Charlie dove for a napkin to wipe his face.

"Uh—we've eaten," he advised, smothering a smile.

"Have you ever! I certainly hope there is going to be a little left over for the nurses."

Ruby nodded, still hiding her face.

"Of course," Charlie agreed cheerfully. "Why, if there wasn't, I'd have to order another one in, wouldn't I?"

"That's the rule," she said sternly, and she left again with the dinner tray. Charlie and Ruby looked at each other and laughed. Charlie finished the rest of his piece, looking at his watch.

"Do you want more?"

Ruby had also finished her last piece. She shook her head. Charlie packed up what was left, and took it out to the nurses. He stopped in at the small bathroom to check his face, and came out with a wet washcloth to take care of Ruby's.

"Let's get the rest of this off," he murmured, and he gently wiped away the encrusted sauce. Ruby smiled her thanks.

"I'll come by again in a few days," he promised.

"S-s-see'ya."

He gave her a quick kiss, and departed. Ruby laid in bed thinking about him.

Ruby watched Stella while Marty went down to the cafeteria to have something to eat. Stella was sitting on the bed with her, facing Ruby, with a couple of toys between them. Ruby watched Stella's movements and fiddled with the toys that Stella wasn't playing with. It seemed like hardly any time had passed when Marty returned.

"Hey, you guys look happy."

Ruby looked up.

"H-hi."

Stella looked up at Marty and babbled to her. Ruby giggled.

"S-s-sound l-like m-m-me."

Marty smiled.

"Yeah, you guys are a lot alike these days."

Ruby concentrated on winding up the music box, and handed it to Stella while it played. Their movements were both uncertain and a little jerky. Marty sat down, watching them.

"Brian is going to come see you sometime soon."

"Y-yeah?"

"Sure. He misses you. It's been ages since either of us spent any time with you. It's been strange not having you around."

"J-jam-m-mie t-too?"

"If you want, I'll give him a call for you."

Ruby nodded.

"B-bored."

"It's not much fun here, is it?"

Ruby shook her head.

"Is Mrs. Winters coming by later?"

"Um-m."

"She's really been a good foster mom for you, hasn't she?"

Ruby shrugged, frowning.

"D-dunn-no."

"She didn't have to come down here when they called her. She just did that because she cares about you."

"Umm."

Stella took a toy away from Ruby and hit one of the other toys with it, enjoying the noise. Dickenson stepped into the room.

"Hello, girls."

Marty looked at her watch.

"It's not time yet."

"I know. I was just in the area and thought I'd stop in to check up on Ruby."

"W-watch," Ruby commanded. She picked up the music box and wound it up again.

Dickenson clapped politely.

"Very good. A grip and twist. I'm impressed."

Ruby smiled, and handed it to Stella.

"You keep playing with that baby," he encouraged, "it's good therapy."

Ruby nodded.

"Umm," she caught herself, "y-yessir."

"How about a 'Yes, Mr. Dickenson'?"

Ruby took a deep breath.

"Y-yes, M-m-is-s-ster-r…" she took another breath and licked her lips, "D-d-dick-cken-n-n-s-s-son-n."

He gave her a thumbs up.

"I'll see you in an hour, and we'll see if we can get you off of the walker today."

Ruby nodded. He nodded and left again. Marty looked at Ruby.

"He thinks you're doing really good, huh?"

"Y-yes-s."

"You can say more than you could before, and you're moving better."

Ruby nodded.

"G-get-ting b-bet-ter."

"You're sure working hard."

~

Ruby walked up and down the parallel bars twice without dragging her feet at all. Dickenson watched her like a hawk for any fault in her posture. Ruby looked at him expectantly for his grade.

"Good," Dickenson proclaimed. "Do you want to give the sticks a try?"

Ruby nodded.

"It's hard," Dickenson warned, "are you sure you're ready for it?"

"I-I'mm t-tough-gh," Ruby said.

He smiled.

"Okay. Stand there while I get them."

Ruby waited for him. He returned a couple of minutes later with the crutches. He took one of Ruby's hands and inserted it through the cuff, showing her how to hold on.

"Steady on that one?"

She nodded.

He helped her to put the other crutch over her other wrist. Ruby leaned on the two crutches, feeling them.

"N-now w-what?"

Dickenson showed her what order to move in. Ruby concentrated on the steps. Suddenly she felt like she was floating, and her vision blurred.

~

She came to on the exercise mat, the crutches still clutched in her hands. Dickenson was bending over her, two firm fingers resting lightly on the pulse point on her neck. He seemed calm.

"Hi. Are you okay?"

Ruby swallowed, her heart speeding up and her breath coming in gasps.

"S-s-stroke?"

"No, it's okay. You had a seizure, but I don't think it was a stroke. Your doctor will be here in a few minutes to check you over. But you just relax, everything will be okay."

Ruby lay still, looking up into his eyes, searching for the truth. His eyes were steady. He took the crutches out of her hands, and held her hand while they waited. It was a couple of minutes before Ruby's doctor came in. He smiled reassuringly.

"Just take it easy, honey. You'll be fine." He pulled up her shirt to place the stethoscope on her chest. "Your heart's going like a little train engine. It's going to be okay. Try to calm down."

He continued to check her over.

"How're you feeling? Dizzy or lightheaded?"

"N-no."

"Confused? Any visual disturbances?"

"N-no."

"Do you think you can stand up?"

"Y-yessir."

Dickenson motioned the doctor back to help Ruby to her feet following the steps they were used to. Ruby felt pretty steady.

"Th-thirsss-sty," Ruby said.

"We'll get you a drink back in your room. How do you feel? Are we going to need a stretcher?"

Ruby shook her head.

"I-I'm o-ok-kay."

"Good for you. Let's get you up to your room. We'll schedule you for some tests this afternoon to make sure this was just your run-of-the-mill seizure and not another stroke."

"W-why?"

"Why would you have a seizure?"

Ruby nodded.

"Y-yessir."

"It's not unusual. A stroke changes the way your brain functions. It can change chemistry, electrical impulses, all kinds of things. It sort of takes a while for your brain to "settle in" completely."

Ruby frowned, nodding. She held onto the walker and headed back to her room with her two escorts.

Ruby slept very restlessly, worrying even though the doctor had told her that the tests showed she hadn't had another stroke. She woke up in the dark, panicking, disoriented. Ruby sat up, and fumbled on the bedside table for the call button. She knocked things on the floor, and jumped every time anything hit the floor, her mind going back to the day that Mike was shot, to Mike knocking stuff off of his bedside table looking for his gun. If he'd found his gun... how would things be different now? She found the button and pressed it. One of the night nurses bustled in after a few minutes.

"Hi, Ruby. You okay?"

"Ss-scared."

"Did you have a bad dream, honey?"

Ruby held the nurse's hand, holding on and closing her eyes, trying to calm herself down. The nurse tousled her hair.

"It's okay. Should I turn on the light?"

"Y-yes."

The small fluorescent light above the bed was switched on. Ruby looked around the room, looking at the familiar shapes and taking deep breaths.

"How about a drink?"

Ruby nodded. The nurse went into the bathroom to fill up Ruby's glass. She came back and gave it to Ruby. She sat on the edge of the bed.

"Are you okay now?"

Ruby nodded.

"I'll leave the light on. You can reach it if you decide you want it back out, right?"

"Y-yes."

"Okay. I'll check back on you in a little while."

CHAPTER Seventeen

When Ruby got back up to her room after physio, there was a man in a suit waiting for her in her room. He was vaguely familiar, but Ruby looked at him for a few moments before remembering he was her new social worker.

"M-miss-ster C-Clive."

It was easier than Mr. Dickenson. Clive nodded and waited while Ruby boosted herself up onto the bed and got settled. Dickenson waved and left. Ruby looked at Clive to find out what he wanted.

"I'm afraid I have some… unsettling news," he said.

Ruby waited without saying anything.

"You father has been killed."

Ruby heard his words and understood their meaning, but felt nothing. She waited for the news to sink in. She took a sip of the lukewarm water beside her bed. Finally, she shrugged.

"Ok-kay."

Clive didn't say anything for a moment, studying her. He lips pressed together, down at the corners.

"I'm afraid there was… foul play."

"M-m-murd-der?"

He nodded.

"Oh."

"Your brother shot him," Clive said.

Ruby was floored.

"W-what? J-jusst-tin?" she questioned in disbelief.

"Yes."

Ruby tried to count back in her head.

"H-he's s-sev-ven!"

"Eight, just recently," Clive confirmed.

"Ac-c-cid-dent...?" Ruby struggled to get the word out.

"No. He admits it was intentional. He said he was protecting June."

Ruby swore. The news was incomprehensible. She couldn't reconcile the picture in her mind of round-cheeked little Justin pulling the trigger of a gun and killing their father.

"You will need to be at the funeral," Clive said. "Once the police release the body."

Ruby nodded.

"And you will probably be subpoenaed to testify at the trial."

"I w-won't."

"If you're subpoenaed, you have to."

"Or w-what?"

"Or you'll be put in jail."

Ruby gestured to her crutches.

"L-like th-thiss?"

Clive didn't want to admit that it was not very likely. He studied her with a sour look.

"Well then, why don't we go over what they would ask you?"

Ruby shook her head. He ignored it.

"Why did you ask to be removed to foster care?" he demanded.

"B-bec-cause."

"Because you father was making improper advances to you?"

"N-no," Ruby shook her head, brows drawn down.

"Did he ever molest you?"

"N-no!"

"Or abuse you in any way?"

"N-n-no."

"Did he ever give you alcohol?"

Ruby was startled by the question. She shook her head again slowly.

"N-no."

"Did your mother ever give you alcohol?"

"N-no."

"Have you ever consumed so much alcohol that you couldn't remember what happened the next day?"

Ruby frowned.

"N-n-n-no."

"I don't think you're being truthful, Ruby."

She said nothing. He could think whatever he liked.

"Were you at home when Chloe went to hospital with alcohol poisoning?"

"N-no. W-when?" she questioned.

"You would have been ten, I think."

Ruby shook her head.

"She didn't ever say anything to you about it?"

"N-no. D-doesn-n-nt d-drink."

"Chloe doesn't drink?"

"N-no."

"So if she went to hospital with alcohol poisoning, it wouldn't be because she went on a binge."

Ruby shrugged, not liking where that was leading.

"D-dunn-n-no."

"What do you know about Ronnie going to the hospital and going to foster care?"

"N-noth-thing."

"You know she did."

Ruby nodded.

"But you two never talked about it?"

"N-no."

Clive stopped asking questions and just looked at Ruby. Ruby looked away from him.

"So you're not going to help keep your little brother out of juvenile," he said.

Ruby didn't answer.

"The other kids are going to be looking to you for what to do. If they see you being loyal to your father instead of telling the truth, they will follow your lead."

Ruby picked up one of Stella's toys off of the night-stand and fiddled with it.

"The police will be here to question you later," Clive said.

"Y-yessir."

"I hope you'll be more cooperative with them than you have been with me."

Ruby shook her head slightly but didn't answer.

"Did you ever live with the twins?" Clive questioned curiously.

"W-when b-born."

"I didn't check the dates on your file, but I thought it must have been around that time that you left."

Ruby wound up the music box, pleased with the ease of movement now. Clive reached over and took it away from her.

"This is very serious, Ruby, I need you to…"

Ruby blew up. She reached her hand over and swiped everything off of the night stand with a crash.

"G-go aw-way!"

"If you behave this way with the police…"

She swore at him, and he stood up.

"I will pick you up for the funeral," he said, looking down at her. Then he left.

The nurse hadn't said anything when she picked everything up off the floor. Possibly she had heard Ruby shouting at Clive. Ruby was still pouting when the police got there. Ruby was surprised to see that it was Merrill and Banks. They sat down to talk.

"Hi Ruby," Merrill greeted.

"H-hi."

"I talked with Mr. Clive on the phone, and he said that he told you about your dad."

Ruby nodded.

"Now you've had a chance to think about it a little."

"Y-yessir."

"Have you thought of anything that might help us with our investigation?"

"N-no."

"We need to know some details about when you were living at home."

Ruby shook her head.

"You were eight when you left."

"Y-yessir."

"Why did you ask to be removed?" he questioned, studying her closely.

"B-bec-cause."

"Because why?"

"I w-wann-t-ted t-to…" Ruby took a breath and concentrated on her words, knowing he wouldn't understand her if she pushed it "b-be innnd-dep-p-p…"

"Independent?"

"Y-yessir."

"Eight is too young to be wanting to leave home for no good reason. What did you want to be independent of?"

Ruby shrugged widely.

"Did you and your dad get along?"

"D-dunno."

"Did you fight?" Merrill persisted.

"N-no."

"Did you do things together?"

"N-no."

"Was he home much?"

Ruby shrugged.

"S-ssomet-times."

"Daytime or night-time?"

Ruby frowned and didn't say anything.

"When he was home, was it while you were at school or after you got home?" Merrill questioned, his eye probing.

"Af-ft-ter s-school," Ruby told him, her stomach tightening uncomfortably.

"Did you ever drink in your home?"

"N-no."

"Never?"

"N-no."

"Was there alcohol kept in your home?"

Ruby hesitated. If she said no, they would know better. The house would have been carefully searched after the shooting. They would know where every drop of alcohol was.

"Y-yessir," she admitted.

"Did your father drink?"

"N-no."

"Your mother did."

"N-no."

"Then who did? Why would alcohol be kept in the house if no-one drank?"

Ruby shrugged, staring at a spot on the wall.

"Did your sisters drink?" Merrill suggested.

"N-no."

Merrill made notes in his notepad, glancing over at Banks, then back at Ruby.

"Do you know your brother Justin?" he questioned, changing the direction of the questioning.

"N-no."

"You don't?"

"N-nev-ver l-l-lived w-with h-him," Ruby explained.

"You never talked to him?"
Ruby shook her head.
"How about June?"
She shook her head again.
"Shall we go over your relationship with your parents?"
"N-no."
"How did you get along with your mother?" he questioned, ignoring her answer.
"D-did-dn't."
"You fought with your mom?"
"Y-yessir."
"What about?"
"Ev-veryth-thing."
"About your father?"
"N-no."
"About your drinking?"
"N-no," she denied again.
"You realize that you are going to be subpoenaed to testify at Justin's trial."
"Y-yessir."
"It would be helpful to Justin if you could talk about what things were like at home—why you left, your relationship with your dad..."
"N-no."
"Why don't you want to help your brother?"
"I-I j-just c-can't," Ruby said flatly.

Ruby was nervous waiting for Clive to pick her up. She didn't have anything appropriate to wear, so she had on blue jeans and a t-shirt, and she had one of the nurses help her brush her hair well and put it back in a ponytail. She had her crutches ready, and stood in the doorway of the hospital room waiting for him.

She saw Clive as he got off the elevator and she started walking towards him. Ruby was still a little unsteady on the crutches, but she could walk with them, and she didn't want to go to the funeral using a walker. Clive saw her coming and waited for her at the nurses' station. He pressed the button for the elevator when she got close.

"How're you doing today?" he questioned phlegmatically.
"F-fine."
"Good. You look nice."

She had lipstick on, and a plain white t-shirt. Clive had only ever seen her in jail and right after an exhausting physio session before. She certainly hoped she looked better than that.

"Th-thanks."

He didn't say anything else, just took her downstairs to his car and opened the door for her. Ruby had difficulty getting herself into the car, but eventually fit herself into place. She held the crutches between her knees. She watched out the window as they drove to an old funeral home near her old neighborhood. Clive had timed it so that she would get there in enough time before the funeral so that they would not interrupt anything. A young man in a suit approached them.

"Friend or family?"

"Daughter," Clive informed him.

"Ah. The immediate family is having a prayer meeting before the service..."

"N-no," Ruby shook her head adamantly.

Clive looked at Ruby for a moment in silence, and then nodded.

"We will just wait in the chapel."

"Please follow me."

They walked behind him to the small chapel. The usher made his way up to the front row, but Ruby sat down on the back row, close to the door. Clive sat down beside her. The usher looked at Ruby in consternation, then smiled thinly.

"Wherever you feel comfortable."

They were a few people already seated in the chapel. Ruby didn't recognize them. They all waited in silence. After some time, the family came in. Ruby watched them choose their seats. Chloe sat down next to her mother, sitting close and putting her arm around her. Justin was being escorted by a police officer, who sat down on one side of him. June sat down on his other side. Ruby wouldn't have recognized the twins. They were no longer baby-faced cuties like she remembered. Justin had a long face and square jaw, and a few scars on his face. He walked with a swagger and had on skin-tight blue jeans, a black tee and a gold chain around his neck. He looked like a little hood. Ruby wouldn't be surprised if he was in one of the teeny-bopper gangs. June was dressed in a tight red dress that was off one shoulder. And she had makeup on.

Ronnie's foster family brought her in. They sat on the second row and Ronnie went up to the front row with the family. She hesitated and sat down beside June. There were several empty spaces between the two halves of the family. The prelude music stopped and a preacher Ruby had never seen before stood up and started to speak.

Ruby was bored with watching the soaps. She saw a movement in the doorway out of the corner of her eye, and looked to see what it was. June stood in the doorway looking at her. Today June was dressed in a halter-top and cut-offs. She had on only lipstick.

"Hi," she said, voice tentative.

"H-hi, J-june."

June wandered into the room, looking around. After a few minutes she turned to face Ruby again.

"How come you won't help Justin?" she demanded.

"C-can't."

"You can too. You just tell them how he was protecting me."

"I d-don't kn-now th-that," Ruby pointed out.

"You know because He did it to you too."

"N-no."

"All you have to do is tell them that you left because Dad was hurting you."

"N-not t-true."

"It is too," June insisted. "Just like he did to Ronnie and tried to do to Chloe. Just like he did to me."

"S-sorry."

"Ronnie's going to testify. But if you won't, then it's three against three, 'cause Chloe won't either. And Mom won't because she helped Him. If you testify, then it's all of us against Mom and Chloe, and they'll believe us."

As if it was just a numbers game. The majority automatically won.

"N-no," Ruby said, shaking her head.

"Come on, Ruby. You remember what it was like."

"N-no. I d-don't."

June stared at her.

"How could you not remember?" she demanded.

Ruby shrugged, like she didn't care.

"I d-don't r-remm-memm-b-ber m-much f-fromm…" she couldn't finish the sentence clearly. June got her meaning. She sat down on the edge of Ruby's bed.

"Why? Because of your stroke?" she questioned.

Ruby shook her head.

"Because of the booze, then," June deduced. When Ruby didn't make any response, she continued. "There's stuff I can't remember too. After you drink a few glasses of booze, things get sort of... hazy."

Ruby frowned. She could remember drinking at home. She didn't remember getting in trouble for it, but she didn't remember anyone giving her alcohol, either. Clive and Merrill had both asked her about drinking. Ruby hadn't figured out then what that had to do with the shooting. But now she was starting to understand. He had used booze to make them compliant, with the added benefit of memory blackouts.

Ruby tried mentally to correct herself. What he had done to June. Or might have done. *Not* what he had done to Ruby.

"Testify anyhow," June suggested, "it doesn't matter what you remember or what happened. Just help us out."

Ruby shook her head.

"N-no. S-sorry."

"What are you afraid of?"

"N-no-noth-thing."

June shook her head in disgust.

"Fine. Be like that, then. If Justin ends up in juvie, it's your fault."

"H-he w-won't," Ruby assured June. They didn't put eight year olds in juvie.

June scowled. Jamie walked into the room, smiling.

"Hi Ruby. How're you doing?" he greeted.

"Hey." Ruby nodded at June. "M-my s-s-ist-ter."

"Hi, I'm Jamie."

"June," she introduced herself tersely.

Ruby motioned to Jamie, the baby in his arms.

"M-my b-b-bab-by."

"Yeah, this is Sheree," Jamie agreed, lifting Sheree slightly.

"Yeah? You're Ruby's boyfriend?" June questioned.

Jamie eyed June.

"We see each other sometimes," he said negligently.

"B-back off," Ruby told Jamie, not liking the way he was looking at June. "Sh-she's eight!"

Jamie raised his brows.

"Eight? I would have guessed twelve."

June fluttered her eyes at him. She looked at Ruby.

"Well, I'll see you 'round," she said, giving up on their conversation.

Ruby watched June walk out the door, then dragged her attention back to Jamie.

Dickenson was reviewing Ruby's file when Sarah Rogers knocked on his door.

"Hi."

"Hi. Thanks for coming by. You ready to meet Ruby?"

"Sure. You want to fill me in?"

"Teenage stroke victim. She retained her language, but has difficulty in speaking. She's good for one or two short words, but she slurs and stutters. I've been working with her in physio and she's improved a lot in gross and fine motor, but hasn't shown much improvement in speech. So, I thought I'd better get you working with her."

"Sounds good. What's she like?"

"Good kid, bad temper. She's really good at four letter words."

Sarah smiled.

"Well, at least that's somewhere to start."

Dickenson closed the file and stood up. They walked up to Ruby's room. She was sitting on the chair in her room, fiddling with one of Stella's baby toys while the TV blared away largely unnoticed. She muted it when she saw Dickenson.

"H-hi, Mmmis-s-t-ter D-dick-ckenns-son."

"Hi, Ruby."

"I'm Sarah Rogers. I'm going to be your speech therapist."

"Oh. H-hi."

"Don't get self-conscious, you're doing great. Mr. Dickenson said you could only manage short words, but Dickenson is not short."

Sarah pretended to glare at Dickenson. He raised his hands in defense.

"That's the one word I've drilled into her. Isn't it, Ruby?"

"Y-yessir."

"What an ego," Sarah commented. "You'll be glad when you're finished with this guy, huh Ruby?"

"H-he's t-tough," Ruby admitted.

"That's how we make you better," Dickenson said with a shrug.

Sarah nodded.

"Well, do you think we could start now, Ruby?"

"S-sure."

Dickenson waved a hand and said goodbye, then left. Sarah sat down on Ruby's bed and looked around for conversation topics.

Merrill picked Ruby up for Justin's trial. Ruby sat down where he indicated, aware that her crutches attracted the attention of the spectators in the courtroom. She kept her head down. She took a quick glance around once she was sitting down. Justin was sitting at one table with a legal aid lawyer. Ronnie and June sat behind him. Their mom and Chloe sat behind the other table. Somebody had dressed June down; she was wearing an oversize white t-shirt and blue jeans. Justin was still dressed the same, looking like a mini hood. Somebody should have had the smarts to make him look like a little kid instead. Ruby studied the others. Ronnie looked pretty normal. Ronnie's foster parents were both there with her, acting like they were her family. Ruby's mom had put on a lot of weight. Her rumpled clothes were several sizes larger than Ruby remembered, and she looked sloppy and dumpy. Chloe too had a full figure and her hair looked uncombed.

Ruby found sitting through the trial difficult. Her muscles cramped and spasmed and a couple of times she had to get Merrill to go out with her to work out her muscles. It meant walking down the aisle with everybody watching her and disrupting the court. But the judge watched her struggle on her crutches didn't say anything. She listened uncomfortably to the details of the abuse that had torn apart the family. The witnesses were convincing. Her mother was not very believable, and Ruby saw a couple of jurors shake their heads when she spoke. Chloe was stubborn and terse, and you didn't get the emotion from her that you got from the younger kids. Then Ruby was called to the stand. She looked at Merrill, and he nodded for her to go up. She got up and slowly approached the witness stand. After having to sit for so long, Ruby was sore and her muscles were uncooperative. She was usually skilled with the crutches now, but after sitting for so long, she could hardly keep her feet. They let her sit down right away, and tried to swear her in. The clerk asked whether she swore to tell the truth, and Ruby shook her head.

"N-no."

The judge looked at her sharply.

"Young lady, this is serious. You must swear to tell the truth."

Ruby shook her head.

"Are you aware of any facts which may have a bearing on this trial?"

"N-no."

"You're not?"

"N-no."

"Then you may state that when you are asked questions. But you must be sworn in."

RUBY, BETWEEN THE CRACKS

Ruby didn't answer. The judge stared at her.

"Will you swear to tell the truth?"

Ruby hesitated. Everyone waited, staring at her.

"Yessir," Ruby said finally.

The judge nodded to the prosecuting attorney to proceed. The man asked several brief questions about whether Ruby had been abused by her father, which Ruby firmly denied. The prosecutor nodded, and turned her over to Justin's lawyer.

"You are the victim's daughter," the lawyer said.

Ruby nodded.

"Y-yessir."

"His oldest daughter."

"Y-yessir."

"And you left home when you were eight."

"Y-yessir."

"The age of the defendant and his twin."

Ruby hesitated. There wasn't any point answering the question, and she couldn't lie or avoid it or he would just point it out to the jury. She shrugged uncomfortably.

"Y-y-yessir."

"And you asked to be removed from your family because of the abuse," he said.

Ruby shook her head adamantly.

"N-no."

"The same abuse that has already been described to the court in detail," he went on.

"N-no."

"Lying to this court will not get you anywhere."

Ruby stared down at her hands and didn't say anything.

"How old were you when you started drinking?" he said after a few moments.

Ruby shrugged.

"I d-dunn-no."

"Before you left home?"

"N-no."

"You never drank at home."

"N-no."

"You realize that your social services file was started before you were removed from your family."

Ruby shifted uneasily.

"And you realize that when the family was investigated, your mother said that one of the ways you were getting into trouble was by drinking."

"Sh-she l-l-lied." Ruby protested.

"So how old were you when you had your first drink?"

"I d-dun-nno."

When she was finished testifying, Ruby was advised she could go sit down. She struggled to get to her feet and walk out, but she couldn't keep her feet. She looked at Merrill. He got up and went up to the stand. He helped her get up and walked her back down the aisle to the door. He put one arm around her to support and steady her. Once outside the courtroom, Ruby stopped for a breather.

"I d-don't have t-to g-go b-b-back?"

"No. That's it," he agreed.

"T-take m-me h-h-home."

"Sure. Are you okay?"

Ruby nodded. Her legs got steadier and she could walk without his support. The walked slowly out to his car.

The trial didn't go on for long. In a few days, it was over and the jury went out. They were out for a couple of days, and from what Ruby understood, that wasn't a good sign. Ruby didn't think they would convict Justin, not after the testimony that she had heard. But they might not like the looks of him, and convict him just because he looked like a punk. Or they might not believe what they heard about what had been going on in the home.

Mrs. Winters was sitting with her while they waited for the phone call that would tell them the verdict. Ruby tried to watch TV and not think about it. She mouthed the words of the commercials, as Sarah had taught her, trying to form the words quickly and without hesitation. Mrs. Winters was studying a crossword puzzle beside her. They didn't talk. Conversations were still too difficult, and she was still leery of Mrs. Winters. She'd come to help Ruby through a rough spot, but Ruby would not go live with her again.

It was late when the phone rang. Ruby had thought that it was too late, and they were going to be out for another day.

"H-hell-lo?"

"It's Mr. Clive. The verdict was just delivered."

"W-what?"

"The jury hung. They couldn't come to a landing."

"N-now w-what?"

"Now they have to decide whether to impanel a new jury and retry Justin."

Ruby was silent, waiting for more explanation.

"If they retry, you'll have to testify again," he said. "If they decide not to, he goes free."

"O-ok-kay. W-what d-do y-you th-think?"

"I don't think they'll retry. No-one really wants to convict an eight year old."

"G-good."

"The twins are in a foster home. We're trying to convince Ronnie's foster parents to take them in so that we can keep the family together as much as possible."

"O-k-kay."

"Are you interested in being placed in the same family with the twins?"

Ruby was surprised. She shook her head automatically.

"N-not w-with R-ron-nnie..."

"You and Ronnie don't get along?"

"N-not her p-parents."

"There was something on your file about that, wasn't there? If the twins don't go live with Ronnie's family, would you be interested in being placed with the same family?"

"I d-dunn-no."

She'd never considered it before. Ruby really didn't want to go to a foster family, but if she had the chance to be with the twins for a little while—her own family...

"Well, we'll talk about it later, when you've had a chance to think it over."

"Ok-kay."

Ruby hung up. Mrs. Winters looked at her.

"Was that the verdict?"

Ruby nodded.

"H-hung j-jury," she explained shortly.

"Oh dear, that's too bad. I was hoping he would be acquitted."

Ruby nodded and shrugged. She turned the volume on the TV back up.

CHAPTER
Eighteen

Brian came to visit with Ruby, arriving at the same time as Marty. He gave her a hug and sat down beside her on the bed.

"Hi, Ruby. Long time no see."

"Y-yeah. How are y-you?"

"Good. Finished with school, finally. Guess I'm going to have to find a job or something now."

"W-what?"

He sighed.

"That's the question, huh? I don't know. I'll look around a bit, but I don't know what I want to do."

Ruby nodded. She held her hands out for Stella, who Marty was holding, and Marty handed her over and went and picked up a few toys.

"She's got a cold today, so she's pretty crabby," she warned.

Ruby put Stella down on the bed and took the toys from Marty. She was to the point now where she could at least match Stella in most of her motor skills. Brian watched them and raised an eyebrow at Marty. Marty shrugged.

"When do you get out of here?" Brian asked.

"W-when th-they d-dec-cide where t-to p-p-put me."

"You're not going to go back to Marty's?"

"I d-dunn-no. Mayb-be a f-foss-t-ter home."

"Why would they put you in foster care again?" Marty challenged. "You can just come live with me. You're old enough to make your own decision, aren't you?"

"T-twins g-going to f-fos-s-ter c-care."

"Twins?" Brian repeated.

"Your brother and sister?" Marty questioned.

Ruby nodded.

"J-june and J-juss-tin."

"How old are they?"

"Eight."

"And you want to live with them? I thought you didn't like kids," Brian said.

Ruby shrugged, looking down at the toys.

"Maybe. I d-dunn-no."

Brian shrugged.

"Well, you've kind of missed your family, you may as well give it a try."

Ruby nodded in agreement.

It was a long time since Ruby had gone willingly to a foster family. But she knew she would regret it if she didn't at least try to live with her siblings again—in a different atmosphere. She hadn't lived with June and Justin since they were infants. She had no idea what they were even like.

Clive picked her up at the hospital and drove her to the house. Ruby tried to sit still without fidgeting. She stared out the window intently but didn't see anything that they went by. She bit her lip and tried to breath normally. Eventually, they pulled up in front of a house. Ruby got out and let Clive go ahead of her to the door. Mrs. Brown opened the door and nodded to her.

"You must be Ruby, then."

Ruby nodded.

"Yes, m-ma'am."

"Come on in. I'll show you your room."

She followed Mrs. Brown to the stairs leading to the second story bedrooms. She stopped at the bottom of the steps and looked up them. She wasn't sure how well she would be able to navigate them—she was just barely off of crutches. Mrs. Brown waited for her at the top of the stairs and watched her slowly climb them.

"I'm sorry—I didn't think about you having problems with the stairs."

"It's ok-kay. I'll g-get it."

She got to the top of the stairs, breathing heavily. She paused for a moment and motioned for Mrs. Brown to go on. The bedroom was just a few steps down the hall. Mrs. Brown opened the door to it. There were two beds in the small room. Ruby put her knapsack down on one of them.

"The twins are at school. You and June will share this room. Justin's is across the hall."

"Ok-kay."

"I have to go talk to Mr. Clive. Go ahead and get settled. Feel free to wander around to see where everything is and make yourself at home."

Ruby nodded. Mrs. Brown left. Ruby sat down for a moment to rest her legs, Then she got up and looked through June's things. The twins had already been there for a while, and June's stuff was in the drawers and the closet. Ruby fingered through everything thoughtfully. She went to Justin's room across the hall and looked through his things too. She took a glance around the master bedroom but didn't go through the drawers or closet. She went back to her room and laid down, savoring the peace and quiet after the constant din of weeks in the hospital. She closed her eyes and rested in privacy.

"Hey, wake up."

Ruby opened her eyes. It was June. She stood looking down at Ruby. Ruby sat up and rubbed her eyes. She hadn't intended to fall asleep, just to relax for a few minutes.

"Hi."

"Hi. So you thought you'd come live with your dear brother and sister, huh?" June said sarcastically.

"Lay off," Ruby snapped.

June looked surprised. She opened her mouth to speak, but didn't make a sound.

"I d-don't h-have any other f-family," Ruby said. "Y-you're it. S-so l-lay off."

June stared at her for a moment, then shrugged.

"Fine. Now you want to be family. You didn't care about it when Justin might go to prison, but you do now. Whatever."

She went to the other side of the room and looked for something in her drawers. She sat down on the bed with a nail file and ignored Ruby.

Ruby didn't see Justin until dinnertime. She studied him covertly as they ate, wondering what gang he belonged to. He and June ate silently, exchanging glances now and then.

"Are you ready to get back to school?" Mrs. Brown questioned Ruby.

Ruby shook her head.

"I d-don't d-do ss-school."

"You're not old enough to be quitting school yet."

"J-just about."

"How old are you?"

"Alm-most s-sixteen."

"You really should try to finish your education."

"I'm not going to school after I'm sixteen," Justin pronounced.

"Me neither," June agreed.

"You see what kind of an example you're being to your siblings?"

Ruby swore at her. Mrs. Brown raised her brows.

"I don't appreciate that kind of language here, Ruby."

She swore again. Mr. Brown shook his head.

"Watch your mouth, young lady," he warned.

Ruby shoved herself back from the table and got up. She swore at him and turned to leave.

"Sit down," he told her, raising his voice.

Ruby considered him for a moment, and then sat down. Mr. Brown nodded, satisfied.

"Now I'd like to hear an apology for…"

Ruby swept all of the dishes that were within her reach off the table and onto the floor. Several of them smashed. Everyone looked at Ruby in shock.

"N-now can I g-go?" Ruby demanded.

They didn't say anything. Ruby got up and walked away. She went to the stairs and struggled up them to her bedroom. It was a while before June came up to the bedroom. She sat down on her bed.

"The Browns are nice folks," she said quietly. "You shouldn't mouth off like that. Or break Mrs. Brown's dishes."

"I d-don't n-need p-parents."

"Then why are you here?"

"T-to b-be with you."

June lay down on her stomach and played with the tufts on the quilt. She looked much younger, her real age for once. She looked, talked and acted like an eight year old.

"I don't even know who you are, Ruby. How can I like you?"

"Y-you d-don't have t-to."
June nodded, intently winding a long tuft around her finger.
"Okay. Long as you don't care."
Ruby shrugged.
"I d-don't know y-you eith-ther."

Ruby tossed and turned for the first half of the night, then gave up on trying to sleep. She was afraid of keeping June awake. Eventually she got up, dressed, and left the room. She went downstairs and outside and walked slowly down the street looking for a bus-stop in the dark. She found one a few blocks down and waited for the late bus.

When it arrived, Ruby asked carefully about transfers, trying to school her tongue so that the bus driver could understand her, and got directions to get over to the area she was familiar with. She went up to Tim's apartment, and tried the door. It was locked, and she didn't have anything to pick the lock with. There was no answer when she knocked, but it was the middle of the night and they were all probably out at a bar or a rumble.

Ruby went back downstairs and out onto the street.

"Hey—Ruby!" It was Terry, one of the younger members of the gang. "Hey, I haven't seen you forever!"

"Hi."

"Where've you been?" he demanded.

"R-re-h-hab."

He raised his brows.

"What's the matter, you drunk already?"

Ruby shook her head.

"S-stroke. Getting b-bett-ter."

"A stroke?" his eyebrows went up as he considered it. "Man, that's weird. Are you going to talk normal again?"

"Yeah. A f-few more w-weeks," Ruby fibbed. She knew it was wishful thinking, but she couldn't admit that it might be a long time before she could talk normally again, if ever.

"Good," Terry approved.

"W-where's everyb-body?"

"Oh, drinking or whatever. Nothing special tonight. Some of them are over playing pool, if you want to go."

"Tim there?"

"Who? Oh, Tim," he looked down at the sidewalk, and his voice got lower. "You ain't been around for a while. He... got hurt in a rumble."

"Hurt?" Ruby repeated, not really wanting to know.

"He got gut-stabbed."

Ruby went cold. She got goose bumps on her arms.

"Tim's dead?"

He nodded, still staring intently at the sidewalk, away from Ruby's face.

"Sorry."

Ruby swallowed and shrugged.

"Y-yeah. G-guess I'll g-go j-join the g-guys."

He nodded.

"I'll walk you over," he suggested, putting an arm around her.

Ruby moved up close to him and they walked over to the pool hall. Terry took her in.

"Hey, guys, look who I found!"

"Ruby! Where'd you come from?"

"Rehab," Terry supplied. "And she had a stroke, so she sounds weird."

Everybody wanted details. Ruby explained as much as she could, and eventually they went back to their games. Ruby tried to order a drink at the bar, but the bartender refused to serve her.

"You've had too much already, honey, and you're under age."

"I'm n-not d-dr-drunk."

"Uh-huh. Sorry."

Ruby went over to one of the boys and picked up his drink. He let her have it without protest. Ruby watched one of the pool games as she drank.

"Where's Ruby?" Mrs. Brown questioned at the breakfast table, frowning.

June shrugged.

"I dunno. She wasn't there when I woke up."

"Wasn't there? When did she leave?"

"She was there when I fell asleep."

"I don't think that girl's going to be around here for long," Mrs. Brown said, shaking her head dubiously.

"Don't call Social Services on her," June begged.

"I have to tell them what's going on."

"Well, don't tell them to take her away."

Mrs. Brown looked at June for a moment, then shrugged.

"I'll let her stay for a while, but I won't put up with this kind of behavior for long."

"She's just settling in," June assured her.

Mrs. Brown smiled.

"You're picking up the lingo pretty quick, aren't you?"

The screen door banged, and Mrs. Brown looked up.

"I guess she's back."

She left the kitchen and went to see. Ruby plopped down on the couch and stretched out.

"Ruby, what are you doing?" Mrs. Brown demanded.

"G-g-go-going s-s-s-sleep."

"Where have you been?"

"Out."

"I can see that. Where?"

Ruby didn't answer. She closed her eyes and shut Mrs. Brown out.

"You need to get up to your own bed. You can't just sleep here."

"C-can't," Ruby said flatly.

"Why can't you?"

Ruby opened one eye briefly.

"T-t-too d-d-drunk."

She closed it again. Mrs. Brown took a minute to think about it.

"Well, I think we should get you upstairs anyway."

Ruby didn't move. Mrs. Brown stood there for a minute, and then walked away.

Justin stood looking at Ruby. He wondered what she was all about. He knew she was his sister, but he had no idea what went on in her head. He hadn't talked to her. June had a couple of times, but still didn't know what to think about Ruby. She was alien to their family. She didn't look like them or talk like them. He couldn't even remember seeing her before the trial. She'd never lived with them before. She seemed so independent and grown-up.

She opened her eyes and saw Justin watching her.

"Hi."

Justin looked around, pretending he hadn't been staring at her.

"Hi." He motioned to her jacket. "Are you in a gang or something?"

Ruby looked at her jacket and realized that she must have borrowed one of the guys' black jackets the night before and come home in it. She was sleeping on the emblazon, so Justin couldn't see it.

"Jags," she said. "W-what about y-you?"

He looked away, ducking his head and flushing.

"I can't get into one until I'm ten. They don't take eight year olds."

"You l-look old-der."

Justin nodded.

"But they know I'm not old enough yet."

"Oh."

Ruby sat up slowly, and got to her feet.

"Y-you'll g-get into one s-soon."

"Do you think so?"

Ruby nodded. Justin grinned.

"I hope so."

Ruby got the standard drinking-is-unacceptable lecture from Mrs. Brown and shrugged it off. She'd heard it all before. Hadn't she just been in rehab? She knew more about alcohol and drugs than they would ever know. Ruby took supper with them, although she wasn't very hungry. It always took some time to get adjusted to a new family's cooking. She ate what she felt like, then pushed herself away from the table.

"Stay a while," Mr. Brown suggested. "We like to spend some time together over supper."

"W-what for?"

"To get to know each other better, spend some quality time with each other."

Ruby rolled her eyes, but stayed where she was seated. She looked at the twins, and took a sip of water.

"You haven't had much to eat," Mrs. Brown said.

"I don't feel good."

"Too much to drink," Mr. Brown pointed out. "If you didn't…"

Ruby swore at him. He didn't look as shocked as he had the day before.

"I don't think that's necessary," he said calmly.

"Then leave her alone," Justin said. "If she wants to get hung over, that's her problem."

Ruby looked at Justin in surprise. She couldn't remember the last time anyone had stood up for her like that. Justin had a strong loyalty to his sisters—and Ruby was now included in that category. June made a motion to Justin to keep quiet. He looked at her and shut his mouth. He turned his attention back to his dinner and ate in morose silence.

Ruby turned her attention to Mr. Brown. She had tried not to pay much attention to him until now. She felt her stomach tighten every time she was in the same room as him, but she tried to ignore him and pretend that he didn't bother her. She looked at him now, his face and hands. He had big hands, like Marty's dad. He wasn't in manual labor, so they weren't calloused like Marty's dad's. But they were large and strong like his. Ruby hadn't thought about Marty's dad for a long time. It had been months since she'd been in the same house as him—not since Sheree was born.

Ruby suddenly felt nauseated and hot. She closed her eyes, trying to get rid of the images that started to flash through her mind. She stood up from the table quickly and went to the bathroom. She hung over the toilet, gagging and retching. She was glad she hadn't had more to eat for supper.

Eventually she managed to settle her stomach and knelt back. There was a light tap on the door behind her, and the door opened. Ruby didn't turn her head to see who it was. There was a hand on her shoulder, and Ruby jerked away at the heavy weight of it. It was Mr. Brown.

"Don't t-touch m-me!" she shouted.

"Hey, relax, I just thought I'd check on how you were doing."

"S-stay away f-from me!"

"Take it easy. I'm not going to hurt you."

He tried to put his hand on her arm again.

"G-get away f-from me!" Ruby shouted, striking out. He took a blow in the gut, and backed off. He stood in the doorway for a moment, then left her alone in the bathroom. Ruby wiped her face with the back of her hand. She was sweating. She stared at the shimmering water of the toilet bowl as footsteps approached down the hall. Ruby looked up to see June standing in the doorway.

"I know how you feel," June offered.

Ruby frowned and shook her head.

"You think I don't feel the same way when he touches me?" June questioned.

Ruby swallowed and couldn't answer. She got unsteadily to her feet and got a drink of water. Justin moved in from somewhere in the hallway.

"I told him to stay away from you," he said through clenched teeth. "You just tell me if he bothers you."

"I t-take c-care of m-myself."

He nodded. Ruby studied the twins, thoughtful. They seemed so old and mature all of the sudden. They were used to dealing with problems together. They were a team, and they took care of things together. It was strange to think of herself as part of their family.

"I n-need a d-drink," she said, breathing out.

Justin glanced over his shoulder.

"Not now. If you still want something tonight, come to my room. After they're asleep. Late."

Ruby nodded.

"Okay."

She fell asleep listening for Mr. and Mrs. Brown to go to bed. But she slept restlessly and woke up when the moon was high in the sky. It was a full moon, and was shining through the window directly onto her pillow. She got up quietly so as not to disturb June in the other bed. She tiptoed to Justin's door, knocked lightly and opened it. The room was on the opposite side of the house, and there was no moonlight.

Justin rolled over and saw her.

"Oh, hi, Ruby," he said lowly. He struggled for a minute to untangle himself, and Ruby did a double-take when she realized that June was in bed with him. Ruby hadn't even looked at June's bed when she got up. Justin reached over to the dresser and rummaged around in one of the drawers. He held a bottle out towards Ruby. She went the rest of the way into the room and shut the door behind her. She opened the bottle and tipped it up to her mouth. June stirred beside Justin, making a little moaning sound. Justin leaned over her.

"June, wake up. It's okay."

She moved around and woke up. She rubbed her eyes and looked at Ruby.

"Oh, give me some too."

Ruby took another gulp, and handed it over. June took a swallow and handed it to Justin.

"You'd think that after what He did, I wouldn't touch this stuff, huh?" she said matter-of-factly. "You'd think after all that, I'd hate booze and boys. Chloe does. But us..." she included Ruby in her gesture, "we're just so screwed up by him." She shook her head.

"Don't talk about it," Justin said.

"Ruby says she doesn't remember. But she's screwed up as bad as me. Maybe she doesn't remember, but he hurt her too."

"Ssh. Go to sleep," Justin told June, pushing her back down to lie down. "I look after her," he informed Ruby.

"I kn-n-ow."

She took the bottle from him and sat on the floor to drink

"Don't finish it," Justin warned. "It's not easy for me to get."

"I'll g-get you another b-bottle."

She leaned back and drank the bottle low.

In the morning, Ruby was gone before breakfast. She couldn't understand the unsettled feelings that June and Justin stirred up in her. It confused her, she couldn't figure out what she was feeling. She caught the bus to Marty's house.

Marty opened the door and smiled.

"Ruby! Welcome home."

Ruby noticed how much weight Marty had lost. Her eyes were dark, like she hadn't slept well for a long time. It had been a while since she'd last visited Ruby at the hospital.

"Are y-you okay?" she questioned in sudden concern. "Y-you l-look s-sick."

"I'm okay. Come on in."

Ruby kicked off her shoes and went in. She looked around. Stella was lying on the carpet on her side, watching Sesame Street on TV. She still looked so tiny. Ruby went over to play with her. Stella continued to stare at the screen paying no attention when Ruby tried to play with her.

"Stella's been sick," Marty said tiredly. "She's still got a fever. She's not interested in much."

"Sick w-with w-what?"

"Flu, pneumonia... a bit of everything."

"Oh."

Ruby withdrew from Stella and went over to Marty.

"I m-miss you."

"It's been so long since we were home together," Marty agreed. She hugged Ruby and kissed her on the cheek. "I've missed you too."

Ruby sat down beside Marty, and they watched TV together.

She didn't know whether to call the Browns. She didn't want them to report her Social Services as a runaway, but she didn't want them to tell her she couldn't stay. Eventually, she picked up the phone and dialed. Mr. Brown answered, and Ruby swallowed.

"I'm s-sleeping over w-with a f-friend."

"Ruby?" he questioned.

As if he didn't recognize her mangled speech.

"Y-yessir."

"I don't think we're to the point yet where you can be trusted to stay out by yourself overnight," he said, voice even and reasonable.

"I'm n-not b-by m-myself."

"Who are you with?"

"A g-girlfriend."

"I really don't think it's a good idea. When you've demonstrated to us that you are responsible enough…"

"I'm n-not coming b-back," she cut him off.

Ruby hung up the phone with a bang. Scowling, she went to find Marty.

"Calm down," Marty said when she looked up at Ruby and saw her expression. "What's the matter?"

"I h-hate him!" Ruby spat out.

"Your foster dad?"

"Uh-huh."

"It's okay. Take it easy. He can't hurt you."

Ruby nodded. She jumped at the sound of the front door opening.

"It's mom," Marty soothed.

Ruby swallowed and listened for her footsteps. She relaxed when she heard high heels. Marty's mom came into the room.

"Ruby, hi! Nice to see you."

Ruby accepted a warm hug.

"Hi."

"How do you feel?" the woman said, studying her closely, meeting her eyes.

"Ok-kay."

"Staying the night?"

"Uh-huh."

"Good. We've missed having you around here. The house has seemed so empty lately."

Ruby nodded, embarrassed.

"Well, why don't you help me make supper while Marty has a rest? How's Stella been today, honey?"

"No better."

"We'd better see the doctor again tomorrow. Lie down and rest for a few minutes while it's quiet. Come on, Ruby."

Ruby followed her into the kitchen. Her movements felt too awkward yet to be of much help, but she tore up lettuce for a salad and put cutlery on the table. Then she sat down and watched Mrs. Rodger get the rest finished.

∼

After the Browns were asleep, Justin heard his door open. He rolled over and lifted the sheets for June to climb in beside him and cuddle up.

"Did Ruby get back?" he said lowly.

June shook her head.

"I don't think she's coming back tonight."

"You don't think she'll tell anyone, do you?" he questioned.

"About what?"

"About you, coming in with me."

"Why would she? She's been with Social Services forever. She knows how stupid they are about things like that."

Justin shook his head.

"It's so dumb," he complained. "You're my sister. What's going to happen?"

"Ruby doesn't care, though. She breaks the rules too. She wouldn't tattle. Where do you think she is tonight? At some shelter?"

"With her boyfriend, I suppose," he admitted.

"And he's cute, too," June giggled.

"How do you know that?"

"I saw him when I went up to see her at the hospital, while you were in jail. He was there with their baby."

"So you don't think she'll say anything?"

"If there's one thing you can say for Ruby, she knows how to keep her mouth shut," June said with a sigh.

"I guess."

They were silent for a while, June holding Justin and trying to find sleep.

"Do you think he hurt her too?" Justin questioned.

June roused herself, snorting slightly.

"What? Jamie?"

"No. Dad."

"Yeah, he did. She won't admit it, but I know he did. Why else would she have left?"

"Then why did she lie about it?"

"She's scared. She didn't have anyone looking out for her, like I did," June said, holding him more tightly. "She doesn't have anyone she can trust."

"Well, she knows she can trust me."

"Not yet. She knows… but she doesn't trust us yet."

Marty was still asleep when Ruby woke up. Usually, Marty was always the first one up. Ruby caressed Marty's arm. It had been so long since she and Marty had been together, since things had been normal. Even now, everything seemed sort of awkward and strained, not quite as comfortable as they had been before Sheree was born.

After a while, Ruby got up, careful not to disturb Marty's sleep. She stood for a minute looking into the crib at Stella. She touched Stella's cheek and withdrew, her brows drawing down in a scowl. Ruby went out to the hallway, and looked around. The light in Mrs. Rodger's room was on. Ruby went in to talk to her. Mrs. Rodger was putting on her makeup at her dressing table.

"Morning, Ruby," she greeted.

"Hi."

"Marty still in bed?"

"Uh-huh."

"And Stella?"

Ruby didn't answer right away. Mrs. Rodger turned around.

"Is Stella still sleeping?"

"Sh-she's c-cold."

"What?"

She got up quickly, and rushed by Ruby to the bedroom. She picked Stella up out of the crib.

"She is cold—and barely breathing! Get an ambulance."

Ruby stood in the doorway for a moment before moving. She hit her wrist on the wall reaching for the wall phone, and tried to slow down and concentrate on her movements. She dialed the phone and tried to talk to the dispatcher. But her tongue was tied. She stammered and couldn't get a coherent word out. Mrs. Rodger heard her and swore. She grabbed the phone from Ruby and talked with the dispatcher, giving her directions. She hung up the receiver with a crash.

"Get Marty up," she ordered.

Ruby went back to the bedroom and shook Marty. Marty pushed her hands away.

"I'm tired, Ruby. You take care of Stella a while," she groaned.

"Sh-she's s-sick," Ruby said.

"Is mom up?"

"G-get up!" Ruby insisted, shaking her hard.

Marty rubbed her eyes and slid out of bed. She looked at the empty crib.

"Where is she?"

Ruby pointed to the door, and Marty went out to the living room, where her mom was leaning over the couch, where Stella was lying, motionless.

"Mom?" Marty whispered.

"I don't know, Marty. She's not good."

"Do you want me to call an ambulance?"

"They're on their way."

"What happened?"

"Ruby found her like this. I guess we should have taken her in yesterday."

Marty hovered over her mother and Stella worriedly. Ruby kept back and opened the front door, watching for the ambulance. Her eyes burned and she tried to swallow the lump in her throat.

They waited at the hospital for some word of how Stella was doing. Marty and her mom sat in the chairs waiting. Ruby was jumpy and couldn't sit still. She walked up and down the room slowly, stretching her muscles and concentrating on her form instead of on Stella's condition. Stella had been so cold.

A young doctor walked into the room when she was close to the door. He nodded at her.

"Are you the sister or..."

"I'm h-her m-m-mom."

His expression changed.

"Maybe if you weren't out drinking, you would have noticed she was sick earlier," he sneered.

Ruby's jaw dropped. She tried to respond, but couldn't get anything coherent out.

"Ruby is not drunk," Mrs. Rodger snapped, coming up behind her and hearing the doctor's comment. "Ruby had a stroke a few months ago. She hasn't had anything to drink."

The doctor looked doubtful.

"And who are you?" he questioned. "Grandma?"

"No. But Ruby and I have joint custody. I'm one of Stella's guardians."

"Well, you've got a very sick little girl. How long has she been under the weather?"

"A couple of weeks."

"You should have brought her in sooner."

"She's seen the doctor three times since she got sick."

"Uh-huh. Why don't you come in and see her while we talk?"

Mrs. Rodger nodded, and she and the doctor went in to see Stella. Marty looked at Ruby, and followed them down the hall. Ruby stayed in the waiting room. She didn't want to see Stella sick and hooked up to all of those machines. She wasn't going to watch the baby die. She had just started to get attached to Stella. She didn't want it to be any more painful than it had to be.

Marty held Stella's hand, and looked up when her mom came in.

"Where's Ruby?" she questioned.

Mrs. Rodger shook her head.

"I don't know. I told her we didn't know how Stella was going to be, and she said she had to go."

"She left?" Marty demanded.

"Yep. I wish I could see inside her mind sometimes," Mrs. Rodger shook her head. "She just looked at me, and said she had to go. Like I had just told her supper would be at six o'clock."

"I just don't get her."

"I know she must be struggling with this. I just wish she could show it."

"Stella will be okay," Marty said, looking down at the tiny form, dwarfed by the big bed. "She'll get better."

Mrs. Rodger swallowed and bit her lip.

"She might not. You heard the doctor."

"She'll make it."

"I hope so, honey."

CHAPTER
Nineteen

Ruby didn't want to go to the gang. There wasn't anyone there she could tell about what was happening in her life. Tim was gone, and half the gang that had been there when she started out were gone. To them she'd been Mike's girl, someone to be looked after; but to the Jags now, she was just Ruby, a tough chick who hung around with them sometimes. It had been a long time since Mike died.

She could go to Jamie, but she'd not had much to do with him since Sheree was born. He knew she had tried to abort Sheree, and Ruby wasn't comfortable around him anymore. And she didn't want to be around Sheree. It would just make her think more about Stella. Marty would be devastated if something happened to Stella. Marty would never forgive Ruby.

So she went back to the foster family. Mr. Brown would be at work. Only Mrs. Brown would be home. She went back to the house and let herself in.

"Where've you been?" Mrs. Brown demanded.

"M-marty's. T-told you y-yes-s-terd-day."

"Doesn't Marty go to school? Where've you been all day?"

"D-doesn't g-go to s-school."

"You've been at her house all day?"

Ruby shook her head.

"H-hos-spit-tal."

"Hospital?" Mrs. Brown repeated with a frown. "What for?"

Ruby shook her head and refused to explain. She went down to the family room and turned on the TV. Mrs. Brown followed her.

"Have you eaten?" she asked.

"Uh-huh."

"Don't watch for too long. I could use some help with chores."

Ruby shrugged and tried to tune her out.

June came and sat down with Ruby when she got home from school. Ruby was sitting on the floor in front of the couch and she patted the floor beside her. June moved over next to her and leaned on her shoulder. They sat together comfortably, like they'd grown up together, comfortable with each other. Ruby stroked June's hair with two fingers.

"Y-you got hair l-like m-mine," she observed.

It was straight and fine, though darker than Ruby's. June ran a hand through her hair on the other side.

"I'm going to get it cut short," she commented. "Really short. What do you think?"

"It'll b-be cute."

June nodded.

"The girls at school are all getting theirs cut. I don't want to be the only one with long hair."

Ruby rolled her eyes.

"S-school-g-girls."

"I know. But I don't want to be different. I'm already the new girl. I don't want to be left out of everything. They've all known each other since kindergarten and everything."

Ruby remembered what it was like to switch schools all the time because you were with a different foster family. Mid-year was the worst, and June had just left behind everyone she knew while she was living at home and moved to a new school in the middle of the year. She'd be introduced to the class and asked questions by the teacher in front of everyone. She'd have to make friends or be left out. Ruby had eventually insisted that she be kept at her old school no matter what foster family or situation she was in. She would bus to get there if she had to, but she wasn't putting up with new schools. Ruby was glad to be past all that now.

Ruby touched June's cheek with her thumb.

"M-makeup?" she questioned.

June rubbed her face with both hands.

"Shhh, Ruby! If they knew I wore makeup at school, they'd kill me!"

"Th-they c-can't s-stop you."

"Does it still show?"

Ruby scrutinized June's face.

"R-red from you r-rubbing it."

June jumped up and ran into the bathroom. Ruby looked back at the TV again. Justin came into the room and stood there staring at her. Ruby looked at him.

"W-what?"

"You said you'd get a new bottle of booze for me," he reminded her.

"F-forgot."

"I want it tonight."

Ruby looked at the clock on the wall, and swore. He was unperturbed.

"Tonight," he repeated, "or next time, you're not having any. You'll have to get your own, and you know they'll search your room."

"Okay."

He nodded and walked back out. Ruby got up, trying to figure out the quickest way to replace Justin's stash. She could try a liquor store, and they might or might not serve her. If not, she'd have to go to one of the gang, or maybe Jamie. Whatever guy she went to would expect her to stick around and be good company. Whatever she did, it was going to be a while before she returned with the loot.

Mrs. Brown answered the phone, and it was Mr. Clive on the other end asking for Ruby.

"Umm, Ruby's not home right now. She took off just before supper and said that she was going shopping or something."

There was silence for a moment.

"I really need to get in touch with her as soon as I can," Clive said. "You don't know where she might be?"

"No. She's only been here for a few days; I don't know her habits yet. She spent last night at a girlfriend's. That's as much as I know about her private life."

"Maybe one of the twins would know something?"

"I'll check."

June just looked at Mrs. Brown blankly when asked if she knew anything. Justin raised his brows.

"How would I know where she went?" he queried.

"I just thought she might have said something to you."

He shook his head. Mrs. Brown picked up the phone again.

"No, the kids don't know anything. Hopefully she won't be back too late, and she could give you a call?"

Mr. Clive hummed and hawed for a moment, then agreed. He gave her his home number.

"Even if she's in late, I have to talk to her."

"Okay. I'll make sure she calls."

Ruby tried to be extra quiet letting herself in. At least they didn't lock her out because it was past dark. She slipped in and shut the door behind her. She headed for the stairs, but Mrs. Brown came out of the kitchen and Ruby froze.

"You're supposed to call your social worker," Mrs. Brown told her.

"Chuck?" Ruby said blankly.

"Mr. Clive."

"Oh—yeah. R-right. B-but it's t-too l-late."

"He left an after-hours number."

Ruby's chest tightened. It was serious when a social worker left his home number. She went into the kitchen and picked up the phone. Mrs. Brown had written the number on the message pad. Ruby dialed carefully. Mrs. Brown hovered nearby, listening in.

"It's m-me," Ruby said, when he answered. There was a pause while Clive composed his thoughts.

"Is Mrs. Brown there, Ruby?"

"I th-thought you w-wanted to t-talk to m-me."

"I do. I just wanted to make sure you're not alone."

"I'm n-not."

"Your friend Marty called me today," he said.

"W-why?"

"You didn't give her a number to reach you at if she needed to get a hold of you."

Ruby gripped the phone receiver more tightly.

"W-what's wr-rong?"

"I think you can probably guess. You were with them at the hospital today."

"S-stella?"

"Yes."

Ruby swore, and gulped, trying to keep herself calm.

"Sh-she's w-worse?" she asked in a high, strained voice that didn't sound at all like her.

"The doctors did everything they could, but she was too sick... I gather she was always sort of fragile..."

It hit Ruby, and she dropped the shopping bag she was holding. Glass shattered. Ruby leaned against the wall. She swore, and tried to catch her breath.

"Oh. Oh, no... oh, no."

Mrs. Brown rushed in and picked up the fallen package. She saw the broken bottle, but didn't get after Ruby.

"Are you okay? What is it, Ruby?"

Ruby shakily hung up the receiver. She stared at Mrs. Brown, unable to focus on what she wanted or what she was saying. Mrs. Brown took her by the arm, with the other hand around her back, and helped her up the stairs to her room. June sat up and turned on the lamp when they entered, and then she saw Ruby's expression.

"What's wrong? What happened?"

"I don't know," Mrs. Brown said, "she just talked to her social worker."

Ruby looked at June's wide eyes.

"M-my b-baby's d-d-dead."

"Your baby? Sheree? What happened?" June questioned.

"N-no. Stella. M-my f-first b-baby."

Ruby let Mrs. Brown sit her down on the bed.

"Are you going to be okay, Ruby? What do you want me to do?"

She shook her head, not wanting Mrs. Brown in her way.

"L-leave me al-lone."

Mrs. Brown didn't want to, but headed towards the door obediently. June looked unsure whether she should follow.

"J-june, s-stay."

June looked relieved. She turned held her arms out to her. Ruby hugged her close, wondering why she wasn't crying. She just held onto June, thinking about Marty. It was Stella who was dead, and Ruby should have thought about Stella, but Ruby had just started to get to know Stella. It was Marty that she was really worried about. Marty would never forgive Ruby for Stella's death. Marty loved Stella, and had said more than once that Stella's medical problems were a direct result of all of the alcohol Ruby had consumed when pregnant. And now Ruby had killed her. Marty was going to be crushed. Marty would never talk to Ruby again. Marty would hate her.

All of the sudden, Ruby started to sob. They sat down, and Ruby wept into June's shoulder. After a while, Ruby realized that June was crying too. She looked at June's face.

"W-why are you c-crying?" she questioned, sniffling.

"Because I don't like to see you hurting. It makes me cry."

Ruby dabbed at her tears, trying to get her composure back for June's sake. She succeeded in stopping for a moment, but it didn't last.

When Ruby awoke, her eyes were scratchy and she was uncomfortable. She realized that she and June had both fallen asleep on Ruby's bed while crying. Justin was standing in the doorway looking at them.

"What's going on?" he demanded.

Ruby covered her face with both hands, trying to keep the fog of sleep from leaving her and making her remember. June sat up.

"Justin—oh—we fell asleep. Ruby was crying—her little girl just died."

Ruby groaned, not wanting to hear it. Justin backed off a little, the belligerence leaving his expression.

"Are you coming in with me?" he said jealously.

"Yeah—as long as Ruby's going to be okay. Are you all right, Ruby?"

She nodded. June hesitated, then left the room with Justin. Ruby pulled a blanket over her face and tried to block everything out.

In the two days before the funeral, Ruby hardly left her bedroom. She ate little if it was brought up to her, and left the room only to go down the hall to the bathroom. She refused to talk to Mr. or Mrs. Brown, or to anyone on the phone. She would talk a little to June, but mostly she just laid in bed trying to make the time pass without thinking. She wanted so much for everything to just be over.

When the day of the funeral arrived, she forced herself to get up and put on a clean t-shirt and pants. Mrs. Brown took her to the chapel, and Ruby asked her to leave. Ruby went in alone, and found Marty and her mom in a room with a tiny casket. Marty looked up with tear-filled eyes when she came in.

"Ruby—I was afraid you wouldn't come." She sniffled. "Are you okay?"

Ruby nodded and hugged Marty, overwhelmed by guilt and sadness over Marty's grief. Marty's mom was more composed, but the pain in her eyes was also clear. She hugged both girls.

"Stella's gone to a better place," she said.

Ruby swallowed around the lump in her throat, tears burning her eyes.

"I'm s-sorry," she choked out.

Marty nodded.

"Me too—we all thought she would get better... but..."

Ruby shook her head, the tears pouring down her face. She should have stayed with Marty when the doctor said Stella might not make it. But Ruby couldn't bear to be beside the tiny form hooked up to IV's and machines.

"Do you want to look at her?" Mrs. Rodger suggested.

Ruby shook her head, but Mrs. Rodger ignored her response.

"It'll help you with closure," she said illogically, and took Ruby over to the casket and opened it. Ruby stared at the baby's body without being able to make sense of it. She was like a doll, all wrapped up in lace and bows. Her face was unnatural and ugly. It even looked as if someone had put rouge on her still cheeks. Ruby looked away, feeling dangerously sick.

"I c-can't," she protested. She grabbed onto Marty and held her tightly, trying to convince herself that she wasn't going to be sick here. She had seen dead bodies before. Bloody, smashed-up bodies. Of people that she had killed herself. And Mike's body too, his face ripped off by a soft-nosed bullet, making him an unrecognizable bloody mess. And though it had made her nauseous, she had not thrown up. Ruby wasn't going to let a clean, prettified little body make her sick now.

"F-fresh air," she said, staggering for the door.

"Marty, you'd better take her outside until she feels better. It's awfully close in here."

Marty nodded and followed Ruby out, taking her by the arm.

"She might have been your baby," Marty said lowly to Ruby as they stood on the sidewalk outside. "But she was *my* daughter. She was *mine*. Pull yourself together, all right?"

Ruby nodded. She swallowed. She breathed, standing there on the sidewalk outside the chapel until she stopped feeling so queasy.

"S-sorry," she apologized.

"It's okay. You just have to get through the service and the graveside, and then we'll go home."

Ruby nodded. They joined Mrs. Rodger again, and then went together into the small room where the service was to be held. Ruby looked around, and saw a couple of people she recognized. Friends and neighbors of Marty's family. She sat down, and half-listened to the somber hymns and to the preacher's blather about eternal life. None of it meant anything to her. Marty and her mom managed to stay dry-eyed and composed throughout most of the service, and Ruby stared at the rug in front of her and took strength from their silence. When Marty started to weep again near the end of the sermon, the tears welled up in Ruby's eyes again. She put her arm around Marty and waited for the preacher to finish.

They were the only ones at the graveside. It was very somber and Marty wept as though her heart would break when the casket was lowed into the cold grave. The preacher was there to offer a few words of comfort, but Ruby looked daggers at him and wished he would just leave them alone. Eventually it was over, and they all got into Mrs. Rodger's car. They were silent on the drive back to the house. It was quiet and empty. Ruby stood in the doorway hesitantly.

"I c-can't s-stay."

"We need you here, Ruby," Mrs. Rodger said. "We can call your foster family, and they'll understand."

Ruby didn't want to stay. The whole house felt like death. They were steeped in it.

"I can't sleep alone," Marty said to Ruby. "You can't go off to the gang or your foster family. I was always here for you when you couldn't sleep alone. Don't desert me now."

Ruby took off her shoes, nodding. They all looked at each other like they didn't know what to do next.

"We'll just watch TV for a while," Mrs. Rodger said finally. "There will be a good movie on tonight."

They all sat down in the front room and tried to anesthetize their pain with the TV.

Ruby couldn't remember having such a hard time sleeping in a long time. Marty was asleep beside her, had fallen asleep hours ago. Ruby listened to her even breathing, expecting it to lull her to sleep. But she had a heavy pain in her chest that kept her awake and her churning thoughts wouldn't let her rest. She tossed and turned and could not find a comfortable position. Eventually, exhausted, she drifted into a troubled sleep as the sky outside started to get lighter.

They slept late into the morning. Marty had never been a late sleeper, but she didn't stir until long after it got light out. She turned over finally and squinted at the window.

"Oh, man... it must be noon. I haven't slept this late since before... before Stella was born."

Ruby hugged her sleepily.

"Go b-back t-to sleep."

"No, I've slept enough. I gotta get up."

Marty touched Ruby's cheek.

"You still look beat, though. Didn't you sleep well?"

"No."

"Why don't you try going back to sleep for a while."

Ruby nodded and snuggled down in the bed. She could hear Marty go out to the kitchen and could hear the rattle of cutlery and dishes. She heard Mrs. Rodger's voice.

"Morning, honey."

"I don't know what to do. I always get Stella's breakfast ready right now."

"I know. Just make something for yourself."

Ruby climbed out of bed, too anxious to sleep any longer. She found herself checking down the hall to make sure that Marty's dad wasn't around. Ruby knew he wasn't there anymore, but it was habit. She joined Marty and her mom in the living room.

"You look horrible, Ruby. Are you okay?"

Ruby nodded.

"Uh-huh."

"Have some coffee. How would you guys like a big pancake breakfast today?"

Ruby put her head down in her arms on the table. They were acting so normal, but Ruby knew how much they were hurting. All because of her.

Marty needed her there. Ruby stayed with her. The Browns knew where she was and it was okay with them. Mr. Clive said that she was old enough to decide where she wanted to stay on her own. Social Services was going to start tapering off their involvement from now on in. The only times that Ruby left Marty home alone was when she went to the graveyard to sit by Stella's tombstone and think. Ruby would go there for hours to apologize to Stella for hurting her by drinking and not being a mommy to her. She didn't tell Marty where she went during the day. Marty thought she was off with the gang or something.

Marty decided to go back to school. She'd been keeping up by correspondence and didn't think she would have a problem getting back into it. Otherwise she would be alone in an empty house every day. The first day she went back to school was the day that Ruby decided to leave. Marty would be okay if she wasn't home alone all the time. And if she couldn't sleep alone at night, her mom had a double bed that she was no longer sharing with anyone. Ruby had carefully thought through her plans, trying to figure out what it was that she wanted.

Charlie was in the locker room changing out of his uniform when one of the others told him someone was waiting for him outside.

"Who?"

"A young lady with a speech impediment."

Charlie frowned, buttoning up his shirt.

"Uh... okay. I'll go see who it is. Thanks."

He tied his shoes and left the locker room. Ruby was pacing across the lobby with her knapsack over her shoulder. Charlie watched her for a minute before she turned and saw him. He had to admire her form, knowing what she'd been through. She walked with such poise and grace. It testified of her perseverance, and of her physiotherapist's. Ruby saw Charlie, and smiled.

"W-want s-some comp-pany?" she questioned.

He put his arm over her shoulders.

"Sure, sweetie. What are we doing?"

"How ab-bout g-going to your p-place?"

Charlie studied Ruby.

"How old are you now, Ruby?"

She didn't answer.

"I don't remember from your file," Charlie said slowly, "but if you tell me you're under eighteen, I really can't do much more than buy you popcorn at the movies."

Ruby shrugged.

"I'm eight-teen."

"Good. My place is a mess—do you mind?"

"No."

"Okay. We'll go home, then."

He put his arm around her and walked her out to his car.

"How are you doing now, gorgeous?"

"Ok-kay."

"I haven't seen you since the hospital. You look a lot better than you did then."

"Uh-huh. J-just my s-speech n-now."

"Yeah. But I can understand you. You just sound a little drunk."

She nodded.

"B-but I'm n-not," she promised.

"I know. You staying off the drugs too?"

Ruby shrugged.

"Yessir."

"Good for you."

He opened the car door for her and she climbed in. Once back at his apartment, Charlie spent a couple of minutes picking things up.

"I told you it was a mess."

"It's okay."

Ruby walked around his apartment looking around. It looked very much like a bachelor's apartment. Not like Chuck's obsessively tidy place or even Wilhelm's. More like Jamie's before the maid got there. She was standing in the doorway of the bedroom when Charlie came up behind her and put his arms around her.

"Tell me again that you're eighteen."

"I'm eighteen."

"Good."

When he turned over to rifle through the drawer of his bedside table, Ruby shook her head.

"You d-don't have t-to. I g-got my t-tubes t-tied."

He looked at her, frowning.

"Did you? I remember you talking about it."

"Uh-huh."

Charlie hesitated, wondering what doctor would perform that procedure on such a young girl. But Ruby had spoken out vehemently about not wanting to get pregnant again, so he nodded and turned back to Ruby.

"Okay. If you say so."

He put her arms around her and pulled her close.

"Come here, you."

Ruby was happy to comply.

Cairns nodded his greeting to Charlie.

"Morning, Charlie."

"Joe."

Cairns stood there and looked at Charlie. Charlie looked up at him after a moment.

"What?"

"I hear you have a new girlfriend."

Charlie grinned.

"News spreads fast around her. Just what exactly did you hear?"

"That she's cute and very young. Met you here after work yesterday. You took her home with you."

"She's eighteen. And who said I took her home?"

"Did you?"

Charlie shrugged, and Cairns laughed.

"You did, didn't you? Where did you meet this girl? Pick her up in vice?"

Charlie felt his face get hot, and kept his head down, tying his shoes.

"Drug rap. I've been keeping track of her for a while."

"Well, well. You'd better be careful."

"Ruby's fine. She's just looking for some company."

Ruby rubbed her belly, lost in thought. She'd always gotten pregnant too easily before. She would be surprised if it took more than a few weeks to get pregnant again. And this time she wouldn't drink too much, and she would be a good mommy, too. Her baby wouldn't die this time. Marty could come see her whenever she wanted to—or maybe Ruby would leave Charlie and go back to live with Marty and her mom again.

"Are you going to get ready to go, precious?" Charlie questioned.

Ruby startled and looked up. Charlie was standing in the doorway watching her sitting on the edge of the bed.

"Oh, yeah. W-what should I w-wear?"

"I picked up a dress for you. It's in the closet."

Ruby got up and opened the closet door. It was a slim black dress, short enough to show off a good bit of thigh. It was a simple cut, with no adornment. Charlie had recently bought her a pair of black heels that Ruby didn't have anything to wear with. She took the dress off the hanger and held it up to herself.

"Will it do, darling?" Charlie questioned with a grin.

Ruby nodded.

"Yeah, I l-like it."

He looked at his watch, and Ruby got the hint.

"I'm g-going."

"Good. Don't want to be late for the ball."

Ruby stripped down.

"D-do I have t-to w-wear n-nylons?" she showed off her long, slim legs.

"I think they look just fine without. Now get dressed."

Ruby pulled the dress on and straightened it. She studied herself in the mirror, turning a bit to look from either side. She slipped on the shoes.

"W-what d-do you th-think?"

"You look good. I don't know if I trust my fellow officers around you."

Ruby smiled. She went into the bathroom to put on a bit of makeup and put her hair up. She looked at herself in the mirror for a minute and joined Charlie. He took her by the arm and escorted her down to the car.

"You're looking mighty fine tonight, sweetheart."

Ruby turned her attention to Charlie's appearance. He was dressed to the nines in a black tuxedo and bow tie.

"You l-look g-good t-too."

"You'll be the belle of the ball. Mind you don't let those other cops dance too close."

Ruby smiled, enjoying the excitement. She'd never gone to a fancy party before—a party with all of those pretty dresses and ballroom music and everything. It was so different being with Charlie. So different from being with Jamie or the gang. Jamie's parties were loud music and drinking, and the gang's parties were just revelry, drugs and booze. She'd only seen fancy parties on TV.

The room was full of gorgeous elaborate dresses and beautiful women. Ruby stuck close to Charlie, feeling out of place. He had bragged up her looks and she hadn't expected all of the extravagance. She felt more like an ugly duckling than the belle of the ball. But the other cops still flirted with her and watched her movements.

"Have we met before?" one of them questioned, studying Ruby with a puzzled look.

Charlie shook his head, then stopped.

"Oh... I guess you probably have. A drug bust months ago. We picked her up."

"Oh." He looked like he would say something further, but he just patted her on the arm and walked away. She looked up at Charlie. He shrugged, and took her over to introduce to a couple of other cops.

Once they'd mixed for a while, Charlie took her out on the dance floor. They hardly even got started when another policeman cut in. Ruby hardly saw Charlie for two minutes at a time after that. She was sure, at the end of the night with throbbing feet that she had danced with every officer in the place—some of them twice. She limped back to the car with Charlie.

"I told you you'd be the belle of the ball. Beauty like yours doesn't need to be overdressed. Simplicity is the way to go."

"I had fun."

"Good. I hoped you would. You certainly got a lot of attention."

"M-my feet hurt."

"You've been dancing for hours. I'm not surprised."

Ruby rubbed her calves and knees and took her shoes off.

"Tired, baby?"

"Uh-huh."

"We'll get you home and to bed."

Ruby sat back and watched out the window. They got to the apartment and Ruby opened her door. She swung her legs out the door and tried to stand up. Her knees shook and she couldn't get out of the car.

"Ch-charlie!"

He came around the car and held his hand out for her.

"Stuck, sweetheart?"

"Uh-huh. Can't g-get up."

He pulled her to her feet. Ruby leaned on him, unsteady.

"I think you overdid it a bit, honey."

"Yeah."

He hung onto her.

"Everybody's going to think I'm bringing you home smashed."

Ruby giggled. It had been quite a night. He helped her into the building and a couple minutes later they were in his apartment. Charlie dropped Ruby on the bed.

"There you go, hon'. I'm going to get a drink, then I'll be right in."

Ruby laid motionless for a minute, and then sat up to get her dress off. She peeled it off and stretched out on the bed and closed her eyes.

Charlie stepped into the room with a can of beer to talk to Ruby while she got ready for bed. She was still on the bed, already asleep. Her dress and her shoes were in a pile on the floor beside the bed. Charlie put down the can and got undressed.

∼

"So," Davidson said casually, "are you and that girl living together?"

"Ruby? Yeah, for a while. Why?" Charlie questioned.

"How old is she?"

"Eighteen."

"Seems like when we arrested her she was only fifteen."

"No, she's eighteen."

"How long ago was that bust? A few months? I'm sure she wasn't even sixteen."

Charlie looked at Davidson.

"Hey. I said she's eighteen, okay?"

"Okay. So what are your plans?"

Charlie shrugged.

"I don't know. Ruby's not the kind that stays in one place for long. I really don't expect her to stay forever."

"Have you guys talked about it?"

"No. We are just taking it one day at a time. You think I want to scare her off?"

"Are you serious? You two looked pretty serious at the ball."

Charlie sighed, shaking his head.

"I like Ruby. But I don't have any expectations. I'll take whatever I can get. One day she's just not going to be there anymore. She's a great kid, but I'm not going to push her, she'll just take off."

"Well... I hope it works out for you. But—be careful, all right? She's so young."

"Ruby and I will be fine."

CHAPTER
Twenty

Ruby stared at the blood, feeling sick. She wasn't pregnant. She had been sure that she would be by now. But her period had arrived, proving her wrong. She'd never been really regular, so she hadn't expected it.

That meant she would be staying with Charlie a while yet. Which was okay; she liked to be with him. He didn't care what she did during the day when he was gone—or at night, if he was on shift. She was always there when he got home, and he didn't ask what she did while he was gone. He reminded her of Marty in ways—he was steady and even, easy to talk to and be around. He didn't have big expectations of her, just liked to spend time with her and enjoy her company. He rarely censured her or told her what to do, and when he did it was with a joke and a grin. He didn't like things to get too serious.

Ruby rubbed her stomach slowly, wincing. She got dressed slowly, and took a beer from the fridge, though she knew that Charlie would ask her about it. He watched her liquor intake pretty closely. Ruby got her knife out of her knapsack and left the apartment.

∽

"So what's your boyfriend do?" Terry questioned.

Ruby looked at him, surprised.

"Wh-what?"

Terry continued to shave his fingernails with his knife, studying them intently and pretending not to be watching Ruby.

"You got a steady guy now, don't you?" he said.

Ruby shrugged and nodded.

"I g-guess."

"Well, he ain't one of the Jags, so what does he do?"

Ruby avoided the question.

"Not m-much. He's n-not in a g-gang," she said.

Terry glanced up at him.

"Just a bum?"

Ruby laughed.

"Yeah."

"He know you're a Jag?"

"No."

"So where does he think you go?"

Ruby wondered fleetingly when she had gone from merely being associated with and protected by the Jags to actually being one of them. There had been no initiation, no clear demarcation, but now she was considered one of them.

"He d-doesn't ask," she told Terry.

Terry nodded. Ruby was silent for a few minutes, watching his busy hands.

"How'd you kn-now I have a s-steady g-guy?" she inquired.

"It's pretty obvious. I mean, you never stay with us for a few days at a time like you did before, you always go home every day. You don't sleep here like you used to with Tim. It's just obvious."

Ruby shrugged. She wasn't nearly as involved with the Jags as she had been at one time. But she still did a lot with them. She wasn't seeing Jamie or Brian any more—couldn't see Marty. She was still planning to go see the twins again, but hadn't seen them since Stella died. Her life had changed a lot.

"I'm thirsty," she told Terry, pushing stray tendrils of hair back from her face.

"You wanna go out for some drinks?"

Ruby nodded.

"Yeah."

"I'll see if any of the others want to come."

Charlie and Davidson got out of the car, both loosening their service weapons in the holsters and unsnapping them.

"Backup coming?" Charlie questioned, casing out the pool hall doors.

"Thirty seconds behind us."

"Let's go in."

Davidson nodded his agreement. They rushed through the front doors and looked around. They were expecting a fight in progress, but things were pretty still. No fight. But no-one was playing pool. The patrons were all focused on the boy on the floor. It looked at first like he'd just been knocked out, but when Davidson rushed forwards and pulled back his jacket, they could see the blood and gore. Charlie looked over the faces of the clientele for the guilty one—the killer, if he hadn't already gotten out the back. The blood was fresh. Two minutes ago it had been called in as a fight in progress. Charlie pulled out his radio with his free hand to tell the back-up units to be on the lookout for a runner, and they would get a description out as soon as they could. Then Charlie froze. At first he hadn't seen the girl towards the back in a black jacket. She was seated on the edge of one of the pool tables, with a good vantage point of the boy on the floor. She had a stein of beer in one hand and was talking to the gang member beside her. She had her eye on Davidson, and then after Charlie spotted her she looked over at him. She froze too.

"Ruby—what's the matter? I think—Ruby?"

Terry tried to get Ruby's attention again, but she was focused on the second cop and didn't hear anything he said. Backup arrived, and the cops started questioning everyone in the place about the fight. Charlie went up to Ruby.

"What are you doing here?"

"Playing p-pool."

Charlie looked around at the other Jags.

"I thought you were finished with these guys."

Ruby shrugged. He'd never asked, and she'd never told him she was. What would be the point in lying to him?

"You're drinking?" Charlie questioned.

Ruby nodded.

"A c-couple."

"Did you see what happened?"

"He g-got himself s-split."

Charlie couldn't believe she was so casual about witnessing a murder.

"He's dead, Ruby."

"I kn-now."

"Who did it?"

She shrugged.

"One of the Jags?" Charlie questioned.

Ruby shook her head.

"No."

Charlie didn't know whether to believe her or not. He was so thrown by seeing her there. But surely the other Jags wouldn't have stuck around if it had been one of them.

"Describe the guy that did it."

Ruby shook her head. Charlie frowned. He looked at her for a minute.

"Don't go anywhere, okay?"

Ruby shrugged. Charlie left her alone and went to question other witnesses. Terry looked at Ruby. A couple of the other Jags moved closer.

"You know this cop?" Terry questioned lowly.

"Yeah."

"He looked surprised to see you here—where do you know him from?"

Ruby giggled and didn't explain. She took another drink, watching Charlie work his way across the room. She didn't generally see Charlie in uniform, but he sure did look good in it. She and the Jags got bored with the investigation and started a new game of pool. The night wore on, and Charlie eventually came up behind her and put his hand on her shoulder.

"Let's go, Ruby."

He was uptight. He never called her Ruby—it was always 'sweetheart', 'honey', 'sunshine' or some other endearment. Ruby looked at him over her shoulder.

"J-just a s-sec."

She carefully lined up her shot, but bungled it up with him standing impatiently behind her. Ruby shrugged.

"S-see-ya, g-guys."

"See you tomorrow, Ruby."

Ruby turned and went with Charlie. He put his hand on her arm and escorted her out of the bar. They didn't say anything when they got outside. Charlie took Ruby over to his car. His partner followed them out of the building. Ruby hesitated when Charlie let go of her arm beside the car. She always rode beside him in the front seat. But Davidson was there too, and she didn't know if Charlie was upset with her or just taking her home.

They all stopped for a moment.

"There's enough room in the front," Charlie said.

Ruby sat between Davidson and Charlie. Charlie put his hand on her knee after a few minutes.

"So what happened, sweetie?"

She shrugged.

"I d-dunno."

"Did you see the boy who killed that kid?"

"Yeah."

"Was it someone you knew?"

"No."

"Could you hear what they were arguing about?"

"M-money. I d-dunno."

"What about money?"

Ruby shrugged.

"D-dunno."

"If you didn't hang around with the gang, you might not end up in quite as much trouble."

"Am I in t-trouble?" she demanded.

He looked at her.

"No. You ended up in the wrong place at the wrong time. At least you weren't knocking off a liquor store somewhere."

Ruby grinned. She tried to relax, as Charlie seemed to have settled down a bit.

"How long have you been involved with the gang?" Davidson questioned.

"Few years."

"So police raids are nothing new to you."

"N-no."

Charlie looked at Davidson and tried to change the subject.

"If you're looking for company while I'm out, why don't you get a job or go back to school?"

"I d-don't like s-school and d-don't wanna job."

"How old are you, Ruby?" Davidson questioned.

Charlie and Ruby exchanged glances.

"Eighteen," Ruby said.

"Funny, I thought you were fifteen or sixteen."

"Eighteen," Ruby repeated firmly.

They pulled up in front of the police station. Ruby got out of the car with the men, though her stomach was tight again with uncertainty.

"You can come in and wait while I finish my shift and change," Charlie told her.

"Okay."

She followed him. He left her in some kind of common room while he went to finish his duties. Ruby hung around, looking at the posters on the wall. Various cops came through the room, and some of them recognized her and stopped to talk for a minute. It was almost an hour before Charlie came back to get her, wearing blue jeans and a white t-shirt.

"Well, kiddo, you ready to go home?"

"Uh-huh."

He put his hand on her back, then lifted it up again.

"Why haven't I seen you wear this jacket before?" he questioned. "Am I that blind?"

"N-no. It's not m-mine. C-can't afford m-my own."

"So you haven't been wearing it around the house and I just didn't notice."

Ruby laughed at the image.

"No. B-been in the c-closet c-couple t-times."

Charlie shook his head. He didn't say anything for a few minutes as they walked out to the car. Charlie was frowning to himself. After a while, he spoke.

"I don't want you to be hiding things from me, okay Ruby? I don't want to find out from some other cop that you were at a pool hall where somebody was killed, okay? I want to hear it from you first."

Ruby eyed Charlie.

"Wh-what?"

"I know you're not going to change just because of me. But I'm not your daddy, I'm not going to punish you or kick you out if you break curfew. I may not approve, but you don't have to hide anything from me. I want to know what you're up to, I don't want to be surprised."

"Yeah, okay."

"Good. Anything I should know?"

"No."

"You sure?"

Ruby shrugged. Charlie didn't say anything further. They got to the apartment and went to bed.

Ruby was awake when Charlie's alarm went off. He rolled over sleepily and turned it off. He laid with his eyes closed for a minute, then opened them, stretching. He noticed she was awake.

"Hey, you're supposed to be fast asleep."

Ruby held her stomach.

"I d-don't feel g-good."

"You got the flu?"

"No."

"Oh." He swung his feet over the side of the bed and got up. "Are you all right? You look upset."

"I'm okay."

"Do you need anything? For your stomach?" he offered.

"Aspirin."

"Okay. Are you staying in bed?"

"For a while."

"I'm going to the gym. I'll see you in a couple hours."

He put on a pair of pants and t-shirt. He left for a minute and came back with a cup of water and a couple pills. Ruby took them. He sat on the bed next to her, watching her face. He touched her cheek.

"What's wrong, sweetie?"

Ruby looked at him. He looked concerned. He could tell there was something on her mind.

"I'm s-sorta d-depressed."

"What about?"

"N-nothing. Just d-down," she looked away from him.

"Do you have a doctor?"

"N-no. Just wh-whoever."

"Can I set you up with my doctor? Remember I told you about Prozac? Otherwise you're going to end up on speed again."

Ruby was doubtful.

"It'll m-make me feel b-better?"

"Better than you're feeling now."

"Ok-kay."

"I'll set up an appointment for you."

Ruby nodded. Charlie patted her on the shoulder.

"You take care of yourself, honey. I don't want you to end up high or suicidal."

He took the cup from her again.

"Get some rest. I won't be too long," he promised.

He left. Ruby listened to the front door click shut behind him. She rubbed her aching stomach, thinking of Stella.

When Charlie got home, Ruby wasn't there. He expected her to still be in bed, but it was cold and unmade. She wasn't usually gone when she knew he would be back soon.

Charlie brushed it off and decided to use the time to tidy up the apartment. It was harder to keep it clean with two people living there. He didn't look at the clock until his stomach started rumbling. Then he realized that Ruby had been gone for a few hours. He called his doctor to set up an appointment for Ruby to see him. He looked at his watch and wondered what she was up to.

Eventually, it was time for him to get ready for his shift. Ruby still wasn't back. He wondered if it had something to do with the night before. Maybe witnessing the murder had upset her more than it seemed. She had acted like she didn't care, but she'd seen one boy kill another in a fight. It couldn't have left her unaffected. He hung around for a few minutes, hoping she would show up, then got his jacket. The Jag jacket that Ruby had been wearing the night before was still hanging in the closet. Wherever she had gone, she wasn't with the gang. Maybe she was with her friend Marty.

Charlie was running late for his shift when he locked up. Then he met up with Ruby in the hall. She seemed a little surprised to see him.

"Oh—Ch-charlie."

"Where've you been, Ruby? I was worried."

She looked up at his face briefly, and Charlie saw how swollen and bloodshot her eyes were. She'd been crying. He cradled her face in his hands, and kissed her gently.

"What is it, sweetie? Are you okay?"

"Uh-huh."

"Where were you? What's wrong?"

She sniffled, considering whether to tell him or not.

"The c-cemetery."

"Oh... I'm sorry. Are you going to be okay?"

Ruby nodded.

"Who died?" Charlie said awkwardly.

"You're g-gonna b-be late."

She moved towards the door and took out her key. Charlie put his hand on Ruby's arm to stop her.

"I don't think you should be alone. You're not going to stay here by yourself, are you?"

"I d-dunno."

"I think you should be with other people."

Ruby stood there for a minute, motionless. Then she shrugged.

"Okay."

"Where do you want to go? I can drop you somewhere."

"N-no. I'll g-get th-the b-bus."

"Okay. You take care of yourself, okay honey? I'm worried about you today."

"Ok-kay."

"That's my girl. See you in the morning."

Ruby unlocked the door to get her jacket, and waved to Charlie. She wrapped the warm jacket around her and closed her eyes. He had called her "his girl" tonight. He'd never called her that before. No-one had ever called her that before. She left the apartment and went to find the gang. Jack was in the cafe they always used to hang out at. Jack wasn't really around the gang that much anymore. He spent more and more time on his own away from them. He saw her as she walked by on the sidewalk outside, and waved for her to come in.

"Hey, Ruby," he greeted as she walked up to him. "How about keeping me company for a while?"

"S-sure."

She sat down beside him and picked up his drink to have a sip. Jack put his arm over her shoulders, sighing.

"I'm leaving, you know," he said.

Ruby looked at him.

"Wh-what? Where?"

"I'm leaving town. Today or tomorrow."

"Oh."

"You want to come with me?"

Ruby looked at Jack, startled. He had never paid that much attention to her. They'd spent some time together now and then, enjoyed each other's company a few times, but she had never considered herself his girlfriend. No-one did. Jack didn't. He said he didn't have a girlfriend. Ruby kind of doubted that he even really liked girls. Ruby shook her head, frowning.

"No. You're k-kidding, r-right?"

Jack laughed appreciatively.

"We'd last about three days together, huh?"

Ruby shook her head.

"I d-don't th-think we'd l-last th-that."

He grinned.

"You're a good kid, Ruby. You're cool."

Ruby smiled. She wondered why he had asked her to go with him. He'd never—as far as she knew—had a steady girlfriend or any long-term relationship.

"Why are you g-going?"

"Oh, you know. I'm too old to be hanging around with these kids anymore. May as well go somewhere that the cops don't know me and I can get a job or something."

"Huh."

"Whose jacket is that?"

Ruby touched it.

"Umm, T-terry's, I th-think."

"Do you want mine?"

She nodded.

"Yeah."

He took it off and handed it to her. He pushed the drink towards her.

"Go ahead and finish it. See ya."

"Bye."

Jack got up and walked away. Ruby watched him go, frowning. She sat there and finished the rest of the drink. She took off Terry's jacket and put on Jack's. She sat there for a while by herself before going to see the rest of the gang.

Ruby was home in bed when Charlie got home. She usually was, but it surprised him now. Things had changed in the last day, and he didn't expect her to be there. He undressed and slipped in beside her.

"Hi, sweetheart."

She stirred.

"Hi, Ch-charlie," she murmured sleepily.

"How was your day?"

"Okay."

"How're you feeling tonight?"

"S-sleepy."

Charlie put his arms around her, snickering.

"Okay, baby. Go to sleep."

He snuggled up close to her and dropped off to sleep.

Ruby was going to see the gang when she saw the cops get out of their car and head purposefully towards her. They were in an unmarked car and plain clothes, but it was obvious they were cops. Ruby looked around quickly to see if there was any way to discreetly avoid them, but there was no way to get away without running. They couldn't pick her up for anything, so Ruby wasn't too worried.

"We want to ask you some questions," one of them told her, pushing her back into the wall of the building behind her. Not roughly, just firmly. Ruby looked them over. She didn't recognize them from any of the places she had gone with Charlie. And obviously they didn't recognize her either.

"Wh-what about?" she said cautiously.

"About Jack Wilson."

"Why? Wh-what'd he d-do?"

"None of your business. Where is he?"

"I d-dunno."

"You were the last one seen with him."

"I haven't s-seen him s-since y-yesterday."

"Yeah, right before he shook his police tail," the cop confirmed. "So where did he go?"

"I d-dunno."

He slapped her. Ruby was startled. She looked from one to the other.

"I d-don't kn-now," she repeated. "He s-said he was l-leaving t-town."

"Where to?"

"I d-dunno."

He slapped her again. Ruby squirmed.

"I w-want my l-lawyer."

"You're not under arrest."

"Then n-no m-more questions."

He slapped her again. Ruby's cheeks flamed, and her lip stung. She licked it and tasted blood. He'd split her lip.

"Do you want to be considered an accessory?" he growled. "Because if you do, you just keep it up."

Ruby shook her head. He moved closer to her, uncomfortably close. Ruby would have moved away if her back wasn't already up against the wall.

"What did you and Wilson talk about when you met yesterday?"

"He s-said he w-was leaving t-town."

"Did you ask him why?"

"Y-yessir."

"What did he say?"

"It w-was t-time to l-leave th-the g-gang. M-move on."

"Why? What had happened?"

Ruby shook her head.

"D-dunno."

"A guy like Wilson doesn't just up and leave his gang without a leader."

Ruby shrugged. That was Jack's business, nothing to do with her.

"Who's the leader of the Jags with Wilson gone?"

Ruby shook her head.

"D-dunno yet."

He slapped her.

"You were the last one to see him, sweet thing. What were his wishes?"

"He d-didn't s-say."

He raised his hand and Ruby moved to protect herself this time. He grabbed her by the throat, right under her jaw, and pushed towards the wall. Ruby struggled for breath and tried to pry his hand away. When she reached for her knife, he squeezed harder.

"Keep your hands where I can see them, or you'll die right here, honey."

Ruby froze. He didn't let go. Ruby felt herself sliding towards darkness, and he finally released her throat. Ruby leaned against the wall, gasping for breath. The cops both seemed to be blurry, on the other side of a thick fog. Ruby's knees buckled, and she blacked out momentarily. When she came to herself, she was still against the wall, with the cop's hands on her shoulders, keeping her on her feet. Ruby straightened, trying to get her equilibrium back. He let go of her shoulders.

"Now, where did Wilson go?" he repeated.

"I d-dunno."

"Why did he give you his jacket?"

They must have been watching from awfully close by if they saw that. Jack must have known about them.

"I w-wanted it. D-didn't have m-my own."

"But now you do."
She nodded.
"Did Jack want you to be the leader of the Jags?"
Ruby laughed. The thought was crazy. Her leading the gang? The leader of the Jags? And going home every day to Charlie? She shook her head.
"You're the last one he saw," the cop pointed out. "He gave you his mantle. It looks pretty obvious from here."
"N-no. N-not m-me."
"He didn't tell you who was to be the next leader of the Jags?"
"N-no."
"But he told you he was leaving and gave you his jacket. And you didn't think anything of it."
"N-no."
The cop pinched the sleeve of the jacket between two fingers.
"You're wearing the commander's stripes."
Ruby looked at the rank insignia on the sleeve. She felt suddenly queasy. She knew Jack had never intended for her to be the leader of the Jags. But it was going to be hard to convince the officers of that.
"Th-they'd n-never let a g-girl b-be their l-leader," she insisted, struggling to get the sentence out clearly.
"It would definitely make some waves. But you're tough enough to make them fall in line, aren't you?"
"N-no," Ruby protested, with a grimace. She could just picture what would happen if she tried.
"Then who's going to take over? Are you going to pick someone?"
"No."
"Where did Wilson say he was going?"
Ruby shook her head. She swallowed, her throat sore and swollen from his strangle hold.
"I d-don't kn-now!" she protested.
His fist drove into her face, and Ruby's head crunched back into the brick wall. Ruby yelped unintentionally, and she brought her hands up to her face to touch her cheek, where he had contacted. Tears started in her eyes, though she tried to hold them back. The cop looked surprised that he had hit her. His fist unclenched and he kept it at his side.
"Let's take her in," the other cop suggested. The partner had stayed out of it until now, saying nothing and not interfering. The first cop grabbed Ruby's arm and pulled her over to the car. He opened the door and shoved her in. They drove to the police station without a word. Not

Charlie's station. Ruby rubbed her sore face, trying to figure out what to say to them.

The cops came back into the room, where Ruby had been sitting waiting. The tough one stripped off his jacket and threw it over a chair. He flexed his hands, and Ruby stared at his bulging biceps. He worked out a *lot*. And he had a tattoo on one of them. He noticed her gaze, and grinned with pride, showing them off.

"Now, are we going to talk?" he demanded, putting both hands flat on the table in front of her and leaning on them.

"I d-don't kn-now anything ab-bout J-jack."

He slapped her across both cheeks, the two slaps echoing in the room like the rapid reports of a gun. Ruby swallowed and clenched her teeth, trying to keep her composure. He waited for her to say something, and when she didn't, slapped her again. Tears started in her eyes again, and Ruby rubbed her eyes, trying to keep them clear.

"What did Wilson tell you?" he questioned.

"He s-said he w-was leaving t-town. He w-was t-tired of th-the Jags."

"Why?"

"He s-said he w-was t-too old."

"Too old for what?"

"The g-gang."

"Why?"

Ruby shrugged hopelessly. Jack had told her next to nothing, and they expected her to be able to get inside his head. He slapped her again. Ruby's mouth was filled with blood, and she spit, staining her t-shirt red. The tough cop slapped her again, spattering blood over the table.

"See what you can do with her," he told his partner, and walked out.

Classic good-cop bad-cop. Ruby hadn't been the subject of the ploy before. The good cop sat down slowly, looking at her.

"Are you okay?"

Ruby made no response. She used her shirt to try to stop the bleeding from her split lip.

"Would you like a coffee or something?"

Ruby ignored him. He was the good cop and he wasn't going to threaten her. He wanted her to get friendly, to let down her guard. They'd get into a casual conversation and he would get the information that he wanted. But it wasn't going to happen. She didn't know what he wanted to find out from her

He sat there looking at her and not saying anything. Ruby dabbed at her face with her shirt.

"Wh-what'd J-jack d-do?" she asked finally. They wanted him for something.

"What do you think he did?"

Ruby shrugged, and looked away from him. They were both silent for a long time. The cop moved his chair closer.

"What's your name?"

"Ruby."

"Were you and Jack close?"

"N-no."

"The two of you didn't spend any time together?"

Ruby hesitated.

"N-no."

He eyed her.

"I don't think you're telling the truth. You're telling me the two of you never spent a night together?"

She shrugged uncomfortably.

"The two of you seemed pretty close yesterday. I'm sure that he wouldn't give his jacket to just anyone."

"He d-didn't t-tell me anyth-thing."

"Mmm. But you admit that you were close?"

Ruby shook her head.

"No."

"If he was leaving town, why didn't you go with him?"

"We w-weren't th-that close."

"Did he ask you to go with him?"

Ruby closed her eyes and didn't answer at first. She opened them, shrugging.

"S-sorta."

"Why didn't you?"

Ruby rolled her eyes.

"If you weren't that close, why did he ask you along?"

"I d-dunno. Was w-weird."

"Are you good with a gun, Ruby?"

So Jack had shot someone. Ruby shook her head.

"We could really use your help, you know," he coaxed.

"I d-don't kn-now anything."

"Stand up."

"What?"

He motioned for her to stand. Ruby got up, and he pushed himself away from the table. He pulled her hands behind her back and cuffed them.

"I w-want my lawyer," Ruby told him.

"Sorry, you're going to lock-up for now."

He tightened the cuffs until they grated against her bones. Ruby bit her lip and didn't say anything. He took her to the cell-block and had her locked up. Ruby glanced around at the other occupants of the cell and leaned against the bars.

"We're not going to hurt you, honey," one of the tough-looking ladies told her. "We're not the enemy."

Ruby hadn't ever been put in a cell with adults before. They'd always been careful to put her in solitary or in with other juveniles before. She was a little nervous about it. The woman looked like a biker chick, with frizzy red hair.

"What's your name?" the woman asked, getting no response from Ruby.

"Ruby."

"Well, Ruby, quit looking at us like we're going to bite you, and come sit down. You look like you're going to faint any second."

Ruby walked over slowly. She sat down on the same bunk as the woman was sitting on.

"I'm Cheryl, Ruby. Oh man, look at you," she touched Ruby's face. "They beat you up."

Ruby pushed her hand away.

"It's n-nothing."

"You won't say that when you sober up. Do you want to lie down?"

Ruby shook her head. She leaned back against the wall, but winced when the bump on her head touched the wall.

"Come on, lie down. Who knows how long you'll have before they want to talk to you again."

Ruby stretched out and closed her eyes.

"Nice jacket," Cheryl commented, touching the emblem on the back of Jack's Jag jacket. Ruby didn't respond. Cheryl left her alone to go to sleep.

When the officer came looking for Ruby again and the guard came to unlock the door, Cheryl went up to the bars.

"You just leave Ruby alone. She's sleeping."

"Get out of the way."

Cheryl didn't move.

"She's been beaten up and you're not seeing her again until you get a lawyer to represent her."

"Move it."

"If you don't get her a lawyer, I'm going to yell from here to kingdom come that you're denying prisoners their rights."

The officer looked her over and looked at the guard.

"Forget it. I'll talk to her later, when this lady has been transferred."

The guard shrugged and pushed the door shut again.

"I want a doctor in here," Cheryl told him.

"You're not hurt."

"No, but the kid is, and she's in a bad way."

He looked over to the bunk where Ruby was sleeping, and shrugged.

"Looks okay to me."

He walked away. Cheryl went back over to Ruby to check on her.

"Ruby, honey. Wake up. I just want to make sure you're okay, then you can go back to sleep."

Ruby eventually stirred and opened her eyes.

"Ch-charlie?"

"Charlie isn't here, honey. Do you want me to call him for you?"

Ruby nodded.

"What's his number? Do you know it?"

Ruby recited it slowly, trying to make her words distinct. Cheryl nodded, repeating it back a few times.

"I'll see if they'll let me call."

She went up to the bars and called for the guard. He came to see her, looking irritated.

"Look, if you keep it up, I'm going to put you in solitary."

"I just want one thing."

"What?"

"One phone call."

"You've already had a phone call."

"It's for Ruby."

"She can make her own."

"She's in too rough a shape to be making calls. But she wants one made."

"If I let you call, will you shut up and behave yourself?"

"Yes."

He unlocked the door and motioned her through. Cheryl went with him to the phone and dialed Charlie's number. Voice mail picked up, and Cheryl left a message. The guard took her back to her cell and locked up again. Cheryl went and sat beside Ruby.

"He wasn't there. I left a message."

Ruby didn't stir.

∼

Charlie told the guard who he was looking for, and he didn't seem surprised. He sighed.

"Yeah, over here," he walked down the cell block and stopped at one. "Ruby Simpson. Someone wants to talk to you."

Another woman, a biker maybe, stood up and came over to the front of the cell.

"Don't you start again," the guard said in exasperation.

"Ruby's not talking to anyone. If you didn't bring a lawyer with you for her, you can just get lost."

Charlie could see Ruby laying on the bunk in the back of the cell.

"Ruby. Come on. It's Charlie."

There was no response from Ruby, but the other woman looked at him, surprised.

"You're Charlie?" she demanded.

"Yeah. Are you the one that left the message?"

"That was me."

She stepped back from the bars so that the guard could unlock the door and Charlie stepped in.

"I thought she was asking for a boyfriend," Cheryl said, watching Charlie suspiciously. "Not a cop. I probably wouldn't have called if I knew that."

Charlie didn't comment on this. He went over to Ruby and shook her. Ruby eventually rolled over onto her back and looked at him through half-closed eyes.

"Charlie?" Her voice was hoarse, faint.

Charlie stared at Ruby.

"What happened? Who hurt her?"

"Your brothers in blue, I expect," Cheryl said.

Charlie stroked Ruby's hair.

"Hey there, precious. Are you okay?"

Ruby could hardly keep her eyes open.

"Let's see if you can get up, okay?" he coaxed her gently into a sitting position. Ruby sat there, hunched over, and didn't do or say anything. Charlie let her just sit and get her equilibrium back, rubbing her back and shoulder encouragingly.

"Are you okay, honey?" He noticed blood in her hair and felt for the cut. She shied away when he touched the swelling bump on the back of her head. "I think we'd better get you to the doctor."

Ruby nodded slightly.

"Okay. Let's stand up."

Ruby leaned on him and he helped her to her feet. She shuffled to the door of the cell, where the guard was still standing. He opened it for them, frowning when he saw Ruby's condition, realizing he could get in trouble for refusing to get her a doctor. They got to the door of the cell, and Ruby stiffened and started convulsing. Charlie couldn't hang onto her and tried to lay her down gently.

"Call an ambulance," he told the guard.

Charlie tried to hold her still and keep her from hurting herself. It seemed like it was going to go on forever. When Ruby finally stopped convulsing, he thought she was dead. He leaned over her to try to hear her breathing. He was relieved to feel her breath. Charlie held her hand and waited for her to open her eyes again. He felt sick. If she'd had another stroke because he hadn't got there in time... he couldn't imagine what he would do if she was worse again. After she had worked so hard to get to where she was.

"Wake up, Ruby. Come on baby... wake up."

She didn't stir. The paramedics got there a little while later. Charlie looked up at them.

"Can you help her?"

"What happened?" one of them questioned, kneeling down and taking her pulse.

"She had a seizure. She has a bump on her head. She had a stroke once before—it wasn't a stroke, was it?"

"No way for us to know yet. How long did the seizure last?"

Charlie shook his head.

"I have no idea. A long time."

"Five minutes," Cheryl advised.

"How long has she been unconscious?"

"Longer. Ten, maybe."

"If it's been ten minutes since the seizure, she shouldn't still be blue," the medic's partner advised.

"Let's get her to the ambulance and get some oxygen going." He pointed to the bruising on her throat. "She's swelling up. I don't want to have to do a trache."

Charlie watched them bring the gurney over and lift Ruby onto it.

"I'm coming with you."

"Is she dangerous?"

"No," Charlie said blankly.

"We'll put hospital security on her. You don't have to come."

Cheryl chuckled softly.

"I think you'd better let him come along, boys. There's more to this than meets the eye."

The medics looked at her quizzically but she didn't explain.

"Well, come on then."

"You'd better report what happened," Charlie told the guard, "or they're going to be wondering what happened to their prisoner."

In the ambulance, they put an oxygen mask over Ruby's mouth and by the time they got to the hospital, Ruby was starting to wake up. She started to move around. She tried to speak, but couldn't get the words past her damaged throat.

"Shh, just take it easy. Don't try to talk."

They took her into the emergency room, and told the doctors what they knew about her condition.

"She's had a stroke?" the doctor repeated.

"The officer knows something about it," the medic nodded towards Charlie.

"Why did she have a stroke?" the doctor questioned.

"She was in a fight," Charlie explained. "Had a blood clot or something."

"How long ago?"

"A few months back."

"Who was she in a fight with today?" the doctor said as he examined Ruby and glanced over the chart.

"I don't know."

"How long ago?"

"I don't know."

"You know how to contact her parents?"

"She doesn't live with them."

"Is she eighteen?"

"Umm, I don't think so," Charlie said awkwardly. "She says she is."

"Can you get a hold of whoever is her guardian?"

"Yeah, probably. Why? She's okay, isn't she?"

"I'm sure she'll be fine. But we'll need authorization to run tests."

"I'll see who I can get."

"There will be forms to fill out to have her admitted, too."

Charlie nodded and went to the admitting desk to make his phone calls. The doctor glanced at the medics, eyebrow cocked.

"What was that about?"

"I don't know."

When Charlie finished filling out papers, he was allowed to sit by Ruby. She had machines hooked up to her monitoring her heartbeat and an oxygen mask over her face. But she was awake.

"Hi, honey. Are you okay?"

Ruby nodded slightly.

"You look horrible."

She grinned a little. He held her hand.

"I'm sorry this happened, baby. I'm going to find out what happened."

She shrugged with one shoulder.

"Do you think you had another stroke?"

Ruby shook her head.

"Just a seizure?"

She nodded.

"Can you talk?"

Ruby touched her bruised throat, shaking her head. A young doctor in a lab coat came in.

"Hi, there. I'm here to take a look at the bump on Miss Simpson's head." He sat down on a stool next to the bed and sat Ruby up to look at the back of her head. "Ouch, that's gotta hurt." He prodded it for a few moments. "We're going to have to put some stitches in there."

"Does it look bad?" Charlie questioned.

"It's nasty, but I've seen worse… we're going to have to shave the area first."

Ruby shook her head.

"Hold still. There's no other way to do it."

He talked to her in a quiet, steady voice as he worked, distracting her attention from what he was doing. When he was finished, he looked at the cuts on her face.

"I'll put a couple of stitches on that one, too. Then you'll be okay. Has anyone given you an anti-inflammatory for the swelling?"

Ruby shook her head.

"We'll put something in your IV."

He walked away from them to give instructions to a nurse. The nurse came over and prepared an injection for Ruby's IV.

"This will probably make you sleepy," she advised. She glanced at Charlie. "Sleep's probably the best thing right now."

Charlie got the hint.

"I guess I'd better go, darling. You sleep. I'll be back before you wake up. Okay?"

Ruby nodded.

"Okay. See you later, precious."

He kissed her on the cheek goodbye, and went back to the police station.

∼

"I want to know who was in charge of the arrest of Ruby Simpson."

The officer looked at Charlie for a moment, then tapped it into the computer.

"When was she arrested?"

"Today."

"It's not logged in yet."

"She was detained in a cell, she had to have been booked."

"Would it have been under another name?"

"No. Don't worry about it, I'll find out from the guard on the cell block."

He nodded. Charlie walked over to the cells, just as if it was his own precinct. The guard knew what he was there about.

"She was okay?" he questioned immediately.

"She woke up," Charlie allowed. "Who arrested her?"

"Dare brought her over. Burns is his partner."

"And their C.O.?"

"Naimath."

"Thanks."

It took a while for Charlie to find either of the officers. He eventually found Dare, who was pretty tight-lipped about everything.

"What did you arrest Ruby Simpson for?"

"Simpson? Doesn't ring a bell. When was she arrested?"

"Today sometime. Young blond kid."

"Oh, her. That's right, she said her name was Ruby. I really didn't have much to do with her, just took her down to the cell to cool off for a bit."

"But what was she arrested for?" Charlie persisted.

"She wasn't. Just brought in for questioning on a murder case."

"You detained her in a cell and she wasn't even under arrest?"

"Sure. She was getting punchy so we wanted to give her a chance to cool down a little bit before we tried again."

"Oh, I see," Charlie nodded. "She was trouble during questioning?"

"Yeah, you know how these gang chicks are. Trouble from the get-go," he chuckled, sharing a joke with Charlie. "But we sort of like them that way, huh?"

"Sure. Keeps things interesting. So did you hit her or Burns?"

Dare pursed his lips, brows drawing down.

"Just what's your interest in this case, anyway?"

"Oh, I've dealt with Ruby before. Thought I might be able to help out a bit."

"Oh. Well, let me see if I can find Burns…"

He sidled off and looked for his partner. Charlie got a coffee and waited. When Dare came back with his partner, they were talking urgently in lowered voices. Charlie grimaced. They'd obviously heard about what happened to Ruby in the cell block.

"Just who are you?" Burns demanded suspiciously. "And why are you asking all of these questions?"

"I'm just trying to figure out what happened here. You're the one who hit her?"

Burns looked quickly at Dare, who shook his head slightly.

"No, I didn't hit her. She'd obviously been in some kind of fight before we picked her up."

He said it smoothly as if it was the truth.

"You want a coffee?" Charlie questioned, going over to the machine. "How do you take it?"

"Black."

Charlie handed him the Styrofoam cup. Burns took it, nodding his thanks and taking a sip. His knuckles were skinned. Dare's were not.

"I'd hate to have to report you if Ruby tells a different story. The doctors at the hospital were careful of forensic evidence, so there will be tests run to see who it was that beat her up."

"What do you care?" Burns demanded. "She's just a gang banger. You've knocked a few of them around in your time, haven't you?"

Charlie exploded. He threw Burns into the wall and held him there with a fistful of his shirt.

"Why do I care? Because she's my girl, that's why! She's not just a gang chick, she's the girl I want to marry! You think you can just pick someone up off of the street and beat them up?"

Burns was speechless. Dare stood there with his mouth open, making no move to help his partner.

"Your girl?" Dare echoed. Charlie nodded grimly. "How were we supposed to know that?"

"You weren't. But maybe you stop and listen to your detainees before you start beating the crap out of them!"

"She didn't say anything about you."

"Well, what did she do to provoke you guys, huh? She tried to run when you picked her up? She swore at you in questioning? What?"

"She's a gang chick," Burns said gruffly, getting his voice back. "Isn't that enough?"

"No, it isn't. What did she do? Was she uncooperative?"

They nodded in unison.

"What did she say?"

Burns cleared his throat.

"She said she didn't know where Wilson had gone."

"Wilson?"

"The leader of the Jags."

"So maybe she didn't know where he had gone!"

"She was lying. She was the last one to see him before he shook his tail. He gave her his jacket."

"She borrows jackets from those guys all the time. So what?"

"Let me go, will you?"

Charlie slowly released him. Burns straightened his collar and composed himself.

"Maybe she was telling the truth, maybe not. How are we supposed to know? We do the best with what we've got," he said.

"Well, after I talk to your boss, what you're going to have is a lot of time on your hands."

They all looked at each other without saying anything.

"You make sure everyone here knows that Ruby's my girl, okay? I thought everyone knew, but obviously not. Nobody touches her or mouths off to her, understand? If you bring her in, you treat her with respect."

"Are you suggesting that we protect her? That she's beyond the reach of the law no because you took a fancy to her?"

"I'm suggesting that you respect her rights like you're supposed to be respecting the rights of every person you bring in."

They had nothing further to say. Charlie scowled at them and went to find Naimath, their boss.

CHAPTER
Twenty-One

When Ruby woke up, Charlie was there as he had promised. When he saw she was awake he took her hand.

"Hey, baby. How're you doing?"

Ruby massaged her throat with one hand, and cleared it painfully.

"Hi," she said softly.

"Try not to strain you voice. It must still be pretty painful."

Ruby nodded.

"One of those cops put his hands around your throat?" she nodded again. "I can't believe it. That is so much against the rules..."

She rolled her eyes. Charlie stroked her hair tenderly.

"I don't see how anyone could hurt my girl like that. I just don't know how they could do it."

"Wh-what d-did Jack d-do?"

Her words were so soft Charlie could barely make them out. He looked at her for a minute trying to figure out what she meant.

"Is Jack this Wilson guy they're looking for?"

She nodded.

"I really didn't look into it. They said it was a murder case, so there you are."

Ruby nodded and made the shape of a gun with her fingers.

"Shot? I guess so. I was more interested in finding out what had happened to you than about the case."

Ruby nodded understandingly. She rubbed her eyes, looking around.

"W-want g-go home."

"I think you might have to spend the night here, baby. I'll find a doctor and see what they say."

She nodded and Charlie went to see if he could find her doctor. After a while they came back.

"I really don't think Ruby should be going home quite yet. I'd like to keep her under observation for a bit."

Ruby shook her head.

"I w-want g-go h-home."

"I'll release you if you insist, but I really advise against it."

Ruby nodded. She slid her feet over the edge of bed.

"L-let's g-go."

"Are you sure you want to do that, honey?"

She nodded decisively. The doctor shook his head.

"Well, go ahead and get changed. I'll get the paperwork started."

Charlie helped Ruby with her clothes. He scowled when he helped her put on her shirt, looking at all of the blood on it.

"Some cops are worse than the criminals we're supposed to be taking care of. Look at that."

Ruby wriggled into the shirt and he helped with her pants and tied her shoes.

Ruby took one of the pills that Charlie's doctor had given her with a glass of water. She looked at herself in the mirror, touching her short hair where she'd gotten the stitches. A couple more weeks and she'd be able to wear her hair normally without the shaved spot showing. She put a ball cap on to cover it up for now. She took a couple of aspirins for her headache and shrugged on her Jag jacket. She stood looking at herself for a minute, put her hands over her stomach briefly, and left the apartment.

Ruby was lonely. Charlie was working long shifts lately, and she missed him. She caught a bus over to find the Jags. The boys were mostly at the cafe making plans for the night. Ruby slid into one of the booths.

"Hi."

"Hey, Ruby."

"Wh-what're we g-gonna d-do?"

"You want to help us get some money?"

Ruby hesitated for just an instant.

"Sure."

"Good. You and Terry, you're gonna have a talk with the old man who runs the little bar on the avenue. He closes early. You up to it?"

"Uh-huh. T-terry g-got'is p-piece?"

Terry nodded, patting his pocket.

"Always do."

"Wh-when's he c-close?"

"Terry'll fill you in."

Ruby nodded and listened to them discussing their other plans. She got up and motioned to Terry. He slid past the other boys and joined her at an empty table a few booths down. Terry sat down and put his arm around her.

"So, baby?"

"Tell m-me about th-the b-bar."

He filled her in on the details, and Ruby listened carefully.

Ruby stood by the door, keeping a lookout. Her hat was pulled down low over her eyes so she wouldn't be easily recognized. She kept one eye on the door and one eye on Terry and the old man.

"You're t-takin' t-too long," she told Terry uneasily. He glanced at her.

"Shut-up," he said tightly.

Ruby shifted her feet nervously, looking out into the darkness for any sign of trouble. Terry was stuffing money into his bag, but Ruby didn't like the look of the old man. He looked up at the door too often. His eyes should have been glued on Terry. His hands should have been shaking. Ruby's heart thumped harder and her chest tightened. She swallowed.

"C-come on."

"Hold your horses."

"Now."

Terry turned and looked at her angrily.

"We'll leave when I'm ready!" he snapped.

Ruby scowled and stared out the window. She spotted reflected blue lights.

"Cops!"

She burst through the doors and sprinted down the street. She had worked on walking a lot with her physiotherapist, but not on running. Her pace felt awkward and unnatural. She glanced quickly over her shoulder for Terry or the cops. No-one had followed her. She hoped that Terry had gotten away unseen. She turned into a side street and saw a police car ahead. She slowed to a walk and stuck close to the shadows in the wall. The last thing to do was look suspicious. They shone their spotlight on her. Ruby stopped walking and didn't move.

"Stay where you are."

Ruby stayed.

"Raise your hands above your head."

Ruby obeyed. One of them got out and cuffed her. The spot moved out of her eyes. The cop looked at her for a minute, frowning.

"Aren't you Charlie's...?"

Ruby nodded.

"You're going to have to come in with us."

"Okay."

"Were you at the bar?"

Ruby looked at him and didn't answer. He shrugged and guided her to the squad car.

They sat her down in one of their offices rather than an interrogation room.

"So where were you tonight?" one of the officers questioned.

"C-can I c-call Ch-charlie?"

"I'll call him for you, if you like."

Ruby nodded in relief. The cop shrugged.

"Is he on shift?"

"Y-yessir."

"I'll track him down. What do you want me to tell him?"

"Th-that I'm here. I asked f-for him."

"All right."

The officer nodded and left her there. Ruby sat back and looked around while she waited.

"What's up? Where's Ruby?" Charlie questioned worriedly.

"I'll take you in to see her in a minute," Devon advised. "Can't you keep her out of trouble?"

"I'm not her parent, keeping her out of trouble isn't my job. What she decides to do in her spare time is none of my business."

"Even if she kills someone, hey?"

Charlie looked at Devon sharply.

"She didn't kill anyone."

"She was involved in heisting a bar. If it went bad, she could just have easily been guilty of murder."

"Was she armed?"

"She was lookout. The bar owner gave a pretty accurate description and we picked her up about two minutes after she fled the scene."

Charlie shook his head.

"Well, let's go have a talk with her."

Devon nodded.

"This way."

Charlie followed him to the office where Ruby was waiting. She looked up, and looked relieved to see him.

"Hi, Ch-charlie."

"Hi, sweetie. How're you doing?"

"Okay."

"What happened?"

Ruby shrugged, and looked at Devon. She wanted him to just spill it all so that she could go home. But Charlie had said before that he wanted her to be honest with him before he heard something from the other officer.

"I w-was at a b-bar," she started out.

"A bar that was being robbed?" Charlie questioned, shaking his head a little, eyebrows up.

Ruby nodded, looking down at the desk.

"Yeah," she admitted.

"Who was with you, baby?"

She shook her head.

"I c-can't s-say."

Charlie looked at Devon.

"Did you get him?"

"Oh, yeah. He didn't even get out the door."

Charlie looked at Ruby.

"So who was it?"

"He c-could be l-lying," Ruby pointed out, eying the unfamiliar officer.

"He's not lying."

"It was Terry Wilkes," Devon offered. "We've got him in the next room."

Ruby nodded.

"Y-yeah."

Charlie shook his head.

"Not very smart, sweetheart," he said.

"I kn-now."

"You want to tell me about it?"

"Wh-what's to t-tell?"

He looked at her for a minute, thinking about it.

"You were standing lookout?"

"Uh-huh."

"How about we write up a statement?"

"Okay."

Charlie nodded.

"Devon will get you a pen and paper."

Ruby shook her head.

"I c-can't write."

"Sure you can, baby."

"N-not since the s-stroke," she explained.

Charlie hesitated.

"We'll have to take it down for you, then."

It was slow work. Prompting Ruby what to say, Ruby's hesitant words, writing down what she said. Ruby tried to talk normally and clearly, but her tongue just couldn't keep up. She kept getting tangled up. It was difficult work. They finally got the statement written up and Ruby signed it.

"C-can we g-go home?" she asked.

Charlie looked at Devon.

"Will you release her to me?"

"Sure, Charlie."

"Okay. Let's go home, darling."

Ruby got up. Charlie took her out to his car. Ruby sat down. She was silent for a while as they drove home.

"Am I g-going t-to jail?" she questioned finally.

Charlie glanced at her and licked his lips while he thought about how to answer her.

"Hopefully we can get you probation. But when they look at your arrest record, they might want to give you juvie for a few months."

Ruby didn't say anything.

"You can handle it, honey. It's no worse than your time in rehab."

She nodded and stared out the window. Charlie wasn't comfortable with the silence.

"It'll go fast, baby. I'll come see you."

"Okay."

He put his arm around her and pulled her close.

∼

Clive sat down with Ruby after the trial.

"You're in a lot of trouble, Ruby," he said, his voice serious, his eyes stern and steady.

Ruby shook her head.

"I pleaded g-guilty," she pointed out.

"And now you're going to juvenile detention."

Ruby shrugged.

"So?"

"I suppose you don't care."

Ruby shook her head.

"If you want to stay out of trouble, stay away from the gang," Clive said. "It's not rocket science, Ruby. All of your criminal charges have been related to your involvement with the gang."

Ruby rolled her eyes. She carefully readjusted her ponytail to make sure it covered the short hair over her scar. Clive watched her impatiently.

"You're just a kid who won't be helped, aren't you?"

Ruby shrugged.

"Well, then... I'll let you get on your way to detention."

"How're J-june and J-justin?" Ruby questioned.

"They're doing pretty well. They're still in foster care."

Ruby nodded.

"G-good."

"It's too bad you couldn't have stayed with them for longer, really gotten to know them."

"Yeah."

They let Charlie be the one to drive Ruby to juvie. He unlocked her cuffs once they got to the car.

"You going to be okay?"

"Uh-huh."

"It's only for a few weeks. Just a couple months."

"I kn-now."

"Then you can come back."

Ruby nodded in agreement. They drove out to the youth detention center.

"Okay, sweetie. This is it. Come on."

He walked her into the reception area and gave the guard her papers. Ruby fidgeted as he read them over and tapped her vital statistics into the computer. He finally looked up, nodding.

"All right. Isn't she restrained?"

"No. She's fine."

"She has to be restrained."

Charlie reached for his cuffs.

"Sorry, darling."

She handed him her pocketknife, and hugged him. Charlie squeezed her gently and kissed her on the forehead.

"Okay, babe."

He slipped the cuffs and put his hand on her back to lead her over to the big door. The admitting guard buzzed them in and took Ruby by the shoulder.

"Thanks. I'll get her processed and be right back."

Charlie nodded.

"See you tomorrow, honey."

The guard took her through another door and down the hall. He took her into a corridor lined with cells where there was another guard on duty, sitting halfway down the hall reading a paper.

"New kid. Take care of her."

The other guard put his paper away noisily and came down and took Ruby by the arm. The other guard left. The new one hustled Ruby down the hall to the shower room.

"Strip down and shower."

Ruby hesitated, looking at him. He unlocked the cuffs over her wrists and checked her pockets. The he stood back, leaned against the wall and motioned to the shower.

"Go on."

Ruby slowly took off her shirt and turned her back to him.

She felt small and insecure when the guard took her to a cell. She was damp and chilled from the shower, and hated wearing a uniform. The guard opened the door and pushed her forward. Ruby stepped in and he shut the door behind her. Ruby sat down on the bunk, looking around. She already missed Charlie. She was used to seeing him every day, sleeping with him at her side. And now she was going to be alone every night. Her stomach felt tight and empty. She just wanted to put her arms around Charlie.

They hadn't given her any sort of orientation. The guard had not said one more word than was absolutely necessary. She didn't know if she was going to be alone all the time, if they were going to let her be around other kids, or whether she would have a cellmate. She lay down and stared up at the ceiling, her heart pounding and stomach twisting.

They brought her a tray for supper. The guard opened the door and put the tray down on one of the bunks and the door shut again. Ruby nibbled at the food half-heartedly, but it was tasteless and sloppy. It made her gag. She left it and laid down again. The guard didn't say anything to her when he collected her tray. Ruby lay there alone until the lights went on and then into the night. She laid there staring at the dim window, tired but too anxious to sleep.

In the morning a guard brought her a breakfast tray and left it without a word. After he was gone, Ruby stood at the door trying to see out the narrow window. All she could see was the other side of the hallway. She sat down and ate the toast and juice that came with her breakfast.

It was mind numbing, being in that little room all by herself, without anywhere to go or anyone to talk to. She tried to talk to the guard when he came to pick up her tray, but he just looked at her without a word.

It didn't matter who Charlie talked to, he couldn't get in to see Ruby. He went every day, but they told him that she was in solitary and couldn't have visitors.

It had been a week when he noticed her pills in the medicine cabinet. He put them in his pocket for when he went to the detention center again. When he got there, he handed them to the guard, explaining that Ruby had accidentally left them at home. The guard shrugged, looking at the bottle.

"We don't allow any pills in the Center."

"They're prescription."

"They're still pills. I'll have our doctor examine her, but if he doesn't concur that she absolutely needs them, she doesn't get them."

"Ruby gets severely depressed. She can't get on without these for long."

"She's made it a full week. Doesn't sound to me like she needs them."

"You can't withhold medication from her," Charlie warned.

"You'd be surprised what we can do. I'll pass these on to the doctor."

"Can I see Ruby today?"

The guard tapped her name into the computer, and shook his head.

"No. But she'll be coming out of solitary tomorrow. You can't see her in the morning, but you could come by towards the end of the day."

"I'll be on shift by then."

"Then come by the day after that." The guard shrugged.

"I hope you realize I will be making a formal complaint about the way Ruby has been treated. You can't tell me why she was put in solitary, and you won't let anyone see her."

"Go ahead. It's Center policy. You're not going to change it."

The door opened and the guard stood there. Ruby waited for him to leave a tray and disappear.

"Come with me," he ordered.

Ruby stood up and followed him out of the cell. He handcuffed her and took her down the hall. They walked by a common room, and Ruby caught a glimpse of other inmates. But they went quickly by. Down to the showers again, to strip and shower quickly in the cold water. Then dry off with a rough, dingy towel and pull on a new prison uniform. When she finished, the guard cuffed her again, and they started back towards Ruby's cell. But they stopped partway down the corridor and he nudged her towards the common room. He stopped her in the doorway and took off the cuffs. Ruby walked into the room, dazed. Her hair was still dripping down her neck and back and she had not expected to be allowed to be around other people. She stood there like an idiot, looking around the room and unable to take anything in.

"Kinda overwhelming, huh?" a heavy girl sitting nearby commented, watching Ruby.

Ruby nodded.

"Uh-huh."

Her voice was hoarse, and she cleared her throat and swallowed, trying to think of something to say.

"That's why they do it. Helps keep newbies from stirring things up."

Ruby nodded again.

"Just sit down and watch TV. That's what you're supposed to do."

Ruby saw the screen anchored to the ceiling over by the wall. She found an empty chair and sat down, staring at the flickering screen. That way she didn't have to talk, didn't have to introduce herself, didn't have to do anything but try to soak up her new surroundings.

"Hey, you. Simpson. Wake up."

Ruby started and raised her head. She had nodded off without even realizing it. She felt like she was shut off inside, like she was a robot just trying to move around like a real person. She straightened up and looked around. The girl who had wakened her, slim and boyish, grinned.

"Hey, don't let them get inside you," she advised. "They can't stop you from being you."

"What?"

"Don't let them get to you. They just want you to be compliant and quiet. But you don't have to be. There's no rule that says you can't talk and mix."

Ruby looked around, wakening a little more.

"I f-feel s-so d-dopey," she said, rubbing her eyes. The other girl's eyes narrowed.

"You didn't take anything, did you? Because they can't make you take pills. They can't force you."

Ruby shook her head.

"N-no. I d-didn't t-take anyth-thing."

"You always talk like that?"

Ruby concentrated on making her words clear.

"Yeah. I had a s-stroke."

"Oh. What was that like?"

"S-scary."

"Huh. But you still look normal. It's just that lisp, or stammer or whatever."

Ruby nodded.

"I'm s-sorta c-clumsy t-too."

The girl's eyes flicked over her.

"You don't look clumsy."

Ruby looked around the room.

"Is th-this everyb-body?" she questioned.

"The whole place is broken into small units like this. Each block has its own schedule. Right now, it's free time. You can be in your cell or in the commons. Sometimes we get to go other places."

"Where else?"

"Outside in the yard, if the weather is nice. Library, weight room, laundry, stuff like that. Kitchen or shop if you have 'privileges'."

Ruby nodded. Some of that was familiar from talking with Jags who had been in juvie before. She tried not to look at the TV, because it seemed to hypnotize her. Whenever she watched it her eyelids started to droop. Ruby rubbed her eyes again and looked at the girl.

"Wh-what's your n-name?"

"Carlton. J.C."

"I'm Ruby."

"Simpson, yeah. It's on the door of your cell."

"Oh."

"Don't worry. You'll get used to this before long. They only keep you isolated in the beginning, or else if you break rules. Otherwise you can go where you want, on the schedule."

"Uh-huh."

"And you'll get to know everyone pretty quick. And some of the time we're scheduled for something at the same time as the guys in block C," she raised her eyebrows, looking sly. Ruby smiled.

"G-great!"

"Yeah."

A guard motioned to Ruby from the doorway.

"Simpson."

Ruby looked around at the other girls to see what to expect. None of them seemed interested. J.C. shrugged at her. Ruby followed the guard out. He handcuffed her and hurried her down the hall. She was shown to a room with a table and two chairs and nothing else. Ruby went in and he shut the door. Ruby sat down on one of the chairs, feeling queasy and uncertain. She waited for the door to open.

When it did, it was Charlie. Ruby jumped up. He stepped in and hugged her, squeezing her tightly.

"Hi, gorgeous. How are you?"

"Charlie."

He kissed the top of her head and held her close, rubbing her back and stroking her still-damp hair.

"There, honey. It's okay. They wouldn't let me see you. I have to go to work. But they wouldn't let me see you until now. I've been trying to get in to see you."

"Th-they had m-me in iso."

"That's what they told me. Are you okay now?"

Ruby nodded.

"Are they giving you your pills?"

Ruby shook her head.

"No. Th-they d-didn't give m-me anything."

"I told them to give you your Prozac. They said the doctor would talk to you?"

"No-one's t-talked to m-me."

"I'll tell them again... I don't want you going off the Prozac, you haven't even been on it for long enough for it to start working."

Ruby nodded. She didn't care about the Prozac, just about feeling his arms around her again. Finally. She had lost count of how long she had been in isolation. It had been so long since she had seen him.

Ruby shook her head.

"It d-doesn't m-matter."

"I want them to take care of you. I don't want you getting down."

"I'll b-be okay."

Charlie backed up a bit and bent down so that he could kiss Ruby. He broke away far too soon.

"I'm sorry. I have to go to work. Already late. I just had to see you before I started. I'll be back after I'm off. In the morning. Then we'll have a real visit."

"Ok-kay," Ruby agreed.

"Bye-bye, sweetie."

"Bye."

She kissed him one more time, and he reluctantly pulled away and left her there, his mouth a grim line and his eyes sad.

∼

The guard came back in.

"Let's go."

There was nobody around when Ruby got back to the common room.

"Wh-where is everyb-body?" she questioned.

"Library or weight room."

"T-take me t-to the w-weight r-room?"

He looked at his watch, sighing in exasperation.

"I suppose."

He took her through the halls past a locked door to a different section, where he led her into the weight room and unlocked her cuffs. He left, letting the door slam shut behind him.

Ruby looked around. A few of the girls she had seen before were there, but mostly it was boys. Ruby admired them as they worked out. One of them noticed her looking at him, and grinned.

"Hey, come spot me," he suggested.

Ruby walked over.

"Wh-what d-do I d-do?"

He gave her instructions.

"You're new," he commented.

"Uh-huh."

"What'd you do?"

"Kn-knocked off a b-bar."

"Mmm." He grunted as he lifted the weight. Ruby watched his muscles work.

"Wh-what's your n-name?"

"Max."

"I'm Ruby."

"Ruby." His eyes flicked over her. "Quite a gem, huh?"

Ruby smiled. She helped him rest the weight back on the rack, and he stretched.

"What do you want to try?" he questioned.

Ruby looked around at the various stations and pointed to one.

"Th-that one."

"Okay. Come on. I'll show you."

Ruby enjoyed the closeness as Max worked with her and demonstrated, and spotted her to make sure that she was working the right muscles. But it made her more aware of how much she was missing Charlie, too. She put it out of her mind and tried to pay close attention to Max and concentrate on just the two of them.

Max was impressed with her discipline and form. Her training with Dickenson had paid off, and although her day-to-day movements were sometimes clumsy, if she was concentrating, her movements were very smooth and well-planned. Dickenson had helped her develop an awareness of all her muscles, and had helped her work on them. The motions that Max showed her were familiar and natural already. And although she wasn't bulky, her muscles were strong. Max was favorably impressed.

"You got a good body," Max commented. "You should work out more."

"G-guess I g-got the ch-chance, n-now."

"Yeah, take advantage of it. If you don't know what to do, there's always someone here who knows."

Ruby nodded. She rested for a moment, and looked around the room.

"N-not a l-lot of g-girls," she commented.

"That's another advantage," he said with a grin.

Ruby smiled.

As usual, Ruby lay awake for a long time. She never seemed to be able to sleep when she wanted to. She hated to sleep alone, and always her thoughts went back to Stella and Marty. And on her failure to get pregnant again. She didn't know what she was being punished for, except that Stella had died, and it was her fault. She couldn't even make up for it. She couldn't do anything to make it right. All she could do was toss and turn and think about her failures.

Charlie was there to see her in the morning. He smothered her with hugs. Ruby pulled away from him after a moment.

"I c-can't breathe," she protested.

He laughed, and realized she was handcuffed.

"What did they do that for?" he gestured to their surroundings, "We're in a locked room with a guard on the door, what're you going to do? They already took my sidearm."

He looked at the cuffs, and dug a key out of his pocket.

"Think that'll do?"

Ruby held still while he unlocked them, then put her arms around her.

"Th-that's b-better," Ruby approved, melting into him.

"How're you doing, sweetie?"

"Okay."

"I sure miss you."

"M-me t-too."

"I don't know how I'm going to wait until you get back. I'm about ready to break you out of here already," he said.

"It's n-not th-that b-bad."

"Are you sure? Have you had any trouble, like in rehab?"

"N-no. N-not yet."

"Good. I don't want you getting in any trouble—or getting hurt."

Ruby rolled her eyes.

"I j-just g-got out of s-solitary."

"No time to get in trouble yet?"

She nodded.

"Yeah."

The long visit with Charlie was good. Ruby got back to the common room and watched TV and talked a little with J.C. When she mentioned meeting Max in the weight room, J.C. grinned.

"Max? He's a good guy to know around here."

"He s-seemed okay."

"Yeah. You wanna make an impression on people around here, you stick with him."

Ruby nodded, understanding.

"Wh-when d-do we s-see him—th-them again?"

"We don't always share with them. Usually we're just by ourselves. Max always works out. Weights, in the yard, whatever. He doesn't do the library or anything."

"So... wh-when...?"

J.C. shrugged.

"A couple days. A week maybe."

"Okay."

"He tell you what he's in for?"

"No."

"Killed a girl."

"How c-come?"

"Why does anyone kill their girlfriend?"

"She w-was m-messing around?"

"Why don't you ask Max?"

Ruby frowned and didn't respond. She turned her attention back to the TV for a while, thinking J.C.'s responses through. She wondered whether she should get more involved with Max, or keep away from him. Ruby wondered what J.C. was trying to do to her—whether she was being friendly or trying to get her in more trouble.

Ruby saw Max a couple of days later outside in the yard. He sauntered over to her.

"Hey, Ruby. Been working out some more?"

Ruby nodded.

He put his hands on her shoulders and squeezed her biceps. He nodded.

"You keep it up. You'd be surprised how a few muscles improve your looks."

"Uh-huh."

He took his hands off her shoulders and leaned on the wall behind her. He was extremely close to her. Ruby shifted, slightly uncomfortable. He bent down and kissed her. Ruby was startled but didn't pull away. He put his arms around her.

"All right, you two, break it up!"

Max pulled away slowly and looked around at the guard.

"Mind your own business."

"No physical contact in the yard."

"I said get lost," Max said tightly, sizing the guard up. He was bigger and stronger, the guard was no match for him if push came to shove.

"You want to go to iso?" the guard demanded. "Is that what you're asking for?"

Max slowly released Ruby from the embrace. The guard nodded.

"I don't want to see you two together again. Just cool off."

Max licked dry lips.

"You can't control who I talk to," he challenged.

"I'm warning you, Terrace, I'm not taking any flak from you. Just try me."

Max stared at him. The guard finally backed off and walked away. Max looked down at Ruby.

"He's bluffing," he assured her. "He can't stop us from talking."

Ruby shrugged. Max continued to look at her.

"Tell the guard you gotta go to the can," he suggested. "Duck into the guys instead of the ladies. Wait for me there."

Ruby stood there for a moment, hesitant, then walked away from Max. She walked around the compound aimlessly for a few minutes until she was sure no-one was watching her. Then she went up to the guard at the door.

"I g-gotta g-go."

He nodded and opened the door for her. The only places to go were the restrooms. There was another security door at the end of the corridor. She opened the door to the men's room slowly, and looked around. It was empty. She tiptoed in, and paced around, trying to find somewhere to stand and wait for Max. She felt awkward, and it seemed like a long time before the door opened. It wasn't Max. The boy looked at her, startled, and backed out again. There was enough time for him to look in confusion at the sign on the door, and he walked back in.

"Uh—you're in the wrong place," he said uncomfortably.

"I'm w-waiting for s-someone."

He stared at her for a moment, then grinned.

"Ah. Lucky guy. Do you mind?"

Ruby turned away from him. He finished his business and left. The next time the door opened, it was Max. He smiled.

"Where's Simpson?"

"Ladies'."

"How long's she been in there?"

Tennyson looked at his watch.

"I don't know. Ten, fifteen minutes."

"Go check on her."

"Probably having female problems."

"Go see."

Tennyson looked around the compound.

"Have Naomi check on her."

Weston looked frustrated, but nodded.

"All right." Tennyson watched Weston walk up to Naomi and talk to her for a moment. Then Naomi came up to the door and entered the building. She was out again a few minutes later.

"Restroom's empty," she told him.

"What?"

"There's no-one there."

Tennyson scowled and followed her inside. The ladies room was empty. But there was a grill on the window and no other way out. Tennyson hurried out of the room and went across the hall to the men's. Simpson and Terrace were against the wall in a full embrace, lip-locked. Terrace saw him, and drew back. Simpson looked around and saw Tennyson and she turned away slightly to do up her uniform. Terrace wiped his mouth with the back of his hand, and did up his uniform with the other hand. Both of them were out of breath. Terrace was sweating.

"All right, lovers. Faces to the wall."

Terrace turned around and put his hands on the wall. Simpson was not as quick, but she got the idea and assumed the position beside Terrace. Tennyson handcuffed both of them. Naomi took charge of Simpson without a word, and Tennyson escorted Terrace back to his cell block.

Ruby sat down on her bunk. She noticed that she'd mis-buttoned her uniform and undid it and buttoned it up again. Max was a fast mover. Ruby was sure the guards wouldn't let them get close to each other again. The guard who had let them in from the yard had been pretty red-faced when he busted them.

She got up and looked out the window on the door. She could see nothing. She went back to her bunk and sat down.

"What is she in solitary for now?" Charlie demanded in exasperation.

The guard tapped a few keys, and shrugged.

"It's not logged in the system."

"I want to know what for," Charlie insisted.

"Sorry." Another shrug.

"How long this time?"

The guard looked at the screen for a moment.

"Just today."

"But you can't find out what for?"

"No."

"You can't call someone up to find out what she did?"

"No."

Charlie shook his head and blew out his breath. He banged his fist down on the counter in frustration.

"I'll be back tomorrow. And she'll be out?"

"Yeah, if you're here this time tomorrow."

Charlie turned and headed for the door. The guard at the desk turned to see who had opened the door behind him. Tennyson stood there and watched Charlie leave.

"What was that about?" he questioned, eyebrows raised.

"Ruby Simpson."

"What about her?"

"Her boyfriend."

Tennyson cocked his head.

"What?"

"He's Ruby Simpson's flame. Comes by every day to see her."

"Well, she's certainly not keeping her fire burning for him."

"Oh? They seemed pretty hot when they met last."

"She's in iso because she was making out with Maxwell Terrace in the little boys' room."

"You're joking."

Tennyson laughed.

"Nope. You want to see hot, you should have been the one to bust in on the two of them. It's been a while since I saw two people quite so... engrossed."

Ruby spotted for Max while he lifted weights. He didn't have much to say, so Ruby just left him to his own thoughts. She was thinking about Charlie's visit after she'd been put in solitary again. He had been a little bit perturbed when she wouldn't tell him what it was for. But she wasn't about to tell him about Max. When she got out of juvie, it would be just her and Charlie again, but until then, it was in her best interests for people to know that she and Max were involved. Some of the other boys talked to her, but they didn't try anything. Max was too well known—he had quite a rep in juvie. Some of the girls sneered at Ruby for getting involved with Max, but Ruby knew they were just jealous of her.

"You're quiet," Max commented, resting between sets.

Ruby glanced down at him.

"S-so're you," she countered.

"Mmm. What're you thinking about?" He hefted the barbell again.

Ruby laughed.

"Ab-bout you."

Max stopped pumping and looked at her.

"About me?"

Ruby nodded. Max looked pleased. He continued with his weights, concentrating on his muscles. When he was finished his set, she helped him to rack the weight. He stood up and kissed her lightly. Ruby glanced around at the guards. One of them was watching them, but made no move to stop them.

"Ignore him," Max advised. "He's not going to do anything."

He took her face in his hands and kissed her again.

"Come with me."

"Where?"

"Back room. Supply cupboard."

Holding her by the arm, he guided her to a room in the back.

"W-won't th-they…"

Max shook his head.

"Nah, they'll let us alone. Relax."

He started to unbutton her uniform. Ruby stopped him, uncertain. Max looked questioning, and when she didn't say anything, he pushed her hand aside and continued. Ruby closed her eyes and imagined he was Charlie.

Tennyson was snickering when Max walked by. Max sneered at the guard.

"What're you laughing at?"

"You, thinking you're Mr. Wonderful with Simpson."

Max held up the orderly procession out of the room.

"What's the matter," he challenged. "You jealous?" .

"Me? That skinny stick of a girl? She's got a nice face, but I don't know what you see in her."

"Then what's your problem?"

Tennyson laughed.

"I'm not the one with the problem."

Max pushed Tennyson into the wall.

"Well, I don't have a problem. So what are you laughing at?" he exploded.

Tennyson's smile disappeared. He straightened his uniform, eying Max.

"She's just playing with you, the same as you play her and all the other girls."

"She's serious," Max assured him, puffing his chest out and lifting his chin. "Believe me, I can tell."

"Tell that to her boyfriend."

"Boyfriend? I don't think so."

"He comes to see her every day. And believe me... they're not just good friends."

Max flushed dark red from his throat up over his face. Tennyson waved to one of the other guards to come over. Max grabbed Tennyson's arm, squeezing tightly.

"What are you talking about?"

"Did I mention he's a cop?"

Max stared at him. Two other guards approached.

"You're holding up the line, Terrace. Move on."

Max slowly released his hold on Tennyson's arm, and glanced over his shoulder looking for Ruby. The few girls who had come to work out had already left, exiting the other direction toward their wing. Max filed out, scowling.

Charlie found Ruby even more depressed next time he saw her. He tried to get her to talk to him, but she was very reticent.

"Are they giving you your Prozac yet?" Charlie questioned.

"No."

"Has the doctor talked to you?" he persisted.

She shook her head.

"No."

Charlie searched her face. She continued to look down, away from him.

"You seem really down, sweetie. Are you okay?"

"Uh-huh."

"Ruby...?"

Ruby looked at Charlie after a moment. There were dark smudges under her eyes. A faint crease in her forehead.

"Ruby, I'm worried about you. Really worried."

Ruby forced a smile, shaking her head.

"It's j-just a few w-weeks," she pointed out.

"That's right. It's not for long."

"Then I'll b-be back w-with you."

"I can't think about anything else. The apartment seems so empty without you."

"I m-miss you t-too."

"I can't wait until you get out of here," Charlie said, clasping her hand.

Ruby nodded, looking away.

"S-so... how's w-work?"

Ruby saw Max on the bench and immediately went over to spot him with his weights. He glared at her. Ruby stopped, uncertain.

"Wh-what's wr-rong?" she questioned.

"I don't like what I've been hearing about you," Max growled.

Ruby shook her head.

"Wh-what?"

"People are talking about us. Say you're two-timing me."

"How c-could I?" Ruby asked with a disbelieving laugh.

"Apparently, you and some cop got a thing going on behind my back. What about that?"

Ruby swallowed. Her mouth went dry.

"Oh. Ch-charlie."

"Charlie?" Max repeated.

Ruby nodded.

"Uh-huh."

"So it's true."

She shrugged.

"Yeah, so?"

Max stared at Ruby.

"I don't like being made a fool of."

"You n-never asked if I had a g-guy on th-the outside."

"I assumed if you did, you wouldn't start anything with me."

"I d-didn't s-st-start it." Ruby rolled her shoulders uncomfortably, looking away.

"How many others have you got on the menu?"

Ruby studied him, uncertain how to answer. She licked her lips, but it did no good.

"N-none right n-now."

"Right now?" Max demanded.

"Yeah."

"What about when you get out?"

"Th-then w-we'll s-see."

Max suddenly started laughing.

"So this is just a casual fling, is that it?"

"Yeah."

He shook his head.

"You're something else, you know that? I never met a girl like you before."

Ruby breathed out, relaxing.

"Ch-charlie's my s-steady," she explained, "b-but I s-still l-like you t-too."

"You're not involved with anyone else here, right? No-one inside?"

Ruby nodded.

"And this Charlie, he doesn't know…?"

"N-no. I d-didn't t-tell him."

"Why a cop? How did you manage to get involved with him?"

"He b-busted me. W-we… k-kept in t-touch."

"I'll say."

Ruby shrugged. Shaking his head, Max went back to his routine.

J.C. sat down next to Ruby. She hadn't paid much attention to Ruby lately, and Ruby figured it was because she was settled in now, not the newbie any more. No longer of interest. J.C. put her arm along the couch behind Ruby.

"So, I guess you and Terrace have patched things up."

"Uh, I guess," Ruby said uncertainly, hearing the teasing note in J.C.'s voice.

J.C. snickered.

"Then you haven't heard what he's saying about you, huh?"

"Wh-what's he s-saying?"

J.C. laughed.

"That you're loose. A player."

Ruby swore succinctly.

"Wh-why would he s-say that?"

J.C. hugged Ruby more tightly around the shoulders.

"Because he's mad at you, why else?"

"He w-wasn't m-mad—w-well, at f-first—b-but n-not after w-we t-talked."

"Well, I'd say he's still mad."

Ruby looked at J.C.

"He's n-not s-saying th-that," she protested.

"You better believe it, baby."

Ruby suddenly got uncomfortable with J.C.'s closeness and physical contact, and drew back slightly. J.C. didn't let her get far.

"What's the matter?" she teased, pulling Ruby back in. "I thought you were easy. Or do you only like boys?"

"L-leave m-me alone," Ruby protested, shifting uncomfortably.

"Aw, you don't have to play hard to get with me, baby. I know your type. Come on, sweetness."

Ruby jerked away and stood up. She looked for some escape, but there was nowhere to go except back to her room. The other girls were turning to watch her, some of them smiling knowingly. Ruby hesitated, then left the common room and went back to her cell.

Ruby was furious with Max. She didn't see him for a week, and she was so hounded by the other inmates that she spent practically all the time in her cell. Even then, if the guards weren't watching carefully, one of the others would slip in to put the moves on her. When Ruby got into the weight room with Max again, she strode up to him and shoved the barbell he was bench-pressing, making him drop it with a crash to avoid injuring himself. He started to swear, sitting up and rubbing his arms where he'd strained his muscles.

"You could kill a person doing that! What are you, crazy?"

"How c-come you're t-talking ab-bout m-me?" Ruby demanded.

"You're crazy! What are you talking about?"

The guards were coming to accost Ruby, but they were in no hurry, taking their time. Ruby slapped Max as hard as she could, leaving the imprint of her hand on his face in bright red. He stood up, grabbing both of her wrists tightly.

"You're getting just what you deserve," Max said furiously, his eyes mean. "You wanted to play the field? Now you can. Anyone you like, they all know all about you."

The guards got to them, but Max didn't let go. He shoved Ruby into one of the weight machines, still holding on. Ruby swore at him fiercely, but couldn't find the words to express herself. Her tongue was tied except to swear at him over and over. She tried to twist out of his grip, but he was too strong.

"And you know what?" Max added. "I don't know why I ever even looked at you twice. You're not worth it."

"Let go, Terrace," one of the guards ordered.

Max eventually released Ruby. The guards went for him first, and in the split second before they could put their hands on her, Ruby lashed out and struck Max's cheek on the other side. It took three guards to hold him back and get him down on the floor to cuff him.

After that, Max was moved to another cell block so that he and Ruby would not end up in the same room again. Ruby went to the weight room when she could anyway, not wanting to give up the weight regimen once she had gotten into the habit. When it was just the girls, the few of them that did weights generally kept to themselves. A couple of them approached Ruby once or twice, but the coolness of her reception deterred them after that. When they shared the weight room with the boys, Ruby had to constantly be on her guard for the hormone-charged guys who figured they could get somewhere with her. They would come up behind her or try to throw her weights off balance to make her vulnerable.

"Hey, Ruby," there was a heavy hand on her shoulder, and Ruby jabbed back with her elbow, pivoting around on her toes and bringing up the dumbbell to use as a weapon. She'd hit him good with the elbow—he hadn't been nimble enough to avoid her. When he managed to straighten up, gasping for breath, Ruby saw that it was Sandy, one of the Jags.

"Oh—I'm s-sorry."

"Man, what do you call that?" Sandy coughed weakly. "I was just—saying hi."

"S-some of the g-guys here... d-don't j-just w-wanna s-say hi."

"Whoa, I'll come from in front next time," he was still breathing irregularly. "I didn't know."

One of the guards walked up.

"You causing trouble again, Simpson?"

Ruby shook her head. Sandy held up his hand.

"No, it was nothing. It was my fault."

The guard nodded and moved away. Sandy sat down on the bench, rubbing his stomach.

"Well great, I'm going to be black and blue in the shower, thanks to you."

Ruby grinned.

"S-sorry."

"You've got some elbow there."

"Have t-to," Ruby agreed, starting her reps again.

Sandy didn't say anything for a few minutes.

"Who's been bugging you?" he questioned after a while. "I'll teach them a lesson."

Ruby shrugged.

"L-lot's of th-them."

"How come? You usually get on okay with everyone."

Ruby preferred not to explain. He shrugged.

"You just point out anyone who causes trouble for you, and I'll take care of it," he instructed, with an emphatic nod.

"Ok-kay."

"I forgot you were here. Don't know why—I guess I didn't think about it because I didn't think I'd see you."

"I haven't s-seen T-terry."

"No, me neither. Couple of other guys should be around too, but they must be in other blocks."

Ruby felt comfortable having him there talking to her. She could let down her guard and just concentrate on her routine and enjoy a casual conversation.

When she saw Sandy again, he had a rainbow bruise over one eye and a split lip. He grinned when he saw her.

"Couple of guys were talking about you," he explained, raising his chin. "I shut them up."

"You d-didn't have t-to d-do th-that."

He shrugged.

"It's good for my rep. You knock a few heads together, and people respect you."

"D-don't g-get in t-trouble."

"What's a day in solitary for another Jag? You gotta show people you can't mess with us. We stick together."

"Thanks."

"No problem. Let's pump some iron," Sandy invited.

"Yeah."

"You're only going to be here a little bit longer," Charlie said encouragingly.

Ruby sighed.

"Yeah, I'll b-be home s-soon."

"It's been too long."

Ruby nodded in agreement. Ruby caught Charlie's eyes roving over her figure, and gave him a quick smile, raising her brows questioningly.

"You're sure looking good, baby," Charlie approved.

Ruby ran her fingers over her biceps, studying them.

"B-been w-working out."

"It looks good on you. You could come to the gym with me, you know, when you get back."

"M-maybe I w-will." Ruby nodded.

"You may as well keep it up."

"Uh-huh."

Charlie took her hand.

"When you get out, everything will be normal again," he promised. "We'll be back together, you'll have your freedom... everything will be fine."

Ruby nodded, looking unconvinced.

"Sure."

"You were okay before the arrest—everything was going good. You were happier then. It was okay."

"Uh-huh."

He looked at his watch.

"I have to go. I'll see you tomorrow, okay?"

"All right."

"You need anything?"

"N-nothing you c-could b-bring."

"Okay. See you later."

He tapped on the door and the guard opened it and came in to get Ruby. He handcuffed her again and took her back to her cell.

~

Ruby showered for the last time and they gave her street clothes back to her. Ruby pulled on her own clothes, savoring the feeling of finally being herself again. They handcuffed her to take her to one of the visiting rooms. Mr. Clive was there with a couple of the juvie administration. Charlie was not there. Ruby sat down where they indicated, looking around and wondering what was going on.

"Well, Miss Simpson, you've served your term. How do you feel about your crime?"

Ruby shifted uncomfortably. She hadn't even thought about "her crime" in weeks.

"N-no-one g-got hurt. It w-was s-stupid w-we g-got c-caught."

"So you're not sorry."

Ruby shook her head.

"I d-don't have t-to b-be s-sorry."

"No, you don't. But I'll be sure to put it on your record, and the next time you get arrested, the judge can take it into consideration."

"I'm s-sorry I g-got c-caught. W-we n-needed m-money. N-no-one g-got hurt."

"It is a condition of your probation that you reside at the halfway house that your social worker has found you a spot at. You have to check in with him weekly, and he will be making unscheduled visits to check up on you. You will not be allowed to have any contact with gangs, and you will occasionally be ordered to be tested for drug use. Alcohol is also off limits. We would like you to enroll in a remedial school program to try to get your high school equivalency. You will not be allowed to carry or possess a weapon. Do you understand all that?"

Ruby stared at him blankly.

"I'm n-not on p-probation. I s-served m-my full t-term."

"And now you're on probation."

"Why?"

"Because you broke the law, Miss Simpson."

"I w-wasn't g-given p-probation," she protested, scowling first at the administrator, and then at Clive.

"You're being put on probation now, at our discretion. Do you understand the terms of your probation?"

"I d-don't have to f-follow them."

"You just try breaking your probation, and find out. Do you understand the terms?"

"I d-don't have t-to…"

"Just answer the question," he growled. "Do you understand the terms?"

"Yessir," Ruby snapped.

"Good. We need some documents signed, and then Mr. Clive will take you to the halfway house."

A number of documents were laid on the table in front of her. Ruby scowled, looking at them.

"W-why d-do I have t-to s-sign these?"

"Do you want to be released?"

"Yessir."

"Then sign the papers and you can get out."

"C-can't he s-sign them?" Ruby gestured to Clive.

"He can sign some of them as guardian," the man admitted hesitantly.

Ruby pushed the pile of papers towards Clive, and he looked at the administrator uncertainly. The man in charge shrugged, and Clive took out a pen. He went through the forms and documents carefully, signing where indicated. When he finished, he still had one document in triplicate that was unsigned. He passed it back to Ruby, clearing his throat.

"You have to sign this one."

Ruby looked at it. It was a thick document, entitled "probation terms".

"Why?"

"Because this one is between the Center and you personally. I can only sign as guardian, not for you personally."

"W-what is it?"

"It's just the terms of your probation, like I told them to you. You just sign to say you understand them."

"I'm n-not on p-probation."

"You told me you understand the terms."

"B-but…"

"If you understand the terms, sign the thing and you can go."

Ruby stared at it.

"I s-served my t-time," she repeated.

"So go to court to get it straightened out," the administrator said. "But if you want to leave, you have to sign it before you can go."

Ruby was becoming more and more uncomfortable with the idea of signing the document. Besides her original reason for not wanting to sign anything because of her awkward, illegible handwriting, she was now starting to suspect there was something shady going on.

"I w-want t-to t-talk t-to my l-lawyer."

"Sign it and you're free to call whoever you like. Until you do, you're still an inmate and you don't have phone privileges."

Ruby reached for the forms that Clive had signed. She looked over the headings and bolded type.

"Th-this s-says I'm released," she said, pointing to one.

They looked at each other. Ruby stood up.

"I w-want to g-go."

Clive stood up too.

"She has been released," he agreed.

"We'll have you back in here tomorrow," the man warned.

"We'll s-see," Ruby retorted.

Clive picked up the documents that she'd refused to sign, shrugging at the others, and he took her out to his car. He unlocked the door for her, and Ruby got in.

"Buckle up."

Ruby obeyed, finding the reach across her body to the buckle extremely awkward. But eventually she snapped it into place. Clive didn't say anything else to her. He started the car and pulled out. He didn't drive her to Charlie's, but to the halfway house that they kept talking about. Ruby looked at it out the passenger side window.

"I w-want t-to g-go home."

"This is where Social Services has placed you. You're getting too old and too wild for foster care, so we'll try this out and see how it works."

"I'm n-not living here."

"You are now. Come on."

He got out of the car, and Ruby slowly undid her seat belt and got out. He took her up to the door. A man answered the door.

"Mr. Clive. And this must be Miss Simpson."

Clive handed him a clipboard to sign the appropriate forms. Ruby always felt like a Fed-Ex package being signed for.

"Come on in. I'll show you around."

"Hang on a sec, Ruby," Clive said, stopping her. He indicated the papers she had refused to sign before. "Let's get these taken care of now."

Ruby took them from him.

"I'll s-sign them l-later."

"Can I pick them up from you tomorrow?"

"Uh-huh."

"I'm sure you don't want to end up right back in juvie. So sign them tonight and we'll keep you out."

Ruby nodded. Clive went back to his car. Ruby let the man show her around the house, even though she wasn't staying.

"Any questions?" the man asked after outlining the house rules.

"Ph-phone?"

"In the kitchen. Who are you calling?"

"M-my l-lawyer."

"Okay, don't be long."

Ruby went to find it. She found the thick city phone book and flipped through it. The pages were thin and she found it difficult to separate them to find the one she wanted. And then she stared at the columns of letters hopelessly. The man came back after a while.

"Are you still on the phone?"

"C-can't find th-the n-number."

"What's his name?"

"W-willhelm."

"Let me see?"

Ruby handed him the book. He flipped through the pages briskly and ran his finger down the column.

"Here it is."

He read the number out to her. Ruby punched it in carefully.

"Thanks."

She waited while the phone rang. Willhelm's voice mail picked up.

"D-does it have another n-number?" Ruby questioned.

"Yeah," he read it out to her.

Ruby hung up and redialed. This time Willhelm answered.

"Hello."

"Hi. It's Ruby S-simpson."

There was silence for a moment before he remembered who she was.

"Ruby. Hi. It's been a long time since I heard from you. Been keeping yourself out of trouble?"

"N-no. I n-need s-some help."

"Where are you?"

"Halfw-way house." Ruby told him where it was.

"Can it wait until tomorrow?"

"N-no. I'll c-come th-there, if y-you w-want."

"I think you'd better stay where you are. I'll be there in an hour or so, okay?"

"Okay."

Ruby hung up, and looked at the man awkwardly.

"Okay. You've had your phone call," he said. "We had supper a while ago, do you want anything to eat?"

Ruby considered.

"Wh-what d-do y-you have?"

"Supper was spaghetti. Get whatever you want from the fridge."

Ruby nodded and went to check it out. He left her alone in the kitchen. Ruby got a bowl of spaghetti for herself and sat down at the table, eating slowly while she waited for Willhelm to get there.

Willhelm was escorted by another teen to the kitchen, and joined Ruby at the table. He sat down, setting his briefcase on the floor.

"So, what did you do to end up here?" he questioned.

"J-just g-got out of j-juvie."

Willhelm frowned.

"I had a s-stroke," Ruby told him, before he could ask if she was drunk. Willhelm raised his brows.

"Really. I'm sorry."

Ruby shrugged and nodded.

"So what were you in juvie for?" he pursued.

"Held up a b-bar."

"Well, that was stupid. But if you're out now, what do you need me for?"

Ruby pulled out the documents she got from Clive, and handed them to him.

"Th-they k-keep t-telling m-me t-to s-sign this."

Willhelm took it from her and flipped through it slowly, his eyes flicking over the pages.

"You didn't sign it?"

"No."

"Good. Do you know what this is?"

Ruby shifted, looking down at it.

"It s-says I unders-stand m-my p-prob-bation t-terms," she said, repeating the juvie administrator's explanation.

"Are you on probation?" Willhelm asked.

"N-no. I s-served m-my full t-term. N-no p-probation."

"Well, if you sign this, you put yourself under voluntary probation. You agree to abide by certain terms."

"I p-put m-myself under p-probation?" Ruby repeated, frowning.

"You got it. If you've been released from juvie and you served your full term, not paroled early, and the judge didn't give you probation time after juvie, you're free. I would suggest that you keep clean, but this—" he threw the agreement down. "You don't have to put yourself under probation."

"S-so I c-can g-go home, they c-can't s-send me b-back t-to juvie for that?"

Willhelm nodded.

"You can do whatever you like, as long as you're not breaking the law."

Ruby looked around. She stood up and went to the phone. Willhelm watched her call Charlie to come get her. He stood up.

"Is that it, then? You'll be all right?"

Ruby nodded.

"If they throw m-me b-back in juvie—I'll c-call you."

"You do that. They can't do anything until you're arrested and sentenced again."

"Okay."

He slapped her on the back and walked out. Ruby went out on the front porch to wait for Charlie.

CHAPTER
Twenty-Two

Ruby awoke with the sun shining in her eyes. She opened them, squinting. She never woke up to the sun in juvie, so she knew she was somewhere else. Her hand was resting on Charlie's muscular chest. She put her arm around him, holding him close. He shifted in his sleep and put his hand over her arm. Ruby rested her head on his shoulder, closing her eyes and counting his breaths. She might not be pregnant yet, but at least she had Charlie. He was a constant, something stable in her life. He would be there for her when she needed him. If she could just get pregnant, she knew she would have a sure hold over him. He would be a dedicated dad. As it was, she had only her hope that he wouldn't get tired of her or meet someone else. If she could have a baby, she could prove that she could be a good mom, that she could make up for what had happened to Stella.

Charlie's breathing quickened, and he moved. He opened her eyes and looked at her.

"Mmm. Morning, sweetheart."

"Hi."

He pulled her into his arms.

"You don't know how good it is to have you back again."

Ruby nodded, snuggling in.

"M-me too"

He kissed her forehead and closed his eyes again. They lay there together, awake, but enjoying the warmth and comfort of each other's bodies too much to move. They just lay still for a long time, and eventually Charlie stirred.

"You going to come to the gym with me today?"

"I g-guess," she agreed.

"Good. I'll whip up some breakfast."

Charlie slowly swung his feet over the edge of the bed and got up to get it ready. Ruby stretched out under the covers, savoring the last few moments in bed.

Charlie came in to get her a while later.

"Breakfast, doll. You're going to have to get out of bed to eat it."

"Mmm. Okay." Ruby didn't move. Charlie pulled back the sheets.

"Come on, up and at'em."

"W-what t-time is it?"

"Time to eat breakfast. Come on."

Ruby grumbled and got up. She pulled on the housecoat he'd gotten her before she was arrested. He took her hand and led her into the kitchen. He'd made pancakes for breakfast. The smell made Ruby queasy, but she smiled anyway. Anything was better than the slop at juvie. She sat down. Charlie sat opposite to her. He pointed at the pill bottle beside her plate.

"Make sure you take your Prozac. I want to get you back on it so you don't get depressed again."

Ruby shrugged and swallowed one. She had a couple of pancakes, and they left the dishes for when they got back. Ruby watched Charlie throw a few items into his gym bag.

"W-what sh-should I t-take?"

"Put a t-shirt and shorts in your knapsack. That's all you need."

Ruby got dressed, put the gym clothes into her knapsack, and joined him.

"I n-need t-to g-get a bag," she told him. "l-like yours."

"Your knapsack is fine. But if you want. I'll watch for a nice one."

"Yeah."

"Ready?"

"Yessir."

Charlie was pleased to have Ruby along with him. He paid for her at the front desk, and promised to get her a membership next time they went on sale. Ruby changed quickly in the locker room, and went out to look for Charlie.

"You want to do weights? Or you want me to show you around a little?" Charlie asked when he found her. Ruby shrugged.

"Weights, I guess."

"Great. Weight room's this way."

It was early in the morning for Ruby, but there were already lots of people there. Ruby took a look around. After the weight room at juvie, the one at Charlie's gym seemed so swank. Lots more weight machines, big fancy ones. Juvie had mostly free weights, ones that had probably been there for thirty years. At the gym, there was music playing, people in chic workout clothes with multi-colored water bottles. At juvie you worked out in your usual uniform, and if you wanted a drink you went to the fountain that everybody else drank from and spit in. And music? If there was no fighting, it was pretty quiet. Just people grunting and sweating, now and then a low conversation going on. Ruby stood there awkwardly. Charlie motioned for her to use whatever she wanted, and Ruby went over to the free weights, which she was most familiar with. Charlie went to one of the weight machines nearby.

"Let me know if you need anything," he told her, "I'll give you a hand."

Ruby started work with the dumbbells. After a while a handsome young man came over to her.

"Hi, there. I haven't seen you here before," he smiled.

Ruby nodded, concentrating on her muscles. He sat down on another bench and picked up a couple of weights.

"Are you a member, or just trying it out?"

"J-just ch-checking it out," Ruby said.

"It's a pretty good club. I've been a member here about five years."

"Uh-huh."

"How long have you been doing weights?" he questioned.

Ruby watched her weights carefully and moved slowly, making sure she worked her muscles the right way.

"Few m-months."

"Not too long, hey? You live close by?"

"Uh-huh."

"I could show you around, if you like. Some of the girls like the aerobics program," he offered, smiling.

"I l-like w-weights."

"Nothing quite like it, is there?"

Charlie approached them.

"Ruby, you want to come spot me for a minute?"

Ruby put her weights down and joined Charlie. He didn't say anything to her about the other man, though Ruby expected him to ask questions. She spotted him for a few minutes until he moved on to his next station.

The other man came over to talk to her again.

"You didn't tell me you were with Charlie," he said reproachfully.

Ruby nodded.

"Uh-huh."

"You don't have much to say, do you?"

"I'm b-busy and t-talking is hard for m-me s-somet-times."

"Strong silent type, huh?"

"I g-guess."

"Nothing wrong with that. Me, I like to talk," he said.

"I n-noticed." Ruby allowed a small smile.

"So you and Charlie are friends?" he suggested.

Ruby looked at him.

"L-live t-together," she said firmly.

"Oh. Too bad." His voice was disappointed, finally accepting that he wasn't going to get anyway with her. He winked at her and walked away. Ruby watched him go, frowning.

Charlie came over some time later, wiping his sweaty face and neck with a towel.

"What did Simon want?" he questioned.

"S-simon?"

"The guy you were talking to."

Ruby shrugged shaking her head.

"A d-date, I think."

"What?" Charlie's voice rose.

"I think he w-wanted a d-date."

Charlie shook his head.

"He doesn't wait to be asked, does he?" he said with a short laugh. "So are you ready to go?"

"Uh-huh."

When Charlie went on shift, Ruby went to find the Jags. Joe and Erwin were at Jack's old apartment.

"Hey, look who's out of juvie," Joe cheered. "How's it going, Ruby?"

"Hi."

"You just get out?"

"Y-yesterday."

"Let's go find some others and celebrate, huh? Celebrate your graduation from juvie hall?"

Ruby nodded.

"Yeah. I'm th-thirsty."

"Atta girl. No drinks in juvie and you get pretty dry, huh?" he acknowledged, giving her a squeeze around the shoulders.

Ruby grinned. Her time in juvie had been so lonely and depressing, she had forgotten how much fun some of the guys were to be with. Joe could always make her smile. It was like the clouds had parted and the sun peeked out.

"Yeah. L-let's g-go g-get those d-drinks," she agreed.

Joe got ready to go, changing his shirt and shoving a gun into his waistband. Erwin put his arm around Ruby's shoulders.

"Things aren't the same when you're not around, Ruby."

Ruby let him pull her closer.

"Wh-where'd y-you g-get the sh-shiner?" she questioned, indicating his face. Erwin touched the bruise tenderly.

"Bar brawl. Good one last night."

"Any r-rumbles l-lately?"

"No. Things have been pretty quiet between gangs lately."

Ruby put her hand over her pocket and swore.

"What is it? What's wrong?"

"M-my kn-nife. I d-don't have it."

Erwin gave her shoulders a squeeze and let her go.

"Lemme see what I got."

He went into the bedroom, and came out a few minutes later with a black switch. Ruby took it from him and switched it open a few times to learn the action.

"Thanks." She opened it again and tested the edge. She frowned. "It's d-dull."

Erwin shrugged.

"That guy down on the corner sharpens knives. We'll take it by there."

"Okay."

"You guys ready?" Joe questioned.

"L-let's g-go."

Ruby was a shade late getting back, arriving just after Charlie got home from his shift. Charlie met her at the door and gave her a welcoming hug.

"Hey, sweetie. You're out late."

Ruby nodded and kissed him. Charlie raised his eyebrows.

"Just how much did you have to drink tonight?"

"T-too m-much," Ruby admitted, holding onto his arm as she walked towards the bedroom. "C-c-celeb-brating."

"Well, let's not make a habit of that, huh?"

Ruby nodded.

"I kn-now."

"Just booze tonight, or have you been popping pills too?" His eyes searched her face.

"J-just b-booze."

Charlie lowered Ruby carefully onto the bed. Ruby bent over to untie her shoes, and nearly toppled over on her face. Charlie steadied her.

"Take it easy, honey, I can do that."

He crouched down and pulled off her sneakers. She was struggling to get her shirt off over her head and get her arms untangled from the sleeves. He helped to straighten her out, and unbuttoned her pants when her fumbling fingers wouldn't obey her instructions. Ruby squirmed out of the jeans and Charlie took them from her to throw over a chair. Her knife fell out of the pocket, and Charlie picked it up and put it on the night table.

"Okay, sugar. You ready for bed?"

Ruby pulled a blanket over herself and shook her head.

"W-wanna w-watch T-T-TV."

"Okay. What do you want to watch?"

Charlie found the remote and flipped the TV on. Ruby didn't answer, and he flipped through until he found an old sitcom that looked good and left it on. Ruby sat staring at the TV, mesmerized. Charlie undressed and sat down beside her, pulling the blanket so it covered him too.

"You let me know when you get tired."

Charlie and Ruby quickly fell back into their old habits and schedules, back to the comfortable routines from before juvie. Charlie made sure that Ruby took her Prozac every day so that she wouldn't get too depressed, but Ruby didn't think it made her feel any better. She was tempted to go back to the uppers that she could so easily get from the gang, but she was afraid that Charlie would notice if she did. He kept a pretty close eye on how she was and what sort of mood she was in, and she knew he would spot it immediately if she was anything more than a little tipsy.

Ruby held onto her hopes of getting pregnant to make up for the wrong she had done to Stella and Marty. She would show everyone that she could be a good mom and take care of a baby properly. That she could be a great mom, not just an average one. And then she saw Marty on the bus, completely unexpectedly. Marty spotted Ruby first.

"Ruby? Ruby, how are you? Where have you been? I never knew what happened to you!"

Ruby shifted uncomfortably, looking around.

"I'm l-living w-with Ch-charlie," she said.

"Charlie?" Marty looked blank.

Ruby nodded.

"Y-you m-met him wh-when I w-was in r-rehab. The c-cop."

"Oh yeah, the cop. Well, you remember, Kate, don't you?"

Ruby looked at the other girl, sitting beside Ruby.

"Oh, K-kate. Sure. Hi."

"Ruby Simpson? I can't believe it! It has been so long! What have you been doing with yourself?"

Ruby shrugged. So everything was back to the way it used to be with Marty and Kate. Kate looked a lot older than Ruby remembered her, and had finally developed the figure that she had so longed for. She was prettier than Ruby remembered too—more sophisticated. Ruby swallowed and tried to keep up a casual conversation with them but not answer Marty's questions about why she had left so abruptly, without a word, and hadn't gone back again. Eventually, they got to Marty's stop, and Marty stood up to go.

"Why don't you come with us?" she invited. "Just for a bit. You don't have to stay if you don't want to."

Ruby shook her head.

"I c-can't."

"Well, you know you can still come by anytime. To crash or visit or whatever."

Ruby nodded.

"Yeah. Thanks."

The bus stopped, and Kate stood up too. It wasn't until then that Ruby realized that Kate's blossoming figure was more than just maturity. Kate's huge tummy had not been visible to Ruby while Kate was sitting down. Ruby watched Marty help Kate off the bus, and walk slowly with her down the sidewalk, Kate moving with the slight side-to-side movement that Ruby remembered from when she was pregnant herself.

Ruby felt suddenly nauseated. It didn't matter to Marty if Ruby got pregnant again. Marty had already replaced her. Marty had taken Kate in and would have her baby to take care of. And from the looks of her, it wouldn't be too far in the future. Marty had forgotten Stella, had put her out of her mind and moved on.

Ruby didn't know where to go. She thought about the graveyard, but couldn't go there now. Not only hadn't she been able to bring life into the world again to show Stella that she could do it, but Marty, the one who had been Stella's real mom, had betrayed her. Had moved on. Ruby didn't get out at the cemetery.

Eventually Ruby decided to go see Jamie. Then she could see how Sheree was doing. Ruby hadn't seen Sheree since she was born. She hadn't wanted to go up and see Jamie, hadn't wanted to see Sheree and be reminded of Marty's dad. But now she had to see that Sheree was okay, that she was a healthy, happy baby with Jamie taking care of her.

A girl answered Jamie's door. Ruby looked at her awkwardly for a moment. She was younger than Ruby, thirteen or fourteen, maybe. Slim and pretty and young. Ruby gulped.

"I'm R-Ruby," she explained.

"Huh?"

"Sh-sheree's m-mom."

The girl shook her head.

"Sorry, I think you have the wrong place." She started to shut the door.

"D-did J-Jamie m-move?"

She stopped.

"Jamie still lives here."

"W-well I'm Sh-sheree's m-mom," Ruby said.

"Who's Sheree?"

Ruby looked at her blankly.

"Jamie's b-baby."

"Jamie doesn't have a baby," the girl said.

Ruby stood there looking at her. She pushed abruptly through the door into the apartment and looked around. It was still Jamie's apartment, but there were no baby things. Nothing that he had gotten in preparation of Sheree's birth was around.

"Wh-where is he?"

"Jamie went to get some groceries. You can't just come in here."

Ruby walked back out. She knew where Jamie got his groceries. She hurried over to the store and looked around for him. Jamie had just checked through. He saw her and froze.

"Ruby. Hey, long time no see," he said in a low, cool voice. He watched her warily, not smiling, not approaching to give her a kiss. None of the old feelings were in his eyes.

"Where's Sh-sheree?" Ruby demanded.

"What do you care? You never wanted her."

"She's my b-baby."

"No, you gave her up a long time ago," he countered.

"Where is sh-she?"

Jamie looked at Ruby for a minute, then shrugged.

"I don't have her any more."

"Why?"

"Social Services took her away. They found out my record and wouldn't let me take care of her anymore."

"Y-your r-record?" Ruby repeated.

"Yeah."

"Wh-what r-record?"

"I've got convictions for molestation," Jamie said with a shrug.

Ruby stared.

"Y-you n-never t-told m-me."

"Yeah right," Jamie snorted. "Hi, cutie. Come on over to my apartment for coffee. Oh, and by the way, I'm a convicted child molester. It's just a juvenile record, anyway. I was more careful after that." Ruby stared at him, not believing it. Jamie studied her, one eyebrow raised. "It's not like you didn't know I like young girls, Ruby."

Ruby thought of the girl back at Jamie's apartment. And she thought of the way Marty had always questioned her about Jamie. Marty had never liked any of the guys that Ruby spent time with, but Jamie in particular had bothered her. Marty had always asked what a college boy wanted with a fourteen year old. And with babies.

Ruby looked at Jamie, not knowing what to say. She'd always thought he was a decent guy. A family man.

"People aren't going to tell you things like that," Jamie advised her. "Those are the things you're supposed to be on the lookout for yourself."

Jamie waited for her response, then when Ruby didn't say anything, he walked by her and left. Ruby stood there until one of the store managers came out and asked her if there was something she needed. Then she walked wordlessly out.

∽

Ruby looked around the pool hall for Joe.

"Hey, Ruby," he came up behind her and put his arm around her shoulders, startling her.

"Oh, hi. I w-was l-looking for you."

"Well, you found me, baby. What do you need?"

"A g-gun."

Joe raised his brows.

"I can find you something," he confirmed. "What do you need?"

Ruby shrugged.

"Somebody getting on your case or something?" Joe questioned.

"N-no. J-just g-got a j-job t-to d-do."

"You just need it once?" Joe confirmed, thinking about what he could get his hands on.

Ruby nodded.

"G-gotta b-be c-clean."

"Mmm. I think I know what to get you. You don't need an automatic, right?"

"N-no," she shook her head, "J-just a p-pistol."

"No problem. I got just what you're looking for."

Ruby nodded, satisfied.

"G-good. Thanks."

Joe nodded.

"I'll have it to you tonight."

∽

Merrill looked around the apartment. Nothing appeared to have been disturbed. Someone had been let into the apartment, had shot the boy, and had walked back out. No fingerprints, no forced entry, no clues. Banks was talking to the officers who were first on the scene. The girl who had discovered the body was having hysterics in the bedroom while the medics tried to get her calmed down.

"Could be a hit," he suggested to Banks, when he finished with the other officers.

"Maybe. But the door wasn't forced."

"Revenge?"

"More likely. Wasn't for money."

"No." The stereo and computer were untouched. Merrill pulled back the plastic sheeting to look at the body again, but he knew what he would find. One bullet in the gut. No exit wound. Lots of blood. The bullet hadn't hit the heart or lungs. He had died of shock and blood loss. Not instantaneous. He'd probably lingered for a quite a while. They would canvas the neighbors, but Merrill didn't expect to get any clues from them.

One of the patrolmen approached Merrill.

"I just ran his name through the computer."

"Find anything?"

"Molestation and a sealed juvenile record."

Merrill and Banks both looked toward the bedroom where the girl who had found the body was. She was young.

"I guess we'd better call her parents."

"And find out if daddy has a gun license."

Both parents had alibis that checked out. And neither had ever owned a gun. There was an older brother too, also a juvenile, and they started investigating him. They questioned the girl, Tara, at her parents' house, later in the day.

"Did Jamie have any enemies?" Merrill questioned.

Besides the families of his victims, of course. They were already starting to check them out. The ones they could track down. Jamie's friends had given them a few names to work with, but mostly they only knew first names. And they had Jamie's record to go by. But they would be missing names, still. You could never track down everyone.

Tara shook her head.

"No, no-one. Everybody liked him."

"You never got any strange phone calls."

"No."

"Or people asking questions about him."

She shrugged.

"No, just my friends."

"No old friends showing up to see him."

Tara frowned suddenly.

"There was this girl who came to the door," she offered, voice uncertain. "She was weird."

"What did she say?"

"She was asking about some baby. I don't know."

"What baby?"

"Jamie's baby, she said. She said she was the mom of Jamie's baby. But that's just crazy, because he didn't have a baby."

"What did she look like?"

"I don't know. A little taller than me. Blond. A couple years older."

"But you don't know her name?"

"She told me, but I don't remember."

"Think about it," Merrill suggested. "You don't remember what she said it was?"

"No. Cheryl or Sherry or something, I'm not sure."

Merrill wrote it down, glancing at Banks to see what he thought. Banks raised a thoughtful eyebrow.

"What did you tell her?"

"That Jamie didn't have a baby."

"And then?"

"She pushed the door open and came in. She was strong, I couldn't stop her. She looked around, and then left."

"Did she say anything else?"

"I don't think so," Tara pushed her hair back over her ear, shaking her head.

"Did she touch anything?"

"No."

"Do you remember anything else at all about her?" Merrill pressed.

"No... just that she sounded drunk, I guess."

"Hmm. Well, we'll look into it. Sounds like it could be promising."

"Did you ever meet any of Jamie's old girlfriends?" Banks suggested.

"No."

"Did he say anything about this girl when you told him about it?"

She shrugged.

"He said not to worry about it. It was nothing."

"So Jamie knew who she was."

Tara thought about it.

"Yeah. He said she was nuts."

∽

Banks brought a printout over to Merrill's desk, reading it as he walked over. He set it down.

"Sheree wasn't the girlfriend, she was the baby."

"What happened?"

"Jamie was her sole guardian. She was removed because of suspected abuse. And because of his past."

"And who was the mother?"

"Sheree's last name is Simpson. I'll see if I can get the mom's name from social services."

"And find out if she's been in contact with them."

Banks nodded and left. Merrill went over the investigation of Tara's older brother, reading over his notes carefully.

When Banks returned, he was frowning.

"The mother's name is Ruby Simpson."

Merrill wrote it down and stared at the name on the page. There was something in the back of his mind that he couldn't quite grasp.

"Where do we know that name from?" he questioned.

Banks sat down, still frowning.

"I've been trying to remember," he said thoughtfully.

"She wasn't a suspect."

"No."

"A witness?"

As soon as he said it, he remembered.

"A Jag that was killed. She was there."

Banks snapped his fingers.

"Oh—that's right. A young girl, like Tara."

"Exactly. So she and Jamie had a baby... She was a witness at her brother's trial, too. That's why Tara thought she was drunk—because of her speech after the stroke."

They both looked at each other.

"It was her. She killed Jamie," Banks said.

Merrill didn't agree or disagree. He tapped his finger on the desk, considering.

"Did you find out whether Ruby has called Social Services to inquire about her baby?"

"No, she hasn't."

"Hmm. So she didn't ask where Sheree is now, didn't call to find out Sheree's status."

"No. Social Services says Ruby voluntarily relinquished custody to Jamie when Sheree was a couple days old, and has never made contact since, to their knowledge."

"She abandoned the baby."

"Practically speaking. But she signed papers."

"Giving custody to Jamie."

Banks nodded.

"I wonder what Jamie told her when she met up with him," Merrill mused.

Marty opened the door and was surprised to see two police officers. They were in suits, not uniforms, but displayed shields and name tags.

"Uh, hi," she greeted uncertainly.

"We're looking for Ruby Simpson," Merrill advised her.

"Ruby doesn't live here anymore."

"Any idea where I could find her?"

Marty shifted, pursing her lips.

"There's a policeman named Charlie. I don't know his last name. She's been staying with him."

"She's living with an officer?"

Marty nodded.

"Yeah. What's this about?" she queried.

"Ruby is part of an investigation we are conducting. Could we maybe come in and ask you a few questions, since we're here?"

"I guess."

Marty opened the door for him to come in. They sat down in the living room.

"How long since you saw Ruby?" Merrill asked.

"I ran into her on the bus not long ago. Before that… not for months."

"Did the two of you have a falling out?"

"Ruby's been through some tough times. I don't know exactly why she left… but it was after her baby died."

"Sheree?" Banks said in surprise.

"Sheree? No. Stella. Stella was older. About a year."

"Oh. I didn't realize she had two kids. Was Ruby taking care of Stella?"

"No. I did. Ruby's never had much to do with her kids."

"Did you know the guy who was taking care of Sheree?"

"Jamie," Marty nodded, "I met him a few times. Never really liked him."

"Why not?"

She shrugged, quirking her mouth.

"Jamie gave me the creeps. I didn't like the way he hung around Ruby and Stella. College guys should chase college girls, not junior high girls."

"But he and Ruby got along?"

"Sure. Ruby liked him."

"Did they ever fight?"

"Not that Ruby told me about. And not that I ever saw."

"So as far as you know, she didn't have any grudges towards him."

"Grudges? No." Marty shook her head, frowning.

"Do you know if they still saw each other?"

"I don't know. I didn't like Jamie, I called him once or twice to find out if he'd seen Ruby after she left, but he hadn't and I stopped calling."

"So as far as you know, they weren't seeing each other anymore."

"But I haven't seen Ruby in a long time, aside from just that chance meeting on the bus. I don't think she saw Jamie much after she gave him Sheree."

"Whose idea was that?"

"Jamie's. Ruby never wanted Sheree. She had an abortion, but it failed."

"Ruby had an abortion? Jamie must have been pretty ticked off."

"He wasn't real happy about it. But there was nothing he could say."

"But if it was his baby…"

"Sheree's not Jamie's baby," Marty interrupted.

"What?"

"Ruby signed custody over to Jamie. But Sheree's not Jamie's baby biologically."

"Who is the father? Or do we know?"

Marty avoided the question.

"You couldn't be one hundred percent sure, with Ruby."

"Why would she give Sheree to someone she wasn't related to?"

"Jamie wanted the baby; I was taking care of Stella and couldn't take on another one. Ruby didn't want her. Jamie wanted her, so Jamie got her."

"Was there ever any sort of agreement that Ruby would take the baby back one day?"

"No." Marty frowned. "Why? Ruby hasn't decided she wants Sheree now, has she?"

"We haven't talked to Ruby yet."

Marty bit her lip, studying them.

"Then what's this all about?"

Merrill looked at Banks, raising his eyebrows. He shrugged and looked back at Marty.

"Jamie's been murdered."

"What? Is Sheree okay?"

"Sheree wasn't there."

"And you think Ruby might have her?"

"No. Sheree was apprehended by Social Services a while back."

"Oh… I had no idea. Does Ruby know?"

Merrill didn't answer.

"You think Ruby did it?" Marty demanded, suddenly understanding. "Ruby couldn't kill anyone!"

"We still have to talk to Ruby. Once we find this 'Charlie' and track her down."

"But you don't seriously think Ruby could have done it? You don't know Ruby!"

"Actually, I do," Merrill said. "That's how I knew to come here. We talked to her when she witnessed a gang member's murder a couple of years back, and then when her father was murdered while she was in hospital after her stroke. So we know Ruby fairly well."

Marty stared at him.

"But you don't know her like I do. Ruby couldn't kill Jamie. She really liked him."

"Loved him?" Merrill suggested.

"N-no… I don't think so. Just liked him a lot."

"Well, we have some information that might have affected her feelings about him."

"What?"

"Sorry. I can't fill you in on that."

Marty shook her head, sending her curls dancing.

"I don't believe that Ruby would kill anyone. Especially Jamie."

"She's already killed once," Merrill pointed out.

"What?"

Merrill raised his eyebrows.

"Ruby never told you? She was arrested for the murder of a boy in one of the other gangs. She pleaded self-defense."

"I never heard anything about that."

Merrill nodded.

"It's not the kind of thing you go home and tell your girlfriend."

"Ruby didn't tell me everything… but I know what kind of a person she is. I don't know... I guess she might defend herself, but kill Jamie? She couldn't."

"It's hard to get into people's minds and understand their motives. I appreciate your input, though."

Marty shrugged. She stood up, and motioned to the door, indicating that the interview was over. Merrill and Banks took their leave.

Charlie was changing after his shift when he was approached by the two plain-clothed men. He stood with his shirt in his hands waiting for them to introduce themselves.

"Charlie? Merrill and Banks, homicide."

"What can I do for you?" Charlie questioned.

"You're the officer that Ruby Simpson is living with?"

"Yeah, sure," Charlie agreed, squaring his shoulders.

"We need to talk with her."

"About a homicide?"

"Unfortunately, yes," Merrill admitted.

"Oh. I'm just going home. I don't know if she'll be there or not."

"We'll just follow you and see if she's there."

Charlie nodded slowly. He pulled on his shirt.

"Who was killed?"

"A young man Ruby used to hang around with."

"Are you questioning her as a witness or a suspect?"

Merrill cleared his throat.

"Ruby is our prime suspect."

Charlie swore quietly.

"Do you know where Ruby was yesterday during the day?" Banks questioned.

"I was on shift. She wasn't with me."

"Do you keep any firearms in the house?"

"No, just my sidearm, and I had it with me."

They started out towards the parking lot. Charlie was thinking about what they had said. He gave them his address when they got out to the parking lot in case they got separated.

"We'll see you there."

Charlie entered the apartment and looked around for Ruby.

"Ruby, are you home?"

She walked in from the bedroom.

"Hi."

"We've got some visitors on their way up."

Ruby shrugged.

"Who?"

"Detectives Merrill and Banks."

"Homic-cide?"

"How did you know that?" Charlie questioned, surprised.

"M-met them b-before."

The detectives got there and walked in the open door.

"Ruby says you've met before," Charlie said, half a statement and half a question.

"We certainly have. Ruby has been a witness in two of our cases. She's also been charged with murder, but got off on self-defense."

"That's right," Charlie said, looking at Ruby. "I remember reading that on your file. A gang banger."

Ruby said nothing.

"So can we count on you to help us out?" Merrill asked Ruby.

Ruby shrugged.

"Have a seat, Ruby. This is going to take a while."

Ruby sat down, and so did they. Charlie stood there for a moment looking uncertain, then sat down.

"Do you know what we're here about?" Merrill questioned.

"N-no."

"Your friend Jamie…?"

"Yeah?"

"He was shot yesterday."

Ruby's eyes widened slightly. She shook her head.

"Who?"

"Well, we don't know for sure. That's why we're talking to you."

Ruby said nothing, waiting.

"You and Jamie were pretty close at one time, weren't you?" Merrill suggested.

"A wh-while back."

"Why did you stop seeing each other?"

"I m-met Ch-charlie."

"So it had nothing to do with your baby?"

"Th-that too," she admitted.

"Was he the father of one of your babies?" Charlie questioned, not understanding.

Ruby shook her head.

"No. B-but he t-took c-care of one f-for a while."

"And you stopped seeing Jamie when he took custody of Sheree," Merrill said.

"Yessir."

"Why?"

"I d-didn't w-want t-to s-see her."

"You didn't want to see Sheree?"

Ruby nodded.

"Why not?"

Ruby shrugged, looking away.

"Who c-cares?"

"Why wouldn't you want to see your own baby? This is important, Ruby."

Ruby scratched the arm of the armchair with her fingernail, not looking at him.

"I d-didn't w-want t-to think ab-bout her d-dad."

"But Jamie wasn't her father."

"No."

"Who was?"

Ruby bowed her head, rubbing her temples.

"I d-don't w-want t-to t-talk about him."

Merrill didn't say anything for a few moments, waiting to see if she would go on. If she would fill the silence. But Ruby said nothing. Merrill went on.

"Okay. You don't want to talk about it. Why did you go to see Jamie last week?"

"I w-wanted t-to s-see him."

"Him or Sheree?"

Ruby considered for a moment, looking at Merrill closely, and then glancing over at Charlie.

"Sh-sheree. B-but she w-wasn't there."

"So then what did you do?"

"I l-left."

"What did Jamie tell you had happened to Sheree?"

"He g-gave her t-to S-social S-services."

"What do you think about that?"

Ruby shrugged.

"N-nothing."

"Have you called Social Services to find out where she is?"

"No."

"You aren't going to try to get custody back?" Merrill persisted.

"N-no."

"What about visitation? You don't want to see her again?"

"I d-dunno. M-maybe."

"You wanted to go see her at Jamie's. Now you don't want to see her?"

"I d-dunno."

"What made you suddenly decide to see her?"

"I d-dunno."

"Come on, Ruby. You had a reason to go see her. What was it?"

They all waited. Ruby folded her arms across her chest.

"J-just w-wanted t-to m-make sure she w-was okay."

"And you found out that she wasn't."

"S-social S-services has her. She's ok-kay."

"This from the girl whose social worker took her to bed," Merrill pointed out.

Ruby looked startled. She looked at him and then glanced at Charlie. She shifted uncomfortably.

"How'd you kn-now about that?"

"It came out during our investigation of Mike's murder, and your subsequent assault. I arrested him myself. So you think Sheree will fare better than you in foster care? She's starting a lot earlier."

"She'll g-get adopted."

"You don't know what her status is. How do you know whether or not she's adoptable?"

"B-babies g-get adopted f-fast."

"But do you know whether they're trying to place her yet? Maybe they're still trying to contact you to terminate parental rights."

"I s-signed all that s-stuff for Jamie."

"You remember for sure that you terminated your parental rights?"

Ruby frowned.

"N-no..."

"Does Social Services know how to get a hold of you?"

"No."

"Then Sheree could be in foster care for a long time while they wait until your abandonment period is up. And then she'll be older and harder to place."

Ruby shook her head.

"I d-don't w-want that."

"Then why didn't you call Social Services to find out what was going on?"

Ruby shrugged.

"I d-didn't kn-now."

"Did Jamie tell you why Sheree was taken away from him?"

"No."

"Are you sure?"

She raised her eyebrows.

"Yessir."

"So you didn't know about his record?"

"No. Wh-what r-record?"

"His convictions for molesting young girls. Social Services took her away because they suspected he was abusing Sheree."

"He w-wouldn't d-do that. He w-was r-real g-good with b-babies. He l-liked t-taking S-stella."

"Were you always with him when he was around Stella?"

"Yeah."

"In the same room at all times, watching him?"

"W-well... n-no."

"So you don't know what he might have done when you weren't looking."

Ruby stared at him, scowling. Merrill went on.

"You met Jamie's newest girlfriend at his apartment?"

"Yessir."

"What did you think of her?"

"I d-dunno."

"Think she was pretty young?"

"I g-guess."

"I wonder how her family felt when they found out she was passing time with an older boy."

Ruby shifted her position and hugged a throw pillow in front of her.

"J-jamie n-never d-did anything. He w-wouldn't d-do anything you d-didn't w-want t-to."

"Maybe with you. But what if you hadn't been interested in a relationship with him like you were?"

"He w-wouldn't have p-pushed m-me," Ruby asserted.

"He was quite a bit older than you. You didn't feel a little pressure to do whatever he suggested?" Merrill suggested.

"No."

"What if he'd tried to force you?"

"He'd r-regret it," Ruby snapped.

"Why, what would you do?"

Ruby didn't answer. Merrill studied her.

"You'd kill him?" he suggested. "Like you killed the Terminator you said tried to assault you?"

Ruby nodded.

"Maybe."

"Ruby," Charlie protested.

She glared at him.

"Anybody t-tried t-to f-force m-me, I'd k-kill'em," she growled. "It's n-not g-gonna happen t-to m-me ag-gain."

Merrill waited for Charlie's response.

"Again?" Charlie repeated softly.

Ruby looked at him and almost answered, but then looked at Merrill and said nothing.

"Is that what happened, Ruby?" Merrill questioned. "As far as you were concerned, you and Jamie were finished. He asked you to come back and talk to him about Sheree when his girlfriend wasn't there. Then he thought he would... renew old acquaintances. You were scared —panicked—maybe even flashed back to the earlier assault—and you killed him."

Ruby shook her head. Her face was pale and hard. Her jaw was set. She swallowed.

"No."

"What happened, then?" Merrill questioned in a lower tone, leaning forward, inviting her confidence.

"N-nothing happened."

"Something happened. Jamie is dead."

"I d-didn't k-kill him."

"I think you did, Ruby."

Ruby shook her head.

"P-prove it," she snapped.

Merrill sat back, watching her.

"Where were you during the day yesterday?" he sighed.

"W-with the J-jags."

"Doing what?"

"Hanging out."

"Who were you with?"

"J-joe and Erwin."

Merrill wrote it down.

"What time were you with them?"

"All d-day. T-til Ch-charlie g-got home."

"Where were you?"

"I d-dunno. Here and th-there."

"You're going to have to be able to verify it."

"Ask J-joe and Erwin. They'll t-tell you."

Merrill nodded.

"Don't worry, we'll be checking your alibi."

Ruby stood up abruptly.

"I'm thirsty."

She retreated to the kitchen and rifled the fridge. Charlie glanced at her over his shoulder, and looked at Merrill and Banks.

"You don't still think she did it," he said very quietly, so Ruby wouldn't hear him.

"You don't?" Merrill returned.

"I don't want to think that Ruby's capable of that."

"She has two possible motives," Merrill counted them off on his fingers. "One, Ruby finds out that Jamie had Sheree taken away from him, and she was angry that he might have abused her daughter. Or two, Jamie tries to start things up with her again, and she panics, lashes out." Merrill cocked his head, considering. "Or, for that matter, she might have been jealous of his new, younger girlfriend. She wanted to start things up again and Jamie didn't. A woman scorned."

"I can't see it," Charlie said, shaking his head. "Self-defense I can understand. But I really can't see Ruby... killing someone—for any other reason."

"Well, maybe she thought she was defending herself."

Ruby walked back in with a beer.

"Are w-we d-done?" she questioned, not sitting back down.

"For now. But we'll be back. Don't leave town," Merrill advised.

Ruby shrugged. She drank her beer and watched them go. After shutting the door, Charlie looked at her.

"Did you kill that boy?" he asked.

Ruby looked at him over the can.

"No."

"I'm not going to run to Merrill with it. If you tell me, it's just between us."

Ruby shook her head. Charlie didn't say anything for a while.

"You don't seem too upset about it."

"I haven't s-seen him for a l-long t-time. I s-stopped s-seeing him."

"So you don't care that someone killed him."

She looked away uncomfortably.

"I d-don't kn-now."

Neither said anything for a while.

"When you said you wouldn't let anyone force you again…" Charlie started off.

"I d-don't w-want t-to t-talk about it."

"Who did you mean? The Terminator that you killed?"

Ruby nodded, then shrugged.

"D-doesn't matter," she said, and then in contradiction. "I d-don't want to t-talk about it."

Charlie swallowed.

"I haven't ever done anything that you didn't want…?" he trailed off.

Ruby looked surprised.

"No! You wouldn't d-do th-that!"

"You would tell me if you felt like I was pushing you, wouldn't you?"

"Uh-huh."

Charlie locked the door and went into the kitchen to get himself a beer.

"You know you can tell me stuff, right?" he asked when he got back in. "I would keep it confidential. I wouldn't turn you in. If something is bothering you…"

"I kn-now."

"You're so used to just keeping things inside," he observed. "I worry you wouldn't tell me if you needed my help."

Ruby shrugged.

"If you want to try to get custody of your baby, I'd help you out. We could work something out."

"D-do you w-want me t-to?" Ruby said, looking at him.

"I thought you might decide you wanted to. It doesn't matter to me what you decide."

Ruby gulped down the rest of her beer.

"I d-don't want t-to t-talk anymore."

She looked at him challengingly. Charlie wanted to carry on the discussion, but he saw that the opportunity was gone. If he pursued it, she would just walk right out. And she might decide not to come back.

"Okay, sweetie. No more talk," he agreed. "What do you want for supper?"

Ruby sat down and turned the TV on.

"D-doesn't matter."

"Okay. I'll surprise you."

~

Joe and Erwin held up well under questioning. Both agreed that one or the other of them had been with her all day. They could each tell him a couple of places they had gone to pass the time, and substantiated each other on the things they had done as a group. If Ruby had done the murder, it hadn't been spur of the moment, in the heat of anger or out of fear. If Ruby had done it, she had carefully made her plans and established her alibi. If she had left Erwin and Joe anytime during the day, she had told them what to say, how to cover for her.

They didn't turn up any murder weapon. There were no fingerprints at the scene of the murder that shouldn't have been there.

"Think we can get a warrant for Ruby's apartment?" Merrill asked Banks.

"On motive only? And a shaky one at that? No."

"I wonder if we could convince Charlie to let us search it voluntarily, without a warrant."

"Do you think she would hide something incriminating there? The gun or bloody clothes?"

"No, but sometimes people get careless in their own homes, where they think they are safe from view."

"Well, it's worth a try," Banks agreed, "but I don't think we'll find anything."

"What we need is someone who saw her there. Or close by."

Banks nodded.

"But the neighbors only ever saw Tara."

"They look similar enough... same build, about the same height. Both blond."

"You think someone mistook Ruby for Tara?"

"It's possible."

"We'll have to look into it."

Charlie hesitated when Merrill asked about searching the house. But he was of the same opinion as the homicide officers—that if Ruby had done the murder, she would not have been stupid enough to leave any evidence in the apartment. He reluctantly agreed to the search. Ruby wasn't around. She had left after their workout at the gym and hadn't yet returned.

"You don't expect to find anything, do you?" he questioned when they started to look around.

"No, but you never know. Sometimes you get a little insight, if nothing else."

They made comments to Charlie as they searched, asking questions as they occurred to them.

"Ruby spend much time with the Jaguars?"

"No, just when I'm out. And I don't know how much of the time she's with them, or when she's somewhere else."

"How long has she had a jacket?"

"Um, for a while, I think. I don't know when she stopped borrowing other people's and started wearing that one."

Merrill touched the stripes on the sleeves thoughtfully, and checked the pockets. Nothing of interest was in the pockets.

"She's on Prozac?" Banks asked when they looked through the bathroom medicine cabinet.

"Yeah."

"No birth control?"

"Uh, no."

Merrill looked at Charlie and didn't comment.

"She likes to go out on the town?" Merrill questioned when he saw Ruby's fancy dresses in the closet.

"We go out together now and then."

"She doesn't go out by herself?"

"Not that I know of."

"She's never away when you get back?"

"Not for long," Charlie said, shaking his head.

"What does she do in her spare time?"

Banks was going through the drawers of the bedside tables, pulling things out to look at them, flipping through books, opening the jackknife he found, and watching carefully for anything that might have a bearing on the case. Charlie sat on the bed watching them.

"She likes to be with other people. She doesn't like to be by herself very much."

"That's why she spends time with the gang."

"I guess so."

They found no weapon, no bloody clothes, and nothing they could use in building their case. Charlie saw them off just as Ruby was coming down the hallway. Ruby looked at them but didn't speak to them. She walked into the apartment and shut the door.

"Wh-what were they here for?"

"To search the apartment."

"Wh-what for?"

Charlie shrugged.

"Any evidence that you were involved in Jamie's murder."

"C-can we g-get p-pizza?"

"Uh, sure. Why not?"

Ruby looked into the bedroom to see if everything had been ransacked, but the detectives had left it tidy. Ruby sat down in the armchair in front of the TV.

"D-do you think I d-did it?" she questioned, not looking at Charlie.

"If you say you didn't, I believe you."

"You think I d-did it," she challenged.

Charlie shook his head.

"I don't think you did it, sweetheart. But I don't know. If you say you didn't do it. I believe you."

Ruby looked at him for a moment. She nodded and turned the TV on.

∽

Ruby glanced around the bar for anyone she knew, and spotted Joe up at the counter. She went up and sat down next to him.

"Hi, J-joe."

He looked up.

"Oh, hey, Ruby. How's it going?" He grinned, pleased to see her.

Ruby shrugged.

"Okay."

"Saw those cops again last night. The homicides asking about you."

Ruby frowned.

"Again? Why?"

"Checking up again I guess. Same questions," he shrugged, shaking his head slightly. "Same answers."

"Huh." Ruby nodded to Joe's glass "You d-drinking already?"

"Why do you think I'm sitting in a bar?"

Ruby grinned. She picked up Joe's glass and had a sip.

"Why'd you kill him?" Joe questioned.

Ruby didn't look at him. She studiously drank down the booze, staring at a spot on the wall behind the bar. Eventually she sighed and looked at Joe.

"He's a p-perv."

"What'd he do?"

She swallowed.

"Maybe n-nothing. Or m-maybe he hurt m-my b-baby."

Joe motioned to the barmaid for another drink.

"I'd have killed him too," he approved.

"Thanks."

"What ever happened to your baby?"

"I d-dunno. She's in foster c-care."

He nodded.

"You did the right thing."

Ruby nodded in agreement.

"I kn-now."

"Don't worry. They're not going to find anything out. They can't prove you weren't with us."

"Unless s-someone s-saw me there."

"No-one saw you. Or you wouldn't be here now."

CHAPTER
Twenty-Three

Ruby lay in bed beside Charlie with her face away from him and her hands over her stomach. She was getting cramps, and knew that meant she wasn't pregnant. She didn't want to get up and go to the bathroom and confirm it. She just wanted to lie there under the warm covers in the safety of Charlie's arms. She had hoped beyond hope that this time she would be pregnant.

The radio alarm went on, and Charlie stirred. He hugged her and kissed her neck.

"Morning, baby."

"Hi."

He rubbed her back and hugged her close. Ruby squirmed away from his grip.

"What's the matter?"

"D-don't feel g-good."

Charlie rubbed her back.

"I'm sorry, sweetie. You're not going to come work out with me, then?"

"N-not t-today."

"Okay. I'll see you after, then?"

Ruby nodded. Charlie got up and got dressed for the gym.

"Would you g-get m-me a T-Tylenol?" Ruby questioned.

"Sure, hon'. I'm gonna miss you at the gym."

He went into the bathroom and came back with a couple of pills and a glass of water.

"Make sure you take your Prozac too."

"Okay."

She listened to him in the kitchen for a few minutes, and then he left. Ruby rolled over and closed her eyes.

⁓

Ruby sat on the examining table waiting for the doctor to come in. She'd waited in the foyer for a couple of hours before they took her into the office.

The doctor finally came in. He picked up her chart and glanced over it. He looked at her over the top of his glasses.

"Well, Miss Simpson… what can I do for you today?"

"I c-can't g-get p-pregnant."

He stared at her for a moment without saying anything. He shook his head.

"You're too young to be worrying about that."

"I w-want a b-baby."

"Miss Simpson… are you married?"

"No."

"Have you finished school?"

"No."

"Could you support a baby on your own?"

"No."

"Then I think you'd better reconsider. Wait until you're older to start having babies."

"I already had t-two. I want another."

"You've had two pregnancies already?"

Ruby nodded.

"T-two b-babies and an abortion."

"When was your abortion?"

"T-tried t-to g-get rid of the l-last b-baby."

"Tried? The abortion was unsuccessful?"

Ruby nodded.

"An improperly performed abortion could have done considerable damage to your reproductive system. I wouldn't count on being able to get pregnant after that."

"Ever?"

He nodded.

"Depending on how badly they botched it."

"C-can't you just g-give me s-some p-pills?"

"I could prescribe fertility drugs, but I don't do that without a full fertility workup, and certainly not to a sixteen year old girl."

"I really n-need them."

"Not in my books, you don't. You have a lot of things left to do in your life before you start worrying about infertility."

"S-says you."

He nodded.

"That's right. That's what I say, and that means you're not going to get any treatment from me. And I guarantee you aren't going to get it from any other reputable doctor either."

Ruby sat there looking at him. He closed her file and took off his glasses.

"That's it. We'll see you again, Miss Simpson."

He walked out of the room. Ruby slid down from the examining table slowly, dazed. She hadn't expected that response from him. He was a doctor, he was supposed to help her out, not make judgments and refuse to treat her. She started for home.

Charlie hurried into the apartment and went to the closet to get his notepad out of his jacket. He saw Ruby's jacket hanging in the closet and called out to her.

"Hi, baby. Forgot my notepad. I'm still on shift."

There was no response. Charlie shrugged and started to head back out the door, then ducked back in and headed for the bedroom.

"How are you feeling, sweetie? Any better?"

The bed was empty. Charlie frowned and looked around. The door to the bathroom was shut. He knocked on the door.

"Honey, are you in there?"

There was no response.

"Ruby? Are you okay?"

The door was locked. Charlie stood there for a moment, listening. All he could hear was water dripping.

"Ruby, are you okay, baby? You'd better answer me, or I'll kick the door in."

He said it jokingly, but he was growing more and more uneasy with her silence. The water continued to drip.

"Ruby!"

Charlie took a couple of steps back and kicked the door beside the handle. It gave most of the way, and he put his shoulder to it and pushed it open. Ruby was in the tub. The water was red and Ruby was ivory white. Choking back his fear, Charlie went to her and felt her neck for a pulse. He was relieved to still be able to feel a weak pounding. He grabbed Ruby by both arms and dragged her out of the tub, trying to unemotionally assess the damage and follow procedure as he'd been taught. He was in uniform and had his radio, so he called for help while he shakily pulled a roll of gauze out of one of the pouches on his belt. He wrapped it as tightly as he could around Ruby's opened wrists. Then he held her close in her arms, whispering softly to her and waiting for an ambulance. She was so white, and her breaths were very shallow. He sat there with her, hearing the tap drip steadily into the bloody water. His partner was there in a moment, having heard his call for help.

"It's Ruby," he said in a shocked tone. "What happened, Charlie?"

"I don't know," Charlie said hoarsely, trying to talk past the lump in his throat. "She's been depressed, she's on Prozac. It's supposed to make her better. Not… this…"

Davidson pulled a towel off of the rack and covered Ruby up with it. Charlie didn't move.

"Is the door open?" he questioned.

"Yeah, I left it open."

"Where are they?"

"It's only a minute since you called. They dispatched an ambulance."

"Why don't they get here?"

"They'll get here," Davidson assured him. Davidson stood up and looked carefully around the bathroom, something that Charlie hadn't done.

"How full was your Tylenol?" he questioned.

"About half, I think."

"It's empty now," he observed. "I don't see a note."

"She couldn't write legibly after the stroke."

Davidson nodded.

"Why did she do it?" Charlie questioned despondently.

There was no answer. Charlie kissed her still face and felt for a pulse again.

"Where are they? She's not going to last long."

"They'll be here in just a minute."

It seemed like an eternity before they heard the voices of the paramedics.

"In here!"

The two young men hurried in. They assessed the situation quickly and went to work, starting an IV drip and examining Ruby's bandaged arms.

"Okay, let's get her down to the truck and get some blood going."

"She's taken a bottle of Tylenol too," Davidson told them.

"She wasn't taking any chances, was she? Okay, let's go."

∼

Ruby's ears were buzzing and she felt sick. She groaned and tried to turn over, but she couldn't move.

"Ruby, are you awake?"

Ruby ignored Charlie's voice and tried to go back to sleep. Her lips and mouth were dry and her throat was sore. It hurt to swallow.

"Come on, baby. Wake up, okay? Please wake up."

She'd never heard him beg like that. Ruby opened her eyes and looked for Charlie. Her eyes were sticky and took a moment to clear. She was in a small white room. A hospital. Then Ruby realized what had happened, and that she had failed. She turned her head to look at Charlie. He moved closer and held her hand.

"Are you okay, sweetie? Are you awake?"

Ruby nodded and swallowed painfully.

"Oh, sweetie... I was afraid we were too late. I thought we were going to lose you."

Ruby was becoming more aware of her surroundings. Of her bandaged wrists, the IV of blood dripping into her arm. The restraints that held her arms down and prevented her from moving or getting up.

"Let m-me g-go," she said.

He shook her head.

"Sorry, darling. You have to be protected until we can get you better and into some kind of program.'"

"I w-won't d-do anything."

"You scared me, Ruby. Why didn't you talk to me? Tell me what was bothering you?"

"I c-couldn't," Ruby protested.

"I thought we had an open relationship. Where we could talk about our problems."

Ruby gazed at Charlie. His eyes were red-rimmed and bloodshot. He'd been crying. Charlie had been crying over her.

"N-not this one."

"Why not? You think I'll be upset about whatever it is? That I'd rather have you die then talk to me about it?"

"No."

"Well then? Tell me what's the matter. What's wrong?"

Ruby turned her head away. The door was shut.

"Am I l-locked in?"

"Yes. You're in the psychiatric wing."

"Why?"

"Because people who try to kill themselves need to be helped. They need professional help. Like I should have gotten for you when I first knew that you were depressed."

"It's n-not your f-fault."

"Well, I feel pretty guilty about it. I didn't know there was anything wrong. I thought we had things under control."

Ruby didn't say anything. Charlie touched her hair.

"I don't know what I would do if I ever lost you, baby."

She turned and looked at him.

"How d-did you…"

"I forgot my notepad at the apartment. I went back for it right after I got on shift."

"Oh."

"How did you think I was going to feel when I came home and found you dead?" Charlie demanded, voice cracking. "How could you do that?"

Ruby sighed.

"I d-didn't want t-to hurt you."

"Well, you did."

"S-sorry."

"I can't live without you, baby. I really couldn't take it if something happened to you."

"I'm t-tired."

Charlie patted her hand, and Ruby closed her eyes and went back to sleep.

"How is she?" the doctor questioned. "Has she been awake?"

"Yes, for a few minutes."

"Did you talk?"

"Yeah. But she really didn't want to discuss it."

"How did she seem?"

"Tired... unemotional. Not like I expected."

"It's pretty draining. And you don't see a lot of strong emotion in a person who's severely depressed. They go through a stage where they are unhappy, tearful maybe, but then they pass that stage, and get to where they hardly feel anymore."

"I don't understand how this happened. She's been a little depressed, but... it wasn't that bad." Charlie shook his head.

"Not to you. But people who are suicidal seldom appear that way. It comes as a shock to everyone around them," the doctor said sympathetically.

"I should have known."

"You are not to blame. She probably hid it very well."

"What can we do now?"

"First we'll switch her medication and see if that helps. She's been on the Prozac for long enough that she obviously is not responding to the treatment. Some teenagers get worse on some antidepressants. And we'll get her into counseling. Maybe keep her in a closed facility for a little while until she's doing better."

"She'll just see it as another jail. She's been through drug rehab and juvenile detention. I don't think any of it helps."

"Maybe not, but she has to be protected until we're sure she won't be a danger to herself."

Charlie nodded. A couple of cops came down the hallway, and Charlie frowned.

"What are you doing here?" he demanded.

"Looking into an attempted homicide," Merrill said quietly.

"You'll just make things worse."

"We'll be very careful, Charlie. There will be no accusations that this was an admission of guilt in Jamie's death. No accusations of anything, just a few discreet questions. We have to investigate."

"You think this was because of Jamie?"

"We don't know what this was about. Has she said anything?"

"No, she won't talk to me about it."

"I'm sorry we have to get in the middle of things. But it is required by law."

Charlie threw up his hands.

"Fine. Whatever. If you can find something out—if you can explain this to me—I'd really like to know what this was all about."

"Great. Thanks. Ruby's been depressed lately?"

"Some times are worse than others. Before we got together, she used uppers to make her feel better. I got her started on Prozac. She told me once she's been depressed since she had an abortion. That was a couple of years ago now."

"I remember seeing the Prozac in your apartment. Sometimes it just doesn't do the job. Has she had any counseling?"

"Not outside of rehab."

"Has she ever told you why she was depressed? Was it related to the abortion?"

"I guess. She's never said though."

"She regretted the abortion?"

"No. She later got her tubes tied so she wouldn't get pregnant again. She's pretty adamant about never having another baby."

"She's sixteen and a doctor tied her tubes? That's pretty radical."

"Well, maybe not after two unwanted babies and an abortion."

"Huh. All the same, I'd like to know what doctor performed the surgery and who signed the parental permissions."

"I guess you'd have to call her social worker."

"Do you have his number?"

"No. But he's been around here and talked to the doctors. They'll have the information."

"Okay. If you think of anything, you'll let me know?"

Charlie nodded.

"Sure. Of course."

"Is she available to talk?"

"She's still unconscious most of the time."

"We'll stop in again tomorrow."

Charlie nodded and watched them turn and walk away again.

Ruby was surprised to see Merrill and Banks again, but was more surprised that they didn't really push her to answer their questions. They weren't the sharp, tough cops that she had talked to so many times before. They were quiet and gentle and were careful of what they said. But she couldn't tell them anything. She hardly knew herself what had happened. To put her finger on what exactly it was that had made her take the steps she did. She only knew how she felt, and what she had done. Why? She wasn't exactly sure.

She was kept under lock and key in the psychiatric section. She hated it worse even than juvie. There, she had been with people like herself. Now if she chose to go out of her room, there were crazy people around her. People who were mentally unbalanced, some of them unpredictably violent. She was afraid to talk to anyone, or to let anyone get close to her. All she wanted was to go home.

Merrill shook hands with Charlie.

"Ruby hasn't told us anything. And as far as Jamie's murder case goes, we don't have enough evidence to charge Ruby."

Charlie nodded.

"So you've finished with your investigation?" he questioned.

"Unless something else turns up."

"Okay. When Ruby gets out... we can start fresh."

"Just one thing," Merrill said.

"Yeah?"

"Use birth control."

"What?"

Merrill shook his head.

"Ruby never had her tubes tied."

Charlie felt the blood drain from his face.

"She didn't...?"

"No."

"Why would she tell me she did?"

Merrill shrugged.

"But I could have... she could have..."

Merrill nodded.

"Be careful."

Charlie nodded uncomfortably.

"Uh, thanks."

Ruby kissed Charlie, and undid his buttons. Charlie put his hand over hers to stop her.

"You lied to me sweetheart."

Ruby bit her lip.

"What?"

"Why did you tell me... you got your tubes tied?"

"I d-did," Ruby said.

"Social Services says not."

"They d-don't know," she dismissed.

"Who did it? What doctor?"

"I d-don't remember his n-name."

"I'm not taking any chances. I thought you didn't want to get pregnant."

"I d-don't."

"Or is that just something you told me to fool me into getting you pregnant? Just part of the plan?"

"No."

"I just can't figure out why you would want to do that. Were you trying to get back at me for something? For arresting you?"

Ruby stood up and walked out of the room. Charlie heard her get her jacket out of the closet and the front door slammed.

Ruby walked for a long time, through the streets, on the bus, wherever she could think of. She didn't want to be with anyone. Not Charlie, and not anyone in the gang. She didn't want to see anyone that she knew. She couldn't stop thinking about Charlie making accusations, not believing what she told him. He was never going to believe anything that she said again. Any time she told him anything, he was going to doubt her.

"Ruby? Hey, what's up?"

Ruby turned and saw Terry.

"When d-did you g-get out?" Ruby said in surprise.

"Just yesterday. How're you doing?"

Ruby shrugged.

"Okay. How ab-bout you?"

Terry grinned and put his arm around her shoulders.

"I'm thirsty and I'm hungry. You?"

Ruby nodded.

"Sure."

"Let's get a drink."

Ruby nodded.

"Or maybe we pick up a couple of six-packs and get a room for the night, huh?" Terry suggested. "I lost my apartment when we got busted, you know."

Ruby shrugged.

"You and your boyfriend break up?" Terry questioned, tilting his head to the side and looking at her.

"Had a fight."

"Ah," he nodded. "Are you going to make up?"

Ruby stared off down the street, scowling.

"I d-don't know yet."

Terry started walking, and Ruby walked beside him, letting him lead the way.

"What was the big fight about?"

"I d-dunno. He d-doesn't t-trust me."

"Dump him then. Who needs that, right? Just drop him."

"Maybe. I d-don't know."

Terry walked into the liquor store. Ruby followed him in. He bought a couple of six-packs of beer, and they each carried one to the motel.

Ruby wasn't back, and Charlie wasn't sure if she would ever be back. He hadn't exactly been kind and tactful. He'd been hurting so much since her suicide attempt, and he just didn't know how to deal with it. Charlie found himself lashing out at Ruby and saying things that he knew would hurt her. He just couldn't understand what was going on in her head. The only thing that he knew for sure was that she had lied to him, and that she had intended to get pregnant. Why, he didn't know. He was afraid it was for money, blackmail. But they both got along so well together, Charlie couldn't believe that it had just been a cover to fool him. However many times she had lied to him, he couldn't believe that she didn't love him, at least on the surface. Maybe it didn't go as deep as he had thought, but he couldn't believe that all the months they had been together and all of the months that they had been separated, that she hadn't cared for him at all. What kind of a girl would spend all that time pretending and scheming. No-one had that kind of patience.

Ruby hated to admit how much she missed Charlie. He was such a part of her life now. The only time that she didn't conform to his schedule was when she was locked up. And even then, they worked visits around his schedule. To be completely away from Charlie for more than a day was disconcerting. She found herself expecting Terry to talk like Charlie did, to say the things that Charlie did and laugh the same way. But Terry was Terry, and however many ways he might be similar to Charlie, he was no replacement.

Ruby stayed with him for a few days, and hung around the gang, but eventually she went back to Charlie's apartment.

Ruby opened the door and found Charlie in the front room conversing with young woman in a suit. Charlie looked up at Ruby, startled. Ruby turned to leave.

"No, Ruby—hang on. Come in. Don't go," Charlie called. Ruby hesitantly went further into the apartment, eying the woman.

"Ruby, this is Miss Carter. She's a social worker."

"Oh."

She should have known. The woman had social worker written all over her. Charlie motioned to Ruby.

"Come here for a minute. I want to talk to you."

He led her into the bedroom, promising Miss Carter that he would return shortly. He shut the door.

"Hi, sweetie. I didn't know if you were coming back."

She stiffly allowed him to hug her and kiss her on the forehead, and then withdrew.

"Miss Carter is here because I wanted to see if we could get your baby," Charlie explained. "I thought maybe if I had custody of Sheree…"

Ruby was baffled.

"What? W-why?"

Charlie shrugged awkwardly.

"I really don't know your agenda, Ruby. But if you're trying to get pregnant again… maybe it would be better to try to take care of the baby you already have."

"They w-won't g-give her t-to m-me."

"Not to you, no. I would be her guardian. When I'm on shift, she could be in a day home or something. They don't particularly like your past history, but I am making some progress with them on having her moved here."

Ruby sat down on the end of the bed, frowning.

"I d-don't know," she said, shaking her head.

"Well, we'll give you some time to think about it, work it through. Maybe we'll do a couple of visits before we make a firm decision. Okay?"

"Okay."

"It was the only thing I could think of, baby. I don't know what it is that you want, but I want you to be happy."

Ruby nodded. Charlie patted her on the shoulder and went back out to talk to Miss Carter. Ruby sat there on the edge of the bed, stunned.

Take care of Sheree? She wasn't even sure if she could look at Sheree. But maybe it would be better than Sheree being in foster care with people that weren't even related to her. Maybe this was a way Ruby could prove that she could still be a good mom.

Charlie took Sheree from the social worker's arms.

"Hi there, little sweetie," he said, looking at her.

She let him hold her, sucking on one finger and studying his face.

"Hi."

"How would you like to come live with me and your mama," Charlie suggested.

She shook her head. Charlie grinned.

"You got a mind of your own, hey?" he chuckled.

It was hard to believe that she was Ruby's little girl. Her hair was so dark it was almost black, and her face was so round and pudgy. Charlie could see none of Ruby in her. When Charlie smiled at Sheree, she smiled widely back.

"You're a real sweetie, you know that?" Charlie said.

She nodded.

"And you are a sweetie," she said slowly and deliberately.

"I am?"

"Uh-huh."

"Then why don't you want to come live with me?"

"I have a puppy," she advised him solemnly.

"If you could bring your puppy, would you like to come?"

"Okay."

Sheree squirmed to be put down, and Charlie set her on the floor. She scampered off. Charlie looked at the social worker.

"I pictured a baby. I knew how old she was, but…"

"Sheree is very advanced for her age. Physically and mentally she is at the top of the spectrum, in spite of her… less than ideal beginnings."

Sheree's foster mom had been watching the introduction.

"Do you really think she should go back to her mother?" she questioned worriedly.

"Ruby never harmed or neglected her. She gave up custody to someone she thought would be better for the job, and her choice was unfortunate. But if it's possible to reunite them, that is what we should be looking for."

"This Jamie guy that Ruby gave her to in the beginning…" Charlie said carefully. "Just how bad was he?"

"It's hard for us to say. He took care of her physical needs, she was never neglected. But she was so young when we took her away from there—she couldn't tell us what happened to her, if anything. We couldn't prove that he had done anything, but when we looked at his record and found out about his convictions, we had to remove her."

"What was it that made you look at his record?"

"The nanny thought things weren't quite right."

"But you never found any corroboration?"

"A doctor examined her and couldn't tell us anything for certain."

"Do you think it's advisable for a man to be her sole guardian again?" the foster mom questioned.

"Charlie won't be the only one there. Ruby is also there, and when Charlie is on shift, Sheree will be in a reputable day home. And we'll be checking up on the situation regularly."

Sheree walked carefully into the room clasping a puppy against her stomach.

"This is Ralph."

"He's very cute," Charlie acknowledged, bending down to look at the pup. He stroked Ralph's head, and the puppy licked him.

Ruby was nervous walking back to the apartment, knowing what she was in for. It was her decision whether or not to go back, but it was going to make a big impact on her life. Ruby steeled herself to open the door and walk in casually. This was the way it was going to be from now on, and she might as well keep cool.

Charlie and Sheree were on the floor watching TV. Charlie looked up at her and smiled.

"Hello, darling. How's it going?"

"Good."

"We already ate. There's spaghetti in the fridge."

"Okay."

Charlie nudged Sheree.

"Say hi to mommy, Sheree."

"Hi," Sheree said obediently, looking at Ruby uncertainly.

"Uh—hi."

Charlie grinned.

"No need to be so nervous. Sheree isn't going to bite you or something."

Ruby moved into the kitchen without saying anything. Charlie left Sheree to watch TV and joined her. He hugged her from behind and kissed her hair.

"It's okay, sweetie. I know you're nervous. But it will be okay."

"Okay."

"Have you even looked at her?" he questioned.

Ruby nodded. She swallowed.

"She looks like her d-daddy."

"And that bothers you?"

"Uh-huh."

"Do you think you can get over that and get to know her? She is a separate person, you know. She's not you and she's not her father. She's a totally separate and complete person on her own."

She nodded. The words made sense. Everything he had said to her from the start had made sense. It was her own feelings that Ruby couldn't understand.

"I d-don't know how t-to b-be a mom."

"Well, I've never been a dad before, either. It's just something we have to take a day at a time and give ourselves a chance to learn. Neither of us is going to be perfect."

Ruby dished up a small bowl of spaghetti and put it in the microwave.

"How was your day today?" Charlie questioned.

"Okay, I g-guess."

"How are you feeling?"

"Fine."

"You know you have an appointment with your therapist tomorrow."

"Uh-huh."

"And you won't miss it."

"N-no."

"Good. Come on over and watch TV with us."

Getting Sheree to bed had taken a while, but Charlie was patient with her and eventually got her to sleep. He came into the bedroom and undressed.

"Well, Sheree's off to never-never land. She's such a cutie."

"You like her?" Ruby questioned, hearing the affection in his voice.

"Sure I do. I think she's very cute and very bright."

"D-do you think I d-did b-bad g-giving her away?"

Charlie answered cautiously.

"She seems like a normal child, doesn't act like she has emotional problems. I think you could have picked a better person to take care of her, but I think things turned out pretty good."

"Jamie always loved b-babies," Ruby explained, "even S-stella."

"Stella was your other baby?"

"Uh-huh."

"Why 'even' Stella? What was wrong with her?"

"She was ugly… and not right. Retarded."

"I didn't know she had problems."

"C-cause I d-drank, Marty s-said."

"Oh, I see. I'm sorry you lost her, Ruby."

Ruby nodded and cuddled up to him as he climbed into bed.

"I wasn't a g-good mom," she admitted.

"We'll work on it. I'm sure it wasn't your fault she died."

Ruby shrugged heavily.

"I d-don't know." She was quiet for a long time, and when she spoke again, Charlie didn't stir, already asleep. "I think G-god must hate me."

CHAPTER Twenty-Four

Ruby tried to close her eyes to the features in Sheree's face that reminded her so much of Marty's dad, and to remember how Ruby had come to enjoy playing with Stella. At the hospital, recovering from her stroke, playing with Stella had been a challenge, and Ruby had enjoyed it. Stella was undemanding, let her work at her own pace, and enjoyed her company.

She could learn to enjoy Sheree that way. She could look past her face and just learn to enjoy playing with her. She could be a good mom. She could prove it to everyone.

Ruby wanted to hold Sheree, but Sheree would have nothing of it. She wasn't a baby and wasn't about to be held like one.

"Then what d-do you d-do?" Ruby questioned impatiently.

"I like to play with Ralph."

Ruby had already been introduced to Ralph.

"Ralph's a d-dog," she said.

"Ralph likes to play," Sheree insisted.

Sheree wandered out of the room and a few minutes later walked back in dragging a string behind her, with the puppy chasing it wildly. Ruby laughed at the romping pup.

"Why's he chasing it?"

"He likes to," Sheree said firmly.

Ruby laughed at her. Sheree was a very strange little girl. She was just a baby, but she acted like she was an adult.

"Why d-did you c-call him Ralph?"

"Because that's his name."

"Why did you name him that?"

"He wanted to be named Ralph."

Ruby watched Sheree make the puppy run in dizzying circles.

"Are you hungry?" she questioned.

"Yes."

Ruby went into the kitchen and looked through the fridge and the cupboards. She pulled out a box of crackers and an apple.

"Come here."

Sheree climbed into one of the kitchen chairs and stood up to see over the counter.

"You have to cut the apple," Sheree instructed.

Ruby got out a sharp knife and sliced the apple carefully. Her movements were awkward. It was a difficult motion to master. Sheree watched her carefully.

"Cut off the yucky parts."

Ruby nodded. She slipped and cut her finger and put it in her mouth.

"An owie?" Sheree questioned.

"Yeah. Ouch."

"Are you bleeding?"

Ruby took her finger out of her mouth and looked at it. She swore.

"Yeah, I am."

Sheree got down from the table and scrambled out of the room. Ruby heard her in the bathroom, and a few minutes later Sheree was back with a band aid. Ruby took it from her.

"Thanks."

Ruby unwrapped the bandage and stuck it over the cut. She put a handful of crackers and apple pieces in front of Sheree. Sheree picked up a piece of the apple.

Charlie walked into the room, rubbing his eyes.

"Hullo, girls. Did I sleep in?" he yawned.

"You slept late," Sheree confirmed. "We've been up forever."

"Sorry. How are you guys getting along?"

"She cut herself." Sheree motioned to Ruby.

Charlie looked at Ruby.

"Are you okay?"

Ruby shrugged.

"Just a little c-cut," Ruby displayed her bandaged finger so he wouldn't be worried.

"Be careful." He surveyed the counter. "Is that breakfast?"

Ruby and Sheree nodded. Charlie picked up a couple of crackers and nibbled on them.

"Are you going to go to the gym with me?"

Ruby motioned to Sheree.

"Who will watch her?"

"They have a kiddie center. They'll watch her while we're working out."

"Oh. Okay."

"So you'll come?"

"Sure."

"Good. How're you feeling today?"

"Okay."

"Did you take your pills?"

Ruby shook her head, and Charlie went into the bathroom to get them from the medicine cabinet. Ruby took them, with Sheree watching alertly.

"What's that for?" she demanded.

"To make me feel better."

"Are you sick?"

Ruby hesitated before answering yes. Charlie got their gym bags from the bedroom and handed Ruby hers.

"Say goodbye to Ralph, Sheree. We have to go out."

"He wants to go outside."

"He has papers in the kitchen."

"But he wants to go outside."

"Okay, get his leash and we'll take him down. Ruby—we'll be right back."

Ruby nodded.

Ruby finished showering and changing before Charlie, and she stood outside the kiddie corral watching Sheree play. Sheree interacted easily with the other children and their supervisors. She was constantly moving and checking out new things. She seemed quite happy to be there.

Charlie came up behind Ruby and put his arms around her.

"She's certainly a little sweetheart, isn't she?"

Ruby felt a stab of jealousy.

"Yeah, I g-guess."

"I can't believe how advanced she is. She is going to be at the top of her class."

"What c-class?"

"In school. Any class."

"She's just t-two," Ruby pointed out.

"I know that. But I'll bet she's reading before she turns three."

"Three year olds c-can't read."

"Ones like Sheree can."

"Foster k-kids are always b-behind."

"That's a big generalization. It can't be true in all cases."

"Foster k-kids are d-dumb. They d-don't d-do g-good."

"You're not dumb, Ruby," Charlie told her.

"All foster k-kkids are d-dumb."

"Who told you that?"

"Nobody had t-to t-tell me."

"You're not dumb," Charlie repeated.

Ruby shrugged and didn't challenge him.

"Let's go get her."

They went into the daycare to get Sheree.

"Sheree was great," one of the supervisors gushed. "She's really fun."

"Well, she'll be a regular here now," Charlie told her.

"Great. We'll see you tomorrow then, Sheree."

"See you," Sheree agreed cheerfully.

They all headed back to the car.

"I'm hungry," Sheree said.

"Well, we'll have a good breakfast when we get back to the apartment."

"What will we have?" she inquired.

"What would you like, honey?"

"I would like cornflakes."

Charlie laughed.

"I think we could manage that."

Ruby put her bag in the car, but didn't get in.

"I'm going out," she told Charlie.

"You don't want to have breakfast first?"

Ruby shook her head.

"I'm not hungry. I g-gotta go."

Charlie nodded.

"All right. Be careful, okay?"

"Yeah. S-see you later."

Ruby left them and went to look for the Jags. Sheree made her feel so uncomfortable. Ruby couldn't separate her desire to be a good mother from her discomfort around Sheree and the feelings collided inside her making her feel tense and sick. And Charlie fawned over her and paid attention to her like Jamie used to cater to Stella. Knowing what she did about what Jamie had really been, that made her feel even more tense. How was she supposed to be a good mom?

∼

Ruby went to Terry's new place when she didn't find the Jags at any of their usual places. Terry's door was unlocked, and Ruby went in. Terry was at the table with another boy with his back to Ruby.

"Hey, baby. Come meet the new guy, he's joining up with the Jags."

The other boy turned to look at her. Ruby swallowed.

"This is—"

"Max," Ruby finished for him. "Hi," she said coolly.

Max stared at her in disbelief. Terry watched the expressions on their faces.

"When did you two ever meet?"

"Juvie. We met in juvie," Max said slowly. "But you never told me that you were in a gang."

Ruby shrugged.

"You never asked. What are you d-doing here?"

"I know a couple of the guys. Things were getting too hot where I was, so I thought I'd join up with the Jaguars."

Ruby eyed him.

"Uh-huh."

Max didn't say anything. He knew that if Ruby wanted to, she could keep him out of the gang. But Ruby knew about loyalty within the gang, and if the other Jags had decided to let Max in, she wasn't going to make waves over it.

Max turned back to Terry slowly. Ruby went to the fridge, leaving them to their conversation.

∼

When they were out shooting pool, Max approached Ruby.

"Hey, Ruby," he said lowly.

She glanced at him, and scowled.

"What d-do you want?"

"I just wanted to talk to you…"

Ruby turned her back on him and went up to the bar to get another drink. The bartender handed her another beer with a warning glance so that Ruby would know that it was the last he would give her. Ruby turned and found that Max had followed her over to the bar.

"Come on, Ruby," he cajoled.

"What?"

"You could'a' said something to Terry to keep me out of the Jags. But you didn't."

Ruby looked at him.

"You ain't in yet," she observed.

"But I will be. Unless you say something."

Ruby shrugged. Max leaned on the bar and lit a cigarette. He rubbed his chin, frowning.

"Look," he said, "you're okay. You ticked me off in juvie. I misread you. And I never knew you were a Jag. I thought you were just some chick…"

Ruby shrugged, and looked away from him. Max was getting frustrated with her. He grabbed her arm.

"I'm telling you I shouldn't have done what I did in juvie. I'm sorry, okay?"

Ruby jerked away from him.

"Are you d-done?"

He shrugged widely and didn't say anything. Ruby went over to where the others were playing. She stood next to Piles and shared a joint with him.

Ruby awoke with her ears buzzing. She put her arm over her head to try to silence it, but the motion only served to make her woozy. It had been a long time since Ruby had been that hung over. She rubbed her temples, trying to clear her head and wake herself up. Charlie moved beside her, and Ruby put her hand over his arm, which was stretched across her.

Her eyes were blurry, and Ruby blinked to try to clear them. She slowly came to realize that she was not in Charlie's apartment. She rolled over slowly, her stomach tightening. If she wasn't in Charlie's apartment, she wasn't in bed with Charlie. She pulled the sheets up to her shoulders and turned to look at… Max.

Max. Ruby drew back from him, feeling sick. She must have gotten pretty smashed the night before to end up in bed with Max.

As she moved away, Max stirred and woke up. He rubbed his eyes and put his arm around her, cupping his hand around her hip.

"Hey, Ruby." He smiled wolfishly.

Ruby pushed his hands away.

"Get off me."

Max grinned and propped himself up on one elbow.

"That's not what you said last night," he laughed.

"I was d-drunk," Ruby snapped.

"You sure were," he agreed.

Ruby sat up, holding the sheets close to her while she looked for her clothes. She untangled them from Max's clothes with one hand. She dressed awkwardly and got up. Max watched her movements.

"You don't have to run away, you know."

"I gotta go home."

"Why, what's at home?"

Ruby ignored him and walked out.

It was still early, and the streets were quiet. Ruby walked part way and grabbed a bus the rest of the way back to Charlie's. Charlie was up making breakfast for Sheree. He looked at Ruby with a frown when she walked in.

"Well, good morning."

Ruby shrugged.

"Hi."

Charlie didn't ask Ruby where she'd been or what she'd been up to. Sheree turned around and looked at Ruby.

"Why did you go away?" she demanded.

Ruby sat down on a chair beside Sheree.

"I fell asleep. S-sorry."

"Why didn't you come home?"

Ruby looked up at Charlie, swallowing.

"I meant t-to. I just g-got... s-sidetracked."

"Why?" Sheree demanded.

"Eat your breakfast, Sheree," Charlie advised her, putting a bowl in front of her. Sheree knelt up to eat. Ruby watched her.

"Is there c-coffee?" she asked Charlie.

He nodded, and got it for her. Ruby sipped it slowly. She couldn't look Charlie in the eye.

"I d-didn't mean t-to be g-gone s-so long," she apologized.

"Where you go is up to you. I didn't say anything."

She knew Charlie was upset, even if he wouldn't say so. He wasn't used to Ruby being away when he got back from his shift. She was always there when he got in.

Ruby went with Charlie to the gym, but he was brooding and quiet. His lips were pressed together in a thin line, and he stared straight ahead as he drove.

Ruby stayed away from the gang, spending the time by herself. As the afternoon drew on, she went to the day home that Sheree stayed at. She rang the doorbell, and a woman answered the door.

"Yes?"

"I c-came t-to g-get Sheree."

"Who are you?"

"I'm her mom."

The woman hesitated, and motioned for her to come in. Ruby looked around. A couple of other children played in the kitchen at the table. Sheree dashed in when she was called.

"Hi."

The woman who had answered the door was looking at a list held in her hand.

"You aren't authorized to pick Sheree up."

"She's my baby. I c-can t-take her where I like," Ruby said.

"You can't take her from here."

Ruby looked at Sheree.

"T-tell her I'm your mama."

Sheree nodded.

"Uh-huh. She's my mom."

"I'm sorry. I can only release her to the people on the list."

Ruby held her hand out for Sheree's.

"Come on. We're g-going home."

Sheree took her hand. The woman grabbed Sheree's other arm.

"You're not taking her anywhere."

Ruby picked Sheree up and wrenched her away. She opened the door and left, with the woman calling after her.

Charlie didn't pay any attention to the call for a squad car to the residential address in his area. It wasn't his call. Ten minutes later when the officer who responded to the call reported that he was on his way to an apartment, and gave Charlie's address, he straightened up and took notice. He looked at Davidson and picked up the CB.

"You want to repeat that address?" he questioned.

The officer repeated the address back slowly.

"That's my place. What's going on?"

"Sounds like an abduction by a non-custodial parent."

"Ruby took Sheree?"

"Yes, that's right."

"I'll meet you over there. Before you go into the apartment."

"Okay. See you there."

Davidson changed course and headed towards Charlie's apartment. Charlie swallowed and tried to regulate his breathing. There was nothing wrong. Ruby had decided to do a little mommying while he was gone. That was all.

The other officer was waiting outside the apartment. He nodded.

"Charlie."

"Hi. I'll see if I can get this straightened out quietly."

"Do you want me to...?"

"Just stay here for a minute."

Davidson and the other officer stayed outside the apartment while Charlie went inside. He opened the door and went in. Ruby was watching TV. Sheree was sitting in her lap, snuggling against her comfortably. Ruby looked up.

"What are you d-doing home?"

"The day home called the police when you picked Sheree up."

Ruby shrugged.

"Why?"

"You don't have custody of Sheree. You're not allowed to be alone with her."

"I'm not d-doing anything wrong."

"I know, honey, but Social Services doesn't think you're ready to have custody of Sheree yet."

Ruby scowled.

"I need to take Sheree back to the day home," Charlie told her.

"But Sheree wants t-to s-stay with me."

"Sheree. Let's go back to daycare."

RUBY, BETWEEN THE CRACKS

Sheree slid away from Ruby.

"I want to bring Ralph," she said.

"Ralph has to stay here. Come on."

Sheree took Charlie by the hand, and led her out of the room without another word to Ruby. He went out into the hallway and closed the door. He held Sheree's hand out for the other officer to take.

"This policeman is going to take you back to daycare, sweetie. You go with him."

"I don't go with strangers," Sheree said stolidly.

"That's right. You don't go with strangers. But if I tell you it's okay to go with someone, you can. And it's okay to go with this policeman."

"Okay."

"I'll see you after work. I'll come pick you up."

Sheree nodded. Charlie knelt down to talk to Sheree.

"Now honey, if Ruby picks you up from daycare, I don't want you to go with her, okay? You wait for me."

Sheree looked disdainful.

"She would just take me anyway."

Charlie grinned.

"She might," he agreed. "Do you know how to call me on the phone if she does?"

"Sure. If you tell me your phone number."

"Do you know how to call 911?"

"Uh-huh."

"If you do that, and you tell them who I am and what happened, they'll be able to find me."

"Okay."

Charlie nodded and patted her on the shoulder.

"Good girl. You go on back to daycare."

"Why did you pick Sheree up from daycare today?" Charlie questioned casually as he and Ruby headed to bed later that night.

Ruby shrugged and didn't look at him.

"I just wanted t-to be with my b-baby."

"You can be with her whenever you want, Ruby. You just can't be with her alone."

"I wanted t-to be alone with her."

"Why?"

"I d-dunno."

Charlie kissed her.

"I don't want to cause trouble. But if you get the police called on you again, Social Services might decide that Sheree shouldn't live with us."

Ruby nodded.

"Whatever."

"You can spend however much time you like with her, as long as I'm here. Or if you want to play with her at the day home, you could do that too."

"Okay."

∼

Ruby was headed towards the bus stop when she saw Max. He was leaning against a lamp-post, watching her.

"What are you d-doing here?" Ruby demanded.

Max grinned slowly.

"I've had my eye on you, girl."

"You s-stay away from me," Ruby growled.

"So you're still with that cop, huh?"

Ruby walked past him without a word. Max followed her and walked beside her.

"You ignoring me?"

She picked up her pace, but Max didn't let himself be left behind. He kept close to her, and put his arm around her shoulders.

"Don't get all pouty on me, miss, just 'cause I'm taking an interest in your little family."

"Get away from me!"

She tried to shake his arm loose, but he was determined to stay with her. Ruby struggled with him, but he just held her tighter.

"Don't fight me, girl. I'm ten times stronger than you, and I'll hurt you."

Ruby stopped trying to wrestle away from him. He relaxed his grip a little, still holding onto her.

"So tell me all about your honey," he coaxed.

Ruby swore at him.

"Is the little girl his?" Max persisted.

"Get lost."

He smiled and continued to walk with her to the bus and to Joe's apartment. Then he let go of her and acted like she was just another Jag.

∼

Charlie got home from his shift, unlocking the door awkwardly with Sheree asleep in his arms. The apartment was dark and Ruby did not seem to be home yet. He reached to put Sheree in her crib, but there was a dark shape in it and he put his hand in to move the toy out of the way before laying her down. He touched something soft and wet and recoiled from it. He put Sheree down on the couch and turned on a lamp. He stared at the crib, feeling sick. It was Ralph. Still and black with blood. There was blood smeared all over the crib, spattered on the wall behind it. He looked down at Sheree, asleep on the couch, to make sure that she was not going to wake up.

Charlie just stood there trying to clear his mind and think of what to do. He looked at the dead puppy, trying to convince himself that it couldn't have been Ruby. Who else could have gotten into the apartment? Who else knew about Sheree's puppy?

He picked Sheree back up and put her down on their bed in the bedroom and shut the door. He had a drink and went to work on cleaning up. The knife that had been used to kill the pup was in the kitchen sink. There were spatters of blood on the white counter top in the kitchen. Ruby came in while he was stripping the sheets out of the crib. She walked in, her gait a little uneven, belying the fact that she had been drinking with the gang.

Charlie saw Ruby look at him uncomprehendingly for a moment, then her eyes widened as they took in the bloody sheets and smeared crib. He anticipated Ruby's reaction only a fraction of a second before she moved. She was on Charlie, with her knife out in an instant.

"Where's my b-baby?" Ruby demanded, as Charlie gripped her wrist tightly, trying to hold her back.

"Sheree's asleep in the bedroom. She's not hurt, Ruby. She's okay. It was Ralph."

Ruby stared at him for a minute, her eyes searching his face. Then she pulled away from him and went to the bedroom. Charlie picked up the sheets he had dropped at Ruby's attack, and waited for her to come back out. She had put away her knife when she came back out of the bedroom. She looked around the room slowly.

"What's g-going on?"

Charlie swallowed and tried to answer unemotionally.

"When I got in, the puppy was in the crib."

"Dead."

Charlie nodded. He was relieved by her reaction, but still uneasy. Someone had been in the apartment, and Ruby was still the likeliest suspect. There was a side of Ruby that he didn't know. Maybe that she herself didn't even know. The side of her that plotted to get pregnant without him knowing. That slit her wrists. That had killed another gang member. That might have killed Jamie. He wouldn't have ever believed any of those things about her, and he wasn't sure if he could believe in her innocence now.

"Who d-did it?"

"I don't know. But I think we should move to a different apartment. We need a second bedroom anyway."

He wondered how ridiculous the whole conversation must sound. The family pet had just been slaughtered and mutilated, someone was trying to terrorize them, and he was talking about moving as if it was just a logistical problem.

Ruby agreed. She headed for the door, and Charlie stopped her.

"Where are you going, Ruby?"

"T-to look around."

She walked out. Charlie realized after she was gone that he hadn't told her to be careful. She was going out to look for some sadistic screw-up who had no compunction about killing, and he didn't tell her to be careful. The butcher could still be hanging around out there, watching for their reaction. Getting his jollies by seeing if they called the police or panicked. He could be out there watching for them, and Ruby could walk right into his arms.

Charlie looked out the window in the kitchen to see if he could see her. Ruby was looking up and down the street, walking along slowly looking around. After a few minutes she walked around the side of the building where he couldn't see her.

Ruby was back half an hour later, and shrugged at him.

"I d-didn't s-see anyone," she said.

"Do you have any idea who might have done this?"

Ruby shook her head.

"You're a c-cop."

"Yes, and you're a Jag. Are you saying that you don't have enemies too?"

"I d-dunno. Not p-personal. This was p-personal."

Charlie considered the suggestion and agreed.

"Yeah, this was personal. So who would have a grudge against you or me?"

Sheree started to cry in the bedroom, and Charlie motioned for Ruby to go get her.

"I have to finish cleaning this up. See if you can get her to go back to sleep in there."

"Okay."

Charlie knew as he washed the wall and the bars of the crib that he would miss some places. They would be finding blood spots for months. If they stayed. He did the best that he could. It would be easier to see in the morning. They were going to have to tell Sheree something. She was going to want to know where Ralph was. For the first time, Charlie wished that Sheree wasn't quite so bright.

He took the bag of bloody sheets and rags and Ralph's ragged little corpse down to the garbage bins behind the building. Charlie wanted everything out of the apartment, out of reach and out of mind. He watched for anyone suspicious in the darkness. Like Ruby, he didn't see anyone.

Sheree was cuddled up to Ruby on the bed, back to sleep. Ruby was not asleep. Her eyes were worried and angry. Charlie slowly got ready for bed.

"I'll put her in the crib now," he offered.

Ruby shook her head.

"I d-don't want her out there."

"It's all cleaned up now. It's okay."

Ruby carefully pulled away from Sheree to undress for bed.

"I want her t-to s-sleep in here," she said stubbornly.

Charlie shrugged and didn't argue any further. They got into bed quietly, trying not to disturb Sheree. As they settled in, Ruby pulled Sheree into her arms and held her close. They both lay awake, still and quiet, for most of the night.

Sheree woke up before either of them in the morning. She squirmed out of Ruby's grasp and tapped Charlie on the arm until he forced his eyes open to look at her.

"I'm up," she told him.

"Hi, sweetie. Why don't you go watch cartoons for a little bit, and then I'll make you breakfast, okay?"

Sheree agreed and Charlie listened for her to put the TV on. There was quiet for a couple of minutes while she wandered out to the front room, and then she started to shriek.

"Charlie, Charlie! Mama!"

Charlie bounded out of bed. Ruby had still been asleep, but she was right behind him. Sheree stood in front of the crib, where Ralph's stiffened corpse was again lying. Charlie picked Sheree up and whirled her around into the bedroom where she couldn't see it anymore. He heard Ruby check out the door into the hallway, then slam the door and lock it. She stalked back into the bedroom.

"You left the d-door open," she accused Charlie.

"I made sure I locked it," Charlie snapped, holding Sheree cuddled tightly in his arms as she cried.

"It was open!"

"Just go take care of things out there."

"What are you going to do?" Sheree questioned, trying to stop her sobbing to talk.

"It's okay. We're just going to clean up so you don't have to see that again."

"What are you going to do with Ralph?"

"Throw him out," Ruby responded, before Charlie could say something more appropriate. This threw Sheree into a fresh flood of tears.

"You can't throw Ralph in the garbage," she protested, clutching Charlie.

"No, we won't throw him in the garbage. We'll put him in a box with his blanket, and we'll bury him someplace special," Charlie assured her.

Sheree just sobbed, holding her face against his chest.

Ruby shrugged and left the room. It was a few minutes before she came back again.

"Let's have b-breakfast," she suggested.

Charlie looked down at Sheree to see how she would respond.

"Why did you do that to Ralph?" Sheree demanded, rubbing her eyes and looking at Ruby.

Ruby opened her mouth and didn't say anything.

"Mama wouldn't hurt Ralph," Charlie said gently, wishing that he believed it one hundred percent, "Mama would never do anything to hurt you."

Ruby nodded.

"I d-didn't d-do it," she said weakly.

"I know you did it," Sheree insisted. "You hurt Ralph."

She was so certain. Charlie looked at Ruby and hoped that she would just go out to the kitchen and make breakfast, and leave him alone with Sheree to find out what made her so sure that Ruby had done it. But Ruby kept standing there, not knowing what do with herself. Charlie rocked Sheree.

"It's okay, honey. Everything will be okay."

"She didn't like Ralph."

"Of course mama liked Ralph."

"She didn't like him. She doesn't like me."

Charlie felt sick. He'd been trying to convince himself since they had taken Sheree in that Ruby really loved her. And Ruby did seem to be getting more attached. But even Sheree knew that Ruby didn't really like her. Even she had noticed.

"Mama loves you very much. Tell her, Ruby."

Ruby seemed relieved to be told what to do. She went over to the bed and sat down on it next to Charlie. She looked down at Sheree.

"I like you, Sheree. You're my b-baby."

Charlie tried handing Sheree to Ruby, although he didn't really want to. Ruby took Sheree into her arms and cradled her.

"It's okay, b-baby."

Sheree closed her eyes and cuddled up tighter, pretending to be an infant.

"Wah. I'm a baby. Wah."

Ruby laughed, thinking it was funny, and she held Sheree closer, rocking her.

"Good b-baby."

Charlie got up.

"Does everybody want a big breakfast?"

Ruby shrugged.

"Wah, baby wants milk," Sheree contributed.

Charlie shook his head and went out to the kitchen. He put on the coffee and while it percolated, he watched the two of them through the door. Sometime that morning, Ruby had gotten out of bed. He just vaguely remembered it. She often got up in the night to go to the bathroom, especially if she'd had a bit to drink. She couldn't have gotten up, changed, gone outside to the back of the building and retrieved the little body. It had to be an outsider. Someone had picked the lock of the apartment and left the body there again. If Ruby hadn't insisted that Sheree stay with them in the bedroom, Sheree would have been a few feet from the door in the crib. Where it could just as easily have been her body as the puppy's.

Or Ruby might have kept Sheree in bed so that the crib would be empty to put the body back in again.

CHAPTER Twenty-Five

Charlie got a paper while they were at the gym, and while he was warming up on the stationary bike, looked through the advertisements for apartments to rent. He wanted to be out of their building by the end of the week.

Ruby stayed with Sheree in the kiddie center instead of doing her weight training. Charlie had suggested that one of them should stay with her and Ruby had volunteered without hesitation. Charlie cut his workout short so that he wouldn't be away from Sheree for too long.

Ruby stayed with them for the drive over to the day home, which she didn't usually do. They dropped Sheree off, and Charlie and Ruby looked at each other.

"Are you g-going to t-tell the c-cops what happened?" Ruby questioned.

Charlie thought about it.

"Yeah, I'm going to make a report."

"Who d-do you think d-did it?"

Charlie swallowed.

"I don't know."

At Ruby's request, Charlie dropped her off at a street near their building before going back on shift.

∼

"Do you think Ruby has psychological problems?" Charlie asked. "I mean, other than the depression?"

Ruby's therapist raised his eyebrows.

"What do you mean?" he questioned.

"I mean... schizophrenia or multiple personalities or something."

"No, I don't think Ruby shows symptoms of any serious disorder like that."

"Some of the things that Ruby's done... I don't understand how she could have. They just don't seem to fit."

"Well, all of us have sides that we hide from other people."

"Do you think that Ruby has an... evil side?"

"I think that's pretty strong. I think she has fears and weaknesses that she tries to hide with her behavior, like anyone else."

"Do you think she has a conscience?"

"Yes, Ruby has an active conscience. She carries around a lot of guilt that weighs very heavily on her."

Charlie nodded. He wondered what secrets of Ruby's the doctor knew that he didn't. He wondered how much Ruby told him and if he could have explained things to Charlie if it wasn't for doctor-patient confidentiality.

"Does she talk much about Sheree?"

The doctor shrugged and didn't answer clearly one way or the other.

"You don't think... that she could ever be a danger to Sheree?" Charlie questioned.

The doctor frowned.

"Has Ruby done something to make you think Sheree is in danger?"

"No... not that I know for sure. But I'm worried that she might have done something... or might be thinking of doing something."

"Ruby has never said anything to make me think that she would set out to hurt Sheree, if that makes you feel better. But you have to remember that Ruby herself had a pretty tough upbringing. She may have different ideas of parenting than you do."

"But you don't think that she would set out to hurt Sheree."

"No, she's never said anything to lead me to believe that."

Charlie breathed out heavily.

"I'm glad to hear that. I guess I'm just an overprotective parent."

"You're there to supervise for a reason. I'm not saying that Ruby would be capable of taking care of a baby on her own."

"I can handle that," Charlie agreed.

When he pulled up in front of the day home, there was a marked police car already sitting there. Charlie's gut tightened and he hurried into the house.

"What's going on? What's wrong?"

A pair of officers was there talking with Ruby and the day home provider. Sheree jumped up and ran to Charlie, hugging him around the legs.

"Where were you?" she demanded.

"I worked late," Charlie said, picking her up. "What's going on here?" he looked pointedly at Ruby. Ruby wasn't supposed to be there. Trying to pick Sheree up on her own again, probably.

"You finished work an hour ago," Ruby accused. "Where've you been?"

"I had some errands to run," Charlie said.

"Ruby was concerned when you didn't show up," the officer explained. "I guess you guys have had a couple of... incidents... and she was worried."

Charlie felt guilty for jumping to conclusions.

"I'm sorry, baby. I wasn't thinking about you getting worried. I shouldn't have taken so long."

"Can we go to McDonalds?" Sheree questioned, breaking the tension. Everybody laughed.

"Yeah, let's go to McDonalds. You want a happy meal?"

"You should have one too," Sheree patted Charlie's hand.

Charlie squeezed her.

"Let's go."

Ruby followed them out to the car.

"Come on, spend a night with us for once," Erwin urged. "Your boyfriend can do without you for one night. We miss you when he's on day shift."

Ruby shook her head.

"I g-gotta get home."

"How come you've been so jumpy lately? You guys having problems or something?"

Ruby shrugged.

"Things aren't g-going so well."

"So have a few drinks and get your mind off of it," he suggested.

"I have to g-go," Ruby repeated.

"When does he swing shifts again?"

Ruby considered it.

"S-Sunday. I think."

"So you'll come out on the town with us then?"

"Yeah."

Erwin shrugged and let her go on. Ruby was stopped at the door by Max.

"Hey, Ruby, where are you goin' so early? The night is still young"

She shoved him.

"G-get lost."

"I'm just inquiring after your health, no need to get snippy."

"S-stay away from me, you g-got it?"

"Um... no." He touched her arm lightly. "Now come on, is that any way to treat a friend?"

Ruby pushed past him.

"How's your little girl?" Max questioned, and Ruby whirled around.

"Leave my b-baby alone."

He shrugged and watched her go.

Ruby looked around the basement suite and shrugged.

"What about animals?" she questioned.

Charlie looked at Ruby in surprise, raising an eyebrow. The landlord hesitated.

"The last people here had a cat..."

"S-so we c-could k-keep our d-dog?"

"I suppose."

They asked a few other questions, and left. Charlie looked at Ruby curiously.

"Our dog?"

"We need a g-guard d-dog."

"I don't know, Ruby..."

"Not a p-puppy like Ralph. A b-big d-dog."

Charlie thought about it for a minute, but didn't fight it.

"Okay, we'll look around."

Charlie glanced over his shoulder towards the bedroom. He hadn't heard Sheree or Ruby for a few minutes. He'd almost fallen asleep watching TV. He got up slowly, stretching out stiff muscles. He'd worked out harder than usual at the gym. He went to Sheree's bedroom and opened the door. Ruby was sitting in a reclined position on the bed. Sheree was standing beside the bed in nothing but her underpants. Sheree saw Charlie first.

"Hi."

Ruby looked up.

"Oh. You were asleep."

"What's going on in here?"

"We're playing dress-up," Sheree said. She picked up Ruby's evening dress and held it in front of her. She slipped it over her head and paraded around.

"It's bedtime for you, honey," Charlie advised.

"I don't want to go to bed."

"I'll read you a story. Come on, let's get you into the tub first."

Sheree pouted.

"We were playing."

"And now it's time for bath and bed."

Sheree headed towards the bathroom in Ruby's dress. Charlie looked at Ruby for a moment, then followed Sheree. He started drawing the bath, and gently encouraged her to take the dress off and had her in the tub a couple of minutes later. Ruby stood in the doorway.

"You shouldn't bath her," she said.

Charlie looked up.

"Why not?"

"C-cause she's g-got nothing on. I should d-do it."

Charlie shook his head.

"She's just fine with me doing it."

Ruby stood there, not moving.

"You shouldn't t-touch her when she's g-got nothing on," she persisted.

"What's the problem? You've never had a problem with this before," Charlie pointed out.

"I d-don't want her t-to g-get hurt."

"I would never hurt Sheree. Would I, sweetie?"

Sheree shook her head.

"Charlie's not hurting me."

Ruby turned and left. Charlie rolled his eyes and continued getting Sheree ready for bed. He took her into her bedroom to put her in the crib. Ruby hung around the doorway.

"C-can she c-come in with us?"

Charlie glanced at her.

"Sheree needs to start sleeping in her own bedroom. She'll be all right."

When he finished reading her a story and kissing her goodnight, Charlie went back to the front room where Ruby had turned on the TV.

"She'll be fine on her own," he advised. "We're safe here."

"I j-just want her with me."

"You can spend time with her during the day."

Ruby watched TV and didn't say anything. Charlie could tell that something was bothering her, but she didn't say what it was.

Ruby couldn't put her uneasiness into words, and Charlie never seemed to listen to her any more. He just told her what to do or not to do and didn't hear what she had to say to him. He gave all of his attention to Sheree, leaving nothing for Ruby. They hardly went out anywhere now, and never anywhere without Sheree.

All the same, she couldn't get rid of the feeling that Sheree was in danger. Whoever it was that had killed the puppy so brutally was watching them still and waiting for the right time to make his move. She didn't like Sheree to be anywhere alone, however much she wanted time to patch things up with Charlie one-on-one. Ruby even found herself suspicious of Charlie and the attention he gave Sheree. She kept hearing Marty's warnings about Jamie giving Stella attention, and then what she had found out about Jamie from his own lips. What did she know about Charlie? Just because he was a cop, that didn't mean that he was an angel. He knew from the start that Ruby wasn't really eighteen, but he ignored the law and stayed with her anyway. He said he wouldn't tell the homicide officers if she had killed Jamie. What other laws and morals was he prepared to overlook if it suited him?

Charlie drove Sheree to the daycare, deep in thought.

"Do you still think your mama doesn't like you?" he questioned after a while.

Sheree and Ruby had been spending more time together, and Charlie wondered if it made a difference to the way Sheree felt about Ruby.

"She makes a face when she looks at me," Sheree answered obliquely.

Charlie snickered.

"What face does she make?" he questioned.

He looked in the mirror at Sheree as she attempted to imitate it, her brows drawn down.

"I think mama's just worried about you," he advised. He wasn't sure whether Sheree's expression was meant to be a scowl or a worried frown.

"Where's my daddy?" Sheree questioned.

Charlie bit his lip.

"Do you mean Jamie?" he questioned carefully, wondering if Sheree remembered him.

"No. A daddy like the other kids have."

"I don't know, sweetie. I don't know who your daddy is."

"I don't either," she agreed with a sigh.

"It's okay. You have Charlie instead. I'll bet none of the other kids have Charlies."

Sheree giggled.

"You're my Charlie," she agreed.

Ruby tied the dog outside the door, looking around for anything suspicious. But there was no-one around. She didn't pat the dog. She didn't want him to be friendly. She wanted him to tear apart anyone who got close.

She went back into the apartment. Charlie was putting Sheree to bed. Ruby stood outside the door where he couldn't see her, listening. She used to like the way he dropped little terms of affection when he talked. Darling, baby, sweetheart... but it grated on her nerves now. He used them when he was talking to Sheree all the time now too. Things were different.

Joe came up and sat on the bar stool next to Ruby after she ordered her drink.

"You got your blade?" Joe questioned.

Ruby nodded.

"Sure."

"Ready for a rumble tonight?"

"Yeah. We g-going ahead?"

"Yeah, Terry just told us. You're around tonight for it, right?"

"I won't miss it," Ruby confirmed.

"Good."

Ruby put her hand in her pocket and touched her knife. It had been a while since she had been in a rumble. She was looking forward to the fight, but she was a bit nervous too. She was always a little nervous before a rumble. Anybody who wasn't crazy or high was nervous before a rumble.

"Where are we meeting them?"

"Over on fourth, you know the field behind the liquor store."

"Oh, sure."

"I'm goin' to the bar. You coming?"

Ruby nodded.

Joe put his arm around Ruby's shoulders, leaning on her to steady himself, pretending that he was just being friendly.

"You're a good rumbler, you know that?" he said conversationally.

Ruby smiled, holding onto him around the waist to keep him from pulling her over.

"So're you, Joe."

"Yeah, but you're—you're a natural. Look at you, you hardly even got a scratch."

Unlike Joe, who had an ugly gash across the forehead that was bleeding pretty profusely. And she had seen him sometime during the middle of the rumble on the ground being kicked in the belly by a couple of big bruisers. Ruby hadn't been able to get to him to help out.

"You're punch-drunk, Joe," she told him.

Joe laughed, nodding.

"Yeah, I am," he agreed. "One of those guys was bouncin' my head off the ground. I thought he'd bust it right open."

"You oughtta see a doctor."

"Maybe."

Ruby looked around at the others to assess the damage the gang had suffered. Joe looked around too.

"How did the new guy do?"

"Max?" Ruby looked for him, a chill going over her. She had seen him before the rumble, but she hadn't noticed him during the rumble or afterward. Why would he disappear right before the rumble? He knew people would be watching him to see how he performed. "Where is he?"

"I don't see him," Joe advised.

"Where would he go? Why would he s-skip out?" Ruby demanded.

"He's around somewhere."

Ruby grabbed Erwin as he came up to them.

"Erwin—take Joe," she tried to transfer Joe's grip over to him. Erwin hung onto Joe uncertainly.

"Why? Where are you going?"

"Has anyone seen Max?"

Erwin shrugged.

"I don't know. What's going on?"

"He ain't here..."

Ruby had been uncomfortable around Max since he had shown up. And with everything that had happened with Sheree, she had become increasingly nervous about Max and his comments and questions about her and her family. Charlie was on shift all night, and Sheree was sleeping at the day home, unprotected.

"I g-gotta go," Ruby said, and let go of Joe. "Make sure he sees a d-doctor."

"Yeah, sure."

There were lights on in the house, which Ruby thought was strange, since it was the middle of the night and all of the houses on the block were dark. She went up to the door and stood there looking into the living room and listening to see what was going on. She could hear Sheree crying, and raised voices. She couldn't make out Max's voice until he walked into the front room. He had Sheree over his shoulder and was shouting at the woman whose house it was. Max burst through the front door before Ruby realized he was headed out. She was against the door, and he bowled her over onto the lawn. He stood there for a moment on the steps, frozen, and stared at her. Ruby got up, a little stunned, feeling for her knife. Max grabbed her wrist and pulled her to her feet.

"Shut up or you're gonna get hurt," he warned, dragging her along with him.

Ruby felt for her knife, but her pockets were empty. She struggled, but Max just tightened his grip and pulled her closer.

"If you try anything, I'm going to hurt this little girl. You hear me?"

Ruby nodded, and stayed close to him while she tried to think of what to do. Sheree was wailing at the top of her lungs, with Max muttering at her to shut up and be still.

Charlie didn't hear the first call that was made calling an officer to Sheree's day home, but shortly after he was called.

"Charlie, your kid was taken from the day home again."

Charlie picked up the CB.

"Ruby picked her up?" he questioned.

"A young man. But the lady says that she thinks Ruby was outside."

"Oh... well, I'll go by the house and see if she's there," Charlie said.

"Let me know what you find out."

Charlie put the CB down, frowning.

"A young man?" Davidson repeated.

Charlie shook his head.

"I don't know. It doesn't make sense."

"Are things okay between you guys?"

"Sure... as much as ever."

"Where's your new place?"

Charlie directed him to the apartment. When he got there, the house was dark, and the dog was in the back yard. Charlie tried to open the back door quietly, in case Ruby was there with someone else, but the dog was barking his head off, warning them if they were home.

The suite was empty. Charlie took a look around, his stomach tied in knots. There was no sign that Ruby had been there lately. But there was no indication either that she didn't intend to come back. Her overnight knapsack was still in the closet. And Sheree's clothes didn't appear to be disturbed. Wherever Ruby had gone, she must not have planned to be away for long. Charlie went back out to the car.

"Let's go to the day home. They're not here."

Davidson followed his directions, and they pulled up behind another squad car in front of the house. Charlie and Davidson went in to talk.

"She didn't go home this time. Can you tell me what happened?"

"This young fellow started banging on the door," Mrs. Clover explained. "He said that Ruby had sent him to pick up Sheree. When I opened the door to talk to him, he just pushed his way in. I shouldn't have opened the door."

Charlie heartily agreed, but he didn't say so.

"Did you see Ruby?" he questioned.

"Not when he came to the door. But I thought I saw her with him when he left. It could have been someone else, I didn't see really clearly, but I assumed..."

"It must have been. Who else would want to take Sheree away?" Charlie said.

Who else indeed? Who had killed the puppy? Charlie tried to block the images out of his mind and concentrate on the matter at hand.

"Do we have a description of this guy?"

Mrs. Clover described him briefly.

"Was he in the gang?"

"He didn't have a jacket on."

"We'll have to check just in case. What exactly did he say about Ruby?"

"Just that she told him to come pick up the baby."

"Did you see what direction they went in?"

"They left on foot," the other officer advised. "But I imagine they had a vehicle close by."

"Do you have anyone looking?"

"There's a couple cars cruising the area."

"You'll come down to the station to look at mug shots?" Charlie suggested to Mrs. Clover.

"Um—yes, I guess I'll have to."

"He's probably known in the area."

She nodded.

"I'm so sorry... I never should have opened the door. I didn't think he would force his way in."

"He probably would have forced the door if you hadn't opened it," the other officer commented. Charlie knew it was true, but he was angry at her for letting him in anyway.

Charlie sat up at home most of the night and on into the morning, hoping that Ruby would bring Sheree back by the time he would normally have gotten off of his shift. She would bring Sheree back unharmed and say that she had just wanted to be with her baby. But Ruby still hadn't returned by daybreak. Midmorning, Charlie got a call from the detective in charge of the case to say that Mrs. Clover had picked out the boy's mug shots.

"The abductor's name is Maxwell Terrace. He's not a Jag. Not even from the city, but he was incarcerated here and apparently stuck around after he got out."

"You don't mean he was at juvie here? He's not a juvenile, right?"

"Sure, he's juvenile. Why?"

"Ruby went to juvie for a few months for that armed robbery."

"You think they met there?"

Charlie shrugged.

"I don't know. You'd better check it out."

"All right. I will. No word from Ruby yet?"

"No. Nothing."

"We'll find them. It's only a matter of time. They're probably at his place or with one of the Jags or something."

"Does he have an address here?"

"Haven't found one yet. But we will. Maybe his PO will know something."

Charlie hung up. He was tempted to call juvie hall himself, but knew better than to interfere with the investigation. He washed up and made sure that someone was watching the house before he went down to the station so that he could be in on any new developments. Bates, who was running the investigation, didn't look pleased to see him.

"You were right. They met in juvie. Apparently had a bit of a romance going on for a while there, but then they broke up. He must have contacted her when he got out a few weeks ago. We've been talking to the beat cops in Jag territory, and apparently Terrace has been seen with them. We're going to start hauling some of the boys in to see what they can tell us."

Charlie nodded.

"I still don't get why Ruby would take off with Sheree like that?"

"Have the two of you been having problems?" Banks questioned.

"No... nothing major."

"You reported an incident a few weeks ago..."

Charlie swallowed and nodded.

"Yes, but I don't think that could have been Ruby."

"But you're not sure."

"No, I guess not."

Bates pulled out the boy's mug shots.

"Did you ever see him around your neighborhood?"

Charlie took the picture, memorizing his face.

"No. I've never seen him before."

"Terrace got out of juvie two weeks before your trouble with the dog."

Charlie shuddered.

"Do you think he did it? What's his background?"

"An all-round bad guy. Gangs, drugs, and murder. We'll have to talk to some of the officers who have had contact with him, see what they know…"

"Why would Ruby get involved with him?"

"Who knows? Ruby has a history of rushing into romances with the wrong people."

Charlie's face got hot and he hoped he wasn't as red as he felt. He cleared his throat.

"I'd like to think that I would have noticed if her… interests were elsewhere."

"Did you notice when she was involved with him in juvie?"

"No, but we didn't see each other very often. And she was depressed, off of her medication. I knew she was unhappy."

Bates nodded.

"Well, maybe you're right. At any rate, Terrace certainly has an interest in Ruby."

They had all been thrown together into an old, noisy car that was a block or so away. Max said nothing to Ruby or Sheree, but he let go of Sheree in order to drive. Whimpering, Sheree crawled into Ruby's arms and cowered there, shaking. Ruby held onto her, stroking her head soothingly, all the while trying to figure out how they were going to get away from Max. She couldn't jump from a moving car with Sheree, the little girl might get hurt. They would have to wait until they stopped for gas or something.

Ruby felt her pockets again for her knife, but it wasn't there. Ruby couldn't figure out where she had lost it. She had folded it up and put it away carefully after the rumble. But it was not there now.

Max drove most of the time with one hand, the other resting in his lap. Ruby was sure he was armed. He had a gun or something in the shadows by his legs, but it was too dark to see clearly. She thought she might try to talk to him, but she couldn't think of anything to say. What was she going to do, talk about the gang? Try to talk him out of what he was doing or find out his motives? If she asked the wrong thing, he could blow her away. Or hurt Sheree. He had no reservations about killing the defenseless. He had to be the one who had killed Ralph and disfigured the little body. For what? For kicks?

She rode in silence, trying to settle Sheree down and stay on top of what was going on.

∽

"Have you ever seen this before?" Bates questioned, showing a knife to Charlie.

"Yeah—that's Ruby's pocketknife. Where did you find that?"

"On the lawn at the house. She must have dropped it."

"Ruby didn't go anywhere without a knife."

"That doesn't mean she can't lose it. So we know for sure she was at the house last night with Terrace. And that she was armed."

"I still can't figure out why Ruby would do this. She didn't even like Sheree that much. They got along, but Ruby didn't… really have strong feelings for Sheree."

"We'll see if any of the Jags can give us some insight. We're having vice pull as many of them in as they can."

"I hope they can help."

Bates looked at Charlie for a moment.

"So do I," he agreed.

∽

Terry watched the officer who came into the room to question him. The cop sat down. The cop didn't look tough, ready to fight, like they usually did.

"Were you with Ruby Simpson any time yesterday?" he questioned.

Terry considered.

"Sure, I saw Ruby yesterday," he agreed.

"You talk to her?"

"A little."

"What about?"

Terry shrugged.

"This and that. Why?"

"Did you talk about anything specific? Unusual?"

"No."

"How did Ruby seem? Nervous? Calm?" the cop prodded.

"What's going on, are you going to tell me?" Terry demanded.

The cop didn't answer right away.

"You know Ruby has a daughter?" he questioned eventually.

"Yeah, I remember when she was born." Terry nodded.

"Her little girl was kidnapped last night."

Terry leaned back in the chair with his arms folded across his chest and looked at the cop, frowning.

"Kidnapped? Is Ruby okay?"

"Ruby's not around."

Terry was uncertain how to respond to this.

"Is she a suspect?"

The cop nodded.

"In kidnapping her own daughter?"

"She didn't have custody. We don't know what happened yet. That's what we're trying to figure out. Think you can help?"

Terry shook his head.

"No... Ruby's been jumpy lately. I dunno why. She took off suddenly last night, didn't say what was going on."

"What was Ruby's relationship with Terrace?"

"Max Terrace? There was something between them." Terry nodded.

"Not a relationship?"

"Ruby didn't like him. She never said why, but she wouldn't stay around him."

"That's not what the other Jags are saying."

Terry shifted and crossed his foot over his knee.

"Some of the guys don't know Ruby real well. She and Max... Max was interested in her, but Ruby didn't like him."

"Did they or didn't they have a relationship?" the cop persisted.

Terry was uncomfortable answering. He cleared his throat and licked his lips.

"They did get together... but Ruby was high. She wouldn't get near him if she was sober."

"But Terrace, he was interested in pursuing a relationship."

"Yeah, sure. They knew each other in juvie. He thought..." Terry shrugged, "he could pick things back up, you know?"

"How did Ruby feel about her daughter, do you know?"

"Ruby didn't talk about her."

"Ever?"

Terry shook his head.

"Not that I remember. Ruby isn't the mommy type."

∼

Bates studied Joe Crenshaw with a frown. The boy had to be practically dragged in. He was pale as a ghost and had a big goose-egg on his head. He moved like an old man. Joe put his head down on the table when he sat down, and closed his eyes.

"Did you and Ruby talk yesterday?" Bates questioned.

"Yeah, sure."

"What did you talk about?"

"Mmm. Don't remember."

"Did Ruby ever talk about her little girl?" Bates suggested.

"Her baby?" Crenshaw's breathing was ragged, like he'd been running. "No, not really…"

"But she did once or twice?"

"I guess."

"How did Ruby feel about her baby?"

"I dunno." Crenshaw shifted, grunting in pain.

"Did she like her? Dislike her?" Bates pursued.

"I dunno. In between."

"Apathy?"

"I dunno."

Bates leaned closer to Crenshaw.

"Are you okay, kid?"

"Yeah, fine."

"You need a doctor."

"Probably," he admitted.

"Have you seen one?"

"No."

"Stay there."

Like he was going to jump up and dance off. Bates left the room to call for the station's doctor.

When they checked into the motel, Ruby's brain went into high gear as she made escape plans. But when Max parked and went to check in, he reached over and grabbed Sheree.

"You stay here and keep quiet," he warned Ruby, and went to the main office. Ruby sat in the car, trapped. Max was a few minutes checking in, and then came back. He motioned Ruby out of the car, and she followed him to their motel room. He put Sheree, drowsy and mostly asleep, down on a chair, and motioned Ruby to the bed.

"Get undressed."

Ruby shook her head, folding her arms across her chest. Max laughed.

"One of you two is coming to bed with me," he advised. "Which is it gonna be?"

Ruby swallowed hard and slowly took off her shirt. Two minors checking into a motel—why were there never cops around when you wanted to be busted?

After Max fell asleep, Ruby slipped carefully out of bed and dressed in the dark. She crept over to where Sheree was sleeping on the chair and picked her up.

"Stay away from the door," Max warned.

Ruby jumped. Max hadn't moved. It was too dark to see whether his eyes were open and whether he was holding his gun. Ruby sat down, cuddling Sheree close and waiting for Max to fall back asleep.

Ruby awoke in the morning with a stiff neck from falling asleep sitting in the chair. Sheree was stirring from sleep. She sat up and put her arms around Ruby's neck.

"Mama... I want to go home."

Ruby rubbed her eyes and looked around. Max was sitting on the bed watching them. He was using a switchblade to trim his nails, and his gun was in easy reach on the side table. Ruby rubbed Sheree's back, holding Sheree close, her head nestled in Ruby's neck.

"I know, s-sweetie," she whispered.

Ruby didn't usually call Sheree sweetie. That was Charlie. Ruby gulped and breathed evenly, trying to keep her emotions from surfacing. Trying to stay calm.

"I want Charlie," Sheree complained.

"Charlie's not here."

Sheree looked over her shoulder at Max. Shuddering, she turned back to Ruby and burrowed into her neck again.

"Why did you take me here?" Sheree asked Ruby, her voice muffled.

"I didn't bring you here. He did," Ruby said.

"You brought me," Sheree insisted.

Ruby tried to ignore the knot in her stomach. What if she got away with Sheree and then Sheree told Charlie it was Ruby who had kidnapped Sheree? What would Ruby do then? What would Charlie do?

"I have to go to the toilet," Sheree said.

"Come on."

Ruby stood up and took Sheree into the tiny bathroom and shut and locked the door. While Sheree sat on the toilet, Ruby started the shower running and investigated their surroundings. The window was small, and when Ruby examined it, she found it was painted shut, and it had a security grill over the outside. Ruby tested the temperature of the shower.

"Do you want to shower with me, Sheree?"

"I don't like showers."

"You wait in here, then. I'll run a bath for you when I'm done."

"I want to go home."

"I know, sweetie… we will," Ruby promised.

"When?"

"I don't know. Soon."

CHAPTER
Twenty-Six

The next few days were nightmarish. They kept on the move, Max giving Ruby no chance for escape. He even got his hands on a pair of handcuffs to ensure that she couldn't go anywhere. Ruby kept between him and Sheree, making sure that he couldn't get his hands on her. Sleeping with Max made her sick, but Ruby refused to let him hurt Sheree.

After a week or so, they finally stopped moving and Max rented a dirty little flat full of cockroaches and rats. There was no phone. No way to contact the outside world. Ruby had always refused to carry a cell. Max occasionally went out for supplies, but brought back more booze than food.

Sheree cried a lot to begin with, but over time, she got listless, eating next to nothing, never talking, and not playing. She just lay around all day, uninterested in anything.

Ruby despaired of ever getting away from Max, and felt herself sinking into deep, dark depression. More and more often, she found herself considering permanent solutions to getting herself and Sheree away from Max's evil influence. Sheree was getting thinner and thinner, no longer a happy, bouncy baby who wanted to know about everything. Max used a straight razor, and Ruby found herself staring transfixed by it in the bathroom, thinking about using it to set herself and Sheree free from their captivity.

Then Sheree got sick. Her forehead was burning hot, but her limbs were cold. She didn't even look at Ruby when she was picked up. Ruby cradled Sheree, her chest suddenly tight. When she looked at Sheree, she saw Stella. Stella before she died. Sheree was going to die, and it would be Ruby's fault again. Ruby took Sheree out to the front room where Max was watching TV. He didn't look at her.

"Sheree's sick," Ruby told him.

"Too bad," he grunted.

"She needs a doctor."

"Kids get sick. She'll be okay in a day or two."

"No," Ruby protested, "she's going to die!"

Max looked at Ruby in amusement, taking a drink from the bottle in his hand. He looked at Sheree, listless, her pink cheek pressed against Ruby's chest.

"How gullible do you think I am? What's she got, huh?"

"I... I don't know. But my other baby... she got sick and died!" Ruby's voice rose as she tried to convince him.

"Nice try, Ruby."

Max turned back to the TV. Ruby took Sheree back to the mattress they slept on and put her down gently.

"You're going to be okay, baby," she soothed. "So that we can go back and see Charlie."

There were tears in Ruby's eyes. She went into the bathroom and got a cold cloth and razor, and sat back down beside the bed, watching over Sheree and sponging her hot face.

Ruby didn't realize she had fallen asleep sitting there, until a crash on the front door woke her with a start. There was shouting in the front room, and before Ruby could get up or look around, there were cops in riot gear at the door of the bedroom. They swarmed in, yelling at her to lie down and put her hands behind her head. Sheree whimpered. Ruby looked at the cops blankly, wondering if she too had a fever and was imagining this.

"Get down!" one of them shouted, and Ruby obediently bellied down beside the mattress. One of them kicked the razor blade away from her, and landed his big boot in the middle of her back while another one screamed at her until she laced her hands behind her head and somebody grabbed her wrists and twisted her arms into handcuffs. They pulled her to her feet and hustled her out of the apartment and down the halls and stairs to the waiting squad cars. Max was being folded into another car. One of the cops was coming out of the building with Sheree in his arms. Ruby sighed in relief and leaned back, closing her eyes.

∼

Bates looked Ruby over. She'd lost weight since the last pictures were taken, and she'd been skinny even then. Ruby's eyes were bruised hollows, her face painfully thin. She had an uncertain, sleepwalker air, as if she wasn't quite sure where she was. They all knew now that Ruby had not been one of the kidnappers, but he had to interview her anyway, get as many details as he could about what had happened.

Ruby stubbed her toe on the table as Bates maneuvered her into a chair. She had been taken from the apartment in her bare feet. But she didn't seem to notice. She sat down acquiescently and didn't look at Bates.

"How are you feeling, Ruby?" he questioned.

"Okay."

"Can I get you a coffee?"

Ruby shrugged. Bates went to the door and had one of the officers go get one for her, then sat down across from Ruby.

"Would you like to tell me what happened?" he said gently.

There was no response.

"Did you know Max was going after your daughter?" Bates questioned.

"No... I just realized that he was gone..." Ruby shook her head, "and I had a feeling..."

"A mother's intuition?"

"I guess."

"You didn't know that he was the one who had been following you, watching your family?"

"No. I should've," she said in a harder voice. "Things he said."

"How did Terrace treat you?"

She shrugged it off, not answering.

"Ruby, did Terrace hurt you? Or Sheree?"

"I didn't let him near Sheree."

"And you?" Bates prompted.

"I took care of her," Ruby reiterated.

"I know you did. You're a good mom. Max had a gun?"

Ruby nodded.

"He threatened the two of you?"

"Uh-huh."

"I'm sorry it took so long for us to track you down."

Ruby didn't say anything. An officer came in with a cup of coffee, and Bates motioned to Ruby. He stood up and left the room, leaving Ruby to drink the coffee. Charlie was watching her on the monitor in the next room. He looked at Bates in concern.

"Can I go talk to her?" he questioned.

"Well, I don't think she's going to tell me anything."

"So I can?"

Bates nodded.

"Sure, go ahead."

Ruby looked up when the door opened again, and saw Charlie. She looked back down at the table, not wanting to meet his eyes. Charlie thought that she had taken Sheree. He thought that she had hurt Sheree, or let Max hurt her.

"Ruby, are you okay?" Charlie whispered.

Ruby glanced up, surprised by his tone of concern.

"I've been so worried about you, baby."

"About Sheree," Ruby corrected.

"I've been worried about you, Ruby. Sheree too, of course. But you're my girl. I didn't know if I'd ever see you again."

Ruby looked at Charlie and met his eyes for the first time. He was telling the truth. She could see the pain and fear in his expression. A lump welled up in Ruby's throat, and her eyes started to burn. She thought about holding the razor blade in her hand just hours earlier, despairing of ever returning to her life with him again.

"I didn't think I'd see you either," she said lowly, trying to keep the tears out of her voice.

Charlie took a few steps towards her, holding his arms out.

"Ruby, honey…"

Ruby got up and put her arms around him. They held each other close, so tightly it hurt. Tears welled up in Ruby's eyes and flooded her cheeks. She couldn't control them.

"Sheree—is Sheree okay? Did you see her?" she begged.

"I haven't seen her yet," Charlie murmured. "They took her straight to the hospital. But the doctor says she's fine, just dehydrated and a bit of a fever. She's sleeping comfortably."

"Not like Stella?" Ruby questioned, pulling back slightly to look up at his face, but still holding on.

"What happened to Stella?"

"She got sick... and she died." Ruby swiped at the tears escaping her eyes.

"Sheree will be home tonight. She's just fine," Charlie assured her.

Ruby rubbed her face in Charlie's shoulder, soaking it with her tears.

"Will I?" she questioned.

"Will you be okay?"

"Will I be home?"

Charlie stroked Ruby's hair, tipping her head back to look at her face.

"Honey, you're coming home with me right now. Why wouldn't you?"

"I didn't know if..." Ruby couldn't even put her fear into words.

"You're my sweetheart. You didn't do anything wrong. I want you to come home."

Ruby hugged him again, hard and tight, trying to convince herself that this was real. That she was really back. She wasn't going to wake up and find herself back in that living nightmare.

"I didn't think I could ever come back," she whispered, her throat aching.

"Sweetie...?" Charlie said.

"Yeah?"

"I want us to be together for good. You, me, and Sheree. I want us to be a family."

Ruby put her face against him again and nodded.

"I do too."

"Do you?"

Ruby nodded.

"Ruby? Look at me for a second."

Ruby looked up at Charlie's face. He kissed her lightly on the lips.

"For good, Ruby. I want to know that you're my girl. Just mine."

"I know."

"I want to be Sheree's father."

Ruby nodded.

"Okay."

Anything he wanted.

"And I want to be your husband."

Ruby swallowed, staring at him, understanding finally dawning. She felt heat wash over her face.

"You want... to get married?" she said finally.

"Will you?" he questioned.

Ruby nodded, unable to find her voice. Charlie grinned and hugged her tightly.

"I'm sorry for how it's been, Ruby. I've been so angry... I didn't realize how much I was just afraid. I don't want to risk losing you ever again. Ever."

Ruby was unable to slow the tears flooding down her face. A detached part of her brain observed that she should have been too dehydrated to cry anymore.

"I never thought anyone would ever want to marry me," Ruby said hoarsely.

"I don't ever want to lose you."

They hugged for a long time, just repeating those words. Finally, Charlie loosened his grip.

"Let's go get Sheree and go home."

Get the next book in the series June & Justin

Did you enjoy this book? Reviews and recommendations are vital to making a book successful.

Please leave a review at your favorite book store or review site and share it with your friends.

Don't miss the following bonus material:
Sign up for mailing list to get a free ebook
Read a sneak preview chapter
Other books by P.D. Workman
Learn more about the author

DON'T MISS A THING! GET THE LATEST NEWS AND A FREE EBOOK

PDWORKMAN.COM/SIGNUP

Preview of June & Justin

CHAPTER
One

Justin woke up groggily. He kept trying to go back to sleep, but the persistent noises wouldn't let him settle back in again. He rubbed his eyes, still disoriented at being wakened out of a heavy sleep.

He tried to sort out the noises. He thought he could hear his mom's and June's voices, and running water. He looked over at the other bed, where June still usually slept, even though their parents had moved her to Ronnie's old bed in Chloe's room ages ago and didn't want her sleeping with her twin. Girls and boys weren't supposed to sleep in the same room anymore once they were school-age.

But the night light provided the light that he needed to see that she hadn't snuck back in. The bed was empty. Unslept in.

Justin swung his feet over the side of the bed and crept down the hallway to the bathroom. His mom's and June's voices were more clear now, and the loud noise of water running into the bathtub. Justin turned the handle and opened the door silently to see what was going on. June was in the tub, their mother sitting on the edge, washing her. The woman turned around, maybe feeling a draft from the open door, or sensing that someone was there.

"Justin. Go back to bed," she ordered.

Justin ignored the command.

"What's wrong?" he asked. "Is June sick?"

"Yes. Now back to bed. Go back to sleep."

"Did she throw up?"

"Bed. Now. You're making it cold in here."

Justin looked worriedly at June. She was crying. She looked small and forlorn, like she was a toddler instead of eight. Her face was washed clean of the makeup that she had started to wear lately. Her dark hair, wet, straggled in rat's tails down her back. Justin ran a hand through his own dark hair, shorter than June's, but still long for a boy's. June didn't look at Justin. He wasn't even sure that she was aware he was there. Their mom told June impatiently to hush, swishing the washcloth in the tub water and wiping the tears from her face.

"Close the door," she told Justin again, raising her voice but not turning around again.

Justin withdrew and closed the door. He stood for a couple of minutes in the hallway with his ear pressed against the door, listening to June sob and their mother repeatedly shush her and tell her she was okay. Eventually, Justin turned around and returned to his room. He pulled the blankets over himself and curled up, trying to warm himself up again. He wiggled his toes under the pile of his old teddy bears and plushies to warm up.

He lay there, listening to the sounds down the hallway, waiting for his mother to take June back to bed.

When he woke up to sun starting to filter into the room through the closed blinds, Justin realized he must have fallen back asleep again while waiting to hear June go back to bed. He stretched and scratched his chin. Justin reached over to his dresser and pulled out a dark hoodie and a pair of socks. He got up and added a gold necklace to the outfit and dragged a comb through his hair. A handful of mousse wet it down and would hopefully keep it in place. Justin paused for a moment to inspect the healing cut above his lip from a fight with Banks, one of the older boys, a fifth-grader. He was pretty sure it would leave a scar.

Justin went to find June.

Chloe's door was shut. Justin didn't bother to knock; he just opened the door and went in. The thirteen-year-old was standing in front of the mirror, primping her shaggy blond hair, and turned to Justin with a scowl, pulling the fallen strap of her pink halter-top back into place. The air was thick with the fumes from her hairspray. Justin coughed.

"You can't just come in here," Chloe growled. "This is my room, not yours."

"It's June's room."

"It's my room too. You have to knock and get permission. Girls need privacy."

Justin shrugged and turned around to June's bed. June eyes were open just a slit, looking at him. She was dressed in a pink nightgown edged with lace that he couldn't remember her ever wearing before. Something their mother must have picked out. June usually liked t-shirts or sweats. June's skin was white, not rosy like usual. Justin sat on the bed and touched her dark, tangled hair.

"Are you okay, June?"

June grunted something.

"Did you puke?" he asked.

June held her hand to her head and rubbed it.

"Don't remember." She burped, and lurched toward him, her other hand on her stomach. "But I think…"

Justin moved quickly out of her way. June staggered out of the bed and stumbled out the door. Justin followed behind her at a distance. June made it safely to the bathroom before throwing up. Justin stayed in the hallway, waiting for her to finish. He suddenly wasn't feeling too hungry for breakfast himself. June rested her head on the edge of the toilet.

"You okay?" Justin asked after a few minutes.

"Uggh. No."

"You must have thrown up last night too."

She turned her head and looked at him. "I don't remember," she repeated.

"Are you done?"

June held her stomach, shaking her head.

"Want me to call Mom?"

"What for?"

Justin shrugged. Chloe came out into the hallway. She had put on a faded denim jacket over her outfit. One side of her blue jeans sagged down below her hip.

"Are you going to school?" Chloe asked June.

Justin looked at her in astonishment. "Are you kidding?" he demanded. "She's too sick to go to school!"

"Sometimes after you throw up, you feel okay," Chloe pointed out, hands on hips.

"She's too sick."

"Let June answer."

Justin scowled at her.

"I'm too sick," June moaned in agreement.

Chloe turned her attention to Justin. "Well, *you'd* better get ready for school then. You don't want to be late." She glanced at the time on her phone and slid it away.

Justin didn't bother to point out that he already was dressed for school. "I'm staying home to look after June."

Chloe looked in at June, frowning. "She's not a baby. She can stay home by herself. You have to go to school."

Justin shook his head. "You can't tell me what to do."

"I'm in charge when Mom and Dad aren't home."

"You can't make me," Justin maintained.

They were interrupted by June throwing up again. They both looked at her. Chloe wrinkled her nose and went into the kitchen to make coffee. Justin stuck around.

"I'm staying home with you," he assured June.

June just moaned.

It was a few nights later; Justin stirred as his door squeaked open. He turned over and saw June creep in and slip into the empty bed. Neither of them said anything. He closed his eyes and went back to sleep again.

But he didn't sleep soundly. June was tossing and turning noisily. Justin drifted in and out of dreams. June's breathing finally settled into a steady rhythm, but she still moved around. Then she started to moan and cry out. Justin slipped out of bed and went over to her. He shook her arm gently.

"June. Wake up. You're having a dream."

She gasped and sat up abruptly. "No. No, Mom!"

"Shh," he quieted her. "I'm here, June. It's Justin. Shh."

"Justy?" June hugged him. "Oh." She breathed out, relaxing in his hold.

"You okay? Have a bad dream?"

"Yeah. I guess."

"Come on over with me," Justin suggested.

June agreed, climbing out of bed. They both went over to Justin's bed. Justin lay down with her, and wrapped his arms around her comfortingly. "There. Now go back to sleep."

With a sigh, June snuggled and drifted quietly off to sleep.

The teacher called on June, and Justin glanced over at her, moving his eyes but not his head. June appeared to be gazing out the window, completely oblivious to Mrs. Mitchell. Some of the other children started to giggle, but June still didn't clue in and turn her attention back to the class. The teacher walked over to June's desk and stopped right beside her. There was silence while everyone waited for June's reaction. Eventually, she turned her attention back to the class, and startled when she saw the teacher at her desk.

"Oh! Mrs. Mitchell." Her eyes were wide, and she looked over at Justin for some sort of clue as to what she should do. She adjusted the shoulder strap that was falling down her arm.

"What are you daydreaming about, June?" the teacher asked.

"Oh... ummm... I just..."

"I need you to focus on what we are doing."

"Okay. Yes."

Justin watched June's feet shift back and forth and cross and uncross. She shot him another look, desperate for help. But there was nothing Justin could do. They had already threatened to put the twins in different classes, and they had both promised to act like they didn't even know each other, and work on their own schoolwork separately, and not talk to each other during class. It was a mistake that had put them both into the same class in the first place. Schools didn't like having siblings in the same room. If Justin interfered with class discipline, they would go ahead and move him to the other grade three class, even if it was mid-year. He swallowed and looked straight ahead at the board, unable to help June.

"Stay in at recess. I want to go over some of your work with you," Mrs. Mitchell directed.

June nodded, looking down at the top of her desk with teary eyes. Justin longed to be able to go over and comfort her. It wasn't fair that he had to ignore her embarrassment. But he stayed stoic, staring straight ahead.

The teacher went back to the front of the class and continued with the lesson. But Justin barely heard a word of it, too distracted by June's sniffles on the other side of the room.

It was lunch time before Justin had an opportunity to talk to June. She'd been kept in all the way through recess, not just for the first few minutes. Once the lunch bell rang and they were both outside the classroom, they immediately joined hands.

"What did she say?" Justin asked.

He gave her hand a squeeze and then let go, not wanting to look like a sissy in front of the other boys. June shook her head. Her eyes filled with tears again. "I didn't get my worksheets done," she explained. "And the stuff that I did was wrong... I just didn't understand it."

"Which worksheets? Math? Phonics? I'll help you."

"All of them," June shook her head and wiped at the corners of her eyes.

"All of them? I'll help you..."

June sighed deeply. "I don't even want to do them," she said.

"But... you have to do them," Justin pointed out.

They got into the cafeteria and looked around for seats. Justin pulled June over to a pair of free seats that were side by side, and they sat down and opened their lunch bags.

"I don't want to do anything, Justy. I just can't do it."

She put her face in her hands, elbows on the table. Justin studied her, frowning to himself. Something was very wrong. He'd known for a while now. There was something she wasn't telling him. And it was getting worse.

"Don't cry at school," he murmured to her, giving her back a quick rub.

"I'm not." But clearly she was. Her body jerked with her sobs.

"Come on, June. It's okay. It's just schoolwork."

She shook her head.

"What, then?" he demanded.

"I don't know. I can't say."

Justin's stomach knotted. Guilt washed over him like a wave. Why couldn't she tell him what was wrong? They shared everything. "What?" he persisted. "Come on. Tell me."

June shook her head again. She rubbed her eyes and lifted her face out of her hands. Without looking at him, she unwrapped her sandwich and poked the straw into her juice box.

"June," he prompted.

She took one glance at him, her face screwed up in an attempt not to cry, and then looked back down at her lunch. Justin held her arm.

"Is it because you've been sick lately?" he asked. "Is that why you're having trouble with the school work? It's okay!"

June shrugged. "I don't want to talk about it anymore," she said.

Justin let it go. He ate his lunch without tasting it, watching her movements covertly. June sniffled a few times, but had nothing more to say. She drank her juice, but only took a couple of bites of her sandwich.

"I'm not hungry," she said, offering it to him.

"You need to eat," Justin said tentatively.

"I don't feel good."

Justin touched her face with the back of his fingers, but she didn't seem hot. "Your stomach again?"

June nodded. Justin took the sandwich from her. She put her head down on her folded arms on the table, and closed her eyes.

"Do you want to go to the nurse's?"

"No."

"Do you want to go home?"

June opened her eyes and looked at him, not answering.

"Do you?"

June nodded. "Yeah. But they won't let us."

Justin shrugged. "It's lunch time. They can't stop us from leaving."

June sat up again. Her eyebrows went up hopefully, eyes widening. "We can go home?"

"Sure. Let's go."

They both got up, leaving the rest of their school lunches on the table, and headed for the door. A supervisor stopped them.

"Where are you guys going?"

"June's sick. I'm taking her to the nurse," Justin said.

The supervisor looked at June, and decided it was okay. She motioned to the door, and the children left.

"I don't want to go to the nurse," June complained.

"We're not. I just told her that. Come on."

They left their schoolbags in the classroom, and just headed out the nearest door. They had only gotten a few steps out the door, when Justin heard a voice calling his name.

"Justin Simpson."

He turned quickly, and was relieved to see it wasn't a teacher, but one of the other boys, affecting a deep voice. Justin shook his head.

"Thought I was in for it!" he complained. "What's up?"

Robbie nodded at him. "Where are you going? Looking for some action?"

Justin motioned for Robbie's cigarette, and when Robbie handed it over, took a quick drag on it, hoping it would help to relax the knot of worry and guilt in his stomach.

"Just headin' home," he explained.

"Why don't we get some of the boys together and do something? Who wants to go home?"

Justin glanced aside at June. "I gotta look after my kid sister. She's sick."

Robbie took the cigarette back, looking June over. "She looks okay to me."

"She's sick," Justin repeated. "I'll have to catch you tomorrow, okay?"

"She can go home by herself."

Justin shook his head. He took June by the arm, and headed across the playground toward home.

"I'm not your kid sister," June muttered.

Justin grinned. "You're twenty minutes younger. I can call you my kid sister if I want."

~

June & Justin, Book #2 of the *Between the Cracks* series by P.D. Workman can be purchased at pdworkman.com

~

About the Author

P.D. Workman is a USA Today Bestselling author, winner of several awards from Library Services for Youth in Custody and the InD'tale Magazine's Crowned Heart award, and has published over 100 mystery/suspense/thriller and young adult books, including stand alones and these series: Auntie Clem's Bakery cozy mysteries, Reg Rawlins Psychic Investigator paranormal mysteries, Zachary Goldman Mysteries (PI), Kenzie Kirsch Medical Thrillers, Parks Pat Mysteries (police procedural), and YA series: Tamara's Teardrops, Between the Cracks, and Breaking the Pattern.

Workman loves writing about the underdog, who the reader may love or hate. She has been praised for her realistic details, deep characterization, and sensitive handling of the serious social issues that appear in all of her stories, from light cozy mysteries through to darker, grittier young adult and mystery/suspense books.

> P. D. Workman, does not shy from probing the deep psychological scars of childhood trauma, mental illness, and addiction. Also characteristic of this author, these extremely sensitive issues are explored with extensive empathy, described with incredible clarity, and portrayed with profound insight.
>
> —KIM, GOODREADS REVIEWER

Some of Workman's titles have been translated into Spanish, French, Portuguese, German, and Italian.

Workman began writing at an early age and is a prolific reader as well as writer. She is also passionate about teaching and learning, expresses her creativity through art and cooking, and loves exploring the Calgary parks and green spaces where the Parks Pat Mysteries are set. She was a legal assistant for many years and has done extensive charitable work.

Workman was born and raised in Alberta, Canada, and is married with one adult son.

Please visit P.D. Workman at pdworkman.com to see what else she is working on, to join her mailing list, and to link to her social networks.

If you enjoyed this book, please take the time to recommend it to other purchasers with a review or star rating and share it with your friends!

tiktok.com/@pdworkmanauthor
facebook.com/pdworkmanauthor
x.com/pdworkmanauthor
instagram.com/pdworkmanauthor
amazon.com/author/pdworkman
bookbub.com/authors/p-d-workman
goodreads.com/pdworkman
linkedin.com/in/pdworkman
pinterest.com/pdworkmanauthor
youtube.com/pdworkman
patreon.com/pdworkmanauthor
reamstories.com/pdworkmanauthor

Find P.D. Workman's books at

PDWORKMAN.COM

Scan the QR code below

www.ingramcontent.com/pod-product-compliance
Lightning Source LLC
Chambersburg PA
CBHW031424160426
43195CB00010BB/604